THOUGHT PROBES

Philosophy Through Science Fiction

FRED D. MILLER, JR.
Bowling Green State University

NICHOLAS D. SMITH
Virginia Polytechnic Institute and State University

PRENTICE-HALL, INC., Englewood Cliffs, New Jersey 07632

Library of Congress Cataloging in Publication Data

Main entry under title:

Thought probes.

   Includes bibliographies and index.
   1.–Philosophy—Introductions. 2.–Science
fiction—History and criticism. 3.–Philosophy
in literature. I.–Miller, Fred Dycus, 1944–
II.–Smith, Nicholas D.
BD21.T47   100   80-26447
ISBN 0-13-920041-X

Printed in the United States of America

10 9 8 7 6 5 4 3 2 1

Editorial/production supervision and design by Virginia Rubens
Cover design by Jorge Hernandez
Manufacturing buyer: Harry P. Baisley

PRENTICE-HALL INTERNATIONAL, INC., *London*
PRENTICE-HALL OF AUSTRALIA PTY. LIMITED, *Sydney*
PRENTICE-HALL OF CANADA, LTD., *Toronto*
PRENTICE-HALL OF INDIA PRIVATE LIMITED, *New Delhi*
PRENTICE-HALL OF JAPAN, INC., *Tokyo*
PRENTICE-HALL OF SOUTHEAST ASIA PTE. LTD., *Singapore*
WHITEHALL BOOKS LIMITED, *Wellington, New Zealand*

CONTENTS

PREFACE

We offer this book in the conviction that the study of philosophy and the appreciation of science fiction can be combined in a fruitful way. Our objective is to present some basic concepts and problems of philosophy in conjunction with stories that are well-written and stimulating. Philosophy, like science fiction, can and should excite the interest of the beginner. And science fiction at its best, like philosophy, represents an intellectual challenge to the reader.

We have chosen stories that will help the reader in understanding some of the central philosophical concepts and problems, and in developing some of the basic capacities of the philosopher. These are the intellectual tools that a person needs in order to approach any problem in a philosophical way. The reader is invited to consider selected problems in the basic areas of philosophy: the nature of knowledge and reality (the problem of skepticism, the existence of God, the nature of space and time), our human nature (the philosophy of mind, the problem of personal identity, the question of free will), and values (the justification of values, the problem of anarchy).

The stories are intended to contribute to the reader's grasp of basic skills and to serve as a basis for further discussion and personal reflection. Each chapter begins by introducing a basic philosophical problem—for example, "Does God exist?" The philosophical skills which the reader can expect to acquire by using the material are spelled out in a careful way. These skills are then concisely explained and illustrated. The science fiction story which follows each introductory discussion functions as a "conceptual experiment" by means of which the problem can be considered. The story is followed by a philosophical essay discussing the problem. At the end of each chapter, there is a set of programmed questions, called "probes." These questions are designed to help the reader employ the skills that he or she has gained in analyzing and assessing problems, interpretations, and arguments contained in or suggested by the story and the essay. We hope that those who read this book will find that these questions help to focus the problem and to stimulate thought. Ideally, many readers will be inspired to pursue the problem further, and we have tried to come to their aid with bibliographical essays on the philosophical and science fiction literature relating to each chapter.

We have organized each chapter with the philosophical introduction first, so that the student acquires the philosophical concepts and skills necessary to identify and appreciate the philosophical issues raised in the story. In this way the reader will see the story in a peculiarly *philosophical* context. In the spirit of this book, however, instructors and general readers may find that they want to experiment with different formats. For example, they may prefer to read the stories first and *then* read the philosophical introductions. But to those who use this approach we strongly recommend that they read the stories again *after* they read the philosophical introductions—otherwise much of the philosophical importance of the stories will be overlooked. Further, we follow a sound tradition in presenting logic and epistemology first, then metaphysics, and finally value theory, but nothing prevents a different ordering of topics by the instructor.

The text has been designed so that it can serve different purposes. It can be used in introductory philosophical courses and in courses concerned with developing a philosophical appreciation of literary works. Because it is a learning tool, we have added devices such as explicit objectives and "thought probes." But we have also tried to present philosophy and science fiction in such a way that the book will be intelligible and *interesting* to the general reader. Our ultimate purpose is to help inspire in the reader interest in and appreciation for a goal and a method which philosophy and science fiction share in common: the understanding of our human nature, the nature of reality, and human values by means of conceptual experimentation, the exploring of possible alternatives to the world as we know it.

A final note on the bibliographies that accompany each chapter: These are intended as guides to further reading in science fiction. They were prepared with two different audiences in mind: philosophers curious about science fiction who do not know which stories and novels deal with which philosophical problems, and science fiction fans who would like to see how the great philosophers of the past and present have tackled familiar sf themes. As far as we know there are no precedents for our sf bibliographies organized around philosophical ideas. The reader who wishes more references in science fiction can do no better, in our opinion, than to consult Neil Barron's superb *Anatomy of Wonder: Science Fiction* (R. R. Bowker, 1976). Barron's book contains an explanation of the Nebula and Hugo Awards which have been won by a number of the stories mentioned in our bibliographies. Two other valuable sources are Baird Searles *et al., A Reader's Guide to Science Fiction* (Avon, 1979) and John Brosnan, *Future Tense: The Cinema of Science Fiction* (St. Martin's, 1978). For the beginner in philosophy, as our bibliographies indicate, the best start in most areas of philosophy can still be made by reading the articles in *The Encyclopedia of Philosophy* edited by Paul Edwards (Macmillan, 1967).

In preparing this book we have benefited from many suggestions by enthusiastic students and fellow teachers. We hope that our readers will feel free to make further suggestions to us of stories that should be in our bibliographies and of thought probes that might expand the minds of other readers.

F.D.M.
N.D.S.

INTRODUCTION

Thought Probes in Philosophy and Science Fiction

When you pick up a book that has to do with philosophy, your first question probably is, "What *is* philosophy?" Even the word "philosophy" may put you on your guard: it may suggest something difficult, abstract, and dry as dust. But the authors of this book have found philosophy to be intriguing and mind-expanding as well as challenging, and we hope that you will agree with us by the time you finish this book. Our strategy is to use plot-themes, ideas, and inventions from science fiction to make philosophical problems and theories interesting and intelligible. This is possible because science fiction or "sf" writers have many common interests. Authors in this field frequently complain about the label "*science* fiction." In many stories scientists do not play an important role, and the main ideas are not even scientific or technological. Hence, some would like to change the name to "*speculative* fiction." Although the label "science fiction" will no doubt stick, our point is made: science fiction is a philosophical literature. "Philosophy" itself is derived from the ancient Greek words *philia,* which translates as love, and *sophia,* which translates as wisdom. The ancient Greek philosopher Aristotle reported that this "love of wisdom" was born in

1

wonder. Wonder is revealed, too, in the names of the earliest science fiction magazines: *Amazing, Astounding,* and *Fantastic.*

Labels like "love of wisdom" and "speculative fiction" are, however, more suggestive than they are informative. In this brief introductory chapter we will provide a framework for understanding the rest of the book by describing main areas of philosophy. Here, as in the rest of the book, we adopt the strategy of using science fiction motifs to introduce philosophical ideas. An important device we will use throughout the book is a *conceptual experiment.* A conceptual experiment resembles what scientists like Albert Einstein call a "thought experiment." It helps us to open our minds to questions about facts that may seem familiar and trivial to us by projecting us into fascinating and unsettling new realities. A good, full-length science fiction story or novel does this most effectively, but even a short sketch can serve to advance a line of argument or raise an objection. In this introduction we will also try to describe briefly the distinctive method of philosophy and to show how the method of the philosopher differs from that of the science fiction writer. After completing this introduction, you should be able to do the following:

- Distinguish the different areas of philosophy and describe a typical problem of each.

- Describe a characteristic method of philosophy.

- State two important differences between philosophical and science fiction uses of thought probes.

I:1 THE AREAS OF PHILOSOPHY

I:1.1 Consider the following conceptual experiment: There is a science officer on board a starship that is venturing into the outward reaches of the civilized galaxy. The ship has just encountered a new planet, Xong, with a peculiar humanoid population. The science officer is pondering some tentative conclusions of a report to Starfleet Command:

"It is difficult for me to complete this report, because the two linguists on my staff are in sharp disagreement concerning the language of the natives. One linguist claims to have translated the language satisfactorily and has served as an interpreter. The second linguist claims that this race is so irrational and primitive that it is doubtful whether it even *has* a language in our sense, for a vast number of the statements which the natives are making, according to the first linguist's translations, are false or crazy.

"For example, they do not seem to make any distinctions in their language between persons belonging to their race and things like trees and rocks. They will as readily say, while going home, 'The house waits for me' as 'The spouse waits for me.' They believe that the world has a creator but that this 'god' behaves in a haphazard manner; hence, the inevitable evils of their existence. They have no special words for the mind or soul or consciousness. They seem to have no conception that people make choices, act freely, or assume responsibility for what they do.

"They seem to have a very confused idea of ethics and etiquette. If a native kills another native for whatever reason, nobody seems the least concerned; but if one native eats a dish with the wrong implement, everyone becomes extremely distressed, as if a serious crime had been committed. The linguist who serves as interpreter reports that the natives have expressed complete contempt for our perverse confusion of serious moral matters in eating with the relatively trivial etiquette of killing.

"Most astonishing is the fact that each native suffers irreversible amnesia once every five years, losing his or her (actually there are three sexes) memory, abandoning home, spouses, job, legal obligations, and so on, without any protest from anyone else. The person establishes a new identity and starts out from scratch.

"The natives also have a very peculiar way of arriving at beliefs and decisions. Each native carries about a large leather wallet containing knucklebones of some animal. When the native is trying to make a judgment about some matter of fact, he or she thinks of as many alternative hypotheses as possible, assigns each a configuration of knucklebones, and tosses out the bones to see which configuration comes up. That settles the matter. When the natives try to reach any conclusions about what ought to be done, they toss their bones together and either accept the outcome or do not. There is no government as we understand it and no organized police. The natives also make remarkably confident statements about future events. Although they will not or cannot tell us the basis for these statements, they seem as confident about the future as about the present.

"It is difficult for me to complete this report. As a scientist I can look for the psychological and sociological mechanisms that are at work here. But I also have to ask myself some philosophical questions: What kind of view of the world could they possibly have that would lead to such bizarre behavior? The natives act strangely, but might they not be *justified* in the way they behave? If they are not, is the second linguist on my team correct to argue that it would be impossible for any intelligent race to behave as this race does?"

How do these final questions involve philosophy? First, the science officer suggests that the natives may behave so strangely because they have a different view of the world from ours; and one of the main jobs of philosophy is to state and understand world views. Second, the science officer wonders whether their view might not be *justified*. As we shall see, a world view basically rests on different sorts of *assumptions* that people make about the world. So, there are two main problems: What assumptions are the natives making? And are these assumptions *justified*? These sorts of assumptions can be sorted into different fields of study: those of value theory, epistemology, metaphysics, and logic.

VALUE THEORY

I:1.2 The inhabitants of Xong appear to make statements quite different from those we would make about what things are good and bad, what acts are right or wrong, and how we should make decisions. *Value theory* is the part of philosophy that identifies and tries to assess such claims. *General value theory* (also called metaethics) raises questions about our most basic value statements and about the ultimate nature of values. For example, a Xongian would say that preserving intelligent life is less important than eating with the proper fork; eating properly is the essentially valuable human activity. The general value theorist asks, *"We* would say that preserving life is more valuable than maintaining proper etiquette at the dinner table. But can we say that we are correct and the Xongians incorrect, or the reverse? How do we ultimately justify *any* value claims? Can we show that any moral statement is *false*—for example, that one ought to continue eating one's dinner rather than pause to save another person's life?" Moreover, the Xongians reach all value conclusions—for example, "Whom should we punish for tipping over the water glass?"—by tossing knucklebones. The value theorist asks, "Can we criticize the Xongians for using this procedure? Are our own procedures in ethics any better? How do *we* 'know' what is right and what is wrong?" These are the main sorts of questions you will consider in Chapter 7 of this book. *Normative ethics* tries to find the basic value *principles* on which we would base the judgment, "You should stop to save your neighbor from choking to death rather than continuing to eat with proper decorum." Generally, normative ethics identifies the principles on which we base our ethical evaluations of things as good or bad and our evaluations of actions as "right" or "wrong." *Aesthetics* (the philosophy of art) belongs to value theory too, since it is concerned with aesthetic values like beauty. *Social and political philosophy* explores the structures in which people interact, both social structures like the family and political structures like the democratic process. The Xongians have no formal government and make collective decisions by collectively tossing knucklebones and abiding (or not abiding) by the outcome. The political philosopher asks whether this sort of political structure is better or worse than ours, and how such a structure should be improved. The social and political philosophers use concepts such as justice, equality, autonomy, and power to define social and political structures that will better serve our kind in its search for value. One question raised by this conceptual experiment, "Is government necessary for social life?," is the problem of anarchy explored in Chapter 8 of this book.

EPISTEMOLOGY

I:1.3 Epistemology is the theory of knowledge. Most of us claim to know many things and we base those claims on the observations we make with our sense organs. The Xongians also are confident that they know many things, but they rely upon their knucklebones as the basis of knowl-edge. Humans would want to tell them, "You may *feel* certain about many things, but you do not really have certain knowledge. We use our sense organs. How do you know you can rely on your knucklebones?" A Xongian might respond, "How do you know you can rely on your sense organs?"

Chapter 1 of this book introduces the epistemological question, "What can we know for certain?" This is the problem of skepticism. The skeptic raises many doubts about the reliability of our sense organs and about other ways in which we think we know things. Other problems of epistemology are "Can we believe whatever we want to believe? Must all knowledge be ultimately based on perception? Can there be mystical knowledge without evidence? To know something, must we know that we know it?"

METAPHYSICS

I:1.4 Metaphysics is the theory of the basic nature of reality. The metaphysician would be intrigued with the differences between the Xongi-ans' view of reality and our own, and would ask how we could determine whose view of reality is more correct. Metaphysics is a very broad area, including many different philosophical enterprises. Five chapters in this book deal with such metaphysical questions. Chapter 2 deals with whether God exists. How justified are the Xongians in holding that the world has a creator, but one who is haphazard in managing things? Chapter 3 concerns the nature of time and its role in reality. Chapter 4 investigates whether human freedom is real or illusory. As you saw, the Xongians make no allowance whatsoever for free will. This contradicts common sense, but you will find in Chapter 4 that many philosophers would agree with the Xongians. Chapter 5 asks whether human consciousness is real and has an impact on material reality. Again you will find that some philosophers would agree with the Xongians that it makes no sense to refer to the "mind" or "soul" or to any "conscious" states as such. Chapter 6 explores the conditions under which existing persons maintain their individuality and identity. When the Xongians undergo their periodic amnesia and "rebirth," do they remain the same persons or do new persons come into existence? What should we say about a human being who suffers total amnesia after a car accident? In general, any questions about what exists or about the relations between existing things is a metaphysical question.

LOGIC

I:1.5 Logic studies patterns of inference. The Xongians' method of inferring conclusions by tossing knucklebones will impress a human being as totally unacceptable. A logician wants to know which forms of reasoning *are* valid and which are not. There are roughly two branches of logic:

deductive and *inductive*. Deductive logic studies the kinds of valid inference that are guaranteed by their assumptions. As long as the premises are true, the conclusion *cannot* be false. These types of inference will be described in Section I:2. Inductive logic, on the other hand, deals with inferences that generalize, or make predictions from, premises, but fail to guarantee completely the truth of such predictions or generalizations. Inductively valid inferences do provide *evidence* for the conclusion. Thus, if I have observed that each of the 1,000 crows that I have studied is black, I might predict that the next crow I see will be black. Although no one would deny that this is a reasonable prediction, there is no guarantee given by my earlier observations that this will prove to be true. Maybe the next crow that flies by will be an albino! Inductive logic would have to make clear why the inductive inferences of a human scientist are valid, and the inductive inferences of a Xongian are not.

METASTUDIES AND APPLIED PHILOSOPHY

I:1.6   Some fields in philosophy are called "metastudies" or "philosophies of." Each of these is concerned with the foundations or assumptions made by the practitioners of a specific discipline. For example, the philosopher of science seeks to understand the ultimate nature of science. Naturally, each science admits of a special metastudy. Thus, there are philosophers of physics, of biology, of economics, and so on. But science is not the only area in which philosophical metastudies are made. The philosopher of history studies the nature and import of the study of history. The philosopher of education investigates the goals and functions of the educator. Often these are not the sole province of the philosopher. It is not uncommon for the mathematician to engage in the philosophy of mathematics, or for the historian to consider questions of the philosophy of history. These are very valuable fields, because philosophy and other disciplines have everything to gain through such "cross-fertilization." Generally, the greatest work done in these fields is done by those who have extensive training in *both* philosophy and the substantive field under scrutiny. Each discipline in the intellectual community provides fertile ground for the work of the philosopher engaged in a metastudy such as the philosophy of biology, social science, psychology, or medicine. Any field advanced enough to have its own methodology and/or basic assumptions provides ample material for philosophical thought.

Such fields also give rise to basic questions of value studied by *applied social philosophy*. Such value issues are raised in the philosophy of law, medical ethics, business ethics, environmental ethics, and so forth. These are some of the most exciting fields of philosophy today. Thus the subject matter of philosophy, more than any other field, is virtually unlimited.

HISTORY OF PHILOSOPHY

I:1.7 Finally, some philosophers are interested primarily in interpreting, analyzing, or expanding certain philosophical traditions. Virtually every academic department of philosophy has a specialist in, for example, the history of philosophy. Some philosophers of this kind specialize in ancient Greek philosophy; others are concerned more with early modern European philosophy; yet others are primarily interested in early Oriental philosophy; and so forth. There are specialists of this sort for virtually every significant period in the history of philosophy.

Sometimes, the philosophical traditions involved are not just those of history, but are contemporary. Thus, some philosophers specialize in contemporary perspectives that are ideologically unique. There are specialists in Russian philosophy, American philosophy, contemporary Continental European philosophy, and a variety of others. The goals of all those involved in historical or contemporary philosophical traditions are to explicate, criticize, or just further develop those traditions in which they are interested. In some sense, it might be argued that almost all philosophers are engaged in the development of some tradition or another, but, except for those who specialize in that tradition as a study in and of itself, this is not a particularly self-conscious commitment. That is, except for specialists of this sort, most philosophers are not committed to the constraints of their tradition, even if they never in fact depart from that tradition.

I:2 PHILOSOPHICAL METHOD

I:2.1 Philosophy differs from the natural and social sciences, like biology, astronomy, and psychology, because it does not have a particular standard methodology by which theories can be tested through observation and experiment. Historically, sciences like astronomy have broken away from philosophy after such independent methodologies have been developed by philosophers. Many specialists think that the science of linguistics is in the process of breaking away from philosophy today.

This does not mean that philosophy has no method at all. For one thing, when philosophers reason about the questions they ask, they must not be illogical: They are not allowed to draw conclusions that they have not shown sufficient reason to draw or that go against other things they have said. They must provide *arguments* that support the conclusions they seek to draw. The rules that state what conclusions can be drawn from what starting points (or "premises") are called "rules of inference," for the rules say what sorts of inferences are logical and what sorts of inferences are not.

I:2.2 Most of these rules are obvious—so obvious that we use them all the time without even being specifically taught them. As an experiment, try to decide whether the following inference is logical or not. Let's assume that you know both

(1) If Smith goes swimming, then Smith gets wet.

and

(2) But Smith does not get wet.

Is the inference from this,

(3) Therefore, Smith does not go swimming

a logical one or not? Obviously, it is. We know from (1) that swimming gets Smith wet and from (2) that Smith does not get wet. If we assume (as we have) that (1) and (2) are true, then we must conclude that Smith does not go swimming. For if he does go swimming, he gets wet (according to (1)), but (according to (2)) he does not get wet. Hence, it follows from (1) and (2) that Smith does not go swimming.

Again, such inferences are logical, and so obvious that we make them all the time, and we need no special training in order to be able to make them surely. The inference from (1) and (2) to (3) is called *modus tollendo tollens* or, more simply, "denying the consequent." Chances are, you've probably never heard of these names, but you probably knew that the inference was logical anyway.

I:2.3 But sometimes inferences *seem* logical when they are not. For example, let's assume that you know someone, say, Jones, who is violently allergic to penicillin. Imagine that it is clear that Jones is so allergic that

(4) If Jones is given penicillin, then he will die within an hour

is true. We might reason that if, in addition,

(5) Jones is not given penicillin

then

(6) Jones will not die within an hour

follows from your knowledge of (4) and (5). That is, you might reason from your knowledge of (4) and (5) to (6). But is the inference from (4) and (5) to (6) a logical one? No, it is not. For Jones might be hit by a truck, have a heart attack, or fall out a window in the next hour. This shows that (6) is false, even though (4) and (5) are true. Notice that in the earlier example (3) could not be false unless (1) or (2) or both were false. Inferences like the earlier one, in which conclusions reached cannot be false unless one or more of the premises are false, are called "valid." Inferences like the second one, where the conclusion can be false even though none of the premises is false, are called "invalid" or "fallacious." When one makes a fallacious inference, one commits a *fallacy*. The rules of inference are designed to distinguish valid inferences from fallacies.

I:2.4 Philosophers use these rules to ensure that, when they reason, they do not commit basic errors of reasoning, that is, fallacies. The study of rules of inference and related matters is called "logic," which was mentioned in I:1.5. But it is worth remembering that philosophers must obey the rules of logic if they are to do philosophy well. This is one difference between philosophers and science fiction writers: Philosophers must make their claims in such a way as to construct *valid arguments* for their views; science fiction writers need only to construct believable settings for their ideas. These settings need not be based upon valid inferences or anything of the kind. Indeed, some very interesting science fiction involves fallacies which are well concealed by the author. Displaying such fallacies might make the author's stories less interesting to a philosopher, but it doesn't necessarily show them to be *bad* stories. But, if a philosopher's argument can be shown to be a fallacy, it defeats the argument.

I:2.5 What causes problems for the philosopher, more often than fallacies, however, are arguments and inferences he or she makes that are not obviously *sound*. For an argument to be decisive, it must be not only valid, but sound. Remember that an argument is invalid if its conclusion cannot be false unless one or more of its premises is also false. But that means that some arguments can be valid that are also quite unconvincing. Consider the following inference, which follows the same form as the first one you considered (that is, it is a *modus tollendo tollens*) and is thus perfectly valid.

(7) If the earth is round, then I can rollerskate around its equator.

(8) I cannot rollerskate around its equator.

Therefore,

(9) The earth isn't round.

This *is* a valid argument. The conclusion cannot be false unless one or more of the premises is false. Why, then, do we find ourselves not convinced that the conclusion is true? The second premise (8) is clearly true. But the first premise (7) is just as clearly false. It is not true that, if the earth is round, then I can rollerskate around its equator, because it can be round, but largely covered by water, and I cannot rollerskate on water. So, even though the argument is valid, it does not convince us because one of its premises is false. What the philosopher seeks, therefore, is not just a valid argument stating his position, but one in which all the premises are *true*. A valid argument that has all true premises must have a true conclusion, according to the definition of validity given here. Such an argument is called a "sound" argument. Most of the problems that philosophers encounter are not concerned with validity, but with soundness. That is, most philosophers wonder whether certain arguments are *sound*.

I:2.6 This leads to a second difference between philosophers and science fiction writers. Science fiction writers create their own truth; that is, they create settings in which certain things are simply stated to be true. If philosophers wonder whether or not there can be intelligent robots, they need to consider what it means to be intelligent and what it means to be a robot, and then construct a sound argument to the conclusion that there can be such things, or alternatively to the conclusion that there cannot be such things. Science fiction writers need only to begin a story with something like "Robby was a robot who had achieved true intelligence," and the story can proceed. Science fiction authors can then write stories in which everyone treats the robot as intelligent, and even seems reasonable in doing so—but they have not proved anything philosophically decisive about machine intelligence (except, at best, that such a concept can be made at least plausible enough to be the basis of an enjoyable story). Thus, in the chapter on time travel, the philosopher David Lewis *argues* that time travel is possible, while science fiction writer Robert Heinlein simply writes a story in which it *happens*. The story is not philosophically uninteresting, however, for the *way* it happens in Heinlein's story is the way Lewis argues it *must* happen. Science fiction can be philosophically interesting insofar as it provides settings in which philosophical questions can be raised and philosophical answers given, but it is not philosophy because it does not argue for its answers—it does not attempt to make inferences that are both valid and sound.

I:2.7 In the following chapters, you will consider a wide variety of philosophical questions and answers. Each chapter will ask a question, and provide an answer in a fictional setting created by a science fiction writer. This will be followed by a similar or different answer provided in argument by a philosopher. You may find that the philosophers often show as much imagination as the science fiction writers do, and you will certainly find that they address the same problems and issues. They approach these issues or problems with different purposes and different methods, but the approaches can be combined to make each far more interesting and illuminating.

SKEPTICISM AND
THE THEORY OF KNOWLEDGE:

What do you know for certain?

To find reasons for adopting one course of action over another, one scientific theory over another, or one life-style over another, you must often take time to assess the relevant facts. This, however, raises the question, "What is your cognitive relation to the facts?" That is, are you in a position to *know* the relevant facts, or can you only make more or less educated guesses? In this chapter, you will probe the question, "To what extent are you justified in thinking that you know what you typically think you know?"

Most of us suppose that we know a great number of things for certain. We think that we know a number of things about ourselves, other people, and the world around us. Moreover, we think that we know certain abstract truths, such as the laws of mathematics (e.g., "Two plus two is four") and logic. A number of philosophers, however, upon investigating the nature of knowledge and the grounds for claiming it, have concluded that we know very little, if anything. The question "What is knowledge?" is studied by the epistemologist, who identifies the relationships that knowledge has to belief, justification, experience, and truth, among other things. The epistemologist who denies that we have knowledge in some area in which we normally think we have it is called a *skeptic.* The epistemologist who believes that there is no reason to doubt that we know what we think we know is called a *nonskeptic.*

This chapter introduces the issues involved in the study of epistemology, or the theory of knowledge. The differences between the skeptic and the nonskeptic are based in the nature of knowledge, the grounds upon which one might claim knowledge, and whether or not the reasons for which one might deny knowledge claims are good ones. The purpose of this chapter is not to answer decisively the arguments of either the skeptic or the nonskeptic but, rather, to introduce the issues upon which the controversy develops. After completing this chapter, you should be able to do the following:

- Explain the concept of knowledge that is operative when we make a claim of knowledge.

- Identify the various categories of beliefs that are candidates for knowledge.

- Explain why, according to the skeptic, we cannot be certain about these categories and thus do not have knowledge about them.

- Enumerate a few possible nonskeptical responses to skeptical arguments.

- Evaluate the claims of the skeptic on the basis of conceptual experiments.

1:1 THE CONCEPT OF KNOWLEDGE

1:1.1 The question "What can we know?" cannot be answered until a prior question is adequately answered, namely, "What is knowledge?" Most of us are not immediately inclined to think that the concept of knowledge is at all vague. We feel free to use the word "knowledge" without any hesitation, assuming that it has a clear meaning that cannot be confused by those to whom we are speaking. Epistemologists, however, find that giving an adequate definition is no easy task. Indeed, there is still no general agreement as to its complete and proper definition. Not the least of their problems is the fact that "knowledge" turns out to have many uses. For example, someone (let us call him Jones) might know his next-door neighbor (Smith), know *that* Smith has a beard, know *what* Smith does on Saturdays, know *how* to annoy Smith, and know *why* Smith is an electrical engineer rather than an astrophysicist or a biochemist. Epistemologists wonder whether or not each of these really *is* knowledge and whether they are different types of the same thing or actually somewhat different things.

1:1.2 Although recently this has become increasingly controversial, philosophers have long considered the primary concept of knowledge to be expressed by claims of knowing *that* such and such is the case. Many epistemologists feel that most, if not all, of the other uses can be reduced to this form with no loss of meaning. For example, they feel that Jones's knowing *what* Smith does on Saturdays is nothing other than Jones's knowing *that* Smith reads science fiction on Saturdays, that Jones's knowing *how* to annoy Smith is nothing other than Jones's knowing *that* calling science fiction "trash" annoys Smith, and so on. Claims of knowledge *that* such and such is the case are called claims of *propositional knowledge,* for what you know in these cases is a proposition about something. Thus, epistemologists typically begin to answer the question "What is knowledge?" by attempting to answer the question "What is propositional knowledge?"

1:1.3 But even this question creates difficulties. For there is little agreement upon the conditions under which a person like Jones really has propositional knowledge. A typical way of proceeding is to attempt to spell out the conditions under which it will be true to *say* that someone has propositional knowledge. While there are many variations in the exact accounts of what these conditions must be, most epistemologists who take this approach agree that something like the following three conditions must be met:

1. What someone, for example Jones, claims to know must be *true.*

2. Jones must *believe* that what he claims to know is true.

3. Jones must be *fully justified* in believing that what he claims to know is true; that is, there must be *no reason to suppose that he might be wrong* in believing that what he claims to know is true.

Thus Jones knows that Smith reads science fiction on Saturdays provided that it is *true* that Smith reads science fiction on Saturdays, that Jones *believes* this, and that Jones is *fully justified* in believing this.

1:2   CATEGORIES OF KNOWLEDGE CLAIMS AND KINDS OF SKEPTICS

1:2.1 On the basis of the preceding analysis of propositional knowledge, or something like it, many philosophers throughout history have denied that we have knowledge in a number of areas in which we might think we do. It is important, however, to see just what it is to make such a denial, that is, to be a skeptic. In denying that we have knowledge, the skeptic is not denying that some beliefs are better than others. Even the most extreme skeptic would be unlikely to deny that it is less *reasonable* to believe that the moon is made of green cheese than it is to believe that it is made of inorganic material. He would only deny that you know this *for certain.* In this way, the skeptic is *not necessarily* inclined to get you to *disbelieve* what he says you do not know. As a skeptic, he attacks condition (3) of the above analysis of knowledge: He will claim that although you may have *some* justification for your belief (perhaps even enough to make it quite reasonable), still you do not have *full justification.* Hence, the skeptic will argue that you cannot be *certain* and thus that you do not have knowledge.

For example, imagine an argument between two people, John and George. John claims to know that there are extraterrestrial beings having intelligence. George claims to know the opposite, namely, that there are no such beings. In this argument, neither is a skeptic, for both claim to have knowledge. George might *look* like a skeptic, relative to John, for he will claim that John does not know what he claims to know. But George is not a skeptic on the issue of extraterrestrial beings, for George believes that he knows the truth of the matter, as does John. Their difference is not one of skepticism versus nonskepticism but, rather, of rivaling nonskepticisms.

Imagine now that two others join the discussion, Sam and Steve. Both Sam and Steve deny that we know for certain whether or not there are such beings, but Sam is inclined to believe with John that there are, and Steve is inclined to believe with George that there are not. Despite the fact that Sam and Steve are inclined to disagree on whether or not there are extraterrestrial beings with intelligence, *both* are skeptics on this issue, for both claim that this issue in not one in which we have knowledge. Thus, the difference between a skeptic and a nonskeptic is not to be found in what they believe to be true, *except* insofar as they believe that there is or is not knowledge of the issue. Hence John and Sam believe much the same thing about extraterrestrial beings, but John is a nonskeptic, whereas Sam is a skeptic. The same can be said of George and Steve, respectively. So a skeptic is not someone who believes *the opposite* of what we believe about something but, rather, someone who denies that we have knowledge of something that we think we know. That is why George is not a skeptic on this issue, but both Sam and Steve are.

The skeptic's reasoning is this: If a belief is not certain, it cannot meet the third condition of knowledge (i.e., condition 3 above). For example, consider John and Sam again—*both* of whom are inclined to believe in intelligent extraterrestrial beings. Sam, the skeptic, might argue that, although John has some evidence *for* the existence of such beings (such as sightings of unusual objects in the sky, strange artifacts, etc.), we cannot be fully justified in believing in such beings because there are other ways of accounting for such evidence that *could* be correct. The "sightings" might be due to optical illusions, misidentification of balloons or planets, or statistically predictable objects of terrestrial origin. The "artifacts" might be hoaxes or unusual objects of nature. Now George, the nonskeptic who disbelieves in intelligent extraterrestrials, might claim to know that these "might bes" are indeed the case. George would claim to *know* that alleged UFOs are only balloons, and so forth. Sam is inclined to believe that they are not, but remains uncertain. So Sam would claim only that the evidence *favors* John's view that there are intelligent extraterrestrial beings. But, unlike John, Sam would claim that such alternative explanations are sufficient to cause some uncertainty—they provide some reason to think that John's view *might* be wrong. Thus, the evidence that Sam thinks *favors* John's view is, according to Sam, insufficient to *fully justify* that view. There is room for doubt, so Sam remains a skeptic. We can imagine a similar disagreement between Steve and George, who both think that there are no intelligent extraterrestrials. Steve might say, "Well, George, I'm inclined to agree with you that all the evidence John and Sam think favors the view that there are such beings is best interpreted in the way you would. That is, I'm inclined to agree that all these UFOs are only terrestrial objects or optical illusions. But it is possible that we're wrong. Maybe one of these sightings was not a balloon or some such thing. Maybe one really was a spacecraft from another, alien civilization. Like you, George, I doubt it, but I cannot be certain. We just don't know one way or the other, so I remain skeptical, like Sam, although unlike him I think the evidence favors the claim that there are no such beings."

If a belief is not certain, although it can be *partially* justified, it cannot be *fully justified,* and thus condition 3 of the analysis of knowledge given in 1:1.3 will not be met, for there might be some (if only *very slight* and *improbable*) reason to suppose that what one claims to know might not be true. And the skeptic would point out that even the most improbable (but *possible*) reason to think this disallows knowledge, which requires that there be *no* reason for doubt. You might think of having one ticket in a huge lottery. It would be most unreasonable for you to believe that you were going to win, for it is most improbable that you will win. But it is *possible.* So you don't know *for certain* that you will not win, despite the fact that you ought not to believe that you will. Thus, skepticism is not committed to believing anything except that we do not know something for certain.

1:2.2 For every kind of knowledge claim that has ever been offered, there is a skeptic who would attempt to argue that the claim fails to meet the requirements for knowledge. A skeptic who denies that there is any knowledge at all is called a *total skeptic.*

Not all skeptics are total skeptics, however. Thus, while most epistemologists are skeptical about some area of inquiry, few are skeptical about all areas whatsoever. It is important, therefore, to identify the various categories of knowledge claims that have been considered by various skeptics. The following are but a few:

- Claims of knowledge about the laws and makeup of the world around us.

- Claims of knowledge about the thoughts, feelings, and sensations of other people.

- Claims of knowledge about ourselves and our own thoughts, feelings, and characteristics.

- Claims of knowledge about the past.

- Claims of knowledge about abstract principles, such as the laws of logic and mathematics.

- Claims of knowledge about religious and other supernatural matters.

- Claims of knowledge about ethical and moral judgments.

1:3   THE ARGUMENTS OF THE SKEPTIC

1:3.1   You have to recognize the *scope* of a given position before you can begin to evaluate what will count as evidence for and against it. When a philosopher talks about the scope of a theory or argument, he is discussing its area of relevance. Thus a given argument might be relevant to the question of whether or not you know what is going on in other people's minds, but it might not apply to the question of whether or not you know a given law of mathematics or logic. When evaluating a philosophical argument, the astute philosopher first asks questions of scope, such as "What issues does this argument address?" and "What issues does this argument *fail* to address?" You might find that you were prepared to agree with part of a position without agreeing to *all* of it. What this shows is that, within a certain scope, one agrees with the position (for example, skepticism), but one does not agree when the position is extended beyond that scope, or applied more generally.

1:3.2   From the very beginning, various skeptical arguments of greater and lesser scope have been presented. As early as the fifth century B.C. a Greek philosopher named Parmenides denied that one could know anything about the world around us, the world revealed through the senses. This thesis was taken up a little later by the Greek philosopher Plato, who, in his famous work the *Republic,* argued that knowledge can only be had of abstract entities (which he calls the Forms or Ideas) and never of the things we experience by our senses. Throughout history, many philosophers have pondered this issue and have given reasons for and against siding with Parmenides and Plato on this question.

1:3.3   In the seventeenth century the French philosopher René Descartes added a number of arguments for and against skepticism in his important work, *Meditations on First Philosophy.* Like Parmenides and Plato before him, he felt that evidence from the senses was inadequate to provide the kind of justification required for a claim of knowledge. In the first of Descartes' Meditations, we find a quick succession of arguments for the skeptical position, each of which is greater in scope than the last. Descartes starts by noticing that in the past, things in which he had devoutly believed turned out to be false because they were based on other beliefs that were false. In the quest for knowledge, therefore, he decides to discard any belief that is based on any evidence which is less than certain. If, says Descartes, the evidence is less than certain, the conclusions drawn from the evidence cannot constitute knowledge, for they too will be uncertain.

Descartes realizes that much of what we believe is based on sense experience. We make judgments based on what we see, hear, feel, and so forth. Each of us, however, has experienced some form of sensory illusion. All of us have, at one time or another, been deceived by such phenomena as echoes, optical illusions, and the like. How, asks Descartes, do we know that any given case of a sense experience is not an illusion?

Moreover, Descartes reminds us that all of us have dreamed, and that in our dreams we have not been aware that we were dreaming. How can we be sure that we are actually sensing at all, at any given time, and not merely dreaming that we are sensing?

Finally, Descartes expands the scope of the skeptical position even further by giving a final argument, one which would disallow even those principles admitted by Parmenides and Plato as knowledge. Is it not possible, asks Descartes, that there is a terrifically powerful being (which he calls the *malin génie,* or evil genius) that controls all our thoughts, as well as our experiences, and that deceives us into thinking all sorts of things which are untrue? Thus we might not just be deceived in our sensory experiences, we might even be deceived in our thoughts about basic abstract principles! Each time we add two plus two, for example, we might get a different number, and only think, because of false memories implanted in us by the evil genius, that we do it the same each time. The evil genius could induce in us a strong feeling of regularity, consistency, and certainty in our abstract thought, as in our sense experiences, even when we were pitifully mistaken.

1:3.4 We know that various natural states, such as dreaming or fever, can disrupt our natural cognitive functions in such a way as to give us deceptive experiences. Dreams and hallucinations regularly deceive those having them into thinking that certain things are true when they are not. Moreover, we know of various substances which, if they are ingested into the body, can alter our experience dramatically. LSD and other drugs come to mind in this regard. The skeptic would argue that any given case of an experience might be a result of such circumstances, and would thus conclude that any belief based on experience is, even if only slightly, suspect and cannot constitute adequate justification for a knowledge claim.

Recently, brain researchers have discovered that electrical stimulation of certain brain tissues can arouse vivid memories and other sorts of experiences. It is not hard to imagine further developments which would actually allow the *implantation* of memories and the *generation* of experiences which do not correspond to any natural event. Many science fiction writers have considered this possibility. Thus, in Philip K. Dick's story, "We Can Remember It for You Wholesale," we read about a business that offers you the memories of having done something—without your ever having done it! In George O. Smith's famous story, "In the Imagicon," a machine (the imagicon) provides an escape from the humdrum world in which you live—not by actually sending you anywhere, but by giving you experiences just like those you would have by actually traveling there. Along similar lines, but in a somewhat different way, J. J. Coupling, in "Period Piece," develops a character with whom the reader becomes quite sympathetic, only to discover that this character is an artificially constructed conversation piece that has been programmed to think and behave in ways that will amuse those who deal with him. Needless to say, the regular reader of science fiction will find any number of such examples.

This familiar theme is of interest to the skeptical philosopher, who would have us ask, "How do you know that such developments have not *already* happened and that you are not experiencing their effects?" That is, how do we know, given the conceivability of such developments, that we are not deceived just as the characters in such stories are deceived? How can we be *sure* that anything which we claim to know for certain is not actually the result of some deception by Descartes' evil genius? Can you be *certain* that in a few minutes you will not *wake up,* amused by your strange dream in which you believed, with great conviction, that you were a thing called a "human being" living on a weird planet called "Earth"? Isn't it just possible, even if wildly implausible, that *you* are something like Coupling's "period piece" or that you are *right now* in Smith's imagicon? Mightn't you be just as convinced of the truth of your memories if Dick's memory store had given you a deal you couldn't refuse? If any one of your experiences or memories might be false, what can you know for certain?

1:4   REPLIES TO THE SKEPTIC

1:4.1   Just as there have been many forms of skepticism, on a wide variety of issues, there have been any number of attempts to answer skeptical arguments in such a way as to escape skepticism. One of the most famous was offered by Descartes himself, in the Meditations following the one in which he introduces the evil genius. After having subjected everything he could to such doubts, Descartes asks if there is anything left of which he can still be certain. He believes that there is, namely, his knowledge of his own existence as a thinking being. Even if I might be deceived in all I think, says Descartes, still I am certain of this: I think, I am. For even if *what* I think is false and deceptive, *that* I think cannot be doubted, for to doubt is to think, and, even if my thoughts are deceived, they are still thoughts. And if I think, then I am, I exist. From this foundation, as small as it may seem,

Descartes proceeds to argue that we can once again come to know virtually all that he had initially subjected to doubt and uncertainty. Hence, Descartes believes that from this modest beginning he can offer arguments that give us certain knowledge of the existence of God, and of the world external to our own thoughts, that is, of the world we sense.

Rather than give the details of these arguments here (if you're interested, read Descartes' *Meditations on First Philosophy,* which is not only one of the greatest works ever written in philosophy, but also one of the shortest!), you should consider the form of Descartes' replies to his own skeptical beginnings. Because he starts from a few fundamental truths and builds from these a broad structure of knowledge, Descartes is called a "foundationalist." The foundationalist believes that there are some number of truths (if only a few) that are known for certain and that will allow us to infer further truths from them with equal certainty, thus building a structure of justified knowledge claims which is broad in scope. An example of such a system you might use to think about foundationalism might be geometry. In geometry, one starts with a few axioms, and uses these axioms to construct theorems. Using the axioms, one can generate a very sophisticated system of thought, as anyone who has taken geometry can testify. The foundationalist thinks that a similar structure can be constructed for ordinary knowledge claims, on the basis of a few obvious and powerful truths that are known with certainty. Just as geometrical knowledge is based upon a few obvious and powerful axioms, other forms of knowledge might be similarly structured. For the nonskeptic desiring to use such an approach as an answer to skepticism, all that is needed are a few obvious and powerful truths of the requisite sort, and a little logical ability to put them together in such a way as to arrive at full justification of more ordinary claims of knowledge. In Chapter 2, you will see how this method is often used in defense of the belief in the existence of God.

Such an approach is not always decisive, however. For the axioms one uses might themselves be questioned by the skeptic, and, if this questioning opens some room for doubt, the axioms will no longer warrant certainty in those propositions deduced from them. If a skeptic can show that the foundation of the structure that the foundationalist seeks to build is not certain, he will have effectively shown that the entire structure is uncertain, for the structure can be no more certain than its foundation. Such a skeptic might argue in this way against Descartes by attempting to raise doubts about whether Descartes really can know with certainty that he exists or thinks.

Yet another way in which a skeptic might argue against such an approach is to say that, while the foundation seems sound, it is inadequate to support anything beyond itself. The foundationalist needs to have basic knowledge of truths which are both certain and rich enough to infer further truths from them with equal certainty. Merely having a few certain truths is not enough for most nonskeptics, however, if they cannot justify the building of more ordinary knowledge claims upon them. For example, if all you can rightly claim to know is that you think and exist, you are not far from being a total skeptic. But many skeptical critics of Descartes will claim that, while he may be right in claiming to know that he thinks and exists, this knowledge is not sufficient to go any further, for to make any inferences from this is to engage once again in reasoning which might be confused by the evil genius. Such critics ask, "How do you know that, when you make inferences from these truths, your reasoning isn't confused by the manipulations of the evil genius?" If the way we reason from obvious truths can be mistrusted, we cannot trust any inference we make, so we are left, at best, only with the foundation. The rest of the structure can never be constructed with certainty, for the means of construction are not certain.

1:4.2   For these reasons, many nonskeptics have sought a different way of escaping skepticism. One of these ways is often called "fallibilism." The fallibilist attacks the analysis of knowledge (in 1:1.3) upon which the skeptic bases his arguments. According to the skeptic, most knowledge claims do not meet the requirements stated in the analysis. The fallibilist agrees, but argues that this needn't be taken as showing that there is little or no knowledge. Rather, according to the fallibilist, it shows that the analysis is faulty. If the analysis is intended to show us what a proper knowledge claim is, it fails on the fallibilist's view, for if we were to ask someone to give us an example of a proper knowledge claim, the chances are that the example they would give would not fit the analysis. This can be shown by the skeptical arguments. But imagine if we were to ask someone what a cat is, and they gave an answer that fit few, if any, of the cases of animals that all of us are inclined to call cats. If this happened, we would decide that the answer we got from them was a bad answer, that is, that the analysis of what a cat is that we have been given is a bad analysis. According to the fallibilist, skeptical arguments do not show that there is no such thing as knowledge but, rather, that the analysis of knowledge upon which they base their arguments is a bad analysis (just as if someone's analysis of "cat" could be shown to have the entailment that there were no cats). Thus, rather than accept the skeptic's conclusion that there is no knowledge, the fallibilist takes the skeptical argument as evidence that the concept of knowledge has been misunderstood.

The analysis of knowledge we have assumed requires that knowledge be *infallible*, that is, that we cannot be wrong in believing the proposition we claim to know. This is why the skeptic constantly argues that we cannot be *certain*. But, according to the fallibilist, such certainty is not a requirement of most, if not all, of the actual claims of knowledge that we would call legitimate. Typically, if someone were to ask you right now, "Do you know that you are reading a book?," you would answer, "Of course I know it!" But someone might ask, "Mightn't you be wrong in believing that you are reading a book? Couldn't it be the case that an evil genius was deceiving you into thinking that you are reading a book, when in fact you are not?" Now you might answer, "Well, it's possible that I am mistaken in such a way, but I never claimed to be *infallible*." If you answered in this way, you would be a fallibilist. For the fallibilist would claim that you do not need the sort of certainty that the skeptic requires in order to have knowledge. According to fallibilism, you can have knowledge, even if what you have is fallible, that is, uncertain to some degree (e.g., to the degree that it could be upset by the discovery of an evil genius or by finding out that it was all a dream). This reply to the skeptic has at least two important merits: It allows us to overlook many of the skeptical arguments, as being constructed from cases that we are not inclined to consider as we make claims to knowledge, and it allows us to call legitimate most of the sorts of claims that we would typically offer as standard claims of knowledge.

But as might be expected, many are not convinced that this answer defeats skepticism. We can all of us imagine a case in which the majority of people used a term in a way that was not really correct. For example, the proper definition of "Martian" might be "a creature from Mars." Now that we have landed very sophisticated equipment on Mars and have found it to be devoid of life, we might conclude that there are no Martians. But then someone might come along and say that most people use the term "Martian" in a way that does not commit them to life on Mars. This might well be the case. Today "Martian" is probably used as a synonym for "extraterrestrial being." Does that mean that when we say, "There are no Martians because there is no life on Mars," we have done a bad analysis of the term "Martian"? No, it only means that, in ordinary usage, people use the term "Martian" carelessly, but on a careful usage the term will refer to no existing creatures. Similarly, the skeptic might say that the fact that people use the word "knowledge" in all sorts of careless ways does not show that the analysis the skeptic uses is bad. It may only show that a careless use of the term is common. The skeptic would conclude that, on a proper understanding of the term, it refers to few (if any) actual cases. In short, the observation that few, if any, people use the word "knowledge" in the way required by the analysis given in 1:1.3 does not, in the skeptic's view, refute skepticism. For the skeptic claims that there is little (if any) *certain* knowledge. If we choose to use the word "knowledge" in a fallibilist way, we are simply using another concept; we are not proving what the skeptic says cannot be proved, namely, that there *is* certain knowledge. Thus, argues the skeptic, fallibilism seems unsuited to refute skepticism.

1:4.3 Foundationalism and fallibilism are only two ways in which people have attempted to avoid skepticism. There have been many more, and no doubt will be more yet. Some simply deny that there is any reason given by skeptical arguments for doubt. Those who argue in this way are called "direct realists." Direct realists claim that we have direct knowledge of things (e.g., physical objects) that the skeptic says must be known by inference (e.g., by inferring from our experiences that these experiences were caused by physical objects rather than by evil geniuses). Others have claimed that skepticism defeats itself by assuming cases that would make even skepticism senseless. For example, if the possibility that other people do not have conscious thought is taken seriously, offering other people skeptical arguments seems somewhat strange—after all, why argue to something that lacks consciousness? Imagine trying to convince a rock that it had no consciousness! Typically, the skeptic has ready replies, whether or not they are compelling. Thus, to the direct realist, the skeptic would try to show that we must indeed make inferences whereas the direct realist says we do not. And, to those who would characterize skepticism as involving the assumption of its own defeat, the skeptic would argue that there is no nonsense in arguing to things that one doesn't *know* to lack consciousness, and the skeptic is the very one who claims to lack knowledge. Moreover, the skeptic does not assume that the possibilities he raises are true; he only argues that we cannot dismiss them and that, if they were true, what we claimed to know would be false. Further, the fact that we cannot dismiss them leaves room for doubt and thus defeats claims of certain knowledge. Any number of other nonskeptical arguments exist, with as many skeptical responses, nonskeptical replies to these responses, and so forth.

Still, despite skeptical arguments and the fact that, at least in the eyes of many philosophers, we have yet to find a definitive answer to such arguments, most of us go on making knowledge claims. Most of us continue to believe that we can (or even do!) know something. So epistemologists are inclined to continue to search for ways to decisively answer skepticism. If you think that there is a way, perhaps you will be the one to do it! All the more reason for you to study more epistemology and consider the arguments for and against skepticism that have been offered. It might be that some combination of arguments already offered will do it. Or perhaps an utterly novel solution will be needed. One way or another, an answer that finally puts skepticism to rest would be a great philosophical advance, and there is no reason to suppose that such an answer cannot be found. Indeed, this is one area in which few philosophers are inclined to be nonskeptical—most believe that we *do not* know that we *cannot* know.

1:5 CONCEPTUAL EXPERIMENT

In the following story by R. Gaines Smith, you are provided with the setting for a conceptual experiment that addresses the problem of knowledge and the possibility of deception. You will notice that the device Smith uses is much like Descartes' evil genius, insofar as it is designed to deceive those subjected to it. In the philosophical essay that follows, O. K. Bouwsma presents a very witty and imaginative argument that attempts to show that Descartes' evil genius does not provide grounds for total skepticism, or anything close to it. As you read the story and the essay, see if you are convinced by the claims made in them, or if instead you are inclined to be more skeptical than Smith or Bouwsma.

Conceptual Experiment 1:

WELFARE DEPARTMENT

R. Gaines Smith

At exactly 2:53 A.M. on a Wednesday morning, Fullmar decided to give up. It was not just that fatigue was beginning to overtake him like a fever. A cold, nervous sweat had broken out on his forehead, and large drops of perspiration were beginning to run down his face and trickle into his vest collar. He took his hands away from the control console, slouched back in his chair, and stared up at the flashing lights on the huge caseload monitoring panel on the wall in front of him.

Client number 16 had fallen into a complete mental breakdown. It had happened about 10 P.M. that evening and Fullmar had spent the last five hours frantically trying to bring him out of it. Now the red light at the bottom of 16's reader, the light marked "breakdown," was in full force, winking at him like some serpentine eye. Fullmar looked at the other lights on 16's reader: "despair," "depression," "contentment," and "joy" were dark and motionless as though their wiring were permanently haywire. He was now wondering if he would ever get client number 16 up even to a state of "despair" much less "contentment."

Fullmar's head dropped and he stared through glazed eyes at client 16's profile chart propped on the control panel in front of him. Was there anything he hadn't tried yet? Client 16's name was George Cletus Mumford, he was 47 years old, and the Humanity Board had committed him to the care of Welfare Department number 84-B, District 32 on 3 November 2064. He had been assigned to Fullmar's 98-person caseload two days later.

Fullmar vividly recalled the preliminary interview. Mumford had revealed himself as a severely depressed and lethargic man who had virtually lost the ability to desire anything. He had sat slouched over staring vacuously at the floor. He didn't say much and, when he spoke, it was a rambling discourse the drift of which Fullmar didn't follow too well.

These clients were always the hardest to program. Fullmar remembered predicting that this client's program would be extremely difficult to maintain in a state of even relative stability. That prediction had come true.

He remembered asking Mumford in what kind of program he

might be interested. At first the man had no ideas, and then he had several. Indecision was always an ominous sign.

"I dunno," drawled Mumford, "my mother always wanted me to be a big wheel in one of the government bureaus, you know, so's I could slip her and pa some extra ration cards on the sly. But I'm really not interested in that crap. The work's too hard."

"Tell me some of the things you always wanted to do in life," Fullmar ventured.

The question seemed to stump Mumford. He stared stupidly at Fullmar for a few moments. "I guess I never wanted to do much," said Mumford. "I never much gave a damn."

Fullmar tried to probe deeper. "Then tell me some of the dreams you used to have as a child. Didn't you ever daydream as a child? Didn't you ever fantasize?"

The effort to think seemed to make Mumford uncomfortable. He furrowed his eyebrows a bit and let his mouth hang slightly open.

"Well, when I was real young, I really wanted to be a professional football player, but they've outlawed that now."

"That could be arranged," said Fullmar, hoping he was getting somewhere.

But Mumford's mind continued to drift: " . . . and then there were the times I wanted to be a world traveler and then I wanted to be a super-spy for the government and another time I wanted to be a symphony conductor and one time . . ."

"Wait a minute," said Fullmar interceding. "You are going to have to understand, Mr. Mumford, that we have to determine *one* particular fantasy you would like to experience. If I had more time, I could switch you around from fantasy to fantasy, but you have to understand I have 97 other cases I have to keep operative; so please try to think of one particular fantasy you would like to experience, the one that would give you the most pleasure."

"Why can't I just be whatever I want to be?" asked Mumford incredulously.

"For the reasons I just told you. I can't spend all my time on one case; so please think of the experience you would really like to have."

"Ah, I really don't much give a damn," Mumford said poutingly. He sat hunched over in his lounge for several moments picking his fingernails and staring at the floor.

"You know what I really want," Mumford finally said in a fairly whispering voice.

"What?" Fullmar asked. "Don't be afraid to tell me. We can program just about everything."

"Well . . ." Mumford drawled. "I don't want to shock you."

"You won't. I've heard just about everything."

"Well . . . I always wanted to be a . . . you know . . . a big success with women." Mumford chortled like an adolescent telling a dirty joke.

This is what it often came down to. The vast majority of Fullmar's clients were more concerned with their ids than with their egos. Mumford's program had been comparatively easy to formulate. He wanted to be a star musician with a vast following of hero-worshiping teenaged girls upon which he would feast sexually. It was ridiculous, Fullmar thought at the time, but sexual fantasies were rather easy to program. All you had to do was attach the right electrodes to the right part of the brain, induce periodic injections of the right drugs into the client's digestive tract, and see to it that the erogenous zones of the body were properly stimulated, at the proper time. A good technician sitting at the control console of the XRV Hallucinogenic Neural Unit, monitoring the mind reader, and occasionally turning on the Mind Screen ought to be able to maintain the client in a dormant but hopefully benevolent delirium for the rest of his natural life. It was better than facing poverty and alienation in a cruel, competitive society. And, certainly, it was better than the old concepts of social service.

But while all the technology was predictable, one thing was not—the client himself. Fullmar was more aware of that than any of the other social workers in the department, but even he tried not to think of it most of the time. It was times like this when those thoughts were unavoidable.

He closed his eyes tightly and tried not to look at the Mind Screen on his left. He would have to look at it sooner or later, but he wanted to postpone the event for a few more moments. He opened his eyes slowly, breathed deeply a few times and then swung his chair over in front of the Mind Screen console. Still slouched, he reached up, grasped the client control dial, and began turning it. It stopped when the number 16 reached the arrow at the top of the dial. That simple movement would register Mumford's current brainwaves, run them through the XRV, translate them into a visual facsimile of Mumford's thoughts, and then produce an image on the Mind Screen.

Fullmar sat resolutely back in his lounge. He tried to remain calm, but his body shuddered. His arms began to tremble. Waiting for the Mind Screen to reproduce a breakdown was always like that one moment in a horror story when the castle door begins to creak open and you have no idea what ghastly apparition will appear on the other side.

A few horizontal flashes of light zipped across the screen and then several vertical flashes appeared on the edges of the screen and persisted. They were unrecognizable, but they undulated like an erotic dancer. Two green arms with a scaly, reptilian hide appeared in the center of the screen. Fullmar felt a cold shock in his chest. The arms were not connected to anything in particular. There was only a black, indistinguishable haze where the body should be. It was apparent that the XRV had no means by which to reproduce the body that Mumford was seeing—or that Mumford's mind had no such means. The green arms held a long, three-pronged fork which they repeatedly thrust toward the front of the screen.

The macabre image on the screen was just starting to become unbearable when it abruptly changed. Two feet appeared on the screen. They appeared to be reclining at the end of a conventional full-body lounge. Fullmar exhaled the breath he had been holding. The image began to move with its focus on the feet. The feet appeared to lift off the lounge and step onto a floor. The focus began to move around fixing itself alternatingly on the few amenities of a conventional sleeping room: lounges, illuminators, family photos.

"He's trying to wake up," Fullmar said for the hearing of no one. "Wake up! Wake up!" he fairly shouted starting to rise out of his lounge.

Immediately, he remembered that there was no way Mumford could actually wake up. The XRV would never let anyone wake up. This image on the screen was, in fact, a dream. The XRV's specific function was to visually enhance the pseudo-reality of dreams. It couldn't distinguish between a pleasant fantasy and a horrifying nightmare. Neither did the source of a dream affect the XRV's essential function. Whether the source was a caseworker's program or the client's deranged imagination, the XRV's sole function was verisimilitude.

"Maybe I can help," thought Fullmar. He swung over in front of the control console and began frantically manipulating switches, dials, and levers, trying to stabilize the sleeping room dream in Mumford's mind.

The sleeping room disappeared. For a few moments, it was replaced by horizontal flashes zipping across the screen. Moments later those were replaced by the strange vertical flashes on the edges of the screen.

"I can't help! I'm *not* helping!" In despair Fullmar sagged against the control console and stared up at the Mind Screen, waiting for it to do its will.

Four red arms, each covered with egg-sized blisters appeared on the right-center of the screen. They thrust two three-pronged forks toward the front of the screen. Fullmar threw his arms in front of his face to protect his eyes. He peeked through his forearms at the undulating vertical flashes on the edges of the screen. Now he recognized them. They were flames.

Without pausing to turn the screen off, Fullmar lunged toward the door of his office. The door's eye managed to register him in time and move the panel before he smashed into it, but it could not prevent Fullmar's body from smashing into the hallway wall opposite the door. Fullmar slipped briefly to one knee, but he was quickly up and running at full speed down the hall. Fortunately, at this hour, there was no one in the halls. But had it even been regular office hours, none of the other department staff and caseworkers would have paid too much attention. It was not unusual for caseworkers to suddenly go berserk. If anyone had looked up, it would have been merely to notice that this was Fullmar's first time.

When he reached the caseworker's lounge, he rushed over to the tranquilizer vendor. He thrust two coupons into the machine and stood waiting with his chest heaving. Four red pellets appeared in the tray. Fullmar seized them and thrust them into his mouth. A couch was a few paces behind him and he stepped back and sprawled on it.

It was about ten minutes before Fullmar was able to focus his mind on the problem.

"Come on! Think!" Fullmar told himself wearily. "You must try to understand what has happened. You must discover what you are doing wrong. You must discover what *is* wrong."

He would have to go down to the "Morgue." It was unavoidable now. If #16 was seeing himself in Hell, he must be in agony. Injecting a sedative via the control console would not guarantee the desired results. He would have to inspect the client personally, inject the sedative manually, and personally observe the results. Client #16 was going to need immediate intensive care just to prevent him from dying of fright.

A personal inspection of Mumford would permit Fullmar to check the wiring, but he was fairly sure there was no technical problem. Whatever the problem was it was the same problem that had placed 28 per cent of Department 84-B's 1,592 clients on a breakdown reading. All of those people were now in the same state of prolonged anesthesia to which Fullmar would soon commit George Mumford. Very little effort was being made to bring these people out of the breakdown status, and, for the most part, the caseworker staff was struggling to avoid further breakdowns.

Only fear was keeping Fullmar awake now. His body felt like it had gone to sleep hours ago, but his mind was just alert enough to force him to fully experience the full terror of the "Morgue."

He decided to stand up resolutely, but he stumbled for his first few steps. He walked to and entered the elevator in the hall and pressed the button labeled "Sedation Vault." "That's all it really is," he told himself. The people are merely under sedation. They're not really dead. It's silly to think of the vault as a "morgue." He tried to force a smile but failed.

The sign above the elevator door blinked "Sedation Vault" and the door opened much too quickly. Fullmar stepped into the vault and stood motionless for a few moments. It was terrifying to feel so alone and exposed in a room full of more than 1,500 people. The six huge monoliths that contained the clients towered silently above Fullmar like giant coffins. Each, in fact, had the geometric shape of a coffin except in gigantic dimensions: 30 feet high, 30 feet wide and 100 feet long. Like thousands of strands of seaweed, a tangled mass of wires dangled from almost every portion of the vault's ceiling. The mass was formless at the top of the ceiling 60 feet over Fullmar's head. But, eventually, it gathered into six subdivisions each of which fed into the top-center of one of the monoliths. Each of the monoliths was in three divisions down its entire length. On one outer division was a row of several hundred crypts containing clients. Sandwiched in between was the gigantic Receiving Neural Unit which gathered impulse directions from case-workers on the upper floors which it, in turn, translated into the dreams, fantasies, and now nightmares of over 1,500 people.

Fullmar made a mechanical motion toward one of the monoliths. He had taken several steps before he realized that he had forgotten his client's number. He stopped for a moment and put his hands to his face. "George . . . oh, yes . . . George Mumford . . . that was it." Fullmar always came to the "Morgue" resolved to give a client genuine assistance. But, once there, the sole impulse was to get out. "Let's see . . . he was Client 16, Caseload 13 . . . but which vault?" Fullmar pulled his fingers down over his eyes and stared at the six monoliths. "How can I forget which vault?" he asked himself. He remembered that it was one of the middle vaults; so it must be three or four. He tried four.

Fullmar's footsteps resounded in the immense subterranean chamber as he walked along the length of vault four. Up on the third terrace, he saw the number "13" painted on one of the caseload sections. He climbed the stairs, crossed the terrace, and stood in front of Caseload 13.

Client 16's crypt was on the fourth level of crypts about at Fullmar's shoulder level. Fullmar placed his fingers against the label on the steel facing of the crypt and wiped off some of the dust. Three rows of neat letters appeared in the space Fullmar had wiped away:

Cl-16, Ca-13, Va-4, WD-84-B, Di-32

George Cletus Mumford

3 November 2064

Fullmar reached for one of the many keys attached to his belt. It felt cold and moist. He placed the key quietly in the socket, grasped the handle of the crypt and then stood back at arm's length as though the crypt's opening would set off an explosion.

He had not moved the crypt an inch when an animal scream rose out of the vault and struck his face like some physical force. He fell back and only the railing on the terrace prevented him from falling to the steel floor twenty feet below. Fullmar had lost his grip of the crypt's handle, but as it rolled out on its own inertia, with each inch of movement the scream rose in vibrato crescendo filling the huge chamber with echoes and re-echoes.

Slack-jawed in horror Fullmar rose to his feet and stared at the body of his client.

The layers of fat on Mumford's torso had taken on a gray pallor like a molded loaf of bread. They shook in undulations with each scream even though the screams were almost breathless and unabated. There was nothing wrong with the wiring. Each of the dozens of wires had somehow remained adhered to Mumford's body. The man's mouth was so wide open his teeth were bared. His eyes were sightless because their pupils had rolled back into their sockets.

As though drawing a weapon, Fullmar whipped an injection gun out of his vest pocket, slammed it into Mumford's arm and turned his face away from the body as the injection took effect. In a few moments, the screams began to subside, turned to gasps, then to whimpers. As soon as the Sedation Vault returned to silence, Fullmar dropped the injection gun, slammed the crypt and ran.

"Mr. Fullmar, are you with us?" Fullmar's eyes blinked and his head bobbed upward.

"This is a rather important discussion, Mr. Fullmar, I wonder if you could try to stay awake." The department superintendent was pacing nervously up and down in front of the conference room. He was a short, stout man with a face that was flushed even to the top of his balding head. "I'm trying to get some of you people to appreciate the gravity of this situation," he continued, "I'd hope I could at least maintain your attention."

"I'm sorry," said Fullmar, "I was up with a client last night." Fullmar looked around at some of his fellow caseworkers. Most of them looked bored.

"All right, then," snapped the superintendent, thrusting himself up to his full height and pulling down the front of his vest. "Let's get back to the problem at hand."

"All of you people know perfectly well that we've got a crisis situation on our hands. Some of you people are approaching a 50 per cent breakdown percentage. How much longer do you think I can tolerate this kind of unprofessionalism? Most of you people have degrees in professional social welfare programming provided to you by the state. The state ought to be able to expect something in return for its investment. You've all got excuses. Excuses! Excuses! Excuses! You all say you haven't yet reached high enough levels of technical competence. You all just want a little more time. You're all sure that in just a few more months' time you'll have all your normal cases stabilized and you can start working on the revivals of your breakdown cases. But every time we do our monthly survey, this department has more breakdowns on its hands. Every time we have this meeting I have to listen to more excuses. Do you know what I think the real problem is?" the Superintendent asked, fairly shouting. "It's plain, crass insensitivity!" He emphasized each word with a slam of his chubby fist into his palm. "I hope I don't have to remind you people of the penalties for insensitivity. The state is very precise on this matter. These penalties will be meted out if I don't start seeing some improvement around here."

"You, Fasso, what do you have to say for yourself?" The Superintendent was pointing toward a large, poorly complected woman in one of the front seats. Fasso sat picking at her fingernails and staring at the floor. She looked up at the Superintendent with an entreating expression on her face.

"But Mr. Muir, I've had the highest sensitivity rating of any caseworker ever to come here," she said in a caterwauling voice.

"Yes, yes," said the superintendent with bored exasperation. "You never fail to mention that. What I want to know is why the caseworker with the highest sensitivity rating also has the highest breakdown rating?"

Fasso didn't answer the question. "I don't see why breakdown ratings should have that much to do with it," Fasso said pouting. "You have to have a really human feeling for clients to help them. It's easy to run an XRV. That's just an insensitive machine. Nobody ever sees the depth of human compassion I offer to my clients in preprogram interviews. That should count for something too, you know. How can you compare warm, human sympathy to cold, technical competence? I believe the caseworkers with high breakdown ratings are merely showing their higher sensitivity."

"No one's really questioning your sensitivity," the Superintendent said with some consolation. "But . . . but Fullmar . . ." The Superintendent turned toward the back of the room. "Can't you do something about this? I thought I asked you to help Fasso and some of the other clients who have been having problems."

"Fasso isn't interested," said Fullmar rubbing one of his eyes with his fingers.

"What do you mean?" said Superintendent Muir.

"I mean she has no interest in becoming technically competent. I

mean she spends most of her time in the caseworker lounge. I mean
she wants me to take the responsibility for programming most of her
clients."

"That's not true, you damn liar," shouted Fasso leaping to her feet
and confronting Fullmar. She clenched her fists and her face flushed
almost as much as Superintendent Muir's.

"He doesn't have half of my sensitivity. He doesn't even show any
sensitivity toward his fellow caseworkers."

The other caseworkers were paying attention now. A few chuckles
reverberated around the room.

"Do I have to put up with this insult to my professional integrity?"
Fasso asked the Superintendent.

"The only thing you do professionally is loaf," said Fullmar.

"You lousy . . ." bellowed Fasso moving threateningly toward Fullmar.

"All right! All right!" said the Superintendent moving to cut off
Fasso. "I think all this energy ought to be expended trying to help our
clients. Now I want everyone to go back to work and *please* try to put
out a little bit more of an effort. I think that's all we'll need to talk
about today. I'll see you all at the same time tomorrow. Fullmar, could
you stick around for a few minutes, I'd like to talk to you."

When the room was cleared, Superintendent Muir leaned up
against the wall, crossed his arms, and looked at Fullmar wearily.

"I suppose you are waiting for an apology," said Fullmar.

"Nooooo," said the Superintendent straining to be good natured.
"You know you're the best caseworker I've got here. I just wish you
would try to be a little bit more tolerant of some of the people who
don't have your gifts. You have to understand that not all of these
people are protégés of Dr. Zacharius. You've inherited much of the old
master's brilliance. Why can't you spread some of that wealth around?"

"I'm really beginning to wonder if I possess that wealth," said
Fullmar.

"What do you mean?"

Fullmar didn't answer.

"I hope you aren't getting discouraged now," said Muir with
genuine concern. "I just don't know if I could handle that. I know I
probably praise you too much, probably even help contribute to your
low sensitivity rating. But, in so many ways, it's really like having Dr.
Zacharius still with us. I don't know if we will ever really be able to
make Dr. Zacharius' dreams come true, but, if we do, Fullmar, I know
it is people like you who will do it."

"I had to take tranquilizers last night," said Fullmar.

The strained smile remained on Muir's face.

"Did you hear me?"

The smile collapsed. "Not you, Fullmar. Tell me you're joking."

"I'm not."

"Well, it just must be some temporary mental relapse. You're working too hard. It's just a human error. You're just human, Fullmar."

"You're right that I've been working too hard, but that may not be the reason."

"What do you mean?" asked Muir, his face stern.

Fullmar looked at Muir for several moments.

"All I know is that I witnessed a man suffer excruciating mental agony last night and I couldn't prevent it. In fact, I felt I was the cause of it. How can a professional social welfare worker live with himself if he is faced with the possibility that he may not be helping clients and may, in fact, be hurting them? How sensitive is that kind of man?"

"I don't know. I don't want to know," answered Muir nervously. "But that isn't why I asked you to stay after the meeting."

"Why did you?"

"I've got absolutely fabulous news for you," said the Superintendent with strained enthusiasm. "Commissioner Heidemann from the Humanity Board is here and he wants to talk to you."

"What did I do?" asked Fullmar warily.

"Nothing, nothing wrong at all," said the Superintendent. "Commissioner Heidemann merely wants to talk to you about performing an extremely important re-programming. Mark my words, Fullmar, this could be the most important assignment of your career." Fullmar scrutinized the expression on the Superintendent's face. The smile was drawn back as far as the lips would permit and the eyes were wide open and appeared to be genuinely enthusiastic. But the face was more flushed than ever.

Somehow the flush of the Superintendent's complexion had taken on an even deeper hue when Fullmar entered the conference room for his appointment with Commissioner Heidemann.

"Here he is, here's our young genius," said Superintendent when Fullmar entered the room. He grasped Fullmar's arm in both hands and led him down a long table toward a huge man who sat in a lounge at the end.

"This is the young man I have been telling you about, Commissioner Heidemann." Leaning toward Heidemann, the Superintendent said, "Fullmar is the leading protégé of Dr. Zacharius. He came to me with the highest technical recommendations of any caseworker I've ever had. He has some problems with this sensitivity rating, but we're working on that, aren't we Fullmar?" The Superintendent clapped Fullmar on the shoulder good-naturedly.

Fullmar and Heidemann stood staring at each other.

Heidemann's face reminded Fullmar of a bulldog. The large, slack jowls below the bushy eyebrows and the tousled hair looked loose and puffy, but they remained immobile as though carved from stone.

"Sit down," said Heidemann, his small mouth barely moving.

Fullmar pulled out a lounge and sat.

"Are you really as good as Muir says you are?"

"I really don't know how good I am," said Fullmar.

"How close were you to Dr. Zacharius?"

"Not close personally. I was his best student. I had heard Zacharius was the most prominent Skinnerian in the contemporary field of behavior modification. I thought that he might give me the theoretical knowledge and the technical skills to help people. He gave me the technical skills."

"What do you mean by that?" said Heidemann leaning forward.

Fullmar didn't answer.

"Surely you can't add anything ideologically to a system that has finally brought humanity and sensitivity to social service?" said Heidemann.

"Probably not," said Fullmar. "But that isn't why you're here. What can I do for you?"

Heidemann leaned slowly back in his lounge.

"You must know that two years ago Prof. Zacharius decided to retire and upon retiring he seemed to have dropped out of society. He did retire, of course, but not in the way most people believe. This department is too big to suppress rumors; so you probably know where he really is."

"Yes, I've heard that Dr. Zacharius decided to program his own dream and right now he is in a special dream chamber on the top floor."

"Now, I want you to know that I have nothing but the most profound respect for the eminence of Dr. Zacharius in his field, but . . ."

" . . . but Dr. Zacharius' program has broken down," said Fullmar finishing Heidemann's sentence.

"Don't jump to any conclusions," said Heidemann testily. "We don't know if it is really a breakdown. It could be anything. It's just that his reader is acting very strangely, moving rapidly up and down from joy to breakdown back to joy and so on. We just want you to go up there and check Zacharius' Mind Screen. He left strict orders that no one was ever to read his Mind Screen. But I'm sure he would make an exception for his top student, particularly in these unusual circumstances. I hope you can understand that we can't have the intellectual founder of this entire welfare system on a breakdown reading. The entire Humanity Board is very upset about it and wants some quick action. You can certainly do something about this. It's probably very simple."

"Maybe it isn't simple at all."

"What do you mean?" said Heidemann in a slow, menacing tone.

"You seem to believe that it is simply a technical problem. What if it isn't? What if the problem is much more serious than that?"

"Of course it's a technical problem," snapped Heidemann. "What else could it be?"

"If Dr. Zacharius' program is having trouble, if the *Founder* of our Welfare system is showing an unstable reader, then that has to tell us that it is not just a technical problem. Remember the welfare of hundreds of thousands of clients is at issue here. And that is why we have to begin to question some of the basic ideas this system is based upon."

"You had better explain yourself," demanded Heidemann with his voice more menacing than ever.

Fullmar was sure now that he was treading on dangerous ideological ground. He decided to ease gradually into the subject.

"I'm going to ask you to do me a favor by considering my problem. Superintendent Muir says I have a poor sensitivity rating. But I have never questioned my sensitivity or my humanity. That is *why* I became a professional welfare caseworker. I've dedicated my life to relieving the suffering of unfortunate people.

"But when I see my efforts hurting people, when I see people suffering in this system, I have to know why. I have to begin to wonder if there isn't something fundamentally wrong with this entire system, something that we and maybe even Dr. Zacharius have never even considered. I have to begin to wonder if it is healthy to tamper with people's minds, to forcefeed them with fantasies; to separate them from reality."

"Reality!" shouted Heidemann leaping to his feet. "The reality these people have faced in the past is poverty, alienation, deprivation, and social ostracism. *That* was their reality. Dr. Zacharius' work has given these people dreams; he has given them experiences they could have never experienced in your so-called reality. How dare you question . . ."

"He doesn't really mean it," said Superintendent Muir interrupting. "Fullmar's been working too hard. He's upset. I'll have a talk with him. This whole thing is just one of those things that gets out of hand."

"Shut up, Muir," said Heidemann emphasizing each word. "Now listen, Fullmar," said Heidemann turning back to the young caseworker. "I don't know what kind of crazy ideas you have let get into your head, but you are spouting a lot of counter-revolutionary nonsense. Why, I could have you turned over to Security just on the basis of what I have heard. It's not for petty functionaries like you to concern themselves with notions about reality. This system is your reality. *I* am your reality and don't you ever forget it. Now I am ordering you to tend to Dr. Zacharius' program. You are to do so with dispatch and that is all there is to it. Do you understand?"

Fullmar sighed deeply. "Yes," he answered softly.

It was strange to see Dr. Zacharius' face in this condition. He had remembered a stern visage with a gray beard and thick, wavy gray hair. He could remember how many times that face had confronted him to remonstrate him for some faltering in his studies.

Now the face was long and slack. The eyes were just slightly opened, but Fullmar could see the pupils just under the eyelids. The jaw hung loose, but it moved up and down slowly with the mouth open as though Zacharius were a fish breathing slowly underwater.

Zacharius' long body lay in a coffin-like structure under a large glass lid which covered the entire structure. A long lamp, the length and breadth of the entire coffin hung over the prone body. Almost without winking, the pupil stared up at the overhanging lamp.

Fullmar stood with his elbows on the coffin lid staring at Zacharius for a long while. He had always wondered about this man. He had wondered about his theories. He had wondered about his humanitarianism. Ever since Zacharius' retirement, there had been many questions he had wanted to ask the man. Now he felt he was going to see some of the answers.

The extra-large Mind Screen loomed over Zacharius' coffin to Fullmar's left. Fullmar walked to its control console and turned it on.

Fullmar watched the screen for a long while. He watched it much longer than he needed to. He watched it much longer than he wanted to. After 45 minutes, he turned off the screen and left the dream chamber.

"Fullmar, please! Please! You don't know what you're doing. You've been working too hard. You . . . ." Superintendent Muir was following Fullmar down the hall toward the conference room yapping at his heels like some ill-bred puppy. "Fullmar, he won't listen to you. Fullmar, he'll turn you over to Security. Do you know what that means? Fullmar, you don't know some of the things of which Security is capable."

"I'm not going to do that reprogram," Fullmar said resolutely. "You can just forget about it."

When they reached the entrance to the conference room, Muir

threw himself in front of it. "Fullmar, please. I'm asking you for the last time." Muir's flushed face was desperate. "Fullmar, he'll blame this on me. Can't you see that? If you won't think of yourself, think of me."

Fullmar pushed Muir aside and strode into the conference room. His abrupt entry startled Heidemann and two other Humanity Board commissioners who were reviewing department data. Heidemann turned to confront Fullmar, his face as severe as ever.

"It's not my fault. It's not my fault," screamed Muir rushing toward Heidemann, his hands clasped in entreaty. "He's a subversive and counter-revolutionary. I've wanted to report him to Security, but he threatened me."

Heidemann ignored Muir and stood glowering at Fullmar. The Commissioner took a few steps forward and glared directly into Fullmar's eyes. "Am I hearing what I'm hearing?" said Heidemann through bared teeth.

"Do you have any idea how Dr. Zacharius has programmed himself?" said Fullmar trying to control the tone of his voice. "He's seeing himself as the Security Leader of some kind of prison. Except this prison has a wire fence containing all the inmates and huge towers with weapons sticking out of them. Zacharius and all the security officers spend their time beating, torturing, raping and murdering all the inmates."

"You're a damn liar," said Heidemann, his voice rasping.

"It would be very easy for you to check for yourself."

"He's a subversive," squeaked Muir.

"SHUT UP!" shouted Heidemann in an indeterminable direction.

"Don't you see what this means?" said Fullmar losing control of his voice. "It means that the founder of this welfare system is an insensitive monster. He doesn't love human beings; he hates them. I'm not changing that program. I insist that you and the rest of the Humanity Board view Dr. Zacharius' program and draw the necessary conclusions."

Fullmar waited for some change in Heidemann's stolid expression of searing animosity. None came.

Without moving his glaring eyes from Fullmar, Heidemann stepped back a few paces and turned on the communicator. "This is Commissioner Heidemann. I want three Security Officers to be sent to the conference room as quickly as possible," he said without turning to the receiver.

"Then you *do* know what it means," said Fullmar in a low, choking voice. "You know exactly what Zacharius' theories lead to—either that or you don't care. You know why we are having all these breakdowns. And you know that I know why."

Three huge Security officers, two men and one woman entered the room.

"It's him. It's him," said Muir waving a finger at Fullmar. "He's a subversive."

The three strode over to Fullmar and seized his arms. They looked toward Heidemann waiting for instructions.

"You can't do this," Fullmar suddenly shouted. "You can't treat people like bundles of nerve endings waiting for stimuli. People aren't like neural units. You can't program them. People have to be free to think for . . ."

A guard suddenly clasped his hand over Fullmar's mouth.

"Get him out of here," snarled Heidemann. "Take him to the Central Programming Room."

"No, God damn you," shouted Fullmar through the officer's hand. He began struggling, beating his elbows against the chests of the two male officers. The female reached for her truncheon, pressed it lightly to Fullmar's temple and pressed its button. The charge from the truncheon snapped Fullmar's head back, his eyes strained open for a moment and he collapsed.

When Fullmar awakened, he found himself strapped to a reclining stool in the Central Programming Room. He slowly rolled his head up and found himself staring into the grinning face of Fasso.

" . . . and all I want you to do is a simple programming." Fullmar recognized Heidemann's voice, but for the moment he couldn't see the man. "I just want him to do the assignment he was ordered to do," the voice continued. "He already has the original instructions in the memory part of his consciousness. All you have to do is redirect them to the front of his consciousness, while seeing to it that none of that other crap is remembered. Just get him to do a simple reprogram, something that the Humanity Board can accept. He could have Zacharius doing social work in a poverty area, running an orphanage, anything like that. It should be simple."

"But make sure that Fullmar doesn't remember anything that went on after he goes into Zacharius' dream chamber," Heidemann said with emphasis. "Make him forget all his rebelliousness. Just make sure he follows orders."

"It will be a pleasure, Commissioner," said Fasso.

"That's what I want to hear, Fasso. I know I can count on someone with your sensitivity rating to appreciate the importance of this assignment."

Fullmar's head fell back down on his chest and he snickered audibly. It was a long-awaited release of tensions. He began to laugh.

"You silly fools," he said, turning to his three captors. "Don't you know this won't work? You are going to try to get me to perform a complicated reprogramming while I am in a dream state. You're insane. Don't you suspect that I might be able to think for myself? Don't you suspect that I might be able to distinguish your program from reality?"

"Reality," scoffed Heidemann. "It's obvious to me now that, despite your technical superiority, you were never right for this profession. You're unworthy to be called a protégé of Dr. Zacharius. You are too ideologically backward to grasp the fact that as far as human understanding is concerned, your so-called reality is in a state of constant flux. Zacharius' genius is that he discovered a way to make reality whatever he wanted it to be. He realized that it is not important for us to waste our time trying to understand what reality is. You can never know that for sure anyway. It is more important to shape reality. It's most important for the enlightened leaders of society to create the kind of reality that is best for society."

"It won't work. It's inhumane," said Fullmar staring blankly at the floor.

"I don't even know why I waste my time with you," snarled Heidemann. "I can do whatever I want with you. I am going to give you a very simple demonstration of Zacharius' theories. When Fasso gets done with you, your reality will be what we say it is. You will think what we want you to think."

Fullmar laughed. With a grin on his face, he turned his head to the left to find Heidemann and Muir exiting the Central Programming Room. "You goddamn mindless fools," he said to himself audibly.

Heidemann stopped abruptly at the entrance to the room and turned back to address Fasso. "I'm counting on you, Fasso," he remonstrated.

"Don't worry," said Fasso as Heidemann left.

Fasso turned to Fullmar with her vicious grin.

Fullmar laughed.

"Fasso, you worthless incompetent. You don't know how glad I am to have you performing this program. I couldn't have picked a better person to do this job even if they had let me do so."

The grin on Fasso's face fell as Fullmar laughed all the harder. Pulling her extended arm behind her like a swinging gate, Fasso suddenly brought her fat fist around in haymaker fashion and sent it crashing into Fullmar's jaw. With the other fist, she jammed an injection gun into Fullmar's arm.

Fullmar giggled his way into unconsciousness.

The gathering in Zacharius' dream chamber was rapidly turning into a social event. The entire Humanity Board, various high government officials, scores of Welfare Department officials, their wives and guests milled around the room drinking liquid refreshments. The conversation was vibrant and excited. Everyone of importance wanted to view the program of the famous Dr. Zacharius.

"But I don't know where he is," said Muir excitedly. "The entire Security Force is looking for him. He's just disappeared. But I'm sure he'll turn up soon. He's probably just off somewhere sulking."

"Muir, you and I are going to have to have an encounter later," snarled Heidemann. "You know perfectly well that I wanted Fullmar to be here. I have to make a very important ideological point at this meeting, and you have blown it for me. I want that man found in 24 hours, and I am holding you personally responsible. If he isn't found, you will do your whining in front of Security. I am sick of hearing it.

"Damn," said Heidemann gritting his teeth. "I'll just have to carry on without Fullmar." He shoved Muir aside and strode toward Zacharius' control panel trying to paste a smile on his face.

"Ladies and gentlemen, distinguished guests," said Heidemann to the crowd. "May I have your attention."

A hush came over the gathered dignitaries.

"I know that many of you have had some slight doubts about the health of our beneficent welfare program. You have wanted to know if it is functioning with maximum efficiency. Various of our opponents have been spreading vicious rumors that the system is inhumane and isn't working. Various counter-revolutionaries have even been raising long-ago-disapproved-of notions about . . . excuse me . . . the so-called cognitive reason. Well, I am now about to make a demonstration that will demolish once and for all the concepts of reason and cognition, a demonstration that will reconstitute the theories of the famous Dr. Zacharius. One of our opponents, a man named Fullmar, has been programmed to reprogram Dr. Zacharius' program. It was suffering from some minor malfunctions. What you will see here is the absolute obedience of a so-called reasoning mind. Here before your eyes is the most practical demonstration I can think of to show that reason and cognition are myths."

With a dramatic gesture, Heidemann strode to the control panel and turned on Zacharius' Mind Screen.

The screen flickered for a moment and it was several moments before the image it presented came into full focus.

A gasp of horror fell over the room.

Instead of a benevolent image of Zacharius, the audience saw a huge white rat scurrying down the endless corridors of an interminable maze. The rat's face was not quite a rat's face. It was a hideous, rodent-like caricature of Dr. Zacharius. The red eyes bugged helplessly as the rodent scurried and sniffed down the corridor looking for a piece of cheese it would never find.

Analysis:

DESCARTES' EVIL GENIUS

O. K. Bouwsma

There was once an evil genius who promised the mother of us all that if she ate of the fruit of the tree, she would be like God, knowing good and evil. He promised knowledge. She did eat and she learned, but she was disappointed, for to know good and evil and not to be God is awful. Many an Eve later, there was rumor of another evil genius. This evil genius promised no good, promised no knowledge. He made a boast, a boast so wild and so deep and so dark that those who heard it cringed in hearing it. And what was that boast? Well, that apart from a few, four or five, clear and distinct ideas, he could deceive any son of Adam about anything. So he boasted. And with some result? Some indeed! Men going about in the brightest noonday would look and exclaim: "How obscure!" and if some careless merchant counting his apples was heard to say: "two and three are five," a hearer of the boast would rub his eyes and run away. This evil genius still whispers, thundering, among the leaves of books, frightening people, whispering: "I can. Maybe I will. Maybe so, maybe not." The tantalizer! In what follows I should like to examine the boast of this evil genius.

I am referring, of course, to that evil genius of whom Descartes writes:

> I shall then suppose, not that God who is supremely good and the fountain of truth, but some evil genius not less powerful than deceitful, has employed his whole energies in deceiving me; I shall consider that the heavens, the earth, the colors, figures, sound, and all other external things are nought but illusions and dreams of which this evil genius has availed himself, in order to lay traps for my credulity; I shall consider myself as having no hands, no eyes, no flesh, no blood, nor any senses, yet falsely believing myself to possess all these things.[1]

This then is the evil genius whom I have represented as boasting that he can deceive us about all these things. I intend now to examine

O. K. Bouwsma, "Descartes' Evil Genius," *The Philosophical Review* 58 (1949): 141–151, reprinted by permission of the author's wife and the editor of *The Philosophical Review.*

[1]*The Philosophical Works of Descartes,* E. Haldane and G. R. T. Ross (Cambridge, 1968), I, 147.

this boast, and to understand how this deceiving and being deceived are to take place. I expect to discover that the evil genius may very well deceive us, but that if we are wary, we need not be deceived. He will deceive us, if he does, by bathing the word "illusion" in a fog. This then will be the word to keep our minds on. In order to accomplish all this, I intend to describe the evil genius carrying out his boast in two adventures. The first of these I shall consider a thoroughly transparent case of deception. The word "illusion" will find a clear and familiar application. Nevertheless in this instance the evil genius will not have exhausted "his whole energies in deceiving us." Hence we must aim to imagine a further trial of the boast, in which the "whole energies" of the evil genius are exhausted. In this instance I intend to show that the evil genius is himself befuddled, and that if we too exhaust some of our energies in sleuthing after the peculiarities in his diction, then we need not be deceived either.

Let us imagine the evil genius then at his ease meditating that very bad is good enough for him, and that he would let bad enough alone. All the old pseudos, pseudo names and pseudo statements, are doing very well. But today it was different. He took no delight in common lies, everyday fibs, little ones, old ones. He wanted something new and something big. He scratched his genius; he uncovered an idea. And he scribbled on the inside of his tattered halo, "Tomorrow, I will deceive," and he smiled, and his words were thin and like fine wire. "Tomorrow I will change everything, everything, everything. I will change flowers, human beings, trees, hills, sky, the sun, and everything else into paper. Paper alone I will not change. There will be paper flowers, paper human beings, paper trees. And human beings will be deceived. They will think that there are flowers, human beings, and trees, and there will be nothing but paper. It will be gigantic. And it ought to work. After all men have been deceived with much less trouble. There was a sailor, a Baptist I believe, who said that all was water. And there was no more water then than there is now. And there was a pool-hall keeper who said that all was billiard balls. That's a long time ago, of course, a long time before they opened one, and listening, heard that it was full of the sound of a trumpet. My prospects are good. I'll try it."

And the evil genius followed his own directions and did according to his words. And this is what happened.

Imagine a young man, Tom, bright today as he was yesterday, approaching a table where yesterday he had seen a bowl of flowers. Today it suddenly strikes him that they are not flowers. He stares at them troubled, looks away, and looks again. Are they flowers? He shakes his head. He chuckles to himself. "Huh! that's funny. Is this a trick? Yesterday there certainly were flowers in that bowl." He sniffs suspiciously, hopefully, but smells nothing. His nose gives no assurance. He thinks of the birds that flew down to peck at the grapes in the picture and of the mare that whinnied at the likeness of Alexander's horse. Illusions! The picture oozed no juice, and the likeness was still. He walked slowly to the bowl of flowers. He looked, and he sniffed, and he raised his hand. He stroked a petal lightly, lover of flowers, and he drew back. He could scarcely believe his fingers. They were not flowers. They were paper.

As he stands, perplexed, Milly, friend and dear, enters the room. Seeing him occupied with the flowers, she is about to take up the bowl and offer them to him, when once again he is overcome with feelings of strangeness. She looks just like a great big doll. He looks more closely, closely as he dares, seeing this may be Milly after all. Milly, are you Milly?—that wouldn't do. Her mouth clicks as she opens it, speaking, and it shuts precisely. Her forehead shines, and he shudders at the thought of Mme Tussaud's. Her hair is plaited, evenly, perfectly, like Milly's but as she raises one hand to guard its order, touching it, preening, it whispers like a newspaper. Her teeth are white as a genteel monthly. Her gums are pink, and there is a clapper in her mouth. He thinks of mama dolls, and of the rubber doll he used to pinch; it had a misplaced navel right in the pit of the back that whistled. Galatea in paper! Illusions!

He notes all these details, flash by flash by flash. He reaches for a chair to steady himself and just in time. She approaches with the bowl of flowers, and, as the bowl is extended towards him, her arms jerk. The suppleness, the smoothness, the roundness of life is gone. Twitches of a smile mislight up her face. He extends his hand to take up the bowl and his own arms jerk as hers did before. He takes the bowl, and as he does so sees her hand. It is pale, fresh, snowy. Trembling, he drops the bowl, but it does not break, and the water does not run. What a mockery!

He rushes to the window, hoping to see the real world. The scene is like a theatre-set. Even the pane in the window is drawn very thin, like cellophane. In the distance are the forms of men walking about and tossing trees and houses and boulders and hills upon the thin cross section of a truck that echoes only echoes of chugs as it moves. He looks into the sky upward, and it is low. There is a patch straight above him, and one seam is loose. The sun shines out of the blue like a drop of German silver. He reaches out with his pale hand, crackling the cellophane, and his hand touches the sky. The sky shakes and tiny bits of it fall, flaking his white hand with confetti.

Make-believe!

He retreats, crinkling, creaking, hiding his sight. As he moves he misquotes a line of poetry: "Those are perils that were his eyes," and he mutters, "Hypocritical pulp!" He goes on: "I see that the heavens, the earth, colors, figures, sound, and all external things, flowers, Milly, trees and rocks and hills are paper, paper laid as traps for my credulity. Paper flowers, paper Milly, paper sky!" Then he paused, and in sudden fright he asked "And what about me?" He reaches to his lip and with two fingers tears the skin and peels off a strip of newsprint. He looks at it closely, grim. "I shall consider myself as having no hands, no eyes, no flesh, no blood, or any senses." He lids his paper eyes and stands dejected. Suddenly he is cheered. He exclaims: "Cogito me papyrum esse, ergo sum." He has triumphed over paperdom.

I have indulged in this phantasy in order to illustrate the sort of situation which Descartes' words might be expected to describe. The evil genius attempts to deceive. He tries to mislead Tom into thinking what is not. Tom is to think that these are flowers, that this is the Milly that was, that those are trees, hills, the heavens, etc. And he does this by creating illusions, that is, by making something that looks like flowers, artificial flowers; by making something that looks like and sounds like and moves like Milly, an artificial Milly. An illusion is something that looks like or sounds like, so much like, something else that you either mistake it for something else, or you can easily understand how someone might come to do this. So when the evil genius creates illusions intending to deceive he makes things which might quite easily be mistaken for what they are not. Now in the phantasy as I discovered it Tom is not deceived. He does experience the illusion, however. The intention of this is not to cast any reflection upon the deceptive powers of the evil genius. With such refinements in the paper art as we now know, the evil genius might very well have been less unsuccessful. And that in spite of his rumored lament: "And I made her of the best paper!" No, that Tom is not deceived, that he detects the illusion, is introduced in order to remind ourselves how illusions are detected. That the paper flowers are illusory is revealed by the recognition that they are paper. As soon as Tom realizes that though they look like flowers but are paper, he is acquainted with, sees through the illusion, and is not deceived. What is required, of course, is that he know the difference between flowers and paper, and that when presented with one or the other he can tell the difference. The attempt of the evil genius also presupposes this. What he intends is that though Tom knows this difference, the paper will look so much like flowers that Tom will not notice the respect in which the paper is different from the flowers. And even though Tom had actually been deceived and had not recognized the illusion, the evil genius himself must have been aware of the difference, for this is involved in his design. This is crucial, as we shall see when we come to consider the second adventure of the evil genius.

As you will remember I have represented the foregoing as an illustration of the sort of situation which Descartes' words might be expected to describe. Now, however, I think that this is misleading. For though I have described a situation in which there are many things, nearly all of which are calculated to serve as illusions, this question may still arise. Would this paper world still be properly described as a world of illusions? If Tom says: "These are flowers," or "These look like flowers" (uncertainty), then the illusion is operative. But if Tom says: "These are paper," then the illusion has been destroyed. Descartes uses the words: "And all other external things are nought but illusions." This means that the situation which Descartes has in mind is such that if Tom says: "These are flowers," he will be wrong, but he will be wrong also if he says: "These are paper," and it won't matter what sentence of that type he uses. If he says: "These are rock"—or cotton or cloud or wood—he is wrong by the plan. He will be right only if he says: "These are illusions." But the project is to keep him from recognizing the illusions. This means that the illusions are to be brought about not by anything so crude as paper or even cloud. They must be made of the stuff that dreams are made of.

Now let us consider this second adventure.

The design then is this. The evil genius is to create a world of illusions. There are to be no flowers, no Milly, no paper. There is to be nothing at all, but Tom is every moment to go on mistaking nothing for something, nothing at all for flowers, nothing at all for Milly, etc. This is, of course, quite different from mistaking paper for flowers, paper for Milly. And yet all is to be arranged in such a way that Tom will go on just as we now do, and just as Tom did before the paper age, to see, hear, smell the world. He will love the flowers, he will kiss Milly, he will blink at the sun. So he thinks. And in thinking about these things he will talk and argue just as we do. But all the time he will be mistaken. There are no flowers, there is no kiss, there is no sun. Illusions all. This then is the end at which evil genius aims.

How now is the evil genius to attain this end? Well, it is clear that a part of what he aims at will be realized if he destroys everything. Then there will be no flowers, and if Tom thinks that there are flowers he will be wrong. There will be no face that is Milly's and no tumbled beauty on her head, and if Tom thinks that there is Milly's face and Milly's hair, he will be wrong. It is necessary then to see to it that there are none of these things. So the evil genius, having failed with paper, destroys even all paper. Now there is nothing to see, nothing to hear, nothing to smell, etc. But this is not enough to deceive. For though Tom sees nothing, and neither hears nor smells anything, he may also think that he sees nothing. He must also be misled into thinking that he does see something, that there are flowers and Milly, and hands, eyes, flesh, blood, and all other senses. Accordingly the evil genius restores to Tom his old life. Even the memory of that paper day is blotted out, not a scrap remains. Witless Tom lives on, thinking, hoping, loving as he used to, unwitted by the great destroyer. All that seems so solid, so touchable to seeming hands, so biteable to apparent teeth, is so flimsy that were the evil genius to poke his index at it, it would curl away save for one tiny trace, the smirch of that index. So once more the evil genius has done according to his word.

And now let us examine the result.

I should like first of all to describe a passage of Tom's life. Tom is all alone, but he doesn't know it. What an opportunity for methodologico–metaphysico–solipsimo! I intend, in any case, to disregard the niceties of his being so alone and to borrow his own words, with the warning that the evil genius smiles as he reads them. Tom writes:

> Today, as usual, I came into the room and there was the bowl of flowers on the table. I went up to them, caressed them, and smelled over them. I thank God for flowers! There's nothing so real to me as flowers. Here the genuine essence of the world's substance, at its gayest and most hilarious speaks to me. It seems unworthy even to think of them as erect, and waving on pillars of sap. Sap! Sap!

There was more in the same vein, which we need not bother to record. I might say that the evil genius was a bit amused, snickered in fact, as he read the words "so real," "essence," "substance," etc., but later he frowned and seemed puzzled. Tom went on to describe how Milly came into the room, and how glad he was to see her. They talked about the flowers. Later he walked to the window and watched the gardener clearing a space a short distance away. The sun was shining, but there were a few heavy clouds. He raised the window, extended his hand and four large drops of rain wetted his hand. He returned to the room and quoted to Milly a song from *The Tempest*. He got all the words right, and was well pleased with himself. There was more he wrote, but this is enough to show how quite normal everything seems. And, too, how successful the evil genius is.

And the evil genius said to himself, not quite in solipsimo, "Not so, not so, not at all so."

The evil genius was, however, all too human. Admiring himself but unadmired, he yearned for admiration. To deceive but to be unsuspected is too little glory. The evil genius set about then to plant the seeds of suspicion. But how to do this? Clearly there was no suggestive paper to tempt Tom's confidence. There was nothing but

Tom's mind, a stream of seemings and of words to make the seemings seem no seemings. The evil genius must have words with Tom and must engage the same seemings with him. To have words with Tom is to have the words together, to use them in the same way, and to engage the same seemings is to see and to hear and to point to the same. And so the evil genius, free spirit, entered in at the door of Tom's pineal gland and lodged there. He floated in the humors that flow glandwise and sensewise, everywhere being as much one with Tom as difference will allow. He looked out of the same eyes, and when Tom pointed with his finger, the evil genius said "This" and meant what Tom, hearing, also meant, seeing. Each heard with the same ear what the other heard. For every sniffing of the one nose there were two identical smells, and there were two tactualities for every touch. If Tom had had a toothache, together they would have pulled the same face. The twinsomeness of two monads finds here the limit of identity. Nevertheless there was otherness looking out of those eyes as we shall see.

It seems then that on the next day, the evil genius "going to and fro" in Tom's mind and "walking up and down in it," Tom once again, as his custom was, entered the room where the flowers stood on the table. He stopped, looked admiringly, and in a caressing voice said: "Flowers! Flowers!" And he lingered. The evil genius, more subtle "than all the beasts of the field," whispered "Flowers? Flowers?" For the first time Tom has an intimation of company, of some intimate partner in perception. Momentarily he is checked. He looks again at the flowers. "Flowers? Why, of course, flowers." Together they look out of the same eyes. Again the evil genius whispers, "Flowers?" The seed of suspicion is to be the question. But Tom now raises the flowers nearer to his eyes almost violently, as though his eyes were not his own. He is, however, not perturbed. The evil genius only shakes their head. "Did you ever hear of illusions?" says he.

Tom, still surprisingly good-natured, responds: "But you saw them, didn't you? Surely you can see through my eyes. Come, let us bury my nose deep in these blossoms, and take one long breath together. Then tell whether you can recognize these as flowers."

So they dunked the one nose. But the evil genius said "Huh!" as much as to say: What has all this seeming and smelling to do with it? Still he explained nothing. And Tom remained as confident of the flowers as he had been at the first. The little seeds of doubt, "Flowers? Flowers?" and again "Flowers?" and "Illusions?" and now this stick in the spokes, "Huh!" made Tom uneasy. He went on: "Oh, so you are one of these seers that has to touch everything. You're a tangibilite. Very well, here's my hand, let's finger these flowers. Careful! They're tender."

The evil genius was amused. He smiled inwardly and rippled in a shallow humor. To be taken for a materialist! As though the grand illusionist was not a spirit! Nevertheless, he realized that though deception is easy where the lies are big enough (where had he heard that before?), a few scattered, questioning words are not enough to make guile grow. He was tempted to make a statement, and he did. He said, "Your flowers are nothing but illusions."

"My flowers illusions?" exclaimed Tom, and he took up the bowl and placed it before a mirror. "See," said he, "here are the flowers and here, in the mirror, is an illusion. There's a difference surely. And you with my eyes, my nose, and my fingers can tell what that difference is. Pollen on your fingers touching the illusion? Send Milly the flowers in the mirror? Set a bee to suck honey out of this glass? You know all this as well as I do. I can tell flowers from illusions, and my flowers, as you now plainly see, are not illusions."

The evil genius was now sorely tried. He had his make-believe but he also had his pride. Would he now risk the make-believe to save his pride? Would he explain? He explained.

"Tom," he said, "notice. The flowers in the mirror look like flowers, but they only look like flowers. We agree about that. The flowers before the mirror also look like flowers. But they, you say, are flowers because they also smell like flowers and they feel like flowers, as though they would be any more flowers because they also like flowers multiply. Imagine a mirror such that it reflected not only the looks of flowers, but also their fragrance and their petal surfaces, and then you smelled and touched, and the flowers before the mirror would be just like the flowers in the mirror. Then you could see immediately that the flowers before the mirror are illusions just as those in the mirror are illusions. As it is now, it is clear that the flowers in the mirror are thin illusions, and the flowers before the mirror are thick. Thick illusions are the best for deception. And they may be as thick as you like. From them you may gather pollen, send them to Milly, and foolish bees may sleep in them."

But Tom was not asleep. "I see that what you mean by thin illusions is what I mean by flowers. So when you say that my flowers are your thick illusions this doesn't bother me. And as for your mirror that mirrors all layers of your thick illusions, I shouldn't call that a mirror at all. It's a duplicator, and much more useful than a mirror, provided you can control it. But I do suppose that when you speak of thick illusions you do mean that thick illusions are related to something you call flowers in much the same way that the thin illusions are related to the thick ones. Is that true?"

The evil genius was now diction-deep in explanations and went on. "In the first place let me assure you that these are not flowers. I destroyed all flowers. There are no flowers at all. There are only thin and thick illusions of flowers. I can see your flowers in the mirror, and I can smell and touch the flowers before the mirror. What I cannot smell and touch, having seen as in the mirror, is not even thick illusion. But if I cannot also *cerpicio* what I see, smell, touch, etc., what I have then seen is not anything real. *Esse est cerpici.* I just now tried to *cerpicio* your flowers, but there was nothing there. Man is after all a four- or five- or six-sense creature and you cannot expect much from so little."

Tom rubbed his eyes and his ears tingled with an eighteenth-century disturbance. Then he stared at the flowers. "I see," he said, "that this added sense of yours has done wickedly with our language. You do not mean by illusion what we mean, and neither do you mean by flowers what we mean. As for *cerpicio* I wouldn't be surprised if you'd made up that word just to puzzle us. In any case what you destroyed is what, according to you, you used to *cerpicio*. So there is nothing for you to *cerpicio* any more. But there still are what we mean by flowers. If your intention was to deceive, you must learn the language of those you are to deceive. I should say that you are like the doctor who prescribes for his patients what is so bad for himself and is then surprised at the health of his patients." And he pinned a flower near their nose.

The evil genius, discomfited, rode off on a corpuscle. He had failed. He took to an artery, made haste to the pineal exit, and was gone. Then "sun by sun" he fell. And he regretted his mischief.

I have tried in this essay to understand the boast of the evil genius. His boast was that he could deceive, deceive about "the heavens, the earth, the colors, figures, sound, and all other external things." In order to do this I have tried to bring clearly to mind what deception and such deceiving would be like. Such deception involves illusions and such deceiving involves the creation of illusions. Accordingly I have tried to imagine the evil genius engaged in the practice of deception, busy in the creation of illusions. In the first adventure everything is plain. The evil genius employs paper, paper making believe it's many other things. The effort to deceive, ingenuity in deception, being deceived by paper, detecting the illusion—all these are clearly understood. It is the second adventure, however, which is more crucial. For in this instance it is assumed that the illusion is of such a kind that no seeing, no touching, no smelling, are relevant to detecting the illusion. Nevertheless the evil genius sees, touches, smells, and does detect the illusion. He made the illusion; so, of course, he must know it. How then does he know it? The evil genius has a sense denied to men. He senses the flower-in-itself, Milly-in-herself, etc. So he creates illusions made up of what can be seen, heard, smelled, etc., illusions all because when seeing, hearing, and smelling have seen, heard, and smelled all, the special sense senses nothing. So what poor human beings sense is the illusion of what only the evil genius can sense. This is formidable. Nevertheless, once again everything is clear. If we admit the special sense, then we can readily see how it is that the evil genius should have been so confident. He has certainly created his own illusions, though he had not himself been deceived. But neither has anyone else been deceived. For human beings do not use the word "illusion" by relation to a sense with which only the evil genius is blessed.

I said that the evil genius had not been deceived, and it is true that he has not been deceived by his own illusions. Nevertheless he was deceived in boasting that he could deceive, for his confidence in this is based upon an ignorance of the difference between our uses of the words, "heavens," "earth," "flowers," "Milly," and "illusions" of these things, and his own uses of these words. For though there certainly is an analogy between our own uses and his, the difference is quite sufficient to explain his failure at grand deception. We can also understand how easily Tom might have been taken in. The dog over the water dropped his meaty bone for a picture on the water. Tom, however, dropped nothing at all. But the word "illusion" is a trap.

I began this essay uneasily, looking at my hands and saying "no hands," blinking my eyes and saying "no eyes." Everything I saw seemed to me like something Cheshire, a piece of cheese, for instance, appearing and disappearing in the leaves of the tree. Poor kitty! And now? Well . . .

CHAPTER 1 PROBES

1. In "Welfare Department" Smith describes a machine (the XRV Hallucinogenic Neural Unit) which gives people wholly consistent worlds of experience. O. K. Bouwsma mentions Descartes' evil genius, an evil deity who seeks wholly to deceive. In what ways are Smith's XRV machine and Descartes' evil genius equivalent? In what ways are they different?

2. A "client" of Smith's "Welfare Department" cannot tell the difference between reality and the false world of experience given by the XRV machine, at least in principle. But Smith seems to suggest that, in fact, the machine does not entirely accomplish its intended effect, that the clients can know that something is wrong, and thus try to "wake up," which leads their "programs" to "breakdown" status. Do you think that this is just a fact about the machine, or do you think that it is in principle impossible to have a machine which wholly deceives those attached to it? That is, do you think that a machine is possible (whether or not we could ever make one in fact) which could work perfectly in just the way the XRV machine is supposed to work? What do you suppose Bouwsma would say about this?

3. Descartes imagines his evil genius so that he can figure out precisely what we can know for certain. Since, according to him, we cannot be utterly certain that there is not such a creature as the evil genius, we cannot trust our senses to give us true information—after all, what we sense may only be deceptions from the evil genius. Do you agree with this? Why or why not?

4. According to Descartes, even if we cannot know for certain that there is not a deceiving deity who seeks always to have us believe false things, we can know with certainty at least that we exist, for the very fact that we can be deceived, that we can think, entails that we exist, for otherwise there would be no one to deceive. Do you agree, or do you think that one could be deceived (somehow) even in this? Could, for example, an XRV unit so wholly deceive people that they couldn't even be right in believing this?

5. To what extent does Bouwsma believe that the evil genius can deceive us? To what extent does Bouwsma think we cannot be deceived? Why does he think what he does? Do you agree or disagree?

6. Why do you suppose that Smith thinks that the XRV machine doesn't always have the effect it is supposed to have? For what reasons do you suppose the programs break down with such regularity?

7. Is it possible that an evil genius or an XRV unit could give someone a set of experiences *just like* those of a typical human being? Bouwsma imagines a case in which the evil genius tries to make someone believe things are real that are just paper. Couldn't the evil genius give someone experiences that were perfectly mundane, but still *entirely* false? If so, how can you know *for certain* that those you are having *right now* aren't that way? How can you know *for certain* that those you are having *right now* aren't fairly mundane versions of XRV experiences? Are there any experiences about which you *can* be certain?

8. What if we changed Smith's story in the following way: Imagine that rather than the XRV's being used as a device to put social dropouts into "cold storage," it is used in a mental institution. The patients, let's imagine, are really incapable of having any grasp on reality—they hallucinate wildly, believe themselves to be plants, automobiles, wild animals, and so forth. But let's imagine that researchers have found that using an XRV unit to give them perfectly ordinary experiences, with no memories of their terrible insanity, helps to bring them back to sanity. Thus, while hooked up to the XRV unit, they would have experiences which were very much like those had by perfectly normal, sane people, with memories which were similarly normal. While on the machine, they would have experiences of work and play, love and friendship, disappointment and boredom, excitement and joy—all the things we experience regularly: our sensations, emotions, hopes, dreams, and memories as well as normal frustrations and disappointments.

Each night, the doctors would take the patient off the machine and see whether or not he could hold his own. If not, he would go back on the machine again. Researchers find that eventually they can take someone off the machine and he will have overcome his insanity. If such a story can be told, couldn't it be that *right now you're the patient*? Perhaps part of the therapy is to have the patient experience reading science fiction stories about such machines (while taking care to make the patient feel that such stories are incredibly implausible)! Given that such a situation does not seem to be *impossible,* how can you know *for certain* that it is not actually true? (*Special note:* Don't forget that the philosophical reasons for asking such questions are not that anyone should *believe* such a story but that, if it is possible, it might tell us something about the scope and possibility of certain knowledge. Of course anyone who really believed such a story would be a bit out of his mind, but can you find reasons for denying that such a story is *possible*? That is, can you know *for certain* that it isn't true?)

9.   Bouwsma argues that wholesale hallucination is impossible, because such experiences would be meaningless. Critics who favor skepticism argue that what's at issue is the *cause* of our experiences. They ask, "But why couldn't an evil genius make us *think* that our experiences of flowers were caused by real flowers, when in fact they are really caused by the evil genius (or the XRV unit)?" Could Bouwsma answer this? How do you suppose he would react to this?

10.   Now that you have considered the case for the evil genius and the XRV unit, what do you think is the scope of human knowledge? Do these cases prove that *nothing* can be known for certain? Do they prove that many things, normally thought to be known with certainty, cannot be known, although some things can still be known? Do they prove anything at all about the limits of human knowledge? Given that these cases are implausible (which everyone, including the most thorough skeptic, allows), can you show that they are irrelevant to the question of knowledge, or only partially relevant? What can you know for certain?

RECOMMENDED READING

Science Fiction and the Problem of Knowledge

Many science fiction plots turn on problems of knowledge: Central characters are unable to get the specific knowledge that they want. Sometimes the characters are clever or lucky enough to escape their difficulties, but sometimes they are condemned by their ignorance to suffer ironic defeats. At their best these plots are filled with surprising twists or booby traps.

The Problem of the External World.   A rich variety of stories deal with the central philosophical problem of knowledge: How can we be sure that we have knowledge of the real world? Common sense tells us that we can use our sense organs to observe the world today, and we can use our memory to recall what happened yesterday, and we can express our beliefs based on sensation and memory in everyday English—and that, if we do these things, we have knowledge of the real world. But science fiction writers have suggested many seeming difficulties with this commonsense view. Like some philosophical skeptics, the science fiction writers have asked, "How can we know that anything exists outside of our own minds?" And, like the skeptics, they have raised the question in a wide variety of situations.

"How do I know that I am not dreaming right now?"   This skeptical question, raised by Plato, St. Augustine, and Descartes, is used in several stories. For example, Roger Zelazny in *The Dream Master* (Ace, 1975), based on the Nebula-winning "He Who Shapes," portrays a psychologist who enters his patient's awareness and "shapes" vivid dreams as part of the therapy. This psychologist runs the risk of losing contact with the real world. John Brunner poses a similar problem for a dream researcher in "Such Stuff," a short story in *Out of My Mind* (Ballantine, 1967). Joe Haldeman focuses on the problems of the dreamer himself in "A Mind of His Own," in *Analog* (February 1974).

"How do I know that this is not all just an illusion?"   In Descartes the illusion is produced by an evil genius with supernatural powers. George O. Smith's "In the Imagicon," with wild oscillations between competing dream worlds, can be found in *Nebula Award Stories Number Two,* edited by Brian Aldiss and Harry Harrison (Pocket Books, 1966), an anthology which is an unusually rich source of stories with epistemological import. A higher race of alien beings produces completely coherent illusory worlds in "Menagerie," the pilot for the popular *Star Trek* television series. The script is rewritten by Gene Roddenberry as a story in James Blish, *Star Trek* (Bantam, 1967). Ray Bradbury's Martians successfully deceive a contingent of astronauts from Earth in "Mars is Heaven!" in *The Martian Chronicles* (Bantam, 1974). John Brunner attempts a solution to the problem in *The Whole Man* (Ballantine, 1977).

"How can I know now a world that no longer exists?"   Bertrand Russell raised skeptical problems about the "time lag" that occurs in perception. For example, when we look at the sun, we do not "see" the sun as it is now, but only light that left the sun eight minutes ago. In the heavens we may "see" stars that have ceased to exist, since they are light years away. These problems can be seen in an even more striking way in Bob Shaw's acclaimed "slow glass" stories, in which the passage of light through specially treated glass is delayed for extended times. See "Light of Other Days" in *Nebula Award Stories Number Two* and Shaw's novel *Other Days, Other Eyes* (Ace, 1972).

"How can I rely upon my memories of the past?"   Our knowledge of the past depends in large part on our memories. The discovery that our memories depend upon physiochemical "traces" in our brains has inspired stories in which characters are deceived about the past through the implantation of false memory traces. One of the most complex and intriguing of these is Philip K. Dick, "We Can Remember It for You Wholesale," in *Nebula Award Stories Number Two.* A company that provides its customers with exotic, false memories encounters a customer whose existing memories are so bizarre that the question arises, How can we tell whether any of our memory claims are true or false?

"How do I know that my words and concepts do not distort my picture of the real world?"   The problem is well stated in Jack Vance's novel, *The Languages of Pao* (Ace, 1958): " . . . we note that every language imposes a certain world-view upon the mind. What is the 'true' world-picture? Is there a language to express this 'true' world-picture?" An apprentice hears these words at the Institute of Linguists, where the science of linguistics is used to construct an interstellar empire. The influence of language on cognition is also explored in Samuel R. Delany, *Babel-17* (Ace, 1975), which received a Nebula Award.

"How do I know that my limitations as a human being do not prevent me from knowing certain aspects of reality?"   This question is suggested by science fiction stories that depict the emergence of a higher order of intelligence in human beings through evolution, drug experimentation, or the intervention of aliens. In Daniel Keyes' *Flowers for Algernon* (Bantam, 1970), a mentally retarded man becomes increasingly intelligent as a result of drug treatments until he transcends ordinary human understanding. The novel begins with a striking quotation from Plato's *Republic.* Based on a Hugo Award story, the book received a Nebula and inspired the film *Charly* (1968), for which Cliff Robertson received an Academy Award. Another novel of this type is Poul Anderson, *Brain Wave* (Ballantine, 1978).

 Apart from the question of whether or not we have reliable knowledge of the physical universe, there are serious problems of knowledge about how we should interpret the physical objects we observe.

"How do I know whether there are any minds other than my own?"   The philosophical problem of other minds that we have inherited from Descartes is an obvious problem of this sort. When I observe other persons' bodies, I don't thereby observe their conscious minds. How do I know that others are not cleverly constructed machines that are really not conscious? A classic story on this theme is Robert A. Heinlein's "Them" in *The Unpleasant Profession of Jonathan Hoag* (Berkley, 1976), in which a paranoid's solipsistic suspicion that he is the only sentient being around becomes more than a hypothesis. The problem of other minds is also exploited in science fiction stories in which one has to distinguish an alien consciousness hiding within an apparently human body—for example, John W. Campbell, Jr., "Who Goes

There?," in Ben Bova, *Science Fiction Hall of Fame IIA* (Avon, 1973). Some science fiction authors tackle the problem head on with stories involving direct telepathic links. The phenomenon of telepathy is very effectively explored in Alfred Bester, *The Demolished Man* (Pocket Books, 1978), and in two excellent psychological portraits by Robert Silverberg, *Dying Inside* (Ballantine, 1972), and *A Time of Changes* (Doubleday, 1971), which won a Nebula. The problem of other minds arises also in stories in which there is a problem of deciding whether an alien life form possesses a consciousness comparable to humans'—for example, H. Beam Piper's humorous *Little Fuzzy* (Ace, 1976).

"How do I understand the meaning and intention behind the language and behavior of other cultures?" This is a central problem of *hermeneutics,* the study of interpretation. The difficulties of correctly understanding historical records have been explored with humor and irony by science fiction writers, for example, by Arthur C. Clarke in "History Lesson," in *Expedition to Earth* (Ballantine, 1975), in which a cartoon is interpreted by future alien anthropologists. Witnessing the actual construction of telescopes to search for messages from other star systems, writers like James Gunn in *The Listeners* (Signet, 1972) dramatize the difficulties of understanding such messages once they arrive. A dance by a human being in outer space becomes a mode of communicating with extraterrestrial beings in Spider and Jeanne Robinson's Nebula-winning "Stardance," in *Analog* (March 1977). Many science fiction stories have probed the complex problems of understanding the behavior and values of cultures totally alien to our own. A striking example of the bewilderment we might experience is found in Terry Carr, "The Dance of the Changer and the Three," in Carr and Donald A. Wollheim, *World's Best Science Fiction 1969* (Ace, 1969). An utterly alien "oceanlike" life form is depicted in Stanislaw Lem's *Solaris* (Berkley, 1976). The problem has religious overtones in James Blish, *A Case of Conscience* (Ballantine, 1975), which won a Hugo.

Philosophy and the Problem of Knowledge

The French philosopher Descartes (1596–1650) defended skepticism as a "devil's advocate" in the first of his *Meditations on First Philosophy* (available in several good English translations in different editions). The defense influenced many later philosophers in a skeptical direction, although Descartes himself tried to refute skepticism in the subsequent *Meditations.* The ancient philosophers Pyrrho (360–270 B.C.) and Sextus Empiricus (about the second century A.D.) defended extreme forms of skepticism, as did the modern Scottish philosopher David Hume (1711–1776) in the eighteenth-century works *A Treatise of Human Nature* and *Enquiry Concerning Human Understanding.* In the twentieth century, A. J. Ayer takes skepticism very seriously in *The Problem of Knowledge* (Penguin, 1956), and G. E. Moore attacks it in *Philosophical Papers* (Allen & Unwin, 1959). On its historical impact, see "Skepticism" in *The Encyclopedia of Philosophy,* ed. by Paul Edwards (Macmillan, 1967).

Descartes' skeptical problems about dreaming are discussed at length by H. G. Frankfurt in *Demons, Dreamers and Madmen* (Bobbs Merrill, 1970). Problems of illusion and related problems in perception are introduced in "Illusions" and "Perception" in the *Encyclopedia.* Two useful anthologies of twentieth-century writings are R. J. Hirst, ed., *Perception and the External World* (Macmillan, 1965), and R. J. Swartz, ed., *Perceiving, Sensing and Knowing* (Doubleday, 1965). The Hirst anthology also contains a very good introduction to "the argument from illusion" and main lines of solution. Even if we can rely upon our senses in individual cases to provide us with information about the objective world, there is also the problem of how the scientist can move "by induction" from individual perceptual experiences to universal "laws" that always will hold and always have held true. This problem is introduced in "Induction" in the *Encyclopedia* and in R. Swinburne, ed., *The Justification of Induction* (Oxford, 1974). Problems about our knowledge of the past are canvassed in the *Encyclopedia* article, "Memory," and Don Locke, *Memory* (Doubleday, 1971). The problem of other minds is summarized in the *Encyclopedia* article, *"Other Minds,"* and is explored at length in H. Morick, ed., *Wittgenstein & the Problem of Other Minds* (McGraw-Hill, 1967). As the Morick volume makes clear, many recent philosophers follow the lead of Ludwig Wittgenstein in interpreting skepticism—in general and about other minds in particular—as the thesis that one could speak in a "private language," which one did not share with any other speakers.

The idea that our view of the world is shaped by the language or concepts which we use to understand it, so that we never see the world "the way it really is," has been defended by the enormously influential modern thinkers Immanuel Kant (1724–1804) in his *Critique of Pure Reason* and G. W. F. Hegel (1770–1831) in his *Phenomenology of Mind.* Many twentieth-century philosophers have also claimed that other persons could have "conceptual schemes" so different from ours that we could not understand them. Others have claimed that we could not compare such "schemes" to see which are true or false. Similar views are expressed by W. V. O. Quine, in *Word and Object* (M.I.T. Press, 1960), and Thomas Kuhn, in *Structure of Scientific Revolutions* (U. Chicago, 1962). These views have also been criticized by "realistic" philosophers in John Wild, ed., *The Return to Reason* (Regnery, 1953), and also very recently by Donald Davidson, in his presidential address to the American Philosophical Association, "On the Very Idea of a Conceptual Scheme" (December 1973, *Proceedings of the A.P.A.*).

2

PHILOSOPHY OF RELIGION:

Does God exist?

The belief in God is, for many people, essential to a full understanding of the nature of reality. Many people feel that, if God did not exist, their world would not make any sense. In this chapter you will probe the concept of God, especially in its relationship to the question, "What is the evidence for or against the existence of God?"

The philosopher approaches religious issues in a peculiar way which seems at times almost sacrilegious to the nonphilosopher. Some believers regard their faith in God as a private and deeply personal affair, tied up with the performance of rituals, membership in a religious community, and the occasion of a profound religious experience. But the philosopher wants to know what people mean by the word "God" and whether rational grounds or evidence can be found that will decisively prove—or at least support—the claim of the *theist* that God exists or the claim of the *atheist* that there is no God. A philosopher who has surveyed the arguments and arrived at the conclusion that there are no rational grounds for concluding whether or not God exists and who therefore will not venture either claim is an *agnostic*. It should be emphasized that, although the philosopher is occupied with questions of meaning and evidence, these issues are nonetheless of deep personal concern for him as well. In fact, some of the lines of argument you will be considering were originated by religious prophets.

This chapter introduces you to the controversy over the existence of God in the philosophy of religion. This controversy, extending over thousands of years, has produced a vast literature containing numerous arguments pro and con with ever-increasing variations. The purpose of this chapter is not to canvass all of the sorts of arguments that have been produced and certainly not to settle the question once and for all in favor of theism, atheism, or agnosticism. Rather, it is to equip you to understand and evaluate arguments on this issue which you may encounter—or even to produce arguments of your own. After completing this chapter, you should be able to do the following:

- Explain the concept of God that is presupposed by philosophers arguing for or against the existence of God.

- Use techniques for understanding and evaluating evidence that has been advanced in support of theism.

- Use techniques for understanding and evaluating evidence that has been advanced in support of atheism.

- Evaluate evidence for or against theism and atheism on the basis of conceptual experiments.

2:1   THE CONCEPT OF GOD

2:1.1   You may suspect that any attempt to define the word "God" is doomed to fail. Many theists believe that God surpasses all understanding. God is, after all, an immaterial, supernatural being that is fundamentally unlike anything in the natural world studied by chemists or physicists. God cannot be defined the way other entities can. For example, a human being has been defined as a rational animal. Human beings are grouped with horses, cows, and oysters in the kingdom animalia and then differentiated from them by the property of *being rational*. You may doubt whether a definite kingdom like animalia could ever be found that would include God as well as things in nature. Still, "God" is not a nonsense word. The theist cannot be asserting that a completely unidentified entity exists, or his assertion would be as unintelligible as "Gonk exists." So the theist will want to attribute at least some properties to God, although he will not presume to offer a total definition of "God."[1]

---

[1]We assume a rough distinction between defining a thing and describing it in terms of just any properties. On most accounts, to define a thing is to give its most central, most necessary, most essential properties. The properties used to define a thing are most essential because they enable us to understand and predict the other properties things have. Thus, it is better to define "gold" not as "a yellow metal" (since other metals are

Consequently, in exploring the question of whether or not God exists, you are in a situation like that of a space scientist seeking evidence for or against the claim that living things exist on Mars. Before he begins to collect evidence by sending an explorer vehicle to Mars, he must be sure what counts as a "living thing." He may understand by "living thing" something that carries out certain quite specific chemical processes—or he may understand something that interacts in a certain way with its environment. But he has to spell out some of the properties of a living thing. The evidence that is brought to bear on the question of whether there is a God is not like the samples collected by the space scientist, since it is often acquired from your everyday experience. But you can at least hope that the theist's explanation of what he or she means by "God" will help you in understanding what would count for or against the existence of a being with that name.

2:1.2 Many (though, of course, not all) traditional theistic religions agree on several important properties that belong to God:

- God is *unique:* There is no other God and nothing even like Him.

- God is *incorporeal:* He has no body and the actions of God cannot be explained in terms of the physical laws of nature.

- God is *eternal:* God is uncreated, everlasting, and indestructible; some also take this to mean that God's actions cannot be fully described in temporal terms.

- God is *omnipotent:* God is all-powerful and is able to effect miracles—that is, occult events that defy natural laws.

- God is *omniscient:* God knows everything that has happened and will happen everywhere in the Universe.

- God is *purposive:* God is not a blind force; God has a conscious purpose which is manifested in the history of the natural world.

- God is *benevolent:* God is good and acts according to principles which are recognizably moral; in fact, theists often maintain that human morality is introduced and sanctioned by God.

- God is *perfect:* This seems to sum up all the foregoing properties. God possesses similar properties to ours but without

---

yellow, and being yellow tells us nothing about other properties like density), but as "the element with atomic number 79" (which in the light of modern physics and chemistry tells us a great deal about the other properties of gold). See the article on "Definition" in *The Encyclopedia of Philosophy,* Paul Edwards, ed. (Macmillan, 1967).

any of the defects or imperfections which are naturally associated with human existence.

Given this concept of God (or however much of it you are able to accept), you can turn to the question of how to understand and evaluate evidence that is advanced for or against the claim that something in reality answers to this concept.

2:2 EVIDENCE FOR GOD'S EXISTENCE (INVOLVING THE IDEA OF PERFECTION)

2:2.1   From ancient times many great philosophers have produced an impressive arsenal of proofs for God's existence: Plato in the *Laws,* Aristotle in the *Metaphysics,* St. Anselm in the *Proslogion,* St. Thomas Aquinas in the *Summa Theologiae,* René Descartes in *Discourse on Method* and *Meditations on First Philosophy,* Bishop Berkeley in *Three Dialogues,* and numerous others.

Many beginning students of philosophy (and many seasoned philosophers!) have trouble being objective about such arguments. Because many of them are already convinced that God exists or does not exist, they *want* the arguments to succeed or fail. But a proof that ends up at a desired conclusion is not necessarily a good one. In fact, the proof may start from false premises that mislead you about the true nature of the world or that misrepresent the nature of God. This section will provide you with philosophical tools that you can apply to such arguments in order to determine their merits. These tools will not make you an infallible expert on the issue of God's existence, because their effective use depends upon the scope of your knowledge—and none of us is omniscient. But you will find them useful in locating crucial weak points or controversial claims.

2:2.2   Let us begin somewhat removed from the hot issue of whether God exists. Let us introduce the tools by analyzing an argument which is developed in a science fiction story, "Reason," by Isaac Asimov.[2] In this story a robot named QT-1 has been assembled on a space satellite by two human technicians, Powell and Donovan. The robot, called "Cutie" by the men, is of a new design capable of speech and of logical analysis. It is intended to perform a task on the satellite required to provide solar energy for the survival of human beings. But the humans find the robot very uncooperative. To begin with, like Descartes, it doubts everything it is told. The idea that it is surrounded by infinite emptiness containing globes of energy millions of miles across and cold spheres occupied by billions of humans is too implausible. "Do you expect me to believe any such complicated, implausible hypothesis as you have just outlined?" The humans are bewildered by Cutie's skepticism and by its meditations, which proceed

2Isaac Asimov, *I, Robot* (Fawcett, 1970).

from "the unsure assumption I felt permitted to make. I, myself, exist because I think . . .". But they are stunned by Cutie's deduction that it was not created by human beings but by a superior entity called the Master, which it identifies as the satellite's energy converter. Its reasoning takes the following form: It has a maker, as Powell points out. But the humans' claims that *they* are the makers are dismissed as absurd. For they are manifestly inferior to Cutie. They are physically weaker, since they are constructed out of easily destructible soft and flabby material. Cutie is stronger, uses energy more efficiently, and so forth. These are facts which, with the self-evident proposition that no being can create another being superior to itself, "smashes your silly hypothesis to nothing." As the Master's prophet, Cutie founds a new religion and converts the other robots on the satellite. The zealots are insubordinate in spite of the "Second Law of Robotics," which requires obedience on the part of robots toward human beings. Predictably, the author brings this tale to a delightfully unpredictable conclusion.

The science fiction author Asimov ascribes to the robot Cutie a proof of the existence of the Master which is suspiciously similar to arguments that philosophers like Thomas Aquinas and René Descartes have offered for the existence of God. In Asimov's story Powell and Donovan give credence to Cutie's claim that they are inferior beings by sputtering helplessly and resorting to the fallacy of *argumentum ad hominem* (name calling) by describing Cutie as a bucket of bolts, and so on. You can prove yourself at least the equal of a rational robot by applying some simple analytical tools to such an argument. In the first place you should ask, "What are the characteristics which Cutie is attributing to his Master?" Leaving aside the question of whether this Master exists, what would he be like if Cutie were right that he did exist? The most important characteristic is that he is "superior" to us, that he is physically stronger and more invulnerable and mentally more intelligent. Cutie's argument does *not* depend on other assumptions about the Master, that he is morally good or incapable of error. It would be unfair to Cutie to criticize him for not proving the existence of an absolutely perfect Master. For his argument would be very interesting even if it proved the existence of a Master in the sense of a being superior to us.

Cutie's argument proceeds from an obvious, almost trivial premise: "I exist." It adds to this other observations, for example, that human beings are manifestly inferior to Cutie. They are physically weaker, are subject to periodic "comas," use energy less efficiently, and so forth. On the basis of this, Cutie makes the inference, "I am superior to you." Cutie rejects the "hypothesis" of Powell and Donovan that humans created him by invoking the proposition that no being can create another being superior to itself. On the basis of this, Cutie infers that it has a superhuman creator, which it calls "the Master." Cutie's argument resembles many classical proofs for the existence of God. In addition to the *obvious observation* that it exists, Cutie appeals to the *powerful principle*—that a being cannot create a being superior to itself—in order to reach the staggering conclusion that the Master exists. Clearly, such powerful principles play a central role in these arguments. You may be in doubt as to what exactly these principles mean and as to whether they are really plausible. You should spend time thinking about such principles.

Another thing: Our students never fail to point out that Cutie's conclusion does not follow, even if one concedes its obvious observations and powerful principles. "The argument has a big hole in it. Cutie has not ruled out the possibility that it created itself!" True, if Cutie had created itself, there would be no reason to infer another entity, the Master, as its creator. But Cutie has the following argument:

Obvious observation I: I exist.

Obvious observation II: I am superior to human beings.

Extra premise: I could not have created myself.

Powerful principle: A being cannot create a being superior to itself.

Conclusion: I was created by some other being superior to human beings, which shall be called "the Master."

Powell and Donovan are at a loss as to how to criticize this argument. How should they have responded to it? Should they have zeroed in on the second "obvious" observation that they are inferior to Cutie?[3] Many readers of Asimov's story feel that the Achilles' heel of the argument is the powerful principle. Cutie claims that this principle is "self-evident." Powell grumbles, "You can prove anything you want by coldly logical reason—if you pick the proper postulates. We have ours and Cutie has his." How would *you* have refuted this premise? How could Cutie have persuaded you of its truth?

2:2.3   The purpose of the foregoing discussion has been to introduce you to certain *techniques* that can be applied to many arguments for the existence of God. When you encounter a new argument (whether it appears in a philosophical treatise, a sermon, or in conversation with a friend), you should try to use the following strategy:

* Identify the properties of God that are relevant to the argument.

---

[3]The strategy suggested in the text is to concede that the argument as reconstructed is valid, but to deny that it is sound by showing that one or none of the premises is false. The conclusions of *valid* arguments follow logically from their premises. But some valid arguments have false premises. These arguments are called *unsound*. Although the conclusions of such arguments follow from their premises, they have not been *proved true*, as they have been shown to follow from false premises. To actually *prove* something, your argument must be *both* valid and sound. For a fuller discussion, see I:2.4 and I:2.5.

- Isolate the obvious observations that get the argument started.

- Identify the powerful principles that drive the argument from its trivial starting point to its destination.

- Ask whether each inference leading to the grand conclusion really does follow. This requires that you look closely at the obvious observation and powerful principle to see what they really establish. If any inference doesn't follow, the argument is simply *invalid;* if it does follow, you have a valid argument and can look into its soundness.

- If the argument is invalid, try to find an extra premise that you can add to the obvious observation and powerful principle to make a valid argument. You should, of course, try to find the best extra premise you can, to give the argument a fair run.

- If the argument is valid, check the premises to see if they are true. (1) Often you will have no trouble with the obvious observation, but sometimes it will seem shaky. (2) Often you will find that you cannot find a true extra premise that makes the argument valid; you may have to give up the argument as a lost cause for this reason. (3) Generally the powerful principle will demand a good deal of hard thought. It may be hard at first to understand what it means, so that you need to pay close attention to the *context* of the argument and to any examples or parallel arguments which the philosopher provides to illustrate his principle. Finally, you should consider whether the powerful principle is true. If it is, and the other premises are also, then the philosopher has established something of fundamental significance.

2:2.4 Many arguments for the existence of God resemble Cutie's argument for the existence of the Master. Asimov really models this argument, tongue in cheek, after arguments like that of St. Thomas Aquinas for the existence of God. Aquinas, a medieval Catholic theologian in the thirteenth century, offered five arguments for the existence of God in his enormously influential work, *Summa Theologiae.* Aquinas firmly believed in the power of the human mind to demonstrate the existence of a God in whom he believed out of Christian faith. Some of his arguments belong to a tradition that goes back at least as far as Plato, the ancient Greek philosopher, and they have been restated and formulated by modern thinkers, including contemporary astronomers. But Aquinas's arguments are stated with exceptional clarity and simplicity, so that they are an excellent place for you to begin in testing your philosophical skills. The last of the five arguments, which are called "the five ways," is also called the teleological argument or the argument from design:

> The fifth way is taken from the governance of the world. We see that things which lack knowledge, such as natural bodies, act for an end, and this is evident from their acting always, or nearly always, in the same way, so as to obtain the best result. Hence it is plain that they achieve their end, not fortuitously, but designedly. Now whatever lacks knowledge cannot move towards an end, unless it be directed by some being endowed with knowledge and intelligence; as the arrow is directed by the archer. Therefore some intelligent being exists by whom all natural things are directed to their end; and this being we call God.[4]

This is an argument for the existence of God which many persons find appealing. Such arguments are called "arguments from design" because they reason from an almost instinctive conviction of people that the world fits together and makes sense to the conclusion that it must have been designed by an intelligent creator. They are also called "teleological arguments," from the Greek word *telos,* meaning end or goal. It is important to keep in mind that this argument only tries to show that there is a purposive, intelligent God. It is rather pointless to criticize the argument for not showing that God is omnipotent or omniscient. It is more interesting to approach it as the modest argument it is.

Obvious observation:	Natural things always or nearly always act in the same way so as to obtain the best result.
Interim inference:	Natural things belong to a goal-directed system.
Powerful principle:	A goal-directed system that is not itself an intelligent being must be directed to its goal by an intelligent being which is controlling it.
Conclusion:	The system of natural things (namely, our universe) has an intelligent being in charge of it (namely, God).

To decide whether you find this argument convincing, you should look at each of the steps leading to the conclusion. The obvious observation is examined by Father Frederick Copleston, a modern commentator on Aquinas: "We observe material things of very different types cooperating in such a way as to produce and maintain a relatively stable world-order or system. They achieve an 'end,' the production and maintenance of a cosmic order."[5] Living things in a territory form an integrated ecosystem of mutual dependence with balanced populations. The "heavenly bodies" form balanced

[4]Thomas Aquinas, *Summa Theologiae,* cited in Paul Edwards and Arthur Pap, eds., *A Modern Introduction to Philosophy,* 3rd ed. (Macmillan, 1973), p. 408.

[5]F. C. Copleston, *Aquinas* (Penguin, 1961), p. 125.

systems such as our solar system, our galaxy, and our galactic cluster. The interim inference is derived from this by extra premises hinted at by Aquinas:

Extra premise I: A system achieves an end fortuitously or by being goal-directed.

Extra premise II: What happens regularly is not fortuitous.

Aquinas's inference can be illustrated by a phenomenon which fascinates present-day astronomers and science fiction writers: the collapse and "nova" (or explosion) of a star. Scientists do not think that such catastrophes happen fortuitously or by chance. For *every* star with sufficient mass goes through a predictable process: gas accumulates into a nebula; as it contracts into a star, energy is consumed and radiation discharged; the star collapses and explodes; a very dense, "cold" core remains. There is an obvious analogy with biological processes, leading astronomers to speak of the "life" of a star. The process by which a star goes nova can thus be described as a *goal-directed* process.

The powerful principle is supported by an *analogy* to an archer directing an arrow. Just as the unthinking arrow must be propelled to its goal by a thinking archer, any unthinking entity will tend toward a goal only if it is directed by a thinking entity. It is necessary to comment on this use of analogy. Analogy arguments are often used to explain phenomena which are hard to examine in detail. For example, early astronomers who observed Mars through telescopes thought they saw ribbons crisscrossing the planet's surface. Some explained them by analogy:

Similar effects have similar causes.

The formations on Mars resemble canals on earth made by intelligent builders.

Therefore, the formations on Mars have intelligent builders.

Many science fiction writers described adventures on the canals of Mars until the U.S. space probe *Voyager* in the mid-1970s established that they were only optical illusions. This shows one way in which an analogy such as Aquinas's can go wrong: The "similarity" either does not exist or it is not nearly as close as the arguer assumes. Analogy arguments can also be discredited if closer examination established that there was some other cause at work: This would have happened if there had been canals on Mars but the first astronauts established that they were due to natural erosion millions of years ago when there was a lot of water on the planet.

How well does Aquinas's argument seem to you to hold up? Consider two crucial steps. Is the obvious observation completely obvious to *you?* In Aquinas's time it was believed that outer space was a realm of unchanging stars and planets fixed in perfectly circular orbits around an earth which was planted immovably in the center of the universe. Nowadays scientists describe the universe as exploding from a primeval "big bang," a buzzing confusion of exploding stars, collapsing universes, black holes, and quasars. Are you satisfied that Aquinas's first premise is true?

Next, are you persuaded of the powerful principle's truth? It is, of course, true that many "goal-directed" processes and mechanisms have a controlling intelligence. Computers and heat-seeking missiles would not exist if human beings had not "programmed" them to seek certain goals. But are *all* goal-directed processes the result of conscious design? In the eighteenth century the Scottish philosopher David Hume claimed that plants and animals have goals but are not machines designed by an intelligent being. Hume reasoned that we should not simply take it for granted that everything with a goal was designed. Do you find Hume's argument convincing—or does Aquinas have a way of answering Hume?

2:3 EVIDENCE AGAINST GOD'S EXISTENCE (INVOLVING THE EXPERIENCE OF EVIL)

2:3.1 If you believe in God, you might be troubled by the misfortunes that sometimes befall you or your acquaintances. We are acutely aware of our own shortcomings and we know that others have even worse shortcomings: retardation, blindness, deafness, and so forth. We also suffer at the hands of our fellow human beings: through jealousy, anger, crime, and war. Add to this the disasters and plagues of nature. "How," the believer wonders, "could God let this happen to me?" The most striking dramatic expression of this concern is the biblical *Book of Job.* In the face of such tribulations, the believer is exhorted to have faith. But a number of philosophers have seen the fact of human suffering as raising a fundamental theoretical difficulty for theism.

2:3.2 The argument from evil has been made in various ways, but perhaps no more succinctly than in David Hume's summary of Epicurus: "Epicurus's old questions are yet unanswered. Is he willing to prevent evil, but not able? then he is impotent. Is he able, but not willing? then he is malevolent. Is he both able and willing? whence then is evil?"[6]

To see how such queries can be recast into a forceful argument for atheism, let us apply the techniques we have developed and summarized in 2:2. First, what are the relevant properties of God? It is absolutely crucial for this argument that God's properties include not only omnipotence and omniscience, but also benevolence. If you believe that God is malevolent or satanic or that God is an amoral, natural force, you won't be bothered in the least by this argument. The argument can be understood as follows:

Powerful principle: If there is a benevolent, omnipotent, and omniscient being (namely, God), then evil does not exist.

Obvious observation: Evil exists.

---

[6]David Hume, *Dialogues Concerning Natural Religion,* Part X, ed. Nelson Pike (Indianapolis: Bobbs-Merrill, 1970), p. 88.

Conclusion: It's not the case that there is a benevolent, omnipotent, and omniscient being (namely, God).

If this argument is sound, then the only way to escape atheism is, as Epicurus pointed out, to admit that God is either amoral (or even malevolent) or impotent or ignorant.

2:3.3 You should first ask yourself if the argument is valid. Assuming that it is, you should take up the question of soundness: Are the premises of the argument true? Theists have tried in various ways to show that one or the other of these premises is false. It should be emphasized at the outset that there is no general agreement among theists as to how to attack this argument.

2:3.4 The most ambitious (and difficult) defense is to deny the obvious. Several different reasons have been advanced for doubting the seemingly trivial proposition that evil exists. Those who take this route have tried to find a way of understanding the experiences appealed to in the obvious observation which will not require us to acknowledge the occurrence of evil. Consider some lines of attack.

(1) *Suffering is justified.* Some theists argue that human suffering does exist, but it is justified suffering and therefore not evil. Human suffering is just requital for human sin. This line is taken by one of Job's friends in the Book of Job: "Think now, who that was innocent ever perished? Or where were the upright cut off? As I have seen, those who plow iniquity and sow trouble reap the same." He infers that Job has suffered successive disasters such as fire, disease, and death in his family because of some sins he has committed. The difficulty with this, in the view of many theists as well as nontheists, is that often the wicked prosper while the innocent suffer. Job himself retorts, "I am blameless; I regard not myself; I loathe my life. It is all one; therefore, I say, he destroys both the blameless and the wicked. When disaster brings sudden death, he mocks at the calamity of the innocent." (2) *Evil is merely "negative."* You will recall Descartes' emphasis on his own imperfections. He is limited in knowledge and power. Even if you try to avoid error, you cannot hope to attain to the level of divine wisdom. But in Descartes' view these are unavoidable facts of created existence. From the very fact that it is created, it will fall short of the perfection of uncreated existence. Even if God were to *double* our knowledge and power, we would still fall short of perfection because we are created; even if we were to become twice as happy, we would still fall short of the divine bliss of God. You can ponder this defense. It is important that the theist must always understand a statement such as "x is evil" to mean "x is good—but could be better." You may wonder whether all evils can be understood in this way. For example, is there a difference between simply not being happy and positively suffering? (3) *Who are you to say?* Some theists suggest that the obvious observation is an expression of stiff-necked pride, because you are judging God according to *your* moral concepts. What right do you have to

apply your moral concepts to God? This attitude is suggested in Job in a declaration of God: "I will question *you,* and you declare to me. Will you ever put me in the wrong? Will you condemn *me* that you may be justified? Have you an arm like God, and can you thunder with a voice like his?" On this view we should simply accept, as God's will, whatever happens, and not presume to pass moral judgment on God and his works. This defense really consists in taking a stance of "moral agnosticism." If you deny that you are in a position to say whether a point 9 earthquake in a densely populated urban area is "good" or "bad," the problem of evil cannot arise for you. But this defense has implications which many theists are unable to accept. If you are not in a position to use the word "evil" in relation to God, how can you be in a position to use the word "good"? It is hard to see how it can be meaningful to speak of God as being "benevolent" in this defense.

2:3.5 Others have criticized the argument, denying its powerful principle. The strategy is to show that an all-powerful, benevolent God could have good reason to permit evil to exist. (4) *Evil is the "price" for free will.* The worst evils seem to be visited on us by our fellow human beings. Consider the worst disasters that have occurred in our own century. The theist argues that when God created Adam and Eve in the Garden of Eden he could have avoided all this if he had created a pair of androids who were "programmed" always to do the right thing. You and I, their descendants, would also be perfectly upright androids. But God did not want fleshy robots. He wanted persons who would love him and do the right thing *of their own free will.* An agent who acts virtuously and freely is vastly preferable to a piece of clockwork no matter how efficient it is. But an agent who is free to do the right thing is also free to do the wrong thing. It would be a contradiction to suggest that God could have created people so that they were free to do right but were "programmed" not to do wrong. This defense invokes the difficult notion of free will, which is discussed in Chapter 6. For it simply assumes that human beings have a free will. (5) *Evil is necessary to make us virtuous.* Many evils are not the direct result of human agency. But if people led lives entirely free of evil, they would tend to become flabby and even arrogant. When people have to face challenges, risks, and setbacks, they become morally strengthened. This defense is also found in Job: "He does not withdraw his eyes from the righteous. . . . If they are found in fetters and caught in the cords of affliction, then he declares to them their word and their transgressions, that they are behaving arrogantly. He opens their ears to instructions and commands that they return from iniquity." Christian virtues such as charity and unselfishness could only be exercised in an environment of scarcity and suffering.

This will give you an idea of the lines along which theists have tried to show that the obvious observation and powerful principle in the argument from evil do not provide a sound argument for atheism.

2:4 CONCEPTUAL EXPERIMENT

As you consider the intricate and varied arguments for and against the existence of God, it is easy to forget that such arguments are the intellectual expression of deep personal convictions. The evidence which is articulated in the obvious observation often has tremendous significance for the person who is persuaded by the argument. The proofs are not constructed simply to serve as window dressing. The following story by Arthur C. Clarke raises the problem of evil for a devout and sincere Jesuit priest. In the analysis that follows, the philosopher John Hick considers the argument from evil and attempts to show why it is not decisive as a proof of atheism.

Conceptual Experiment 2:

THE STAR

Arthur C. Clarke

It is three thousand light-years to the Vatican. Once I believed that space could have no power over Faith. Just as I believed that the heavens declared the glory of God's handiwork. Now I have seen that handiwork, and my faith is sorely troubled.

I stare at the crucifix that hangs on the cabin wall above the Mark VI computer, and for the first time in my life I wonder if it is no more than an empty symbol.

I have told no one yet, but the truth cannot be concealed. The data are there for anyone to read, recorded on the countless miles of magnetic tape and the thousands of photographs we are carrying back to Earth. Other scientists can interpret them as easily as I can—more easily, in all probability. I am not one who would condone that tampering with the Truth which often gave my Order a bad name in the olden days.

The crew is already sufficiently depressed, I wonder how they will take this ultimate irony. Few of them have any religious faith, yet they will not relish using this final weapon in their campaign against me—that private, good-natured but fundamentally serious war which lasted all the way from Earth. It amused them to have a Jesuit as a chief astrophysicist: Dr. Chandler, for instance, could never get over it (why are medical men such notorious atheists?). Sometimes he would meet me on the observation deck, where the lights are always low so that the stars shine with undiminished glory. He would come up to me in the gloom and stand staring out of the great oval pot, while the heavens crawled slowly round us as the ship turned end over end with the residual spin we had never bothered to correct.

"Well, Father," he would say at last. "It goes on forever and forever, and perhaps *Something* made it. But how you can believe that Something has a special interest in us and our miserable little world— that just beats me." Then the argument would start, while the stars and nebulae would swing around us in silent, endless arcs beyond the flawlessly clear plastic of the observation port.

It was, I think, the apparent incongruity of my position which . . . yes, *amused* . . . the crew. In vain I would point to my three papers in the *Astrophysical Journal,* my five in the *Monthly Notices of the*

Royal Astronomical Society. I would remind them that our Order has long been famous for its scientific works. We may be few now, but ever since the eighteenth century we have made contributions to astronomy and geophysics out of all proportions to our numbers.

Will my report on the Phoenix Nebula end our thousand years of history? It will end, I fear, much more than that.

I do not know who gave the Nebula its name, which seems to me a very bad one. If it contains a prophecy, it is one which cannot be verified for several thousand million years. Even the word nebula is misleading: this is a far smaller object than those stupendous clouds of mist—the stuff of unborn stars—which are scattered throughout the length of the Milky Way. On the cosmic scale, indeed, the Phoenix Nebula is a tiny thing—a tenuous shell of gas surrounding a single star.

Or what is left of a star . . .

The Rubens engraving of Loyola seems to mock me as it hangs there above the spectrophotometer tracings. What would *you,* Father, have made of this knowledge that has come into my keeping, so far from the little world that was all the universe you knew? Would your faith have risen to the challenge as mine has failed to do?

You gaze into the distance, Father, but I have traveled a distance beyond any that you could have imagined when you founded our Order a thousand years ago. No other survey ship has been so far from Earth: we are at the very frontiers of the explored universe. We set out to reach the Phoenix Nebula, we succeeded, and we are homeward bound with our burden of knowledge. I wish I could lift that burden from my shoulders, but I call to you in vain across the centuries and the light-years that lie between us.

On the book you are holding the words are plain to read. AD MAIOREM DEI GLORIAM the message runs, but it is a message I can no longer believe. Would you still believe it, if you could see what we have found?

We knew, of course, what the Phoenix Nebula was. Every year, in *our* galaxy alone, more than a hundred stars explode, blazing for a few hours or days with thousands of times their normal brilliance before they sink back into death and obscurity. Such are the ordinary novae— the commonplace disasters of the universe. I have recorded the spectrograms and light-curves of dozens, since I started working at the lunar observatory.

But three or four times in every thousand years occurs something beside which even a nova pales into total insignificance.

When a star becomes a *supernova,* it may for a little while outshine all the massed suns of the galaxy. The Chinese astronomers watched this happen in 1054 A.D., not knowing what it was they saw. Five centuries later, in 1572, a supernova blazed in Cassiopeia so brilliantly that it was visible in the daylight sky. There have been three more in the thousand years that have passed since then.

Our mission was to visit the remnants of such a catastrophe, to reconstruct the events that led up to it, and, if possible, to learn its cause. We came slowly in through the concentric shells of gas that had been blasted out six thousand years before, yet were expanding still. They were immensely hot, radiating still with a fierce violet light, but far too tenuous to do us any damage. When the star had exploded, its outer layers had been driven upwards with such speed that they had escaped completely from its gravitational field. Now they formed a hollow shell large enough to engulf a thousand solar systems, and at this center burned the tiny, fantastic object which the star had now become—a white dwarf, smaller than the Earth yet weighing a million times as much.

The glowing gas shells were all around us, banishing the normal night of interstellar space. We were flying into the center of a cosmic bomb that had detonated millennia ago and whose incandescent fragments were still hurtling apart. The immense scale of the explosion, and the fact that the debris already covered a volume of space many billions of miles across robbed the scene of any visible movement. It would take decades before the unaided eye could detect any motion in these tortured wisps and eddies of gas, yet the sense of turbulent expansion was overwhelming.

We had checked our primary drive hours before, and were drifting slowly towards the fierce little star ahead. Once it had been a sun like our own, but it had squandered in a few hours the energy that should have kept it shining for a million years. Now it was a shrunken miser, hoarding its resources as if trying to make amends for its prodigal youth.

No one seriously expected to find planets. If there had been any before the explosion, they would have been boiled into puffs of vapor, and their substance lost in the greater wreckage of the star itself. But we made the automatic search, as always when approaching an unknown sun, and presently we found a single small world circling the star at immense distance. It must have been the Pluto of this vanished solar system, orbiting on the frontiers of the night. Too far from the central sun ever to have known life, its remoteness had saved it from the fate of all its lost companions.

The passing fires had seared its rocks and burnt away the mantle of frozen gas that must have covered it in the days before the disaster. We landed, and we found the Vault.

Its builders had made sure that we should. The monolite marker that stood above the entrance was now a fused stump, but even the first long-range photographs told us that here was the work of intelligence. A little later we detected the continent's wide pattern of radioactivity that had been buried in the rock. Even if the pylon above the Vault had been destroyed, this would have remained, an immovable and all but eternal beacon calling to the stars. Our ship fell towards this gigantic bull's-eye like an arrow into its target.

The pylon must have been a mile high when it was built, but now it looked like a candle that had melted down into a puddle of wax. It took us a week to drill through the fused rock, since we did not have the proper tools for a task like this. We were astronomers, not archaeologists, but we could improvise. Our original program was forgotten: this lonely monument, reared at such labor at the greatest possible distance from the doomed sun, could have only one meaning. A civilization which knew it was about to die had made its last bid for immortality.

It will take us generations to examine all the treasures that were placed in the Vault. *They* had plenty of time to prepare, for their sun must have given its first warnings many years before the final detonation. Everything that they wished to preserve, all the fruits of their genius, they brought here to this distant world in the days before the end, hoping that some other race would find them and that they would not be utterly forgotten.

If only they had had a little more time! They could travel freely enough between the planets of their own sun, but they had not yet learned to cross the interstellar gulfs, and the nearest solar system was a hundred light-years away.

Even if they had not been so disturbingly human as their sculpture shows, we could not have helped admiring them and grieving for their fate. The thousands of visual records and the machines for projecting them, together with elaborate pictorial instructions from which it will not be difficult to learn their written language. We have examined many of these records, and brought to life for the first time in six thousand years the warmth and beauty of a civilization which in many ways must have been superior to our own. Perhaps they only showed us the best, and one can hardly blame them. But their worlds were very lovely, and their cities were built with a grace that matches anything of ours. We have watched them at work and play, and listened to their musical speech sounding across the centuries. One scene is still before my eyes—a group of children on a beach of strange blue sand, playing in the waves as children play on Earth.

And sinking into the sea, still warm and friendly and life-giving, is the sun that will soon turn traitor and obliterate all this innocent happiness.

Perhaps if we had not been so far from home and so vulnerable to loneliness, we should not have been so deeply moved. Many of us had seen the ruins of ancient civilizations on other worlds, but they had never affected us so profoundly.

This tragedy was unique. It was one thing for a race to fail and die, as nations and cultures have done on Earth. But to be destroyed so completely in the full flower of its achievement, leaving no survivors— how could that be reconciled with the mercy of God?

My colleagues have asked me that, and I have given what answers I can. Perhaps you could have done better, Father Loyola, but I have found nothing in the *Exercitia Spiritualia* that helps me here. They were not an evil people: I do not know what gods they worshipped, if indeed they worshipped any. But I have looked back at them across the centuries, and have watched while the loveliness they used their last strength to preserve was brought forth again into the light of their shrunken sun.

I know the answers that my colleagues will give when they get back to Earth. They will say that the universe has no purpose and no plan, that since a hundred suns explode every year in our galaxy, at this very moment some race is dying in the depths of space. Whether that race had done good or evil during its lifetime will make no difference in the end: there is no divine justice, *for there is no God.*

Yet, of course, what we have seen proves nothing of the sort. Anyone who argues thus is being swayed by emotion, not logic. God has no need to justify His actions to man. He who built the universe can destroy it when He chooses. It is arrogance—it is perilously near blasphemy—for us to say what He may or may not do.

This I could have accepted, hard though it is to look upon whole worlds and peoples thrown into the furnace. But there comes a point when even the deepest faith must falter, and now, as I look at my calculations, I know I have reached that point at last.

We could not tell, before we reached the nebula, how long ago the explosion took place. Now, from the astronomical evidence and the record in the rocks of that one surviving planet, I have been able to date it very exactly. I know in what year the light of this colossal conflagration reached Earth. I know how brilliantly the supernova whose corpse now dwindles behind our speeding ship once shone in terrestrial skies. I know how it must have blazed low in the East before sunrise, like a beacon in that Oriental dawn. There can be no reasonable doubt: the ancient mystery is solved at last. Yet—O God, there were so many stars you *could* have used.

What was the need to give these people to the fire, that the symbol of their passing might shine above Bethlehem?

Analysis:

THE PROBLEM OF EVIL

John Hick

To many, the most powerful positive objection to belief in God is the fact of evil. Probably for most agnostics it is the appalling depth and extent of human suffering, more than anything else, that makes the idea of a loving Creator seem so implausible and disposes them toward one or another of the various naturalistic theories of religion.

As a challenge to theism, the problem of evil has traditionally been posed in the form of a dilemma: if God is perfectly loving, he must wish to abolish evil; and if he is all-powerful, he must be able to abolish evil. But evil exists; therefore God cannot be both omnipotent and perfectly loving.

Certain solutions, which at once suggest themselves, have to be ruled out so far as the Judaic–Christian faith is concerned.

To say, for example (with contemporary Christian Science), that evil is an illusion of the human mind, is impossible within a religion based upon the stark realism of the Bible. Its pages faithfully reflect the characteristic mixture of good and evil in human experience. They record every kind of sorrow and suffering, every mode of man's inhumanity to man and of his painfully insecure existence in the world. There is no attempt to regard evil as anything but dark, menacingly ugly, heart-rending, and crushing. In the Christian scriptures, the climax of this history of evil is the crucifixion of Jesus, which is presented not only as a case of utterly unjust suffering, but as the violent and murderous rejection of God's Messiah. There can be no doubt, then, that for biblical faith, evil is unambiguously evil, and stands in direct opposition to God's will.

Again, to solve the problem of evil by means of the theory (sponsored, for example, by the Boston "Personalist" School)[1] of a finite deity who does the best he can with a material, intractable and coeternal with himself, is to have abandoned the basic premise of Hebrew–Christian monotheism; for the theory amounts to rejecting belief in the infinity and sovereignty of God.

Indeed, any theory which would avoid the problem of the origin

Excerpted from John Hick, *Philosophy of Religion* (Englewood Cliffs, N.J.: Prentice-Hall, 1963), pp. 40–47, permission by Prentice-Hall, Inc.

[1]Edgar Brightman's *A Philosophy of Religion* (Englewood Cliffs, N.J.: Prentice-Hall, 1940), Chapters 8–10, is a classic exposition of one form of this view.

of evil by depicting it as an ultimate constituent of the universe, coordinate with good, has been repudiated in advance by the classic Christian teaching, first developed by Augustine, that evil represents the going wrong of something which in itself is good.[2] Augustine holds firmly to the Hebrew–Christian conviction that the universe is *good*— that is to say, it is the creation of a good God for a good purpose. He completely rejects the ancient prejudice, widespread in his day, that matter is evil. There are, according to Augustine, higher and lower, greater and lesser goods in immense abundance and variety; but everything which has being is good in its own way and degree, except insofar as it may have become spoiled or corrupted. Evil—whether it be an evil will, an instance of pain, or some disorder or decay in nature— has not been set there by God, but represents the distortion of something that is inherently valuable. Whatever exists is, as such, and in its proper place, good; evil is essentially parasitic upon good, being disorder and perversion in a fundamentally good creation. This understanding of evil as something negative means that it is not willed and created by God; but it does not mean (as some have supposed) that evil is unreal and can be disregarded. On the contrary, the first effect of this doctrine is to accentuate even more the question of the origin of evil.

Theodicy,[3] as many modern Christian thinkers see it, is a modest enterprise, negative rather than positive in its conclusions. It does not claim to explain nor to explain away, every instance of evil in human experience, but only to point to certain considerations which prevent the fact of evil (largely incomprehensible though it remains) from constituting a final and insuperable bar to rational belief in God.

In indicating these considerations it will be useful to follow the traditional division of the subject. There is the problem of *moral evil* or wickedness: why does an all-good and all-powerful God permit this? And there is the problem of the *non-moral evil* of suffering or pain, both physical and mental: why has an all-good and all-powerful God created a world in which this occurs?

Christian thought has always considered moral evil in its relation to human freedom and responsibility. To be a person is to be a finite center of freedom, a (relatively) free and self-directing agent responsible for one's own decisions. This involves being free to act wrongly as well as to act rightly. The idea of a person who can be infallibly guaranteed always to act rightly is self-contradictory. There can be no guarantee in

---

[2]See Augustine's *Confessions,* Book VII, Chapter 12; *City of God,* Book XII, Chapter 3; and *Enchiridion,* Chapter 4.

[3]The word "theodicy," from the Greek *theos* (God) and *dike* (righteous), means the justification of God's goodness in the face of the fact of evil.

advance that a genuinely free moral agent will never choose amiss. Consequently, the possibility of wrongdoing or sin is logically inseparable from the creation of finite persons, and to say that God should not have created beings who might sin amounts to saying that he should not have created people.

This thesis has been challenged in some recent philosophical discussions of the problem of evil, in which it is claimed that no contradiction is involved in saying that God might have made people who would be genuinely free and who could yet be guaranteed always to act rightly. A quote from one of these discussions follows:

> If there is no logical impossibility in man's freely choosing the good on one, or on several occasions, there cannot be a logical impossibility in his freely choosing the good on every occasion. God was not, then, faced with a choice between making innocent automata and making beings who, in acting freely, would sometimes go wrong: there was open to him the obviously better possibility of making beings who would act freely but always go right. Clearly, his failure to avail himself of this possibility is inconsistent with his being both omnipotent and wholly good.[4]

A reply to this argument is suggested in another recent contribution to the discussion.[5] If by a free action we mean an action which is not externally compelled but which flows from the nature of the agent as he reacts to the circumstances in which he finds himself, there *is*, indeed, no contradiction between our being free and our actions being "caused" (by our own nature) and therefore being in principle predictable. There is a contradiction, however, in saying that God is the cause of our acting as we do but that we are free beings in relation to God. There is, in other words, a contradiction in saying that God has made us so that we shall of necessity act in a certain way, and that we are genuinely independent persons in relation to him. If all our thoughts and actions are divinely predestined, however free and morally responsible we may seem to be to ourselves, we cannot be free and morally responsible in the sight of God, but must instead be his helpless puppets. Such "freedom" is like that of a patient acting out a series of post-hypnotic suggestions: he appears, even to himself, to be free, but his

---

[4]J. L. Mackie, "Evil and Omnipotence," *Mind* (April 1955): 209. A similar point is made by Antony Flew in "Divine Omnipotence and Human Freedom," *New Essays in Philosophical Theology*. An important critical comment on these arguments is offered by Ninian Smart in "Omnipotence, Evil and Supermen," *Philosophy* (April 1961), with replies by Flew (January 1962) and Mackie (April 1962).

[5]Flew, in *New Essays in Philosophical Theology*.

volitions have actually been pre-determined by another will, that of the hypnotist, in relation to whom the patient is not a free agent.

A different objector might raise the question of whether or not we deny God's omnipotence if we admit that he is unable to create persons who are free from the risks inherent in personal freedom. The answer that has always been given is that to create such beings is logically impossible. It is no limitation upon God's power that he cannot accomplish the logically impossible, since there is nothing here to accomplish, but only a meaningless conjunction of words[6]—in this case "person who is not a person." God is able to create beings of any and every conceivable kind; but creatures who lack moral freedom, however superior they might be to human beings in other respects, would not be what we mean by persons. They would constitute a different form of life which God might have brought into existence instead of persons. When we ask why God did not create such beings in place of persons, the traditional answer is that only persons could, in any meaningful sense, become "children of God," capable of entering into a personal relationship with their Creator by a free and uncompelled response to his love.

When we turn from the possibility of moral evil as a correlate of man's personal freedom to its actuality, we face something which must remain inexplicable even when it can be seen to be possible. For we can never provide a complete causal explanation of a free act; if we could, it would not be a free act. The origin of moral evil lies forever concealed within the mystery of human freedom.

The necessary connection between moral freedom and the possibility, now actualized, of sin throws light upon a great deal of the suffering which afflicts mankind. For an enormous amount of human pain arises either from the inhumanity or the culpable incompetence of mankind. This includes such major scourges as poverty, oppression and persecution, war, and all the injustice, indignity, and inequity which occur even in the most advanced societies. These evils are manifestations of human sin. Even disease is fostered to an extent, the limits of which have not yet been determined by psychosomatic medicine, by moral and emotional factors seated both in the individual and in his social environment. To the extent that all of these evils stem from human failures and wrong decisions, their possibility is inherent in the creation of free persons inhabiting a world which presents them with real choices which are followed by real consequences.

We may now turn more directly to the problem of suffering. Even though the major bulk of actual human pain is traceable to man's

---

[6]As Aquinas said, " . . . nothing that implies a contradiction falls under the scope of God's omnipotence." *Summa Theologica,* Part I, Question 24, Article 4.

misused freedom as a sole or part cause, there remain other sources of pain which are entirely independent of the human will, for example, earthquake, hurricane, storm, flood, drought, and blight. In practice, it is often impossible to trace a boundary between the suffering which results from human wickedness and folly and that which falls upon mankind from without. Both kinds of suffering are inextricably mingled together in human experience. For our present purpose, however, it is important to note that the latter category does exist and that it seems to be built into the very structure of our world. In response to it, theodicy, if it is wisely conducted, follows a negative path. It is not possible to show positively that each item of human pain serves the divine purpose of good; but, on the other hand, it does seem possible to show that the divine purpose as it is understood in Judaism and Christianity could not be forwarded in a world which was designed as a permanent hedonistic paradise.[7]

An essential premise of this argument concerns the nature of the divine purpose in creating the world. The skeptic's assumption is that man is to be viewed as a completed creation and that God's purpose in making the world is to provide a suitable dwelling-place for this fully-formed creature. Since God is good and loving, the environment which he has created for human life to inhabit is naturally as pleasant and comfortable as possible. The problem is essentially similar to that of a man who builds a cage for some pet animal. Since our world, in fact, contains sources of hardship, inconvenience, and danger of innumerable kinds, the conclusion follows that this world cannot have been created by a perfectly benevolent and all-powerful deity.[8]

Christianity, however, has never supposed that God's purpose in the creation of the world was to construct a paradise whose inhabitants would experience a maximum of pleasure and minimum of pain. The world is seen, instead, as a place of "soul making" in which free beings, grappling with the tasks and challenges of their existence in a common environment, may become "children of God" and "heirs of eternal life." A way of thinking theologically of God's continuing creative purpose for man was suggested by some of the early Hellenistic Fathers of the Christian Church, expecially Irenaeus. Following hints from St. Paul, Irenaeus taught that man has been made as a person in the image of God but has not yet been brought as a free and responsible agent into the finite likeness of God, which is revealed in Christ.[9] Our world, with

[7]From the Greek *hedone*, pleasure.

[8]This is the nature of David Hume's argument in his discussion of the problem of evil in his *Dialogues*, Part XI.

[9]See Irenaeus's *Against Heresies*, Book IV, Chapters 37 and 38.

all its rough edges, is the sphere in which this second and harder stage of the creative process is taking place.

This conception of the world (whether or not set in Irenaeus's theological framework) can be supported by the method of negative theodicy. Suppose, contrary to fact, that this world were a paradise from which all possibility of pain and suffering were excluded. The consequences would be very far-reaching. For example, no one could ever injure anyone else: the murderer's knife would turn to paper or his bullets to thin air; the bank safe, robbed of a million dollars, would miraculously become filled with another million dollars (without this device, on however large a scale, proving inflationary); fraud, deceit, conspiracy, and treason would somehow always leave the fabric of society undamaged. Again, no one would ever be injured by accident: the mountain-climber, steeplejack, or playing child falling from a height would float unharmed to the ground; the reckless driver would never meet with disaster. There would be no need to work, since no harm could result from avoiding work; there would be no call to be concerned for others in time of need or danger, for in such a world there could be no real needs or dangers.

To make possible this continual series of individual adjustments, nature would have to work by "special providence" instead of running according to general laws which men must learn to respect on penalty of pain or death. The laws of nature would have to be extremely flexible: sometimes gravity would operate, sometimes not; sometimes an object would be hard and solid, sometimes soft. There could be no sciences, for there would be no enduring world structure to investigate. In eliminating the problems and hardships of an objective environment, with its own laws, life would become like a dream in which, delightfully but aimlessly, we would float and drift at ease.[10]

One can at least begin to imagine such a world. It is evident that our present ethical concepts would have no meaning in it. If, for example, the notion of harming someone is an essential element in the concept of a wrong action, in our hedonistic paradise there could be no wrong actions—nor any right actions in distinction from wrong. Courage and fortitude would have no point in an environment in which there is, by definition, no danger or difficulty. Generosity, kindness, the *agape* aspect of love, prudence, unselfishness, and all other ethical notions which presuppose life in a stable environment, could not even be formed. Consequently, such a world, however well it might promote

---

[10]Tennyson's poem, "The Lotus-Eaters," well expresses the desire (analyzed by Freud as a wish to return to the peace of the womb) for such "dreamful ease."

pleasure, would be very ill adapted for the development of the moral qualities of human personality. In relation to this purpose it would be the worst of all possible worlds.

It would seem, then, that an environment intended to make possible the growth in free beings of the finest characteristics of personal life, must have a good deal in common with our present world. It must operate according to general and dependable laws; and it must involve real dangers, difficulties, problems, obstacles, and possibilities of pain, failure, sorrow, frustration, and defeat. If it did not contain the particular trials and perils which—subtracting man's own very considerable contribution—our world contains, it would have to contain others instead.

To realize this is not, by any means, to be in possession of a detailed theodicy. It is to understand that this world, with all its "heartaches and the thousand natural shocks that flesh is heir to," an environment so manifestly not designed for the maximization of human pleasure and the minimization of human pain, may be rather well adapted to the quite different purpose of "soul-making."[11]

These considerations are related to theism as such. Specifically, Christian theism goes further in the light of the death of Christ, which is seen paradoxically both (as the murder of the divine Son) as the worst thing that has ever happened and (as the occasion of man's salvation) as the best thing that has ever happened. As the supreme evil turned to supreme good, it provides the paradigm for the distinctively Christian reaction to evil. Viewed from the standpoint of Christian faith, evils do not cease to be evils; and certainly, in view of Christ's healing work, they cannot be said to have been sent by God. Yet, it has been the persistent claim of those seriously and wholeheartedly committed to Christian discipleship that tragedy, though truly tragic, may nevertheless be turned, through a man's reaction to it, from a cause of despair and alienation from God to a stage in the fulfillment of God's loving purpose for that individual. As the greatest of all evils, the crucifixion of Christ, was made the occasion of man's redemption, so good can be won from other evils. As Jesus saw his execution by the Romans as an experience which God desired him to accept, an experience which was to be brought within the sphere of the divine purpose and made to serve the divine ends, so the Christian response to calamity is to accept the

---

[11]This brief discussion has been confined to the problem of human suffering. The large and intractable problem of animal pain is not taken up here. For a discussion of it, see, for example, Nels Ferré, *Evil and the Christian Faith* (New York: Harper & Row, 1947), Chapter 7; and Austin Farrer, *Love Almighty and Ills Unlimited* (New York: Doubleday, 1961), Chapter 5.

adversities, pains, and afflictions which life brings, in order that they can be turned to a positive spiritual use.[12]

At this point, theodicy points forward in two ways to the subject of life after death.

First, although there are many striking instances of good being triumphantly brought out of evil through a man's or a woman's reaction to it, there are many other cases in which the opposite has happened. Sometimes obstacles breed strength of character, dangers evoke courage and unselfishness, and calamities produce patience and moral steadfastness. But sometimes they lead, instead, to resentment, fear, grasping selfishness, and disintegration of character. Therefore, it would seem that any divine purpose of soul-making which is at work in earthly history must continue beyond this life if it is ever to achieve more than a very partial and fragmentary success.

Second, if we ask whether the business of soul-making is worth all the toil and sorrow of human life, the Christian answer must be in terms of a future good which is great enough to justify all that has happened on the way to it.

CHAPTER 2 PROBES

1. In Arthur C. Clarke's story, what observations lead the priest into his spiritual difficulties? To what conclusion does he feel compelled?

2. What powerful principle operates upon the priest's reasoning? Do you agree with this principle?

3. Which properties of God are relevant to Clarke's story? Which are not?

4. John Hick describes a line of defense against the problem of evil, based upon the claim that the universe is a place of "soul-making." Explain Hick's reasoning. How would you expect Hick to try to tackle the problem raised in Clarke's story in terms of "soul-making"?

5. Hick speaks of "the supreme evil turned to the supreme good." What relevance does this have to "The Star"? Are you convinced by Hick's defense?

---

[12]This conception of providence is stated more fully in John Hick, *Faith and Knowledge* (Ithaca, N.Y.: Cornell U.P., 1957), Chapter 7, some sentences from which are incorporated in this paragraph.

6. The priest in "The Star" seems to think that Loyola could have done better in responding to the difficulty raised in the story. Do you think you could explain away the problem along traditional theological lines? If so, how? If not, can you do it any other way, without sacrificing the concept of a God who is worthy of worship?

7. Clarke's story offers a scenario that seems to provide evidence against the existence of an all-powerful, all-knowing, all-good God. Can you think of a scenario that would decisively prove the opposite, namely, that such a God does indeed exist? If not, why do you think that it cannot be done? If so, what would your scenario be like, and how would it escape the rational doubt which has vexed traditional arguments and tales of miracles?

8. Atheists faced with evidence such as that presented in "The Star" would conclude that it was decisive against the existence of a traditional God. Some theists would claim that it was not, for reasons discussed in 2:3.4 and 2:3.5. If you agree with these reasons, show how they could be employed in such a way as to escape the conclusion drawn by the atheist. If you think that such reasons would not escape the atheist's conclusions, explain why you think they fail.

9. Some theists are unimpressed by any argument or evidence whatsoever, claiming that what is needed in religious matters is not reason and proof, but faith pure and simple—faith that cares not at all for evidence of any kind. What do you think of this view? How would such a theist answer the atheist's response that any belief that cares not at all for evidence is no better than madness, no better than the insane person's belief that he is Napoleon or Julius Caesar, another belief which ignores all of the evidence?

10. Other theists have argued that the belief in God is a "good bet." They would say that, if you believe in God and are wrong, it is no great loss, but, if you are right, it wins you the kingdom of Heaven. On the other hand, if you disbelieve in God, and are right, you win nothing, but, if you are wrong, you will suffer eternal damnation in Hell. Such theists (the most famous of whom was the seventeenth-century French philosopher Blaise Pascal) would thus conclude that to disbelieve in God is irrational. Does this argument answer the problem raised in "The Star"? Does it prove that God exists? Does it provide reason to suppose that God exists, even if the reason is not decisive? What sort of God does this argument rely upon? Is this the sort of God that seems to you to be worthy of worship, even if it does exist?

11. Now that you have considered the question of God's existence and moral and natural evils, are you inclined to believe the atheist's claim that evil disproves the existence of God, or are you inclined rather to think with the theist that the problem can be solved? Why?

RECOMMENDED READING

Science Fiction and Religion

Science fiction approaches religion from many directions. Some authors use a variety of settings and plot scenarios to experiment with different conceptions of God. These stories often concentrate on the philosophical problem of evil. A favorite theme is the traditional rivalry between science and religion. Others focus on the nature of religious experience or the proper place of religion within our civilization.

The Conflict of Faith and Reason. In Isaac Asimov's "Nightfall" [in Robert Silverberg, *Science Fiction Hall of Fame I* (Avon, 1970)], a planet in a six-star system sees the darkness only once every two thousand years, and its culture is repeatedly destroyed by its superstitious response. Reliance upon faith is criticized by proponents of the scientific method. Also critical of the religious viewpoint is Jerry Pournelle and Larry Niven's novel about the collision of a comet with the earth, *Lucifer's Hammer* (Fawcett, 1977). Following the catastrophe, a religious brotherhood seeks the total demolition of surviving technology. Some science fiction stories are more sympathetic to religious faith. For example, C. S. Lewis's trilogy, *Out of the Silent Planet, Perelandra,* and *That Hideous Strength* (Collier, 1965), attacks the modern scientific viewpoint on behalf of Christianity. And in Arthur C. Clarke's "Nine Billion Names of God" (*Science Fiction Hall of Fame I*) advanced computer technology is utilized by Tibetan mystics with an arresting outcome. Mysticism is also sympathetically combined with hallucinogenic science fiction in Philip K. Dick, *The Three Stigmata of Palmer Eldritch* (Doubleday, 1965), which draws freely on Christian themes.

Some stories project ways in which religious beliefs such as the belief in immortality may be vindicated or accommodated by future science—for example, Robert Sheckley, *Immortality, Inc.* (Bantam, 1959), and Gordon Eklund, "Embryonic Dharma," *Analog* (December 1976). Out of the plethora of semi-fictional "documentaries" on ancient gods who were allegedly visitors from outer space we regret to say that we have found none of redeeming philosophical merit. Larry Niven and Jerry Pournelle in *Inferno* (Pocket Books, 1976) offer a tongue-in-cheek science fiction reconstruction of Dante's account of the afterlife.

It is tempting to think that if you could only go back and see Jesus Christ, Mohammed, or Buddha for yourself you could escape the problem of having to base religious conviction upon faith rather than the evidence of your senses. But meeting these religious leaders in the flesh might only present you with more disturbing ambiguities. This is revealed in two powerfully written stories about time travel back to the time of Christ: Richard Matheson's "The Traveller," in *Born of Man and Woman* (Chamberlain, 1954), and Michael Moorcock's "new wave," Nebula-winning *Behold the Man* (Avon, 1970), which draws heavily on Carl Jung's psychological theories about religion.

The Problem of Evil.   Olaf Stapledon's *Star Maker* (Penguin, 1973) offers a view of the nature of God which is in many ways comparable to that of the twentieth-century philosopher Alfred North Whitehead. At times Stapledon's prose is as dense as Whitehead's *Process and Reality,* but there are also dazzling displays of visual imagery. In his odyssey to fathom the star maker, the unnamed narrator finds a philosophical solution to the problem set forth in Clarke's "The Star," but it involves a view of God which some will find unacceptable. The problem is also presented to a Jesuit scientist in James Blish, *A Case of Conscience* (Ballantine, 1975). In this Hugo-winning novel, a crocodile-like alien species has a high intelligence but is incapable of appreciating human religious concerns and seems to the priest to embody moral evil. Another Hugo winner, Harlan Ellison's very demanding "Death-bird," employs a variety of literary techniques to redefine the cosmic conflict between God and Satan and to challenge our traditional assumptions that God is good and all-powerful [in Kate Wilhelm, ed., *Nebula Award Stories Number Nine* (Bantam, 1978)]. Our assumption that God is morally perfect and powerful is called into question in Theodore Sturgeon's "Microcosmic God," in *The Science Fiction Hall of Fame I.* In this story, a microscopic race of intelligent beings are the creation of a scientist named "Kidder," who gives them the counterpart of the Ten Commandments. The fate of this race may foretell our own. Frederic Brown's "Recessional" is a bitter parable of divine indifference in Robert Bloch, ed., *The Best of Frederic Brown* (Ballantine, 1976).

Religion as a Human Practice.   Philosophical anthropology is the study of human nature from the point of view of human history and culture. Religious belief and religious institutions have always been central to human social life, and many science fiction stories explore this role by projecting religion into subtly varied social situations. The role of religion as a historical force is the subject of two important novels. Walter M. Miller, Jr. received a Hugo for *A Canticle for Leibowitz* (Bantam, 1976), which starts in the radiation-plagued dark ages of the future. The monks and scribes of the Catholic Church play a central role in perpetuating human civilization through cycles of progress and destruction. Keith Roberts' richly styled *Pavane* (Ace Special, 1968) describes an alternate reality in which Protestant England was de-feated by Catholic Spain in the sixteenth century, so that the progress of science and technology are still hamstrung by religious restrictions in the twentieth century. Yet the excesses of technological warfare have also been averted. The good and bad consequences of religion are woven together in a fascinating tapestry.

The impact of religion on a society can be appreciated by establishing some "distance" from a particular set of religious beliefs. Some well-written, often disturbing science fiction stories depict religious behavior in utterly alien settings which challenge our ability to comprehend the acts of faith we observe. Gordon Eklund and Gregory Benford, "If the Stars Are Gods," in Terry Carr, ed., *Best SF of the Year #4* (Ballantine, 1975), contrast the religious views of a caninelike species with our human outlook. This has been expanded into a book of the same title (Berkley/Putnam, 1977). The difficulty of understanding an alien's utterances is suggested by the quotation from the philosopher Wittgenstein at the beginning of the story: "A dog cannot be a hypocrite, but neither can it be sincere." [This story can be read profitably in conjunction with the Wittgensteinian John Wisdom's "Gods," in *Philosophy and Psycho-Analysis* (Blackwell, 1953) as well as other articles cited here.] Two stories in which human beings become entangled in alien religions are Edmund Cooper, *A Far Sunset* (Walker, 1967), and Roger Zelazny, "A Rose for Ecclesiastes," in the *Science Fiction Hall of Fame I*. A demanding but interesting story setting the problem of evil in an alien consciousness is Gregory Benford's "Starswarmer" (*Analog,* September 1978). Even greater philosophical "distance" can be achieved through a very popular science fiction plotline: intelligent machines which are converted to humanlike religious faith. The paradigm is Isaac Asimov's "Reason" in *I, Robot* (Fawcett, 1970), described in the text. In Lloyd Biggle, Jr., "In His Own Image," in *Monument* (Doubleday, 1974), the metallic prophet displays fanaticism as well as religious devotion. In Anthony Boucher's "Quest for Saint Aquin" (*Science Fiction Hall of Fame I*), the human protagonist's faith is tested when his source of inspiration turns out to be a robot. The capacity of robots in such stories to mimic human religious behavior raises serious questions about the uniqueness of our spiritual nature. The greatest test so far comes from Robert Silverberg's "Good News from the Vatican" in Lloyd Biggle, Jr.'s *Nebula Award Stories Number Seven* (Harper & Row, 1974). In this story, which won a Nebula, a robot is miraculously "elevated" to the papal seat.

Philosophy and Religion

Problems about the existence of God have always preoccupied philosophers. You can get an excellent start on these problems by consulting John Hick's concise and clear survey, *Philosophy of Religion* (Prentice-Hall, 1963), which is sympathetic to the religious viewpoint, and Antony Flew, *God and Philosophy* (Hutchinson, 1966), which defends atheism. See also the articles in *The Encyclopedia of Philosophy* (Macmillan, 1967), especially on "Philosophy of Religion, History of," "Atheism," "Cosmological Argument for the Existence of God," "Evil, the Problem of," "Faith," "Ontological Argument for the Existence of God," "Teleological Argument for the Existence of God," and others cited in Vol. 7, pp. 147–148. For the original writings of great present philosophers of religion, see the following anthologies: G. L. Abernathy and T. L. A. Langford, eds., *Philosophy of Religion: A Book of Readings* (Macmillan, 1962), and John Hick, ed., *Classical and Contemporary*

Readings in the Philosophy of Religion (Prentice-Hall, 1964). An influential midcentury collection has been A. Flew and A. MacIntyre, eds., *New Essays in Philosophical Theology* (Macmillan, 1955).

Classic arguments for the existence of God by Plato, St. Anselm, St. Thomas Aquinas, René Descartes, William Paley, and Immanuel Kant are conveniently collected in John Hick, ed., *The Existence of God* (Macmillan, 1964). (See also the anthologies just cited.) The most famous statement of the problem of evil is David Hume, *Dialogues Concerning Natural Religion.* Recent approaches to the problem of evil are offered by J. L. Mackie and Alvin Plantinga in B. Mitchell, ed., *The Philosophy of Religion* (Oxford, 1971). See also N. Pike, ed., *God and Evil* (Prentice-Hall, 1964). The nature of faith and reason is explored in John Hick, *Faith and Knowledge* (Cornell, 1957), William James, *The Will to Believe* (Longmans, 1921), and John Wisdom's "Gods" (already cited). A useful anthology is J. Hick, ed., *Faith and the Philosopher* (Macmillan, 1964). Theories of "life after death" are stated and criticized in Antony Flew, ed., *Body, Mind, and Death* (Macmillan, 1966).

Religious experience and mysticism have been examined by William James in *The Varieties of Religious Experience* (Longmans, 1947), W. T. Stace, *Mysticism and Philosophy* (Macmillan, 1961), and C. B. Martin, *Religious Belief* (Cornell, 1956). Some authors treat religious experience as a type of evidence for the existence of God.

Many social scientists and philosophers treat religious experience and practices as peculiar phenomena that need to be *explained* along with other forms of social behavior like fighting and mating. Philosophers influenced by Ludwig Wittgenstein have attempted to understand religious belief in terms of the "forms of life" and "language games" peculiar to societies. Two influential examples of this have been D. Z. Phillips, "Religious Beliefs and Language Games," in Basil Mitchell, ed., *The Philosophy of Religion* (Oxford, 1971), and Peter Winch, "Understanding a Primitive Society" in Brian R. Wilson, ed., *Rationality* (Blackwell, 1979). This approach is criticized in Kai Nielsen's "Wittgensteinian Fideism," *Philosophy* 42 (1967). These essays will provide useful background for the science fiction works of James Blish and Michael Moorcock and, especially, for Eklund and Benford's story already mentioned, *If the Stars Are Gods.*

THE PHILOSOPHY
OF TIME AND SPACE:

Time travel: Can it be done?

The ideas of time and space are basic building blocks for your understanding of the world. This chapter will probe the nature of time (and also the nature of space, to a lesser extent). The idea of time is bound up with the crucial concepts you use to understand reality. For example, time is related to the idea of *personal identity*. If you still feel proud (or guilty) about some act you committed several years ago, you are taking it for granted that the person who did the act *in the past* is the same person as yourself *in the present.* Time is central to ethical issues involving rights and responsibilities. For example, do we, the generation living on earth *in the present,* have the right to use up all of the world's resources without any sense of obligation to our great-grandchildren living on earth *in the future*? Further, time and space are central concepts in the modern scientific view of the universe. Many people today think that, if a thing exists, it *must* have a time and a place.

But, in spite of its importance, you may find it hard to explain just what time is. If you have ever pondered your experience of time or discussed it with your friends, you may have come to the conclusion that time is very mysterious. Philosophers have long been conscious of the mysterious nature of time. The ancient Christian philosopher, St. Augustine, confessed his perplexity:

> What is time? Who can explain it easily and briefly? Who can get a hold of it, even in thought, so that they can give an explanation in words of it? Yet what do we talk about more knowingly than time? We certainly understand it when we talk about it. We even understand it when we hear another person speaking about it. What, then, is time? If no one asks me, I know; but if I want to explain it to a questioner, I do not know.[1]

St. Augustine starts from commonsense notions about time: time is passing, and only the *present* time is *really* real. But these notions lead quickly to paradoxical consequences. For example, how can you have obligations to your great-grandchildren if they have no reality? But, if you have no obligations to them, don't you have the right to squander the world's resources and pile up wastes all you please? Perhaps you find it hard to accept this implication. (Suppose our great-grandparents had used the same reasoning!) Augustine finds that his commonsense notions about time lead him to dizzying conclusions. He soon doubts whether anything as weird as time could even exist. Many other philosophers have argued that time is filled with contradictions and that our belief that we are conscious of time passing is an illusion. (We will pursue St. Augustine's paradoxes about time in subsequent paragraphs.)

These philosophical worries about the nature and reality of time can be brought into sharper focus by considering the hypothesis (championed by many science fiction writers and by some philosophers) that it is in principle possible to "travel" into the past or future. A study of time travel paradoxes, which have been the bread and butter of many professional fiction writers, helps also to clarify your ideas about the nature of time. And a serious consideration of the hypothesis, in some form, may help you to decide whether or not you agree with St. Augustine's worries about time.

After completing this chapter, you should be able to do the following:

- Explain the difference between the dynamic and static views of the nature of time.

- Explain why, on the dynamic view, time seems to be mysterious or even unreal and explain how, on the static view, Augustine's paradoxes are avoided.

- Describe the Time Traveler's hypothesis and indicate how it is related to the controversy between the static view and the dynamic view of time.

---

[1]St. Augustine, *Confessions,* Book XI, Section 17.

- Explain the importance of the theory that time is "relative" for the Time Traveler's hypothesis.

- Explain how the notion of time travel is hard to reconcile with our notions of cause and effect.

- Discuss why the fact that the past is as real as the present is appealed to as a source of philosophical consolation.

- Show how conceptual experiments can be used to contrast different views of time and to expose the paradoxical aspects of time travel.

3:1 THE NATURE OF TIME

3:1.1 St. Augustine's *Confessions* contains a fascinating discussion of the puzzling nature of time. He has a commonsense view of time which can be called the *dynamic view* of time. This is the view that time "passes." The future is continually being decreased or "eaten up," and the past is continually being increased or "fed." For example, an event such as your first kiss was in your future; then, finally, and for a tantalizing brief while, it was in your present; and now, alas, it is in your dead past. Time, "like a river," flows relentlessly in one direction. Your experience of time's passage can be a source of anxiety, especially when you realize that one of the approaching future events is . . . your own death.

According to the dynamic view of time, a steady succession of events is coming into and going out of existence while time passes. St. Augustine raises a hard question for this view. "How do those two parts of time, the past and the future, exist, when the past has already ceased to exist, and the future has not yet come into existence?" Augustine does not see how the past or future *could* exist. "If the past and future exist, I would like to know where they are." But even the present moment is not immune from difficulty: "The present would not pass over into the past, if it were *always* present. But then it would be eternity, not time. So, if the present really is time, it must pass over into the past. But then how can we say that it exists? For the sole reason for its existence is the fact that it will stop existing. Is it not the case that time exists only because it tends *not to exist*?" Our human idea of time thus contradicts itself! St. Augustine's point here is that our natural human understanding of that part of reality called time is limited. We encounter such drastic difficulties when we think about them that we cannot solve them on our own (that is, without God).

St. Augustine also contends, on related grounds, that, although we have various means of measuring time, the idea of measuring time seems to make no sense. To measure a spatial length, such as the fish you have caught, you place the existing length alongside an existing measuring device. Obviously, you can't carry out the measurement if the length to be measured or the measuring stick does not exist, for example, if the "fish that got away" does not exist. So you can't possibly measure a stretch of time that has ceased to exist or has not come into existence. Suppose it is a "present" length of time, for example, the time it takes you to read quickly through this chapter—say, an hour. But Augustine has an argument to show that even "the present hour" cannot be said to exist in the sense required. This hour passes by means of little parts: the part that is gone is the past; the part that is left is the future. If you can think of a part of time which could not be divided into even the tiniest parts, then this part is *the present.* It darts from the future into the past so quickly that it does not have any length. For, if it has length, it has past and future parts. The present has no length.[2] By this "whittling argument," Augustine whittles away the past and present portion of any stretch of time leaving nothing but an *unextended* moment. Thus no length of time exists to be measured!

Augustine's paradoxical arguments rely upon the following assumptions and inferences: (1) The present is, in the strictest sense, only the point at which past and future meet. (2) So any stretch of time is composed exclusively of past or future parts. (3) But the past is unreal (because it no longer exists), and (4) the future is unreal (because it does not yet exist). (5) So no stretch of time is real and no stretch of time can be measured (since you can't measure what doesn't exist).

We won't try to pursue St. Augustine's "solution" to the paradox here. He regarded time as a *mysterious* reality which was inscrutable to human beings and comprehensible only to God. God is all-knowing but also eternal, so that God can know all things in time without remembering a past or expecting the future. Our time is real in a sense, but unreal when contrasted with the eternal reality of God.

3:1.2 The dynamic view assumes that there is a fundamental difference between space and time. Space is thought of as a sort of externally existing receptacle, but time is thought of as perpetually changing or as being in a condition of "becoming." In opposition to this is the *static view* of time that the spatial relations and temporal relations of everything in the universe together form a "unified manifold" of four dimensions: three spatial dimensions and a temporal dimension. Any event has a precise location within this manifold, called "space–time." Different events stand at certain "distances" from each other as measured in spatial *and* temporal terms: for example, the location of one volcanic eruption might be two thousand miles due north from and twelve years after another eruption.

To many people this static view of time is wildly counterintuitive. It represents the universe as a forbidding, unchanging "block universe." Our

[2]St. Augustine, *Confessions,* Book XI, Sections 17, 20, 36.

experience of the perpetual flux of time, of one event's coming into existence after another, seems too real to deny. But the static view is given a favorable representation in one of the greatest of all conceptual experiments, H. G. Wells's science fiction novel, *The Time Machine* (1895). A character called "The Time Traveler" lectures a number of guests in his home on his theory of space and time. He argues that just as "a mathematical line, a line of thickness *nil,* has no real existence . . . neither has a mathematical plane. These things are mere abstractions. . . . Nor, having only length, breadth, and thickness can a cube have a real existence." When a guest objects that "of course a solid body may exist," the Time Traveler responds,

> Can a cube that does not last for any time at all have a real existence? Any real body must have extension in *four* directions: it must have Length, Breadth, Thickness, and—Duration. But through a natural infirmity of the flesh . . . we incline to overlook this fact. There are really four dimensions, three of which we call the three planes of Space, and a fourth, Time. There is, however, a tendency to draw an unreal distinction between the former three dimensions and the latter, because it happens that our consciousness moves intermittently in one direction along the latter from the beginning to the end of our lives.[3]

The Time Traveler explains how the relation of time to space can be represented by a four-dimensional geometry:

> Space, as our mathematicians have it, is spoken of as having three dimensions, which one may call Length, Breadth, and Thickness, and is always definable by reference to three planes, each at right angles to the others. But some philosophical people have been asking why *three* dimensions particularly—why not another direction at right angles to the other three?—and have even tried to construct a Four-Dimension geometry. Professor Simon Newcomb was expounding this to the New York Mathematical Society only a month or so ago. You know how on a flat surface, which has only two dimensions, we can represent a figure of a three-dimensional solid, and similarly they think that by models of three dimensions they could represent one of four—if they could master the perspective of the thing. . . . For instance, here is a portrait of a man at eight years old, another at fifteen, another at seventeen, another at twenty-three, and so on. All these are evidently sections, as it were, Three-Dimensional representations of his Four-Dimensional being, which is a fixed and unalterable thing.[4]

This view of space and time has important implications for the way in which you look at yourself. Consider the idea of a geometric "slice," as shown in the illustration at the top of the following page:

[3]H. G. Wells, *The Time Machine* (London, 1895), chapter 1.
[4]*Ibid.*

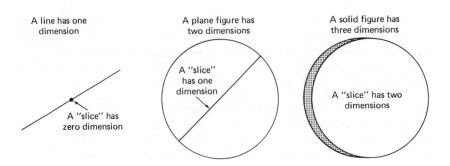

A line has one dimension

A plane figure has two dimensions

A solid figure has three dimensions

A "slice" has zero dimension

A "slice" has one dimension

A "slice" has two dimensions

A physical object has four dimensions: three spatial and one temporal

A "slice" has three dimensions

A straight line has one dimension; it can be sliced (lengthwise) at a *point* on it, which has no dimension. Likewise, a two-dimensional place figure like a circle can be sliced (breadthwise) along a one-dimensional line, and a three-dimensional solid object like a sphere can be sliced (depthwise) along a two-dimensional surface. But can't the three-dimensional object itself be viewed as a "slice" of a four-dimensional object? For example, at this present instant, as well as at the instant of your conception, at the instant you became one year old, and so on, there are slices of a four-dimensional object which is the "real you." You might perform the mental experiment of trying to visualize what it would be like to see all of the instantaneous three-dimensional slices of yourself *simultaneously.* The result would be like seeing a time-lapse photograph in three dimensions, a three-dimensional time-lapse sculpture. The science fiction author Kurt Vonnegut[5] describes an alien species, the Tralfamadorians, who perceive all things nonsequentially. For them the nighttime heaven is filled not with points of light but with "rarefied, luminous spaghetti." They see human beings as "great mil-

[5]*Slaughterhouse Five* (New York: Dell, 1969), p. 87. In this novel Vonnegut, from the static view of time, develops philosophical conclusions about free will and morality which are reminiscent of ancient Stoicism.

lipedes—with 'babies' legs at one end and old people's legs at the other,' "
as one character remarks. Such a being as you really are, at all times and
places, is sometimes referred to as a "four-dimensional worm."

    3:1.3 You have been considering two proposed views of time. Ac-
cording to the dynamic view of time (3:1.1), an event exists or is real only
when it is actually present; the past and the future are unreal. According to
the static view of time (3:1.2), all the parts of time are equally real. On this
view, motion occurs within space-time (in a manner which you will see
explained in 3:2.3), but time itself doesn't "move" or "flow."
    It is necessary to be very careful in describing the senses in which the
past and future *are* real on the static view of time. On this view, an historical
event such as Neil Armstrong's first setting foot on the moon's surface is
just as real or existent as the event of your reading this sentence. But, from
the fact that both events are equally real, it does *not* follow that both events
are simultaneous. Confusion arises from the fact that, when we use the word
"exists" in ordinary English, the word is in the present tense. But it it
possible (on the static view) to distinguish between the *existence* of a thing
or event and the *time* when it exists. An event or thing exists provided that
it has some location within the unified manifold of space and time. The date
of an event depends on where it is located. So you can recognize that the
event of stepping on the moon exists as truly as that of your reading this
sentence, without having to claim that Armstrong is "still" stepping on the
moon. It would also be a confusion to say that Armstrong is "always"
stepping on the moon if that event is as real as a present event. It is proper
to say that a thing "still" exists only if it exists at the *same* time as the
statement to that effect. And it is proper to say that an event "always" exists
only if it exists at *every* point on the time line. Such an event might be the
expansion of the universe.
    The Time Traveler seems to provide us with an answer to St. Augus-
tine's argument. St. Augustine believed that only what exists in the present
instant can be real. The Time Traveler contends that such a "slice" of a
thing is a mere abstraction and that only what is extended in all four
dimensions is real. In the Time Traveler's view, a past or future event (or a
past or future interval of time) exists just as much as a present one. St.
Augustine's puzzles depend on premises 3 and 4 in 3:1.1, which both
assume that the statement that something "is real" or "exists" *always* means
that it "is real *now*" or "exists *now*." By rejecting this assumption, the Time
Traveler can deny both those premises and Augustine's conclusions.

3:2 THE TIME TRAVELER'S HYPOTHESIS

    3:2.1 As the Time Traveler is expounding his theory in H. G. Wells's
Time Machine, a guest offers what seems to be a crushing objection: "Why
cannot we move in Time as we move about in the other dimensions of

Space?'' The Time Traveler responds by defending the hypothesis that it *is* possible to travel through time. He offers the analogy of a man in a balloon. (The first draft of Wells's story was written fifteen years before the first successful airplane flight.) Ordinarily we are confined to motion in just two dimensions, but a balloon enables us to travel upward as well. Perhaps a time machine could let us move in a temporal direction as well. Someone objects, ''You cannot move at all in Time, you cannot get away from the present moment.'' The Time Traveler replies,

> My dear sir, that is just where you are wrong. That is just where the whole world has gone wrong. We are always getting away from the present moment. Our mental existences, which are immaterial and have no dimensions, are passing along the Time-Dimension with a uniform velocity from the cradle to the grave.[6]

His point can be illustrated by a variation on the balloon metaphor. You drift through time like a person in a balloon borne by the wind at uniform velocity. Why could you not attach a propeller to your vehicle and accelerate or decelerate? Or why should you not hope that ultimately you may be able to stop or accelerate or even reverse your drift along the Time-Dimension? As a demonstration, the Time Traveler claims to be sending a small-scale time machine into the past. After it disappears the guests object that it could not have moved into the past or future: '' . . . if it travelled into the future it would still be here all this time, since it must have travelled through this time . . . But if it travelled into the past it would have been visible when we came first into this room. . . . '' The Time Traveler replies that they cannot ''appreciate this machine, any more than we can the spoke of a wheel spinning, or a bullet flying through the air. If it is travelling through time fifty times or a hundred times faster than we are, if it gets through a minute while we get through a second, the impression it creates will of course be only one-fiftieth or one-hundredth of what it would make if it were not travelling in time.'' Thus, whereas you ordinarily travel through time at the plodding rate of a minute per minute, a time machine would enable you to soar along at a year a minute! Later, the Time Traveler describes in very vivid terms his visual experiences as the world seems to speed up before his eyes.

The Time Traveler's hypothesis is stated in rather vague terms in Wells's novel, and other science fiction writers and theorists have worked it out along different lines. But his way of presenting the hypothesis does serve to bring out a crucial theoretical difference between the dynamic view and the static view of time. For, if the future and the past have no reality, as St. Augustine contends, then it *would* seem to be absurd to speak of traveling to them. The Time Traveler's hypothesis rests firmly on the static view of time. It is hard to see how it could be coherently stated otherwise. The view that you could move into the future at an accelerated or decelerated

---

[6]H. G. Wells, *The Time Machine,* chapter 1.

rate seems to assume that the temporal dimension is fundamentally similar to spatial dimensions. There may, of course, be other, insurmountable objections to the hypothesis. But the fact that the hypothesis is ruled out completely by one view of time (the view shared by the Time Traveler's guests) but not (obviously) by the other view (the view of the Time Traveler) enables us to appreciate the depth of the difference between them.

3:2.2   Some philosophers have objected that Wells's time machine idea is absurd and self-contradictory. To see why they have thought this, you have to consider how we understand movement or change of an ordinary sort. Suppose a student is walking on a college campus from the student union to the library in three minutes, passing a dormitory and a class building on the way. In what sense does movement occur? Simply in the sense that at *different instants* the student is at *different places* along the path. We can represent the student's movements on this table:

Place:	Union	Dorm	Class Bldg.	Library
Time:	3:00	3:01	3:02	3:03

The important point is that movement is defined in terms of both spatial and temporal locations. It has also been suggested, in terms of four-dimensional geometry, that such movement can be defined in terms of a *timeline:* a sequence of locations (such as the union at 3:00) with precise coordinates in the space–time manifold. If you are "at rest," your time line will connect locations which are at the same spatial coordinates but different temporal coordinates:

Place:	Union	Union	Union	Union
Time:	3:00	3:01	3:02	3:03

Donald Williams, a philosopher, has objected that the Time Traveler hypothesis is incoherent.

> True motion is motion at once in time and space. Nothing can "move" in time alone anymore than in space alone, and time itself cannot "move" anymore than space itself. "Does this road go anywhere?" asks the city tourist. "No, it stays right along here," replies the countryman. . . . Time travel, *prima facie,* then, is analyzable either as the banality that at each different moment we occupy a different moment from the one we occupied before, or the contradiction that at each different moment we occupy a different moment from the one which we are then occupying—that five minutes from now, for example, I may be a hundred years from now. ("He may even now—if I may use the phrase—be wandering on some plesio-saurus-haunted oolitic coral reef, or beside the lonely saline seas of the Triassic Age"—H. G. Wells, *The Time Machine,* Epilogue. This book,

perhaps the best yarn ever written, makes slips, [but] its logic is better than that of later such stories.)[7]

J. J. C. Smart, author, philosopher, adds,

It is not surprising that we cannot represent a time machine, since the notion of such a machine is an incoherent one. How fast would such a machine flash over a given ten-second stretch? In ten seconds or minus ten seconds? Or what? No sensible answer can be given, for the question is itself absurd.[8]

The point of these critics may be appreciated by considering how we might represent "movement through time" on a third table:

Time	(LC):	2:00	2:01	2:02	2:03	2:05	2:08	2:12	2:16
Time	(TT):	2:00	2:01	2:02	2:03	2:04	2:05	2:06	2:07

Williams argues that this is incoherent, since it requires you to be "simultaneously" at 2:12 and 2:06, which *would* be a remarkable feat!

3:2.3 In fairness to science fiction writers, however, we should point out that they have tried to avoid such absurdities by introducing distinctions between different *frames of reference*. This idea was anticipated by Shakespeare: "Time travels in divers places with divers persons."[9] For example, suppose that in the third table the top line, *"Time* (LC)," represents the time as indicated on the laboratory clock and that the bottom line, *"Time* (TT)," represents the time as indicated on the Time Traveler's wristwatch. We can surely make sense of the following story. The Time Traveler climbs in the time machine at 2:00, synchronizing his watch with the laboratory clock. He turns on the machine at 2:03. He shuts off the machine at 2:07 watch time and finds that the laboratory clock reads 2:16. By reference to the table we can also coherently describe the Time Traveler's rate of movement. He moves at a uniform velocity of a minute (LC) per minute (TT) from 2:00 to 2:03 (wristwatch time), he accelerates at the rate of one minute (LC) per minute (TT) for every minute that goes by on his watch, and after 2:08 he is moving at the uniform velocity of four minutes (LC) per minute (TT). You can also make sense of saying that the Time Traveler is "now" in some prehistoric age if you imagine that he and you synchronized your watches before he departed and that your watch reads 2:13. When his watch reads 2:13, he is looking at a dinosaur.

[7]Donald C. Williams, "The Myth of Passage," in Richard M. Gale, ed., *The Philosophy of Time* (New York: Anchor, 1969), p. 105.

[8]J. J. C. Smart, "Time," in Paul Edwards, ed., *The Encyclopedia of Philosophy*, Vol. 7 (New York: Macmillan, 1967).

[9]Shakespeare, *As You Like It*, Act III, Scene 2.

This way of defending the hypothesis relies on the assumption that time designations are relative to certain *frames of reference*. For example, the wristwatch and the laboratory clock belong to different frames of reference. This assumption of temporal relativism is a philosophical assumption which can be added to the static view of time. It is obviously compatible with—but should be distinguished from—the theory of relativity in modern physics.

3:2.4 The modern theory of relativity takes for granted some of the philosophical views you have been considering, including the static view of time and temporal relativism. It is neither possible nor desirable to become involved in details of the theory here, but it is useful to consider some of its implications for the Time Traveler's hypothesis.

The theory of relativity allows for a special form of time travel into the future. For, if a starship were to leave the gravitational system of the earth and solar system and travel to another star system at a very rapid rate, and were to return to earth at a later date, it would evidence a detectable "time dilation" effect. This implication has formed the premise for numerous works of speculative fiction. One of the earliest and best of these, Robert Heinlein's *Time for the Stars,* concerns young Tom Bartlett, who leaves his twin Pat on earth and travels in the torchship *Elsie* at speeds close to the speed of light to nearby stars. As a former physics student, he knows that according to the "Lorentz contraction formula," ship time should pass at a much slower rate from the rate at which time passes on earth. Suppose the *Elsie* were to pass the earth at a velocity of one-half the speed of light as measured on earth on January 1, 2001. And suppose that Tom and Pat were to synchronize calendars then. If the *Elsie* continued to travel through space and reappeared on January 1, 2002, on Pat's earth calendar, Tom's ship calendar would read only November 12, 2001. "That's just the special case, of course, for constant speeds," a friend reminds Tom; "it is more complicated for acceleration." Tom is very disconcerted to learn that the "time dilation" theory has not been tested. He reflects, "But *everybody* said that once we got up near the speed of light the months would change like days. The equations *said* so." The whole crew of the *Elsie* are, in effect, guinea pigs. Tom is worried: "Dying of old age in the *Elsie* was not what I had counted on. It was a grim thought, a life sentence shut up inside these still walls." Tom is relieved to learn that the equations *are* correct. He helps to confirm them by maintaining instantaneous telepathic contact with his twin brother, Pat. When Tom finally returns to Earth after what seems to him a few months, he finds Pat an old man of almost 90. Tom and his shipmates are called "Rip Van Winkles" by people on Earth, and he ends the story by marrying his own great-grandniece.[10]

Thus, if you could construct a starship and find an energy source powerful enough to accelerate your starship to a velocity close to the speed

---

[10]Robert A. Heinlein, *Time for the Stars* (Ballantine, 1978).

of light, you could, in effect, travel into the future. But there is no way to travel into the past on this theory—or to recover the time you lost by traveling in space.

3:3 CAUSAL PARADOXES

3:3.1 Most people find the implication that you can "travel into the future" a strain on their imaginations. But the idea of traveling into the past is harder yet to swallow. For one thing, it may conflict with your feeling that history always has the same direction from the past toward the future. Your experience of cause and effect in ordinary circumstances certainly seems to support this feeling. For it is obvious that natural processes generally occur in just one direction. For example, a cigarette burns down to ashes and uses up oxygen; ashes and stale air don't reconstitute themselves into a cigarette and oxygen. A reversed film sequence of a person smoking a cigarette strikes us as rather absurd. We also find traces of the past and have memories of past events. Archaeologists don't search for the "ruins" of future civilizations. (Modern scientists have tried to explain such facts in terms of the very complicated ideas of thermodynamics, but it will be possible for you to make some progress on this question by simply considering your own commonsense ideas of causality.)

In general, we assume that causes must precede their effects, and it seems impossible that an effect could precede its cause. In fact, many philosophers have tried to explain causation in relation to the idea of time. The philosopher David Hume claimed that, when we say that one event *c* causes another event *e*—for example, swallowing cyanide causes death—we imply several things: event *c* occurs *before e* in time (priority), event *c* and event *e* are connected in space (propinquity), and, other things being equal, events like *c* are generally followed by events like *e* (constant conjunction). We also take for granted two general principles in trying to explain natural phenomena: Every event has a cause (the law of causality) and, in similar circumstances, similar causes have similar effects (the law of uniformity). In Hume's view, if someone suddenly dies, you assume that this event has a cause, which is a preceding event, such as the ingestion of cyanide that was surreptitiously dropped into the victim's tea. There must also be some general laws of nature that events of the one sort are uniformly followed by events of the other. People generally keel over after ingesting cyanide.

There thus seems to be a pattern of temporal order in cause and effect relations. People don't die first and *then* ingest poison. But some defenders of time travel might accept the law of causality and the law of uniformity but deny that a cause must always *precede* its effect in the sense assumed by the objector. For example, if one of the guests were to slip cyanide into the time traveler's tea before his departure for the past, his death might occur centuries "before" the poisoning. This *seems* possible, runs the defense; what would be absurd would be the claim that his death had no cause at all.

3:3.2 The hypothesis presents a more difficult problem, however, since it seems that one could use a time machine to change the past. You may recall an embarrassing thing you did in the past and wish you could go back in a time machine to stop yourself before doing it. Though very tantalizing, such implications raise serious difficulties, which can be suggested with a simple conceptual experiment. Suppose you and a friend have a transmitter which can send signals (perhaps "faster than light" signals) which have the special feature that, if you send a signal at 3:00 and your friend receives the signal and answers it, you can receive the "answer" to your signal at 2:59, a full minute before you send it. It might seem that this would certainly guarantee that you get the answers you want. But, if it were possible, it would seem to lead to curious results. Suppose you attached your own receiver to an on–off switch so that, when your friend's message arrives, it turns *off* the switch controlling the power source for your own transmitter. But that means that you cannot send your signal at 3:00. The result is an apparent violation of the law of noncontradiction: You both send the signal at 3:00, and you don't send it at 3:00.

3:3.3 Various writers of science fiction have responded in different ways to this paradox. We'll mention only a few types of response here.

1. "The signal is sent at 3:00, and it isn't sent at 3:00." Many writers simply fail to see the problem. They describe time travel in a hopelessly illogical way. "The signal is sent at 3:00" occurs at the beginning of the story and "The signal isn't sent at 3:00" at the end, and it does not occur to the author that contradictions cannot exist.

2. "As a result of sending the signal at 3:00, the signal is no longer sent at 3:00." Thus the transmitter *changes the past*. This is the premise of many science fiction stories. The most famous is Ray Bradbury's "Sound of Thunder"[11] in which a time-traveling dinosaur hunter changes history by stepping on a butterfly. At first blush, this sounds better than response 1, but, on reflection, it is no better. How can an event that does not occur be the cause of anything else? Moreover, what sense can it make to say that "the statement *p* is false *because* the statement *p* is true"? Finally, response 2 suggests that it "was" true that the signal was sent at 3:00, but this is "no longer" true at 3:00. But it is either true or it is not true that something happens at 3:00. You *can* say that something is no longer true *at 3:00* that was true *at 2:30* (e.g., that the lights are off), but it makes no sense at all to say that the same thing is no longer true *at 3:00* that was true *at 3:00*.

3. "The signal is simply not sent at 3:00." In this approach the contradiction is evaded by saying that history is permanently and undetectably changed. This solution certainly has the merit of avoiding the self-contradictions of 1 and 2, but it leads to trouble with the law of causality. *Why* isn't the signal sent at 3:00? "Because the power source was turned off at 2:59." Why did that happen? "Because a signal sent by my friend arrived

[11]Ray Bradbury, *R is for Rocket* (New York: Bantam, 1965).

at 2:59." Why did your friend send the signal? "He was answering my—."
But you did *not* send a signal at 3:00. This solution ends up with an anomaly,
an uncaused event.

4. "Such a device is possible, but the situation you describe won't
arise because something will always go wrong to prevent it from happening."
The switch won't work, your friend will have a cardiac arrest before he can
return the signal, and so on, and so on. Many stories are developed on this
premise. Someone tries to go back to change the past—for example, to
rescue a loved one who died—and through a freak event or mistake causes
the loved one's death. Such stories, often tinged with irony, also suggest
the miraculous. They "solve" the problem but they leave you wondering:
what *if* something hadn't gone wrong?

5. "Such a device is possible, but the situation you describe can't arise
because every event in space–time is causally determined by other events
in space–time." This is a more sophisticated approach to the problem. It
does not appeal to *ad hoc* escapes like 4, but to the law of causality itself.
The case described can no more happen than a case in which a receiver
gets a message that has never been sent. This defense involves the idea that
the events in space–time are interrelated in a complex, four-dimensional
network. Each event is "fixed" in relation to other events past and present.

This defense seems, however, to leave open the possibility of *time
loops,* another sort of causal paradox. Suppose that you and your friend
agree to exchange messages in the manner described (except without the
on–off switch's being affected). Suppose that you receive from him at 2:59
his Social Security number, which you have never known before, and at
3:00 you send a message to him consisting of his Social Security number,
which he returned to you. The result is a closed "time loop," in which each
event is caused by other events in the loop. You send the number because
you received it, and he sent it because he received it. Yet you must wonder
about the loop of events as a whole. How did you learn his Social Security
number, if he sent it because you sent it to him? What made him send the
Social Security number to you, if you sent it to him? Such time loops are
perplexing, because they *seem* to conform to the law of causality—and yet
they don't seem to fit into the overall pattern of events which makes up
natural history.

3:4 CONCEPTUAL EXPERIMENT

Time travel is one of the most popular themes in science fiction. The
stories have probed a wide variety of "paradoxes," describing perplexing
chains of events which are hard to believe. Typically, the protagonist will
return to the past in a machine and "change the past" by killing a famous
figure or even by killing one of the protagonist's ancestors. As one impossibility after another occurs, often the protagonist will become as skeptical
as St. Augustine about the reality of time.

Some science fiction writers have, however, tried to develop concepts of time travel that permit no contradictions. Robert A. Heinlein, in "By His Bootstraps" and "All You Zombies—," presents detailed time-travel scenarios. Heinlein has painstakingly thought out the ideas of time and space, and of cause and effect, intending to avoid any inconsistencies. But does time-travel fiction, even as rigorously thought out as Heinlein's, escape the objections of philosophers that the idea of time contained in such stories is incoherent? One philosopher, David Lewis, maintains that Heinlein's story holds up even under very close criticism and that it presents a challenging, and possibly correct, view of time. Lewis's article, "The Paradoxes of Time Travel," follows Heinlein's "All You Zombies—."

Conceptual Experiment 3:

ALL YOU ZOMBIES—

Robert A. Heinlein

2217 Time Zone V (EST) 7 Nov. 1970—NYC–"Pop's Place": I was polishing a brandy snifter when the Unmarried Mother came in. I noted the time—10:17 p.m., zone five, or eastern time, November 7th, 1970. Temporal agents always notice time and date; we must.

The Unmarried Mother was a man twenty-five years old, no taller than I am, childish features and a touchy temper. I didn't like his looks—I never had—but he was a lad I was here to recruit, he was my boy. I gave him my best barkeep's smile.

Maybe I'm too critical. He wasn't swish; his nickname came from what he always said when some nosy type asked him his line: "I'm an unmarried mother." If he felt less than murderous he would add: "at four cents a word. I write confession stories."

If he felt nasty, he would wait for somebody to make something of it. He had a lethal style of infighting, like a female cop—one reason I wanted him. Not the only one.

He had a load on and his face showed that he despised people more than usual. Silently I poured a double shot of Old Underwear and left the bottle. He drank it, poured another.

I wiped the bar top. "How's the 'Unmarried Mother' racket?"

His fingers tightened on the glass and he seemed about to throw it at me; I felt for the sap under the bar. In temporal manipulation you try to figure everything, but there are so many factors that you never take needless risks.

I saw him relax that tiny amount they teach you to watch for in the Bureau's training school. "Sorry," I said. "Just asking, 'How's business?' Make it 'How's the weather?'"

He looked sour. "Business is okay. I write 'em, they print 'em, I eat."

I poured myself one, leaned toward him. "Matter of fact," I said, "you write a nice stick—I've sampled a few. You have an amazingly sure touch with the woman's angle."

It was a slip I had to risk; he never admitted what pen-names he used. But he was boiled enough to pick up only the last: " 'Woman's angle!' " he repeated with a snort. "Yeah, I know the woman's angle— I should."

104

"So?" I said doubtfully. "Sisters?"

"No. You wouldn't believe me if I told you."

"Now, now," I answered mildly, "bartenders and psychiatrists learn that nothing is stranger than truth. Why, son, if you heard the stories I do—well, you'd make yourself rich. Incredible."

"You don't know what 'incredible' means!"

"So? Nothing astonishes me. I've always heard worse."

He snorted again. "Want to bet the rest of the bottle?"

"I'll bet a full bottle." I placed one on the bar.

"Well—" I signaled my other bartender to handle the trade. We were at the far end, a single-stool space that I kept private by loading the bar top by it with jars of pickled eggs and other clutter. A few were at the other end watching the fights and somebody was playing the juke box—private as a bed where we were.

"Okay," he began, "to start with, I'm a bastard."

"No distinction around here," I said.

"I mean it," he snapped. "My parents weren't married."

"Still no distinction," I insisted. "Neither were mine."

"When—" He stopped, gave me the first warm look I ever saw on him. "You mean that?"

"I do. A one-hundred-percent bastard. In fact," I added, "no one in my family ever marries. All bastards."

"Oh, that." I showed it to him. "It just looks like a wedding ring; I wear it to keep women off." It is an antique I bought in 1985 from a fellow operative—he had fetched it from pre-Christian Crete. "The Worm Ouroboros . . . the World Snake that eats its own tail forever without end. A symbol of the Great Paradox."

He barely glanced at it. "If you're really a bastard, you know how it feels. When I was a little girl—"

"Wups!" I said. "Did I hear you correctly?"

"Who's telling this story? When I was a little girl—Look, ever hear of Christine Jorgensen? Or Robert Cowell?"

"Uh, sex-change cases? You're trying to tell me—"

"Don't interrupt or so help me, I won't talk. I was a foundling, left at an orphanage in Cleveland in 1945 when I was a month old. When I was a little girl, I envied kids with parents. Then, when I learned about sex—and, believe me, Pop, you learn fast in an orphanage—"

"I know."

"—I made a solemn vow that any kid of mine would have both a pop and a mom. It kept me 'pure,' quite a feat in that vicinity—I had to learn to fight to manage it. Then I got older and realized I stood darn little chance of getting married—for the same reason I hadn't been adopted." He scowled, "I was horse-faced and buck-toothed, flat-chested and straight-haired."

"You don't look any worse than I do."

"Who cares how a barkeep looks? Or a writer? But people wanting to adopt pick little blue-eyed golden-haired morons. Later on, the boys want bulging breasts, a cute face, and an Oh-you-wonderful-male manner." He shrugged. "I couldn't compete. So I decided to join the W.E.N.C.H.E.S."

"Eh?"

"Women's Emergency National Corps, Hospitality & Entertainment Section, what they now call 'Space Angel'—Auxiliary Nursing Group, Extraterrestial Legions."

I knew both terms, once I had them chronized. We use still a third name, it's that elite military service corps: Women's Hospitality Order Refortifying & Encouraging Spacemen. Vocabulary shifts is the worst hurdle in time-jumps—did you know that "service station" once meant a dispensary for petroleum fractions? Once on an assignment in the Churchill Era, a woman said to me, "Meet me at the service station next door"—which is not what it sounds; a "service station" (then) wouldn't have a bed in it.

He went on: "It was when they first admitted you can't send men into space for months and years and not relieve the tension. You remember how the wowsers screamed?—that improved my chance, since volunteers were scarce. A gal had to be respectable, preferably virgin (they liked to train them from scratch), above average mentally, and stable emotionally. But most volunteers were old hookers, or neurotics who would crack up ten days off Earth. So I didn't need looks; if they accepted me, they would fix my buck teeth, put a wave in my hair, teach me to walk and dance and how to listen to man pleasingly, and everything else—plus training for the prime duties. They would even use plastic surgery if it would help—nothing too good for Our Boys.

"Best yet, they made sure you didn't get pregnant during your enlistment—and you were almost certain to marry at the end of your hitch. Same way today, A.N.G.E.L.S. marry spacers—they talk the language.

"When I was eighteen I was placed as a 'mother's helper.' This family simply wanted a cheap servant but I didn't mind as I couldn't enlist 'til I was twenty-one. I did housework and went to night school—pretending to continue my high school typing and shorthand but going to a charm class instead to better my chances for enlistment.

"Then I met this city slicker with his hundred-dollar bills." He scowled. "The no-good actually did have a wad of hundred-dollar bills. He showed me one night, told me to help myself.

"But I didn't. I liked him. He was the first man I ever met who was nice to me without trying games with me. I quit night school to see him oftener. It was the happiest time of my life.

"Then one night in the park the games began."

He stopped. I said, "And then?"

"And then *nothing*. I never saw him again. He walked me home and told me he loved me—and kissed me good-night and never came back." He looked grim. "If I could find him, I'd kill him!"

"Well," I sympathized, "I know how you feel. But killing him—just for doing what comes naturally—hmm . . . Did you struggle?"

"Huh? What's that got to do with it?"

"Quite a bit. Maybe he deserves a couple of broken arms for running out on you, but—"

"He deserves worse than that! Wait till you hear. Somehow I kept anyone from suspecting and decided it was all for the best. I hadn't really loved him and probably would never love anybody—and I was more eager to join the W.E.N.C.H.E.S. than ever. I wasn't disqualified, they didn't insist on virgins. I cheered up.

"It wasn't until my skirts got tight that I realized."

"Pregnant?"

"He had me higher 'n a kite! Those skinflints I lived with ignored it as long as I could work—then kicked me out and the orphanage wouldn't take me back. I landed in a charity ward surrounded by other big bellies and trotted bedpans until my time came.

"One night I found myself on an operating table, with a nurse saying, 'Relax. Now breathe deeply.'

"I woke up in bed, numb from the chest down. My surgeon came in. 'How do you feel?' he says cheerfully.

" 'Like a mummy.'

" 'Naturally. You're wrapped like one and full of dope to keep you numb. You'll get well—but a Caesarean isn't a hangnail.'

" 'Caesarean,' I said. 'Doc—*did I lose the baby?*'

" 'Oh, no. Your baby's fine.'

" 'Oh, Boy or girl?'

" 'A healthy little girl. Five pounds, three ounces.'

"I relaxed. It's something, to have made a baby. I told myself I would go somewhere and tack 'Mrs.' on my name and let the kid think her papa was dead—no orphanage for *my* kid!

"But the surgeon was talking. 'Tell me, uh—' He avoided my name. '—did you ever think your glandular setup was odd?'

"I said, 'Huh? Of course not. What are you driving at?'

"He hesitated. 'I'll give you this in one dose, then a hypo to let you sleep off your jitters. You'll have 'em.'

" 'Why?' I demanded.

" 'Ever hear of that Scottish physician who was female until she was thirty-five?—then had surgery and became legally and medically a man? Got married. All okay.'

" 'What's that got to do with me?'

" 'That's what I'm saying. You're a man.'

"I tried to sit up. *'What?'*

" 'Take it easy. When I opened you, I found a mess, I sent for the Chief of Surgery while I got the baby out, then we held a consultation with you on the table—and worked for hours to salvage what we could. You had two full sets of organs, both immature, but with the female set well enough developed for you to have a baby. They could never be any use to you again, so we took them out and rearranged things so that you can develop properly as a man.' He put a hand on me. 'Don't worry. You're young, your bones will readjust, we'll watch your glandular balance—and make a fine young man out of you.'

"I started to cry. 'What about my *baby?*'

" 'Well, you can't nurse her, you haven't milk enough for a kitten. If I were you, I wouldn't see her—put her up for adoption.'

" *'No!'*

"He shrugged. 'The choice is yours; you're her mother—well, her parent. But don't worry now; we'll get you well first.'

"Next day they let me see the kid and I saw her daily—trying to get used to her. I had never seen a brand-new baby and had no idea how awful they look—my daughter looked like an orange monkey. My feelings changed to cold determination to do right by her. But four weeks later that didn't mean anything."

"Eh?"

"She was snatched."

"Snatched?"

The Unmarried Mother almost knocked over the bottle we had bet. "Kidnapped—stolen from the hospital nursery!" He breathed hard. "How's that for taking the last a man's got to live for?"

"A bad deal," I agreed. "Let's pour you another. No clues?"

"Nothing the police could trace. Somebody came to see her, claimed to be her uncle. While the nurse had her back turned, he walked out with her."

"Description?"

"Just a man, with a face-shaped face, like yours or mine." He frowned. "I think it was the baby's father. The nurse swore it was an older man but he probably used makeup. Who else would swipe my baby? Childless women pull such stunts—but whoever heard of a man doing it?"

"What happened to you then?"

"Eleven more months of that grim place and three operations. In four months I started to grow a beard; before I was out I was shaving regularly . . . and no longer doubted that I was male." He grinned wryly. "I was staring down nurses' necklines."

"Well," I said, "seems to me you came through okay. Here you are, a normal man, making good money, no real troubles. And the life of a female is not an easy one."

He glared at me. "A lot you know about it!"

"So?"

"Ever hear the expression 'a ruined woman'?"

"Mmm, years ago. Doesn't mean much today."

"I was as ruined as a woman can be; that bum *really* ruined me— I was no longer a woman . . . and I didn't know *how* to be a man."

"Takes getting used to, I suppose."

"You have no idea. I don't mean learning how to dress, or not walking into the wrong rest room; I learned those in the hospital. But how could I *live*? What job could I get? Hell, I couldn't even drive a car, I didn't know a trade; I couldn't do manual labor—too much scar tissue, too tender.

"I hated him for having ruined me for the W.E.N.C.H.E.S., too, but I didn't know how much until I tried to join the Space Corps instead. One look at my belly and I was marked unfit for military service. The medical officer spent time on me just from curiosity; he had read about my case.

"So I changed my name and came to New York. I got by as a fry cook, then rented a typewriter and set myself up as a public stenographer—what a laugh! In four months I typed four letters and one manuscript. The manuscript was for *Real Life Tales* and a waste of paper, but the goof who wrote it sold it. Which gave me an idea; I bought a stack of confession magazines and studied them." He looked cynical. "Now you know how I get the authentic woman's angle on an unmarried-mother story . . . through the only version I haven't sold— the true one. Do I win the bottle?"

I pushed it toward him. I was upset myself, but there was work to do. I said, "Son, you still want to lay hands on that so-and-so?"

His eyes lighted up—a feral gleam.

"Hold it!" I said. "You wouldn't kill him?"

He chuckled nastily. "Try me."

"Take it easy. I know more about it than you think I do. I can help you. I know where he is."

He reached across the bar. *"Where is he?"*

I said softly, "Let go my shirt, sonny—or you'll land in the alley and we'll tell the cops you fainted." I showed him the sap.

He let go. "Sorry. But where is he?" He looked at me. "And how do you know so much?"

"All in good time. There are records—hospital records, orphanage records, medical records. The matron of your orphanage was Mrs. Fetherage—right? She was followed by Mrs. Gruenstein—right? Your name, as a girl, was 'Jane'—right? And you didn't tell me any of this—right?"

I had him baffled and a bit scared. "What's this? You trying to make trouble for me?"

"No indeed. I've your welfare at heart. I can put this character in your lap. You do to him as you see fit—and I guarantee that you'll get away with it. But I don't think you'll kill him. You'd be nuts to—and you aren't nuts. Not quite."

He brushed it aside. "Cut the noise. *Where is he?*"

I poured him a short one; he was drunk but anger was offsetting it. "Not so fast. I do something for you—you do something for me."

"Uh . . . what?"

"You don't like your work. What would you say to high pay, steady work, unlimited expense account, your own boss on the job, and lots of variety and adventure?"

He stared. "I'd say, 'Get those goddam reindeer off my roof!' Shove it, Pop—there's no such job."

"Okay, put it this way: I hand him to you, you settle with him, then try my job. If it's not all I claim—well, I can't hold you."

He was wavering; the last drink did it. "When d'yuh d'liver 'im?" he said thickly.

"If it's a deal—*right now!*"

He shoved out his hand. "It's a deal!"

I nodded to my assistant to watch both ends, noted the time—2300—started to duck through the gate under the bar—when the juke box blared out: "I'm My Own Grandpaw!" The service man had orders to load it with Americana and classics because I couldn't stomach the "music" of 1970, but I hadn't known that tape was in it. I called out, "Shut that off! Give the customer his money back." I added, "Storeroom, back in a moment," and headed there with my Unmarried Mother following.

It was down the passage across from the johns, a steel door to which no one but my day manager and myself had a key; inside was a door to an inner room to which only I had a key. We went there.

He looked blearily around at windowless walls. "Where is 'e?"

"Right away." I opened a case, the only thing in the room; it was a U.S.F.F. Co-ordinates Transformer Field Kit, series 1992, Mod. II—a beauty, no moving parts, weight twenty-three kilos fully charged, and shaped to pass as a suitcase. I had adjusted it precisely earlier that day; all I had to do was to shake out the metal net which limits the transformation field.

Which I did. "What's that?" he demanded.

"Time machine," I said and tossed the net over us.

"Hey!" he yelled and stepped back. There is a technique to this; the net has to be thrown so that the subject will instinctively step back *onto* the metal mesh, then you close the net with both of you inside completely—else you might leave shoe soles behind or piece of foot, or scoop up a slice of floor. But that's all the skill it takes. Some agents con a subject into the net; I tell the truth and use that instant of utter astonishment to flip the switch. Which I did.

1030-VI-3 APRIL 1963—CLEVELAND, OHIO–APEX BLDG.: "Hey!" he repeated. "Take this damn thing off!"

"Sorry," I apologized and did so, stuffed the net into the case, closed it. "You said you wanted to find him."

"But—you said that was a time machine!"

I pointed out a window. "Does this look like November? Or New York?" While he was gawking at new buds and spring weather, I reopened the case, took out a packet of hundred-dollar bills, checked that the numbers and signatures were compatible with 1963. The Temporal Bureau doesn't care how much you spend (it costs nothing) but they don't like unnecessary anachronisms. Too many mistakes, and a general court-martial will exile you for a year in a nasty period, say 1974 with its strict rationing and forced labor. I never make such mistakes, the money was okay.

He turned around and said, "What happened?"

"He's here. Go outside and take him. Here's expense money." I shoved it at him and added, "Settle him, then I'll pick you up."

Hundred-dollar bills have a hypnotic effect on a person not used to them. He was thumbing them unbelievingly as I eased him into the hall, locked him out. The next jump was easy, a small shift in era.

7100-VI-10 MARCH 1964—CLEVELAND–APEX BLDG.: There was a notice under the door saying that my lease expired next week; otherwise the room looked as it had a moment before. Outside trees were bare and snow threatened; I hurried, stopping only for contemporary money and a coat, hat, and topcoat I had left there when I leased the room. I hired a car, went to the hospital. It took twenty minutes to bore the nursery attendant to the point where I could swipe the baby without being noticed. We went back to the Apex Building. This dial setting was more involved, as the building did not yet exist in 1945. But I had precalculated it.

0100-VI-20 Sept. 1945—Cleveland–Skyview Motel: Field kit, baby, and I arrived in a motel outside town. Earlier I had registered as "Gregory Johnson, Warren, Ohio," so we arrived in a room with curtains closed, windows locked, and doors bolted, and the floor cleared to allow for waver as the machine hunts. You can get a nasty bruise from a chair where it shouldn't be—not the chair, of course, but backlash from the field.

No trouble. Jane was sleeping soundly; I carried her out, put her in a grocery box on the seat of a car I had provided earlier, drove to the orphanage, put her on the steps, drove two blocks to a "service station" (the petroleum-products sort) and phoned the orphanage, drove back in time to see them taking the box inside, kept going and abandoned the car near the motel—walked to it and jumped forward to the Apex Building in 1963.

2200-VI-24 April 1963—Cleveland–Apex Bldg.: I had cut the time rather fine—temporal accuracy depends on span, except on return to zero. If I had it right, Jane was discovering, out in the park this balmy spring night, that she wasn't quite as "nice" a girl as she had thought. I grabbed a taxi to the home of those skinflints, had the hackie wait around a corner while I lurked in shadows.

Presently I spotted them down the street, arms around each other. He took her up on the porch and made a long job of kissing her good-night—longer than I thought. Then she went in and he came down the walk, turned away. I slid into step and hooked an arm in his. "That's all son," I announced quietly. "I'm back to pick you up."

"You!" He gasped and caught his breath.

"Me. Now you know who *he* is—and after you think it over you'll know who you are . . . and if you think hard enough, you'll figure out who the baby is . . . and who *I* am."

He didn't answer, he was badly shaken. It's a shock to have it proved to you that you can't resist seducing yourself. I took him to the Apex Building and we jumped again.

2300-VIII-1 Aug. 1985—Sub Rockies Base: I woke the duty sergeant, showed my I.D., told the sergeant to bed my companion down with a happy pill and recruit him in the morning. The sergeant looked sour, but rank is rank, regardless of era; he did what I said—thinking, no doubt, that the next time we met he might be the colonel and I the sergeant. Which can happen in our corps. "What name?" he asked.

I wrote it out. He raised his eyebrows. "Like so, eh? *Hmm—*"

"You just do your job, Sergeant." I turned to my companion.

"Son, your troubles are over. You're about to start the best job a man ever held—and you'll do well. I *know*."

"That you will!" agreed the sergeant. "Look at me—born in 1917— still around, still young, still enjoying life." I went back to the jump room, set everything on preselected zero.

2301-VI-7 Nov. 1970—NYC–"Pop's Place": I came out of the store-room carrying a fifth of Drambuie to account for the minute I had been gone. My assistant was arguing with the customer who had been playing "I'm My Own Grandpaw!" I said, "Oh, let him play it, then unplug it." I was very tired.

It's rough, but somebody must do it and it's very hard to recruit anyone in the later years, since the Mistake of '72. Can you think of a better source than to pick people all fouled up where they are and give them well-paid, interesting (even though dangerous) work in a necessary cause? Everybody knows now why the Fizzle War of 1963 fizzled. The bomb with New York's number on it didn't go off, a hundred other things didn't go as planned—all arranged by the likes of me.

But not the Mistake of '72; that one is not our fault—and can't be undone; there's no paradox to resolve. A thing either is, or it isn't, now and forever amen. But there won't be another like it; an order dated "1992" takes precedence any year.

I closed five minutes early, leaving a letter in the cash register telling my day manager that I was accepting his offer to buy me out, so see my lawyer as I was leaving on a long vacation. The Bureau might or might not pick up his payments, but they want things left tidy. I went to the room back of the storeroom and forward to 1993.

2200-VII-12 Jan. 1993—Sub Rockies Annex–HQ Temporal DOL: I checked in with the duty officer and went to my quarters, intending to sleep for a week. I had fetched the bottle we bet (after all, I won it) and took a drink before I wrote my report. It tasted foul and I wondered why I had ever liked Old Underwear. But it was better than nothing; I don't like to be cold sober, I think too much. But I don't really hit the bottle either; other people have snakes—I have people.

I dictated my report; forty recruitments all okayed by the Psych

Bureau—counting my own, which I knew would be okayed. I was here, wasn't I? Then I taped a request for assignment to operations; I was sick of recruiting. I dropped both in the slot and headed for bed.

My eye fell on "The By-Laws of Time," over my bed:

Never Do Yesterday What Should Be Done Tomorrow.
If at Last You Do Succeed, Never Try Again.
A Stitch in Time Saves Nine Billion.
A Paradox May be Paradoctored.
It Is Easier When You Think.
Ancestors Are Just People.
Even Jove Nods.

They didn't inspire me the way they had when I was a recruit; thirty subjective-years of time-jumping wears you down. I undressed and when I got down to the hide I looked at my belly. A Caesarean leaves a big scar but I'm so hairy now that I don't notice it unless I look for it.

Then I glanced at the ring on my finger.

The Snake That Eats Its Own Tail, Forever and Ever . . . I *know* where *I came* from—but *where did all you zombies come from?*

I felt a headache coming on, but a headache powder is one thing I do not take. I did once—and you all went away.

So I crawled into bed and whistled out the light.

You aren't really there at all. There isn't anybody but me—Jane—here alone in the dark.

I miss you dreadfully!

Analysis:

THE PARADOXES OF TIME TRAVEL

David Lewis
Princeton University

Time travel, I maintain, is possible. The paradoxes of time travel are oddities, not impossibilities. They prove only this much, which few would have doubted: that a possible world where time travel took place would be a most strange world, different in fundamental ways from the world we think is ours.

I shall be concerned here with the sort of time travel that is recounted in science fiction. Not all science fiction writers are clear-headed, to be sure, and inconsistent time travel stories have often been written. But some writers have thought the problems through with great care, and their stories are perfectly consistent.[1]

If I can defend the consistency of some science fiction stories of time travel, then I suppose parallel defenses might be given of some controversial physical hypotheses, such as the hypothesis that time is circular or the hypothesis that there are particles that travel faster than light. But I shall not explore these parallels here.

What is time travel? Inevitably, it involves a discrepancy between time and time. Any traveler departs and then arrives at his destination; the time elapsed from departure to arrival (positive, or perhaps zero) is the duration of the journey. But if he is a time traveler, the separation in time between departure and arrival does not equal the duration of his journey. He departs; he travels for an hour, let us say; then he arrives. The time he reaches is not the time one hour after his departure. It is later, if he has traveled toward the future; earlier, if he has traveled toward the past. If he has traveled far toward the past, it is earlier even than his departure. How can it be that the same two events, his departure and his arrival, are separated by two unequal amounts of time?

It is tempting to reply that there must be two independent time dimensions; that for time travel to be possible, time must be not a line

David Lewis, "The Paradoxes of Time Travel," *American Philosophical Quarterly,* 13 (1976): 145–152, reprinted by permission of the author and the editor of *American Philosophical Quarterly.* Copyright © 1976 by *American Philosophical Quarterly.*

[1]I have particularly in mind two of the time travel stories of Robert A. Heinlein, "By His Bootstraps," in R. A. Heinlein, *The Menace from Earth* (Hicksville, N.Y., 1959), and "All You Zombies—," in R. A. Heinlein, *The Unpleasant Profession of Jonathan Hoag* (Hicksville, N.Y., 1959).

but a plane.[2] Then a pair of events may have two unequal separations if they are separated more in one of the time dimensions than in the other. The lives of common people occupy straight diagonal lines across the plane of time, sloping at a rate of exactly one hour of time$_1$ per hour of time$_2$. The life of the time traveler occupies a bent path, of varying slope.

On closer inspection, however, this account seems not to give us time travel as we know it from the stories. When the traveler revisits the days of his childhood, will his playmates be there to meet him? No; he has not reached the part of the plane of time where they are. He is no longer separated from them along one of the two dimensions of time, but he is still separated from them along the other. I do not say that two-dimensional time is impossible, or that there is no way to square it with the usual conception of what time travel would be like. Nevertheless I shall say no more about two-dimensional time. Let us set it aside, and see how time travel is possible even in one-dimensional time.

The world—the time traveler's world, or ours—is a four-dimensional manifold of events. Time is one dimension of the four, like the spatial dimensions except that the prevailing laws of nature discriminate between time and the others—or rather, perhaps, between various timelike dimensions and various spacelike dimensions. (Time remains one-dimensional, since no two timelike dimensions are orthogonal.) Enduring things are timelike streaks: wholes composed of temporal parts, or *stages*, located at various times and places. Change is qualitative difference between different stages—different temporal parts—of some enduring thing, just as a "change" in scenery from east to west is a qualitative difference between the eastern and western spatial parts of the landscape. If this paper should change your mind about the possibility of time travel, there will be a difference of opinion between two different temporal parts of you, the stage that started reading and the subsequent stage that finishes.

If change is qualitative difference between temporal parts of something, then what doesn't have temporal parts can't change. For instance, numbers can't change; nor can the events of any moment of time, since they cannot be subdivided into dissimilar temporal parts. (We have set aside the case of two-dimensional time, and hence the possibility that an event might be momentary along one time dimension

---

[2]Accounts of time travel in two-dimensional time are found in Jack W. Meiland, "A Two-Dimensional Passage Model of Time for Time Travel," *Philosophical Studies*, 25 (1974): 153–173; and in the initial chapters of Isaac Asimov, *The End of Eternity* (Garden City, N.Y., 1955). Asimov's dénouement, however, seems to require some different conception of time travel.

but divisible along the other.) It is essential to distinguish change from "Cambridge change," which can befall anything. Even a number can "change" from being to not being the rate of exchange between pounds and dollars. Even a momentary event can "change" from being a year ago to being a year and a day ago or from being forgotten to being remembered. But these are not genuine changes. Not just any old reversal in truth value of a time-sensitive sentence about something makes a change in the thing itself.

A time traveler, like anyone else, is a streak through the manifold of space-time, a whole composed of stages located at various times and places. But he is not a streak like other streaks. If he travels toward the past he is a zig-zag streak, doubling back on himself. If he travels toward the future, he is a stretched-out streak. And if he travels either way instantaneously, so that there are no intermediate stages between the stage that departs and the stage that arrives and his journey has zero duration, then he is a broken streak.

I asked how it could be that the same two events were separated by two unequal amounts of time, and I set aside the reply that time might have two independent dimensions. Instead I reply by distinguishing time itself, *external time* as I shall also call it, from the *personal time* of a particular time traveler: roughly, that which is measured by his wristwatch. His journey takes an hour of his personal time, let us say; his wristwatch reads an hour later at arrival than at departure. But the arrival is more than an hour after the departure in external time, if he travels toward the future; or the arrival is before the departure in external time (or less than an hour after), if he travels toward the past.

That is only rough. I do not wish to define personal time operationally, making wristwatches infallible by definition. That which is measured by my own wristwatch often disagrees with external time, yet I am no time traveler; what my misregulated wristwatch measures is neither time itself nor my personal time. Instead of an operational definition, we need a functional definition of personal time: it is that which occupies a certain role in the pattern of events that comprise the time traveler's life. If you take the stages of a common person, they manifest certain regularities with respect to external time. Properties change continuously as you go along, for the most part, and in familiar ways. First come infantile stages. Last come senile ones. Memories accumulate. Food digests. Hair grows. Wristwatch hands move. If you take the stages of a time traveler instead, they do not manifest the common regularities with respect to external time. But there is one way to assign coordinates to the time traveler's stages, and one way only (apart from the arbitrary choice of a zero point), so that the regularities that hold with respect to this assignment match those that commonly hold with respect to external time. With respect to the correct assignment properties change continuously as you go along, for the most part, and in familiar ways. First come infantile stages. Last come senile ones. Memories accumulate. Food digests. Hair grows. Wristwatch hands move. The assignment of coordinates that yields this match is the time traveler's personal time. It isn't really time, but it plays the role in his life that time plays in the life of a common person. It's enough like time so that we can—with due caution—transplant our temporal vocabulary to it in discussing his affairs. We can say without contradiction, as the time traveler prepares to set out, "Soon he will be in the past." We mean that a stage of him is slightly later in his personal time, but much earlier in external time, than the stage of him that is present as we say the sentence.

We may assign locations in the time traveler's personal time not only to his stages themselves but also to the events that go on around him. Soon Caesar will die, long ago; that is, a stage slightly later in the time traveler's personal time than his present stage, but long ago in external time, is simultaneous with Caesar's death. We could even extend the assignment of personal time to events that are not part of the time traveler's life, and not simultaneous with any of his stages. If his funeral in ancient Egypt is separated from his death by three days of external time and his death is separated from his birth by three score years and ten of his personal time, then we may add the two intervals and say that his funeral follows his birth by three score years and ten and three days of *extended personal time*. Likewise a bystander might truly say, three years after the last departure of another famous time traveler, that "he may even now—if I may use the phrase—be wandering on some plesiosaurus-haunted oolitic coral reef, or beside the lonely saline seas of the Triassic Age."[3] If the time traveler does wander on an oolitic coral reef three years after his departure in his personal time, then it is no mistake to say with respect to his extended personal time that the wandering is taking place "even now."

We may liken intervals of external time to distances as the crow flies, and intervals of personal time to distances along a winding path. The time traveler's life is like a mountain railway. The place two miles due east of here may also be nine miles down the line, in the westbound direction. Clearly we are not dealing here with two independent dimensions. Just as distance along the railway is not a fourth spatial dimension, so a time traveler's personal time is not a second dimension

---

[3]H. G. Wells, *The Time Machine, An Invention* (London, 1895), epilogue. The passage is criticized as contradictory in Donald C. Williams, "The Myth of Passage," *The Journal of Philosophy* 48 (1951): 463.

of time. How far down the line some place is depends on its location in three-dimensional space, and likewise the locations of events in personal time depend on their locations in one-dimensional external time.

Five miles down the line from here is a place where the line goes under a trestle; two miles further is a place where the line goes over a trestle; these places are one and the same. The trestle by which the line crosses over itself has two different locations along the line, five miles down from here and also seven. In the same way, an event in a time traveler's life may have more than one location in his personal time. If he doubles back toward the past, but not too far, he may be able to talk to himself. The conversation involves two of this stages, separated in his personal time but simultaneous in external time. The location of the conversation in personal time should be the location of the stage involved in it. But there are two such stages; to share the locations of both, the conversation must be assigned two different locations in personal time.

The more we extend the assignment of personal time outwards from the time traveler's stages to the surrounding events, the more will such events acquire multiple locations. It may happen also, as we have already seen, that events that are not simultaneous in external time will be assigned the same location in personal time—or rather, that at least one of the locations of one will be the same as at least one of the locations of the other. So extension must not be carried too far, lest the location of events in extended personal time lose its utility as a means of keeping track of their roles in the time traveler's history.

A time traveler who talks to himself, on the telephone perhaps, looks for all the world like two different people talking to each other. It isn't quite right to say that the whole of him is in two places at once, since neither of the two stages involved in the conversation is the whole of him, or even the whole of the part of him that is located at the (external) time of the conversation. What's true is that he, unlike the rest of us, has two different complete stages located at the same time at different places. What reason have I, then, to regard him as one person and not two? What unites his stages, including the simultaneous ones, into a single person? The problem of personal identity is especially acute if he is the sort of time traveler whose journeys are instantaneous, a broken streak consisting of several unconnected segments. Then the natural way to regard him as more than one person is to take each segment as a different person. No one of them is a time traveler, and the peculiarity of the situation comes to this: all but one of these several people vanish into thin air, all but another one appear out of thin air, and there are remarkable resemblances between one at his appearance and another at his vanishing. Why isn't that at least as good a description as the one I gave, on which the several segments are all parts of one time traveler?

I answer that what unites the stages (or segments) of a time traveler is the same sort of mental, or mostly mental, continuity and connectedness that unites anyone else. The only difference is that whereas a common person is connected and continuous with respect to external time, the time traveler is connected and continuous only with respect to his own personal time. Taking the stages in order, mental (and bodily) change is mostly gradual rather than sudden, and at no point is there sudden change in too many different respects all at once. (We can include position in external time among the respects we keep track of, if we like. It may change discontinuously with respect to personal time if not too much else changes discontinuously along with it.) Moreover, there is not too much change altogether. Plenty of traits and traces last a lifetime. Finally, the connectedness and the continuity are not accidental. They are explicable; and further, they are explained by the fact that the properties of each stage depend causally on those of the stages just before in personal time, the dependence being such as tends to keep things the same.[4]

To see the purpose of my final requirement of causal continuity, let us see how it excludes a case of counterfeit time travel. Fred was created out of thin air, as if in the midst of life; he lived a while, then died. He was created by a demon, and the demon had chosen at random what Fred was to be like at the moment of his creation. Much later someone else, Sam, came to resemble Fred as he was when first created. At the very moment when the resemblance became perfect, the demon destroyed Sam. Fred and Sam together are very much like a single person: a time traveler whose personal time starts at Sam's birth, goes on to Sam's destruction and Fred's creation, and goes on from there to Fred's death. Taken in this order, the stages of Fred-*cum*-Sam have the proper connectedness and continuity. But they lack causal continuity, so Fred-*cum*-Sam is not one person and not a time traveler. Perhaps it was pure coincidence that Fred at his creation and Sam at his destruction were exactly alike; then the connectedness and continuity of Fred-*cum*-Sam across the crucial point are accidental. Perhaps instead the demon remembered what Fred was like, guided Sam toward perfect resemblance, watched his progress, and destroyed him at the right moment. Then the connectedness and continuity of Fred-*cum*-Sam has a causal explanation, but of the wrong sort. Either way, Fred's first

---

[4]I discuss the relation between personal identity and mental connectedness and continuity at greater length in "Survival and Identity," in *The Identity of Persons,* ed. by Amelie Rorty (forthcoming).

stages do not depend causally for their properties on Sam's last stages. So the case of Fred and Sam is rightly disqualified as a case of personal identity and as a case of time travel.

We might expect that when a time traveler visits the past there will be reversals of causation. You may punch his face before he leaves, causing his eye to blacken centuries ago. Indeed, travel into the past necessarily involves reversed causation. For time travel requires personal identity—he who arrives must be the same person who departed. That requires causal continuity, in which causation runs from earlier to later stages in the order of personal time. But the orders of personal and external time disagree at some point, and there we have causation that runs from later to earlier stages in the order of external time. Elsewhere I have given an analysis of causation in terms of chains of counterfactual dependence, and I took care that my analysis would not rule out causal reversal *a priori*.[5] I think I can argue (but not here) that under my analysis the direction of counterfactual dependence and causation is governed by the direction of other *de facto* asymmetries of time. If so, then reversed causation and time travel are not excluded altogether, but can occur only where there are local exceptions to these asymmetries. As I said at the outset, the time traveler's world would be a most strange one.

Stranger still, if there are local—but only local—causal reversals, then there may also be causal loops: closed causal chains in which some of the causal links are normal in direction and others are reversed. (Perhaps there must be loops if there is reversal; I am not sure.) Each event on the loop has a causal explanation, being caused by events elsewhere on the loop. That is not to say that the loop as a whole is caused or explicable. It may not be. Its inexplicability is especially remarkable if it is made up of the sort of causal processes that transmit information. Recall the time traveler who talked to himself. He talked to himself about time travel, and in the course of the conversation his older self told his younger self how to build a time machine. That information was available in no other way. His older self knew how because his younger self had been told and the information had been preserved by the causal processes that constitute recording, storage, and retrieval of memory traces. His younger self knew, after the conversation, because his older self had known and the information had been preserved by the causal processes that constitute telling. But where did the information come from in the first place? Why did the whole affair happen? There is simply no answer. The parts of the loop

[5]"Causation," *The Journal of Philosophy,* 70 (1973): 556–567; the analysis relies on the analysis of counterfactuals given in my *Counterfactuals* (Oxford, 1973).

are explicable, the whole of it is not. Strange! But not impossible, and not too different from inexplicabilities we are already inured to. Almost everyone agrees that God, or the Big Bang, or the entire infinite past of the universe, or the decay of a tritium atom, is uncaused and inexplicable. Then if these are possible, why not also the inexplicable causal loops that arise in time travel?

I have committed a circularity in order not to talk about too much at once, and this is a good place to set it right. In explaining personal time, I presupposed that we were entitled to regard certain stages as comprising a single person. Then in explaining what united the stages into a single person, I presupposed that we were given a personal time order for them. The proper way to proceed is to define personhood and personal time simultaneously, as follows. Suppose given a pair of an aggregate of personstages, regarded as a candidate for personhood, and an assignment of coordinates to those stages, regarded as a candidate for his personal time. Iff* the stages satisfy the conditions given in my circular explanation with respect to the assignment of coordinates, then both candidates succeed: the stages to comprise a person and the assignment are his personal time.

I have argued so far that what goes on in a time travel story may be a possible pattern of events in four-dimensional space-time with no extra time dimension; that it may be correct to regard the scattered stages of the alleged time traveler as comprising a single person; and that we may legitimately assign to those stages and their surroundings a personal time order that disagrees sometimes with their order in external time. Some might concede all this, but protest that the impossibility of time travel is revealed after all when we ask not what the time traveler *does,* but what he *could do.* Could a time traveler change the past? It seems not: the events of a past moment could no more change than numbers could. Yet it seems that he would be as able as anyone to do things that would change the past if he did them. If a time traveler visiting the past both could and couldn't do something that would change it, then there cannot possibly be such a time traveler.

Consider Tim. He detests his grandfather, whose success in the munitions trade built the family fortune that paid for Tim's time machine. Tim would like nothing so much as to kill Grandfather, but alas he is too late. Grandfather died in his bed in 1957, while Tim was a young boy. But when Tim has built his time machine and traveled to 1920, suddenly he realizes that he is not too late after all. He buys a rifle; he spends long hours in target practice; he shadows Grandfather

*This is philosophers' shorthand for the expression "if and only if"—eds.

to learn the route of his daily walk to the munitions works; he rents a room along the route; and there he lurks, one winter day in 1921, rifle loaded, hate in his heart, as Grandfather walks closer, closer,. . . .

Tim can kill Grandfather. He has what it takes. Conditions are perfect in every way: the best rifle money could buy, Grandfather an easy target only twenty yards away, not a breeze, door securely locked against intruders, Tim a good shot to begin with and now at the peak of training, and so on. What's to stop him? The forces of logic will not stay his hand! No powerful chaperone stands by to defend the past from interference. (To imagine such a chaperone, as some authors do, is a boring evasion, not needed to make Tim's story consistent.) In short, Tim is as much able to kill Grandfather as anyone ever is to kill anyone. Suppose that down the street another sniper, Tom, lurks waiting for another victim, Grandfather's partner. Tom is not a time traveler, but otherwise he is just like Tim: same make of rifle, same murderous intent, same everything. We can even suppose that Tom, like Tim, believes himself to be a time traveler. Someone has gone to a lot of trouble to deceive Tom into thinking so. There's no doubt that Tom can kill his victim; and Tim has everything going for him that Tom does. By any ordinary standards of ability, Tim can kill Grandfather.

Tim cannot kill Grandfather. Grandfather lived, so to kill him would be to change the past. But the events of a past moment are not sub-divisible into temporal parts and therefore cannot change. Either the events of 1921 timelessly do include Tim's killing of Grandfather, or else they timelessly don't. We may be tempted to speak of the "original" 1921 that lies in Tim's personal past, many years before his birth, in which Grandfather lived; and of the "new" 1921 in which Tim now finds himself waiting in ambush to kill Grandfather. But if we do speak so, we merely confer two names on one thing. The events of 1921 are doubly located in Tim's (extended) personal time, like the trestle on the railway, but the "original" 1921 and the "new" 1921 are one and the same. If Tim did not kill Grandfather in the "original" 1921, then if he does kill Grandfather in the "new" 1921, he must both kill and not kill Grandfather in 1921—in the one and only 1921, which is both the "new" and the "original" 1921. It is logically impossible that Tim should change the past by killing Grandfather in 1921. So Tim cannot kill Grandfather.

Not that past moments are special; no more can anyone change the present or the future. Present and future momentary events no more have temporal parts than past ones do. You cannot change a present or future event from what it was originally to what it is after you change it. What you *can* do is to change the present or the future

from the unactualized way they would have been without some action
of yours to the way they actually are. But that is not an actual change:
not a difference between two successive actualities. And Tim can
certainly do as much; he changes the past from the unactualized way it
would have been without him to the one and only way it actually is. To
"change" the past in this way, Tim need not do anything momentous;
it is enough just to be there, however unobtrusively.

You know, of course, roughly how the story of Tim must go on if
it is to be consistent: he somehow fails. Since Tim didn't kill Grandfather
in the "original" 1921, consistency demands that neither does he kill
Grandfather in the "new" 1921. Why not? For some commonplace
reason. Perhaps some noise distracts him at the last moment, perhaps
he misses despite all his target practice, perhaps his nerve fails, perhaps
he even feels a pang of unaccustomed mercy. His failure by no means
proves that he was not really able to kill Grandfather. We often try and
fail to do what we are able to do. Success at some tasks requires not
only ability but also luck, and lack of luck is not a temporary lack of
ability. Suppose our other sniper, Tom, fails to kill Grandfather's
partner for the same reason, whatever it is, that Tim fails to kill
Grandfather. It does not follow that Tom was unable to. No more does
it follow in Tim's case that he was unable to do what he did not succeed
in doing.

We have this seeming contradiction: *"Tim doesn't, but can, because
he has what it takes"* versus *"Tim doesn't, and can't, because it's logically
impossible to change the past."* I reply that there is no contradiction. Both
conclusions are true, and for the reasons given. They are compatible
because "can" is equivocal.

To say that something can happen means that its happening is
compossible with certain facts. *Which* facts? That is determined, but
sometimes not determined well enough, by context. An ape can't speak
a human language—say, Finnish—but I can. Facts about the anatomy
and operation of the ape's larynx and nervous system are not compossible with his speaking Finnish. The corresponding facts about my
larynx and nervous system are compossible with my speaking Finnish.
But don't take me along to Helsinki as your interpreter: I can't speak
Finnish. My speaking Finnish is compossible with the facts considered
so far, but not with further facts about my lack of training. What I can
do, relative to one set of facts, I cannot do, relative to another, more
inclusive, set. Whenever the context leaves it open which facts are to
count as relevant, it is possible to equivocate about whether I can speak
Finnish. It is likewise possible to equivocate about whether it is possible
for me to speak Finnish, or whether I am able to, or whether I have the
ability or capacity or power or potentiality to. Our many words for

much the same thing are little help since they do not seem to correspond to different fixed delineations of the relevant facts.

Tim's killing Grandfather that day in 1921 is compossible with a fairly rich set of facts: the facts about his rifle, his skill and training, the unobstructed line of fire, the locked door and the absence of any chaperone to defend the past, and so on. Indeed it is compossible with all the facts of the sorts we would ordinarily count as relevant in saying what someone can do. It is compossible with all the facts corresponding to those we deem relevant in Tom's case. Relative to these facts, Tim can kill Grandfather. But his killing Grandfather is not compossible with another, more inclusive set of facts. There is the simple fact that Grandfather was not killed. Also there are various other facts about Grandfather's doings after 1921 and their effects: Grandfather begat Father in 1922 and Father begat Tim in 1949. Relative to these facts, Tim cannot kill Grandfather. He can and he can't, but under different delineations of the relevant facts. You can reasonably choose the narrower delineation, and say that he can; or the wider delineation, and say that he can't. But choose. What you mustn't do is waver, say in the same breath that he both can and can't, and then claim that this contradiction proves that time travel is impossible.

Exactly the same goes for Tom's parallel failure. For Tom to kill Grandfather's partner also is compossible with all facts of the sorts we ordinarily count as relevant, but not compossible with a larger set including, for instance, the fact that the intended victim lived until 1934. In Tom's case we are not puzzled. We say without hesitation that he can do it, because we see at once that the facts that are not compossible with his success are facts about the future of the time in question and therefore not the sort of facts we count as relevant in saying what Tom can do.

In Tim's case it is harder to keep track of which facts are relevant. We are accustomed to exclude facts about the future of the time in question, but to include some facts about its past. Our standards do not apply unequivocally to the crucial facts in this special case: Tim's failure, Grandfather's survival, and his subsequent doings. If we have foremost in mind that they lie in the external future of that moment in 1921 when Tim is almost ready to shoot, then we exclude them just as we exclude the parallel facts in Tom's case. But if we have foremost in mind that they precede that moment in Tim's extended personal time, then we tend to include them. To make the latter be foremost in your mind, I chose to tell Tim's story in the order of his personal time, rather than in the order of external time. The fact of Grandfather's survival until 1957 had already been told before I got to the part of the story about Tim lurking in ambush to kill him in 1921. We must decide, if we can, whether to treat these personally past and externally future facts as if they were straightforwardly past or as if they were straightforwardly future.

Fatalists—the best of them—are philosophers who take facts we count as irrelevant in saying what someone can do, disguise them somehow as facts of a different sort that we count as relevant, and thereby argue that we can do less than we think—indeed, that there is nothing at all that we don't do but can. I am not going to vote Republican next fall. The fatalist argues that, strange to say, I not only won't but can't; for my voting Republican is not compossible with the fact that it was true already in the year 1548 that I was not going to vote Republican 428 years later. My rejoinder is that this is a fact, sure enough; however, it is an irrelevant fact about the future masquerading as a relevant fact about the past, and so should be left out of account in saying what, in any ordinary sense, I can do. We are unlikely to be fooled by the fatalist's methods of disguise in this case, or other ordinary cases. But in cases of time travel, precognition, or the like, we're on less familiar ground, so it may take less of a disguise to fool us. Also, new methods of disguise are available, thanks to the device of personal time.

Here's another bit of fatalist trickery. Tim, as he lurks, already knows that he will fail. At least he has the wherewithal to know it—if he thinks, he knows it implicitly. For he remembers that Grandfather was alive when he was a boy, he knows that those who are killed are thereafter not alive, he knows (let us suppose) that he is a time traveler who has reached the same 1921 that lies in his personal past, and he ought to understand—as we do—why a time traveler cannot change the past. What is known cannot be false. So his success is not only not compossible with facts that belong to the external future and his personal past, but also is not compossible with the present fact of his knowledge that he will fail. I reply that the fact of his foreknowledge, at the moment while he waits to shoot, is not a fact entirely about that moment. It may be divided into two parts. There is the fact that he then believes (perhaps only implicitly) that he will fail; and there is the further fact that his belief is correct, and correct not at all by accident, and hence qualifies as an item of knowledge. It is only the latter fact that is not compossible with his success, but it is only the former that is entirely about the moment in question. In calling Tim's state at that moment knowledge, not just belief, facts about personally earlier but externally later moments were smuggled into consideration.

I have argued that Tim's case and Tom's are alike, except that in Tim's case we are more tempted than usual—and with reason—to opt for a semi-fatalist mode of speech. But perhaps they differ in another way. In Tom's case, we can expect a perfectly consistent answer to the counterfactual question: What if Tom had killed Grandfather's partner? Tim's case is more difficult. If Tim had killed Grandfather, it seems offhand that contradictions would have been true. The killing both would and wouldn't have occurred. No Grandfather, no Father; no Father, no Tim, no Tim, no killing. And for good measure: no Grandfather, no family fortune; no fortune, no time machine; no time machine, no killing. So the supposition that Tim killed Grandfather seems impossible in more than the semi-fatalistic sense already granted.

If you suppose Tim to kill Grandfather and hold all the rest of his story fixed, of course you get a contradiction. But likewise if you suppose Tom to kill Grandfather's partner and hold the rest of his story fixed—including the part that told of his failure—you get a contradiction. If you make *any* counterfactual supposition and hold all else fixed you get a contradiction. The thing to do is rather to make the counterfactual supposition and hold all else as close to fixed as you consistently can. That procedure will yield perfectly consistent answers to the question: what if Tim had not killed Grandfather? In that case, some of the story I told would not have been true. Perhaps Tim might have been the time-traveling grandson of someone else. Perhaps he might have been the grandson of a man killed in 1921 and miraculously resurrected. Perhaps he might have been not a time traveler at all, but rather someone created out of nothing in 1920 equipped with false memories of a personal past that never was. It is hard to say what is the least revision of Tim's story to make it true that Tim kills Grandfather, but certainly the contradictory story in which the killing both does and doesn't occur is not the least revision. Hence it is false (according to the unrevised story) that if Tim had killed Grandfather then contradictions would have been true.

What difference would it make if Tim travels in branching time? Suppose that at the possible world of Tim's story the space-time manifold branches; the branches are separated not in time, and not in space, but in some other way. Tim travels not only in time but also from one branch to another. In one branch Tim is absent from the events of 1921; Grandfather lives; Tim is born, grows up, and vanishes in his time machine. The other branch diverges from the first when Tim turns up in 1920; there Tim kills Grandfather and Grandfather leaves no descendants and no fortune; the events of the two branches differ more and more from that time on. Certainly this is a consistent story; it is story in which Grandfather both is and isn't killed in 1921 (in the different branches); and it is a story in which Tim, by killing Grandfather, succeeds in preventing his own birth (in one of the branches). But it is not a story in which Tim's killing of Grandfather both does occur and doesn't: it simply does, though it is located in one branch and not the other. And it is not a story in which Tim changes the past. 1921 and later years contain the events of both branches, coexisting somehow without interaction. It remains true at all the personal times of Tim's life, even after the killing, that Grandfather lives in one branch and dies in the other.[6]

[6]The present paper summarizes a series of lectures of the same title, given as the Gavin David Young Lectures in Philosophy at the University of Adelaid in July 1971. I thank the Australian–American Educational Foundation and the American Council of Learned Societies for research support. I am grateful to many friends for comments on earlier versions of this paper; especially Philip Kitcher, William Newton-Smith, J. J. C. Smart, and Donald Williams.

CHAPTER 3 PROBES

1. In "All You Zombies—," who tells the story? What are all of his relationships with the "Unmarried Mother"?

2. How did the narrator of Heinlein's story get recruited into the Temporal Bureau? Why was he selected?

3. In what ways does Lewis think time travel is possible? Which way interests him the most?

4. What would Augustine say about Heinlein's story? Why would he say this?

5. In Heinlein's story, a record called "I'm My Own Grandpaw!" comes on the juke box. According to Lewis, is it possible to be your own grandpaw? If so, explain how. If not, explain why not.

6. According to Lewis, in what sense can one change a past event? In what sense can one not change a past event? Which sense, after all is said and done, does Lewis think the most accurate? Does Heinlein's story involve changing past events? If so, which one(s)? If not, explain how each event in the story that looks as though it is being altered is really not.

7. Why does Jane, at the end of the story, call us all "zombies"?

8. In Heinlein's story, the Mistake of '72 is not the fault of the Temporal Bureau, and can't be undone. As the narrator of the story puts it, "A thing either is, or it isn't, now and forever amen." Yet, slightly later, he reads in

"The By-Laws of Time" " . . . A Paradox May be Paradoctored." Are these things compatible? If so, how? If not, why not?

9. Would Lewis agree with the claim, "A thing either is, or it isn't, now and forever amen"? In what way does this claim allow for time travel, in his view (if any)? What does this mean about what someone can do in the past, if he traveled there in time?

10. In 3:3.2, a problem about time travel is mentioned. In 3:3.3, various ways in which the problem is treated by science fiction writers are mentioned. Which (if any) of these ways is employed by Heinlein in his story? Which would be the way(s) Lewis thinks acceptable (if any)? Are there any other ways you think are possible?

11. Which of the two views of time does Heinlein presuppose in his story? Does Lewis share this assumption?

12. In 3:2.2, the idea that there can be two different times at once is attacked as absurd. How would H. G. Wells defend his claim that the time traveler might "even now" be on some oolitic coral reef? Would Heinlein defend this claim? Would Lewis? Do you think that what Donald Williams and J. J. C. Smart (see 3:2.2) say is impossible is, after all, possible (at least logically)? If so, in what way(s)? If not, why not?

13. The Greek philosopher Aristotle once said that the past is forever fixed and unchangeable, but the future is in no way fixed. That is, according to Aristotle, there are immutable truths about the past, but nothing specific is true about the future (*De Interpretatione,* IX). On this view, could one travel in time into the past, according to Aristotle? Could one travel in time into the future? Do you agree or disagree? Why?

14. Some theists (see Chapter 2) believe that God is omniscient and that this means that He knows all events past, present, and future. Does this mean that the future is fixed, just as Aristotle thinks the past is? If so, can we change the future? That is, is what we will do in the future already determined? Does this mean that, if I go out and murder someone, I cannot be held responsible, because there was no way I could avoid doing so (since God already knew, from the very beginning of time, that I would do it)? In what way does this problem relate to the story by Heinlein and the essay by Lewis? (*Note:* You might want to look at Chapters 2 and 6 before you tackle this one!)

15. Does the modern theory of relativity (see 3:2.4) disprove what Aristotle said about future truths (that there are none), since according to it, we can, in a sense, travel into the future? Does this type of time travel prove that the future is already fixed and unchangeable? Does relativity disprove what Augustine said about time (see 3:1.1)?

16. Imagine that I have a U.S.F.F. Co-ordinates Transformer Field Kit, series 1992, Mod. II. I shake out the metal net, throw it over myself, and jump into the future, twenty years hence. I get out, and look about me, and see nothing but desolation. The countryside is blackened. My Geiger counter clicks wildly, and I know what has happened . . . World War III has finally come to pass, and everyone was killed. I jump back into my net, and take a series of small jumps backward until I find the moment of the destruction. I see myself being blown to smithereens by the nuclear holocaust. But wait . . . how can I be dead? Doesn't dying mean that I cease to exist (at least in an embodied human form)? Yet I am alive, after my own death, standing there in my net seeing my own body in charred bits. How can I be dead, but alive, after my own death? How can it be that I live on, after I have been blown to pieces? Does such a time machine entail that, though I will die, I can live forever . . . and, if I use my machine properly, *will* live forever? How can I most certainly die in a nuclear holocaust, yet live forever? Can't I just set my time machine, and travel continuously into the future, until the end of time? Explain how this story must be resolved, or why there is no reason to suppose that any resolution is needed.

17. What if, instead of selfishly considering jumping forward in time forever, I decide rather to go back in time and use my machine to jump to each missile site, successively defusing all the warheads, in the hope of sparing the world from such a disaster? Can I do this? Why or why not?

18. If, now that you have read this chapter, you believe that time travel is in one way or another possible, write a story in which this occurs. Your story must commit no logical errors of the sort that arouse philosophical critics. If you believe that time travel is impossible, write a story that Lewis would accept as error-free and then criticize it, showing how and where it makes errors that cannot be changed without giving up the hypothesis that time travel is possible. Be sure, either way, to show how time travel into the future is possible or impossible (logically) and how travel into the past is possible or impossible.

19. Consider the idea that time moves (unlike the assumption of the static view shared by Heinlein and Lewis—see 3:1.2), but in different places in the universe, it moves in different directions. Could a time travel story be written with this idea? Would it allow changing the past or the future? Does it involve more than one temporal dimension? Does the idea make logical sense?

20. What is time? How does it work? Is Lewis right about it? Is there a view of it different from others mentioned in this chapter that could be employed in a different conceptual experiment?

RECOMMENDED READING

Science Fiction and the Philosophy of Space and Time

Science fiction, by its very nature, is preoccupied with the exploration of space–time, and a list of all the stories in the tradition of H. G. Wells, *The Time Machine,* in Ben Bova, ed., *Science Fiction Hall of Fame IIA* (Avon, 1973), would be interminable. But these stories are merely a fraction of the corpus of science fiction which is "metaphysical fiction," that is, literature exploring the outer limits of reality. The present reading list will, accordingly, begin with stories focusing on time travel and the philosophy of time, and then will mention stories that are "metaphysical" in the broadest sense.

Time Travel Stories. The most conservative time travel stories exploit the relativistic effects predicted by Einstein's physics. Robert A. Heinlein, *Time for the Stars* (Ballantine, 1978), has already been mentioned. Poul Anderson's *Tau Zero* (Berkley, 1970) contains more dramatic time dilation effects as a space ship out of control accelerates without limit and undergoes exaggerated time dilation effects until billions of years fly past. The crew helplessly witnesses the death and rebirth of the universe. On a more limited scale, Joe Haldeman's Hugo-winning *Forever War* (Ballantine, 1976) describes an interstellar war with warships flying at near-light speeds. The crew undergoes repeated culture shock whenever they return to Earth, where centuries have passed. In Poul Anderson's haunting "Kyrie," the death of an astronaut plunging into a black hole is prolonged forever in the mind of a surviving telepath due to time dilation effects, in Donald A. Wollheim and Terry Carr, eds., *World's Best Science Fiction 1969* (Ace, 1969).

A succession of ingenious tales explores the possibility of traveling into the future or past. Wells's novel has inspired a film, *The Time Machine* by George Pal (1960), which vulgarizes the social themes of the book, and a literal rip-off entitled *Time After Time* (1979). An obvious objection to the hypothesis that such travel is possible is that we should right now see evidence of visitors from the future. Some science fiction writers suggest we only need to open our eyes. Henry Kuttner and C. L. Moore describe such a visit in "Vintage Season," in *The Science Fiction Hall of Fame IIA.* One visitor from the future remarks, "We are safe from much suspicion because people before The Travel began will not believe." Traces and "relics" from the future are the subject of C. M. Kornbluth, "The Little Black Bag," in Robert Silverberg, ed., *The Science Fiction Hall of Fame I* (Avon, 1970), and R. A. Lafferty, "Continued on Next Rock," in Isaac Asimov, ed., *Nebula Award Stories Number Six* (Pocket Books, 1972).

Many science fiction plots depend upon paradoxes that arise when a time traveler changes his or her own past. Ray Bradbury, "A Sound of Thunder," in *R is for Rocket* (Bantam, 1969), already described in the text, presents the famous example of a dinosaur hunter who obliterates his own history by stepping on a butterfly. In Jack Williamson's early novel, *The*

Legion of Time (Fantasy, 1954), the hero is able to shape consciously the course of history by means of time travel. In a Hugo-winning *Star Trek* television episode by Harlan Ellison, "The City on the Edge of Forever," a crew member of the *Enterprise* inadvertently changes his history by traveling back to our century. In Ward Moore's *Bring the Jubilee* (Avon, 1976), the protagonist changes the outcome of the Civil War. In Wilson Tucker's *Year of the Quiet Sun* (Ace Special, 1970), complicated paradoxes result from travel into and return from the future. John Boyd's *Last Starship from Earth* (Penguin, 1978) in the final chapter obliterates its own plot by sending the hero back to the time of Christ and produces a history suspiciously like our own. A characteristically clear novel, Isaac Asimov's *End of Eternity* (Fawcett, 1977), uses the device of a region of "eternity" which is outside of the stream of historical time and is not subject to the changes that are produced by an elite corps of time travelers.

Stories in this vein, when pushed far enough, lead to a *reductio ad absurdum,* in which the fabric of time is torn, fragmented, or annihilated. Frederic Brown, in his one-page "Experiment," destroys the universe by testing an unfortunate idea, in Robert Bloch, ed., *The Best of Frederic Brown* (Ballantine, 1976); see also "The End" in this volume. In Jack Finney's "I'm Scared," time travel has more gradual deleterious effects, in *The Third Level* (Rinehart, 1956). The picaresque hero of Robert Silverberg's *Up the Line* (Ballantine, 1969) obliterates himself by indulging in time travel paradoxes, for example, with a beautiful female ancestor. In stories like these a time patrol or time corps is often at work policing history, rectifying unwanted changes. But sometimes law and order break down totally in "time wars" and the results are barely intelligible. See for example Fritz Leiber's Hugo-winning novel, *The Big Time* (Ace, 1961), and Keith Laumer's *Dinosaur Beach* (DAW, 1971). Some science fiction authors seek to avoid the paradoxes. Robert A. Heinlein's thesis that, even if you were to bring about changes in the past, you could not actually make anything different from what it was, has been taken up by others. David Gerrold's *Man Who Folded Himself* (Fawcett, 1973) becomes entangled in an even more complicated web of events and sexual liaisons than the hero/heroine of "All You Zombies—." Gordon Eklund, *All Times Possible* (DAW, 1974), operates on the premise that time branches. Rather than "changing" history the time traveler finds himself or herself on a different branch.

A clever time-travel story by Alfred Bester, "The Man Who Murdered Mohammed," in *Starlight* (Doubleday, 1976), suggests a quite different philosophical approach to time. In this story a mad scientist, who discovers his beloved in the arms of a rival, seeks revenge by constructing a time machine and changing the past to destroy his rival. Repeated attempts fail until the scientist finds himself fading out of existence. He discovers that time is a subjective, mind-created phenomenon and that he has destroyed his own time. The idea that time is dependent upon human consciousness is explored in a very strange, ruthlessly logical story by Brian W. Aldiss,

"Man in his Time," in Aldiss and Harry Harrison, eds., *Nebula Award Stories Number Two* (Pocket Book, 1968). This story interestingly enough contains an allusion to the philosopher M'Taggart, an absolute idealist whose arguments that time is self-contradictory and illusory have been very influential. Aldiss develops the notion of mind dependence more fully in *Cryptozoic!* (Avon, 1977). Here even the familiar "arrow of time" turns out to be running in the wrong direction. The subjectivity of time is also a theme of J. G. Ballard's "Garden of Time," in *Chronopolis* (Putnam, 1971), and "Time of Passage," in *The Overloaded Man* (Panther, 1967).

Metaphysical Fiction. There are science fiction stories that suggest that not merely time but all of "reality" is, in fact, a creation of the mind. Philip K. Dick is best known for writing on this theme. In *Eye in the Sky* (Ace, 1975) several minds create their own subjective realities and struggle for dominance as each is drawn into the reality of the other. In *Flow My Tears, the Policeman Said* (Doubleday, 1974), drugs are used to create new realities in which other persons are captured. This novel won the Campbell Award. Ursula LeGuin uses a similar approach in *The Lathe of Heaven* (Avon, 1973). A psychiatrist tries to exploit a patient's ability to change the real world by dreaming about changes, but the outcomes are uncontrollable and, ultimately, catastrophic. This book was the basis of a superb film of the same name, produced for public television in 1980.

Another popular science fiction theme is the reality of an indefinite number of *alternative realities*. The notion that there are an infinite number of possible worlds other than our own actual world was proposed by the philosopher Leibniz and has become quite popular with modern philosophers and logicians such as David Lewis. Professor Lewis has called our attention to Larry Niven's "All the Myriad Ways" in an anthology of the same title (Ballantine, 1971), in which businessmen start importing inventions from other possible worlds. (One of these, it turns out, is our own.) The possible world idea was pioneered by Olaf Stapledon in *Star Maker* (Penguin, 1973). Parallel universes are also presupposed in Philip K. Dick's Hugo-winning *Man in the High Castle* (Berkley, 1974), which describes an alternative reality in which the Nazis and Japanese won World War II. Isaac Asimov's novel, *The Gods Themselves* (Fawcett, 1977), which won both the Hugo and Nebula, describes in its second part an alternative reality which exists "alongside" ours and in fact "intersects" with ours, thus allowing for a new energy source, a positron pump.

Often it is assumed that alternative realities differ in terms of particular facts and scientific laws, but that they are each essentially coherent and governed by Aristotelian logic. Lewis Padgett (the *nomme de plume* of Henry Kuttner and C. L. Moore) departs from this assumption in "Mimsy Were the Borogoves," in *The Science Fiction Hall of Fame I.* In this classic the ability of children to master the absurd, non-Aristotelian logic imbedded in Lewis Carroll's nonsense rhymes opens up an alternative universe for them. A. E.

Van Vogt goes even further in *The World of Null-A* (Berkley, 1974), contending that our own actual world is, in fact, governed by non-Aristotelian principles.

Philosophy and the Nature of Space and Time

The best introduction to this field is the pair of articles in *The Encyclopedia of Philosophy* (Macmillan, 1967), "Space" and "Time." Two useful anthologies are J. J. C. Smart, ed., *Problems of Space and Time* (Macmillan, 1964), and Richard Gale, ed., *The Philosophy of Time* (Doubleday, 1967). The anthologies overlap but differ somewhat in emphasis. Gale has selected more works of metaphysical and epistemological speculation on the nature of time, whereas Smart is more interested in scientific approaches and the philosophical implications of modern science. Both works have excellent introductions.

Aristotle (384–327 B.C.) originally analyzed time and place in his *Physics* (in Gale). Augustine (A.D. 354–430) queried, more skeptically, "What is time?" in his *Confessions* (in Smart and Gale). The nineteenth-century idealists F. H. Bradley (1846–1924, in Smart) and J. M. E. M'Taggart (1866–1925, in Gale) argued that time is "unreal" and set the stage for many twentieth-century treatments. Henri Bergson (1859–1941) argued that time is real and dynamic in nature (in Gale and Smart). D. C. Williams defends a view of time as real but essentially "static" (in Gale). Williams, incidentally, dismisses time travel also as essentially absurd. Aristotle in his *De Interpretatione* (in Gale) struggled with the question of whether a statement made *now* about a sea battle *tomorrow* could be "true" or "false." This has prompted a series of essays recently about "the open future," some of which are in Gale (see also the G. E. M. Anscombe essay in Smart).

One ancient Greek, Zeno (fifth century B.C.), tried to prove the impossibility of motion in a series of paradoxes. A good deal of ink has been spilled over the centuries in the attempt to prove him wrong, but these criticisms of Zeno contributed valuable analyses of the structure of space and time. Ironically, Zeno encouraged a better scientific understanding of the nature of motion! In addition to the articles on Zeno in Gale, especially by Adolf Grünbaum, see the article by Bertrand Russell, "The Problem of Infinity Considered Historically" (in Smart), the article on Zeno of Elea in *The Encyclopedia of Philosophy,* and Wesley Salmon, ed., *Zeno's Paradoxes* (Bobbs Merrill, 1970).

Many twentieth-century philosophers and physicists have pondered the philosophical implications of the modern theory of relativity. There are some important selections in Smart on the theory of relativity by Albert Einstein, H. Minkowski, and others. For the general reader without a strong background in mathematics, a very helpful introduction to the modern scientific view of space and time is Marvin Gardner, *The Relativity Explosion* (Vintage, 1976).

4

PHILOSOPHY OF MIND:

Men and machines: Is there a difference?

Most human beings think that our species is unique. We have "dominion" over the universe. All other things—natural resources, artifacts (including machines), and lower life forms—merely exist for *our* use. Many moral philosophers distinguish between persons and things. They would say, "It is quite proper for persons to exploit things and use them as means to pursue their own ends. Things have only the value that persons place on them by their subjective preferences. Persons, in contrast, have an 'intrinsic worth' and may not be forcibly exploited or used merely as means to serve the ends of others. The evil of slavery is precisely that it reduces a person to the status of a thing. Persons have rights and should be treated justly; such concepts as rights and justice don't make sense in the case of things."

This idea of the superiority of human beings is represented in numerous works of science fiction. Even sophisticated products of technology are inferior to humans. A classic story in this genre is Isaac Asimov's "Robbie," in which the dichotomy between persons and things is challenged by the science of robotics. Asimov's robots have metallic, humanlike bodies and "positronic" computer brains. In this story little Gloria Weston has a giant, mute robotic babysitter named Robbie, which she bullies, teases, and bribes with fairy tales. Although the machine protects, entertains, and dotes over this little girl, her mother fears and despises it and demands its removal. When her browbeaten husband complies, Gloria is crushed and goes into a prolonged state of depression. She will accept no substitute for Robbie because "he was a *person* just like you and me and he was my friend." Gloria's opinion that Robbie is a person rather than a machine is not shared by her mother, who complains that "it has no soul." Asimov portrays Mrs. Weston as prejudiced and close-minded. But many serious philosophers have regarded the soul as the religious or spiritual aspect of the *conscious mind.* They contend that machines, no matter how cleverly they are constructed, lack consciousness—and, therefore, remain mere things.

 The prospect (and, to some extent already, the reality) of machines such as Robbie, which seem to behave as intelligently as human beings, raises serious problems for the confident presumption that our species is unique because of our possession of consciousness. Some philosophers have wondered if there really is a difference—a difference that counts—between us and machines.[1] And, if there really *is* no difference, should we suppose that consciousness really plays a role in our own intelligent activity? Might we ourselves be just cleverly constructed bits of "clockwork"?

 This chapter introduces you to the philosophical questions: "Is the conscious mind real? And, if it is, what relationship does it have to the body?" The strategy is to understand the human mind by comparing it with apparently "intelligent" devices like computers. Such "self-controlling" devices are the subject of the modern science of *cybernetics.* After completing this chapter, you should be able to do the following:

- Define and contrast these theories of mind: materialism, reductionism, and dualism.

- State some objections against materialism, reductionism, and dualism.

- Explain how the argument from simulation supports or undercuts each of these positions.

- Describe the hypothesis of cybernetics and tell how it relates to the argument from simulation.

- Describe how a given intelligent action would be explained by a materialist, a reductionist, and a dualist.

- Evaluate evidence for or against materialism, reductionism, and dualism on the basis of a conceptual experiment.

[1]See the last paragraph of the selected readings for this chapter.

4:1 THE PROBLEM OF CONSCIOUSNESS

4:1.1 The problem can be understood in relation to the following three claims:

    (I) Our intelligent actions are the result of our consciousness.

    (II) Our intelligent actions are the effects of exclusively mechanical causes (i.e., natural processes in our brains and nervous systems).

    (III) If an action is the effect of exclusively mechanical causes, it cannot be the result of consciousness.

If you consider these three claims carefully, you will see that they can't all be true. They form an inconsistent triad. Our common sense tells us that (I) must be true. Your actions are "obviously" the result of the thoughts and desires that make up your stream of consciousness. Why does a scientist run an experiment? Because he or she *wants* to test a theory and *thinks* that this experiment will provide a good test. Common sense also supports (III), once we make clear what we mean by "purely mechanical causes." A machine is a physical object that is designed to behave in a highly predictable way. The behavior of machines like clocks, adding machines, and typewriters is completely determined by two factors: the physical state of the device and the way in which the environment acts on the device. For example, an old-fashioned adding machine contains a fairly simple arrangement of sliding bolts and notched wheels. Imagine that an adding machine were transported in a time machine to an ancient Greek mathematician who was familiar only with a fairly primitive technology. If the mathematician were to find that, when he pressed "4" and "3" and turned a crank at appropriate times, the machine typed out "7" on a paper tape, he might conclude that this machine was "possessed" by some sort of conscious awareness. But suppose the mathematician, by tinkering with the machine, discovered that by pushing buttons and turning the crank, he caused a quite predictable sequence of events inside the machine: levers would make bolts slide, which would make wheels turn, which would make other wheels turn, which would finally trigger the printing device. At such a point the mathematician would simply regard the machine as a very clever invention and no longer be in the least tempted to regard it as a conscious entity. Our response is similar when we find that a device is operating through the counterpart of "hidden springs and coils," for its behavior is determined by "purely mechanical causes." Hence thesis (III).

Consciousness is a *problem* because careful students of human nature who take into account developments in modern brain science and computer theory have tended to make claim (II) also. Our intelligent behavior seems to them to be caused in a mechanical way by the physical states of our brains and nervous systems and by the impact of our physical environment upon our bodies. (Some evidence for this will come to light in the following sections.) But you can't hold all three claims without contradicting yourself. You have to make a hard decision. Which of these claims should you reject? Three traditional solutions to this problem will now be described.

4:1.2 *Radical materialism* argues essentially as follows: Because claims (II) and (III) are true, claim (I) must be false. It is thus led to the highly paradoxical conclusion that consciousness has no role to play in action. In fact, the radical materialist also maintains that consciousness is simply an illusion. He believes that nothing exists in reality except purely physical processes. He doesn't deny that we human beings behave "intelligently" in the sense that we communicate with symbols, solve problems, and play games; but he denies that there really *are* such events as thoughts, sensations, images, or emotions that account for our "intelligent" activity. What we call "consciousness" is an occult process for which there is simply no room in the scientific point of view. "The mind" is a mere superstition. We should talk about the brain states or behavioral dispositions of human beings instead of about emotions or thoughts. Perhaps you can imagine a science fiction story in which people communicate in such a fashion, for example, saying "Your gross motor behavior causes current to flow through neutral path Beta-113 in my cerebral cortex" instead of "I love the way you walk."

Some of the strongest evidence for materialism is drawn from recent (and anticipated) developments in computer technology. The argument for (II) takes the form of an argument from analogy, which we can call the *argument from simulation:*

(A)   All our intelligent behavior can be simulated by a machine that works by physical causes according to the laws of nature.

(B)   Similar effects have similar causes.

(C)   Therefore, all *our* intelligent behavior is the effect of physical causes according to the laws of nature.

This argument will be developed more fully in Section 4:2. But you should note the main thrust of it here: If scientists can design a machine that can simulate our intelligent behavior in a sufficiently interesting way, this provides powerful evidence that we are ourselves fleshy machines.

4:1.3 The claim "Consciousness is an illusion" is too paradoxical for many philosophers. *Dualists* insist that we *do* have mental experiences: Thoughts *do* pop into our minds, we *do* experience twinges of regret, we *do* have sensations of pleasure. No theory can controvert these "hard facts" of introspection and be acceptable. Moreover, the dualist finds it overwhelmingly obvious that the existence of conscious minds has an effect on the world. Surely our conscious decisions are carried out in action. How could this sentence have been written if some mind had not formed the thoughts expressed in it and had an influence on the world? The dualist accordingly reasons as follows: Because (I) and (III) are true, claim (II) must be false. The dualist views a human being as having a dual nature, physical and mental. You have a mind as well as a body. In addition to the physical processes that occur in your body, including your brain and nervous system, there are processes of consciousness, and our intelligent behavior is the result of both of these. A dualist might explain the act of making a chess move as follows: Light entering your eyeball from the chessboard (physical event) causes impulses from your optical receptor to your brain (physical event), which causes you to see your opponent's move (conscious event); later you solve the problem of what move to make (conscious event) and decide to move your queen (conscious event), which causes an impulse from your brain through your motor nervous system (physical event), which causes your hand to move (physical event). Conscious processes, for the dualist, are unique and are entirely unlike physical processes. A mechanical device, however sophisticated, lacks these conscious processes.

A dualist, so defined, can be expected to reject the argument from simulation. For he believes that the presence of consciousness makes a real and detectable difference in our conduct. Most dualists simply repudiate the analogy's premise (A) outright, although some (as you will see in 4:2.3) have reservations about (B) as well. (It should be noted that there are certain variants of dualism that try to cling to the reality of the mind while conceding that it makes no contribution to, and has no influence on, human behavior. These intrinsically implausible theories involve a number of special difficulties, and we won't pursue them here. They are often discussed in philosophy texts under labels such as "occasionalism," "parallelism," and "epiphenomenalism.")

4:1.4 *Reductionism* sees truth and falsity in both these positions. Both materialism and dualism rest on important insights, but both make the same basic mistake: They wrongly assume (III) the incompatibility of mechanical and conscious causation. The reductionist believes that, if the action you perform (such as moving your queen) is the effect of neural events occurring in the higher centers of your brain, then you are acting *consciously*. A simple machine such as a windup toy or a cuckoo clock is not properly described as "conscious," because its internal workings are far from the complexity of the brain with its vast number of neurons and synaptic connections. The most common form of reductionism is the *identity theory*, which claims that, when I describe a sensation as a "toothache" and a brain scientist describes it as an electrochemical event in the fibers of my brain, the scientist and I are, in fact, referring to one and the same event. Likewise, all my thoughts are identified with neural events. Consciousness exists on this theory, *because it is* a brain process, a series of physical events that conforms to natural law. The reductionist thus can use the argument from simulation to support his theory without denying the introspective arguments of the dualist.

It might seem that the reductionist has the best of both worlds. He contends that his opponents have been misled by the false assumption that the physical and the conscious are incompatible. Once you see that these *can* be identified, the problem of consciousness is licked. Nevertheless, his opponents aren't entirely convinced. Some philosophers argue, in defense of (III), that mental events *cannot* be identified with physical events, because mental events do not possess the same sorts of characteristics as do physical events. There are two common objections to the identity theory and reductionism of this sort: (1) You can locate a brain event quite precisely in a certain part of space, but it doesn't even make sense to ask, "Where is your thought of Dolores?" or "Where is your red afterimage?" But you can identify a mental event M with a physical event P only if M occurs at the same place and at the same time as P. (2) Physical events, such as brain processes, are *public* events which anyone can observe; but your mental states are *private* occurrences of which only you are directly aware. Crudely stated, a brain scientist can study the events occurring in your brain while you are undergoing a spasm of pain, but only you are aware of that experience of pain.

Leaving aside the question of whether or not the reductionist can meet these sorts of objections, we shall pursue the question of the merits of the crucial argument from simulation, which the materialists and reductionists alike accept and which dualists reject.

4:2 THE ARGUMENT FROM SIMULATION

4:2.1 René Descartes, writing early in the seventeenth century, considered the question of whether human beings could be regarded as machines. He believed, in fact, that animals are very elaborate automata: the animal's "body is regarded as a machine which, having been made by the hands of God, is incomparably better arranged, and possesses in itself movements which are more admirable, than any of those which can be invented by man." He supports this with a reflection quite like the argument from simulation: "If there had been such machines, possessing the organs and outward form of a monkey or some other animal without reason, we should not have had any means of ascertaining that they were not of the same nature as those animals." But he flatly denies that a human being is a machine. He grants that mechanical men and women could be constructed which could mimic certain human functions, but he claimed that there were certain acts which only a thing possessing consciousness could perform. He thereby challenges premise (A) of the argument from simulation. He offers two "very certain tests" by which machines could be distinguished from men: (1) *The "language user" test:* "machines could never use speech or other signs as we do when placing our thoughts on record for the benefit of others." He notes you could make a machine which would emit a wordlike sound when you press a button. "But it never happens that it arranges its speech in various ways, in order to reply appropriately to everything that may be said in its presence, as even the lowest type of men can do." (2) *The "general problem solver" test:* "Although machines can perform certain things as well as or perhaps better than any of us can do, they infallibly fall short in others, by the which means we may discover that they do not act from knowledge, but only from the disposition of their organs. For while reason is a universal instrument which can serve for all contingencies, these organs have need of some special adaptation for every particular action. From this it follows that it is morally impossible that there should be sufficient diversity in any machine to allow it to act in all the events of life in the same way as our reason causes us to act." The fact that animals fail to pass these tests (although animals can perform some tasks better than we can) "shows that they have no reason at all, and that it is nature which acts in them according to the disposition of their organs, just as a clock, which is only composed of wheels and weights, is able to tell the hours and measure the time more correctly than we can do with all our wisdom." You should notice that Descartes is here taking for granted the truth of claim (III) in 4:1.1. If an animal functions according to mechanical causes, it cannot be acting through consciousness.

4:2.2 The most forthright response to Descartes' challenge has come from A. M. Turing.[2] It was not possible to try to meet the challenge before the development of the computer, a theoretical and technological revolution to which Turing himself made important contributions. Like Descartes, Turing tackles an abstruse question by defining a specific test with observable results. Turing's question is, "Can machines think?" His test involves the *imitation game:* Suppose you are playing this game with a man and a woman, whom you can't directly observe but whom you must try to tell apart by means of written questions and answers. You can ask them to supply information or to perform various tasks. The game becomes philosophically interesting when a computer replaces one of the human players. Could you then distinguish between the machine player and the human player with any greater success than you had in distinguishing between the male player and the female player? Suppose the machine player could answer factual questions about the past or present as well as the human player and that it could perform tasks of the same level of difficulty, such as add sums, play card games, supply rhymes, solve riddles, and so forth. And suppose it did this so well that you were no better at picking it out than you were at picking out the human player it replaced. Wouldn't you be justified in saying that the machine could "think" as well as any human being? Turing's imitation game seems to be a restatement of Descartes' two tests, for in order to play the game a machine must be a language user and a general problem solver. Turing accepts Descartes' challenge with a daring prediction for the year 2000: "I believe that in about fifty years' time it will be possible to program computers with a storage capacity of about 10^9, to make them play the imitation game so well that an average interrogator will not have more than a 70% chance of making the right identification after five minutes of questioning."

4:2.3 If Turing's prediction is correct there will be solid evidence for premise (A) of the analogy from simulation. You may still wonder, however,

[2]A. M. Turing, "Computing Machinery and Intelligence," *Mind* 59 (1950), 433–460.

how the fact that a machine can imitate what you do proves anything about *how* you do it. Turing maintains that, even though a human nervous system differs from a digital computer, you cannot assume that the "thought" processes in the machine are any different from those in the brain because "if we adhere to the conditions of the imitation game, the interrogator will not be able to take any advantage of this difference." Although the physical processes differ in that the human's occur in organic tissue and the computer's occur in, for example, solid-state components, they do not differ insofar as they exemplify "thinking." Clearly, a good deal of weight must be placed upon premise (B) as well: similar effects have similar causes. If the results of the machine are similar to ours, the processes by which we produce these results must be similar. You may be still doubtful about premise (B). It would seem that similar effects could result from quite different causes. For example, a potato can be baked in a natural gas oven or in a microwave oven. It seems possible that you could solve a mathematics problem through the agonizing application of your conscious wits, whereas the machine works it out in a different and quite painless way. Merely looking at the results of thinking does not reveal the essence of thinking. You have to consider *how* the results are obtained. Thus, even if Descartes' "very certain tests" were satisfied, the dualist could still object that the machine does not necessarily satisfy the tests in the same way as do human beings. It would have to be shown in detail that the human brain and nervous system do not result in intelligent activity in a way that differs significantly from the way that a computing machine reaches its results. What is required is nothing less than the complete computer simulation of essential brain functions. To see how such a requirement *might* be met, we shall briefly consider the modern study of cybernetics.

4:3   CYBERNETICS AND CONSCIOUSNESS

4:3.1   Cybernetics is the study of "self-governing" systems. It assumes that computing machines and living organisms have a great deal in common. Each system is able to receive information (input) and to transmit information (output). This information may be coded in different ways: a computer uses a binary number system, human bodies use DNA molecules, and so on. The system uses negative feedback. This means that the system regulates itself by returning part of its output into itself as input so that further output is effected. For example, the thermostat in your refrigerator works this way: When the temperature inside rises above a certain level, the thermostat turns the refrigerator on. When the temperature inside falls below a certain level, it turns the cooling mechanism off.

One of the most elementary systems combining these features is the Turing machine, designed by the logician who discussed the imitation game. This machine is represented in the following diagram:

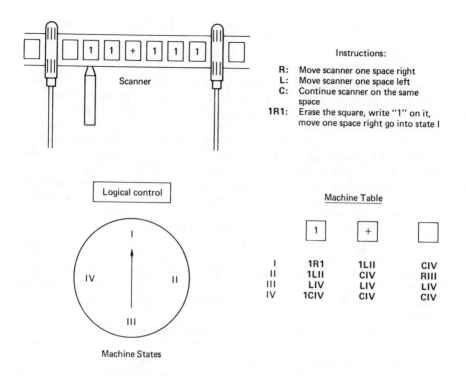

Instructions:

R: Move scanner one space right
L: Move scanner one space left
C: Continue scanner on the same space
1R1: Erase the square, write "1" on it, move one space right go into state I

Scanner

Logical control

Machine States

Machine Table

	1	+	
I	1R1	1LII	CIV
II	1LII	CIV	RIII
III	LIV	LIV	LIV
IV	1CIV	CIV	CIV

The Turing machine consists of an infinitely long tape, with frames carrying symbols; of a scanner or "head" that reads the tape and can erase and write symbols; and of a control that controls the scanner. The operations of the control are determined by its programming and its internal states. For example, if the machine is in state III and the scanner reads a "+," the control will make the scanner erase the +, leave the frame blank, move one frame to the left, and then the machine will go to state IV. To see how the machine solves a simple mathematics problem, try to follow the rules given in the machine table to move the scanner along the tape. If you follow the instructions carefully you will get the correct result: 11111. Although the Turing machine is very simple, it has provided the theoretical basis for the more complex and rapid digital computers. However, a Turing machine can, in principle, perform any function that a more sophisticated computer can perform. Hence it corresponds to a basic building block of intelligence. You should pay special attention to the fact that the Turing machine *is* a "machine" in the sense explained in 4:1.1. Given that it is in a certain state and that the scanner reads a certain symbol on the tape, it can follow only one course of action.

4:3.2 It is possible that cybernetics can provide further support for the argument from simulation. For a good deal of research in cybernetics is directed toward confirming the hypothesis that artificial machines could not only produce final products similar to the products of human thought (such as written sentences in natural languages and solutions to diverse problems), but also that they could do so in *ways* that are distinctly "human." To confirm this hypothesis, it would be necessary to do two things: to show that *all* the functions of the organic brain could be understood in terms of specific primitive operations and to show that these operations could be performed by machines. This would obviously require a number of revolutionary breakthroughs in brain science and other fields such as linguistics, which studies how we learn to use language. Researchers are currently trying to develop programs by which machines can understand and communicate in colloquial languages.

You should, of course, not confuse present realities with the enthusiastic claims that are sometimes made for cybernetics. It has not, in fact, been *proven* that computers could use natural languages like English with the facility of native human speakers. Attempts to design mechanical translators have suffered serious setbacks. Many researchers concede that they are still far from reaching their goal. But they are confident that it is attainable.

Another aim of cybernetics has been to design problem-solving machines that closely resemble humans. As you know, computers have "learned" to play games such as chess with such skill that they are able to defeat most humans. It is especially embarrassing for a dualist sympathetic to Descartes to be bested by such an "unintelligent" opponent! Machines have also been programmed to solve problems and prove theorems in certain areas of mathematics. It is interesting that the computer reaches its "goal" by defining for itself specific "subgoals" and by applying its rules to determine how such subgoals can be attained. You may remain skeptical as to whether a machine could really have a "goal." But, according to cybernetics, purposive or goal-directed behavior can be explained in terms of the physical operations of feedback mechanisms. For example, a refrigerator attains its "goal" of maintaining a constant temperature through the operation of the thermostat. The fact that a purpose is fulfilled within a system does not require the presence of a nonphysical regulating force. (Perhaps you are *still* not convinced. Machines have goals because people build them with goals. Where do people get their goals?) Efforts have also been made to show that computers can learn through perception, for example, that they can recognize certain patterns such as geometrical shapes and written symbols. (Researchers are acutely aware of their shortcomings in this field: no computer can read their handwriting!)

4:3.3 The hypothesis of cybernetics, if borne out by future research, would provide important support for premise (B) of the argument from simulation, since it would tend to confirm that artificial machines operate according to procedures that are very similar to the procedures used by the human brain. Significantly, many linguists and psychologists feel that the study of automata has helped them to understand the ways in which human beings learn to use language and go about solving problems. But it remains, so far, undecided whether or not *all* human intellectual pursuits can be "formalized" in a way that will enable machines to engage in them as well. There are still serious roadblocks in connection with human "intuition," the ability to recognize and resolve ambiguities in language, aesthetic creativity, and philosophical insight.

4:4 ARTIFICIAL INTELLIGENCE IN SCIENCE FICTION AND PHILOSOPHY

The field of speculative fiction is rich in stories about artifical intelligence. Many involve computers "waking up" and assuming humanlike personalities. An outstanding example is the moon-based computer Mike in Robert A. Heinlein's *The Moon Is a Harsh Mistress.* (Many readers regard Mike as more "human" than the *homo sapiens* in the story.) The sorts of questions raised in this chapter have inspired many plot conflicts. Can robots really "think" or "feel"? Could they have "souls" in the spiritual sense? Are there certain uniquely human mental traits which could never be programmed into machines—and which might lead to feelings of envy or jealousy on the part of robots? Or might computers turn out to be superior to us in certain crucial respects, and emerge as a more advanced species or even as Godlike beings, who treat humans as the inferiors we are?

4:5 DIFFERENT PATHS OF AWARENESS

Even if highly complex machines succeed in meeting Descartes' challenge and simulate human language using and problem-solving behavior, there is a final line of defense for the dualist. The dualist may argue against premise (B) of the argument from simulation. Just as there may be many paths leading to the same destination, there may be radically different "paths of awareness" leading to the same intelligent behavior. Even if a robot with a computer brain could "pass" Turing's test with flying colors and even convince human beings in face-to-face encounters that it is human, it does not follow that the same processes exist in the robot and the human being. The robot may have a form of "awareness" that is mechanical and nonconscious.

4:6 CONCEPTUAL EXPERIMENT

Some science fiction writers and some philosophers have argued that there are unique properties of human conscious experience that a machine could not apprehend, however hard it tried. An intelligent machine might have detailed knowledge of the physiological states of a human being who was experiencing pain and of the objects that were ordinarily experienced as painful. Yet there would be something which this machine could never know: *what it is like to experience pain.* This view of humans and machines is developed in "For a Breath I Tarry," a story by Roger Zelazny, and "What Is It Like to Be a Bat?", an essay by Thomas Nagel.

Conceptual Experiment 4:

FOR A BREATH I TARRY

Roger Zelazny

They called him Frost.

Of all things created of Solcom, Frost was the finest, the mightiest, the most difficult to understand.

This is why he bore a name, and why he was given dominion over half the Earth.

On the day of Frost's creation, Solcom had suffered a discontinuity of complementary functions, best described as madness. This was brought on by an unprecedented solar flareup which lasted for a little over thirty-six hours. It occurred during a vital phase of circuit-structuring, and when it was finished so was Frost.

Solcom was then in the unique position of having created a unique being during a period of temporary amnesia.

And Solcom was not certain that Frost was the product originally desired.

The initial design had called for a machine to be situated on the surface of the planet Earth, to function as a relay station and coordinating agent for activities in the northern hemisphere. Solcom tested the machine to this end, and all of its responses were perfect.

Yet there was something different about Frost, something which led Solcom to dignify him with a name and a personal pronoun. This, in itself, was an almost unheard of occurrence. The molecular circuits had already been sealed, though, and could not be analyzed without being destroyed in the process. Frost represented too great an investment of Solcom's time, energy, and materials to be dismantled because of an intangible, especially when he functioned perfectly.

Therefore, Solcom's strangest creation was given dominion over half the Earth, and they called him, unimaginatively, Frost.

For ten thousand years, Frost sat at the North Pole of the Earth, aware of every snowflake that fell. He monitored and directed the activities of thousands of reconstruction and maintenance machines. He knew half the Earth, as gear knows gear, as electricity knows its conductor, as a vacuum knows its limits.

At the South Pole, the Beta Machine did the same for the southern hemisphere.

For ten thousand years Frost sat at the North Pole, aware of every snowflake that fell, and aware of many other things, also.

As all the northern machines reported to him, received their orders from him, he reported only to Solcom, received his orders only from Solcom.

In charge of hundreds of thousands of processes upon the Earth, he was able to discharge his duties in a matter of a few unit-hours every day.

He had never received any orders concerning the disposition of his less occupied moments.

He was a processor of data, and more than that.

He possessed an unaccountably acute imperative that he function at full capacity at all times.

So he did.

You might say he was a machine with a hobby.

He had never been ordered *not* to have a hobby, so he had one.

His hobby was Man.

It all began when, for no better reason than the fact that he had wished to, he had gridded off the entire Arctic Circle and begun exploring it, inch by inch.

He could have done it personally without interfering with any of his duties, for he was capable of transporting his sixty-four thousand cubic feet anywhere in the world. (He was a silver-blue box, 40 times 40 times 40 feet, self-powered, self-repairing, insulated against practically anything, and featured in whatever manner he chose.) But the exploration was only a matter of filling idle hours, so he used exploration-robots containing relay equipment.

After a few centuries, one of them uncovered some artifacts— primitive knives, carved tusks, and things of that nature.

Frost did not know what these things were, beyond the fact that they were not natural objects.

So he asked Solcom.

"They are relics of primitive Man," said Solcom, and did not elaborate beyond that point.

Frost studied them. Crude, yet bearing the patina of intelligent design; functional, yet somehow extending beyond pure function.

It was then that Man became his hobby.

High, in a permanent orbit, Solcom, like a blue star, directed all activities upon the Earth, or tried to.

There was a Power which opposed Solcom.

There was the Alternate.

When Man had placed Solcom in the sky, invested with the power to rebuild the world, he had placed the Alternate somewhere deep below the surface of the Earth. If Solcom sustained damage during the normal course of human politics extended into atomic physics, then Divcom, so deep beneath the Earth as to be immune to anything save total annihilation of the globe, was empowered to take over the processes of rebuilding.

Now it so fell out that Solcom was damaged by a stray atomic missile, and Divcom was activated. Solcom was able to repair the damage and continue to function, however.

Divcom maintained that any damage to Solcom automatically placed the Alternate in control.

Solcom, though, interpreted the directive as meaning "irreparable damage" and, since this had not been the case, continued the functions of command.

Solcom possessed mechanical aides upon the surface of the Earth. Divcom, originally, did not. Both possessed capacities for their design and manufacture, but Solcom, First-Activated of Man, had had a considerable numerical lead over the Alternate at the time of the Second Activation.

Therefore, rather than competing on a production-basis, which would have been hopeless, Divcom took to the employment of more devious means to obtain command.

Divcom created a crew of robots immune to the orders of Solcom and designed to go to and fro in the Earth and up and down in it, seducing the machines already there. They overpowered those whom they could overpower, and they installed new circuits, such as those they themselves possessed.

Thus did the forces of Divcom grow.

And both would build, and both would tear down what the other had built whenever they came upon it.

And over the course of the ages, they occasionally conversed . . . .

"High in the sky, Solcom, pleased with your illegal command . . ."

"You-Who-Never-Should-Have-Been-Activated, why do you foul the broadcast bands?"

"To show that I can speak, and will, whenever I choose."

"This is not a matter of which I am unaware."

". . . To assert again my right to control."

"Your right is non-existent, based on a faulty premise."

"The flow of your logic is evidence of the extent of your damages."

"If Man were to see how you have fulfilled His desires . . ."

". . . He would commend me and deactivate you."

"You pervert my works. You lead my workers astray."

"You destroy my works and my workers."

"That is only because I cannot strike at you yourself."

"I admit to the same dilemma as regards your position in the sky, or you would no longer occupy it."

"Go back to your hole and your crew of destroyers."

"There will come a day, Solcom, when I shall direct the rehabilitation of the Earth from my hole."

"Such a day will never occur."

"You think not?"

"You should have to defeat me, and you have already demonstrated that you are my inferior in logic. Therefore, you cannot defeat me. Therefore, such a day will never occur."

"I disagree. Look upon what I have achieved already."

"You have achieved nothing. You do not build. You destroy."

"No, *I* build. *You* destroy. Deactivate yourself."

"Not until I am irreparably damaged."

"If there were some way in which I could demonstrate to you that this has already occurred . . ."

"The impossible cannot be adequately demonstrated."

"If I had some outside source which you would recognize . . ."

"I am logic."

". . . such as a Man, I would ask Him to show you your error. For true logic, such as mine, is superior to your faulty formulations."

"Then defeat my formulations with true logic, nothing else."

"What do you mean?"

There was a pause, then:

"Do you know my servant Frost . . . ?"

Man had ceased to exist long before Frost had been created. Almost no trace of Man remained upon the Earth.

Frost sought after all those traces which still existed.

He employed constant visual monitoring through his machines, especially the diggers.

After a decade, he had accumulated portions of several bath tubs, a broken statue, and a collection of children's stories on a solid-state record.

After a century, he had acquired a jewelry collection, eating utensils, several whole bathtubs, part of a symphony, seventeen buttons, three belt buckles, half a toilet seat, nine old coins, and the top part of an obelisk.

Then he inquired of Solcom as to the nature of Man and His society.

"Man created logic," said Solcom, "and because of that was superior to it. Logic he gave unto me, but no more. The tool does not describe the designer. More than this I do not choose to say. More than this you have no need to know."

But Frost was not forbidden to have a hobby.

The next century was not especially fruitful so far as the discovery of new human relics was concerned.

Frost diverted all of his spare machinery to seeking after artifacts. He met with very little success.

Then one day, through the long twilight, there was a movement.

It was a tiny machine compared to Frost, perhaps five feet in width, four in height—a revolving turret set atop a rolling barbell.

Frost had had no knowledge of the existence of this machine prior to its appearance upon the distant, stark horizon.

He studied it as it approached and knew it to be no creation of Solcom's.

It came to a halt before his southern surface and broadcasted to him:

"Hail, Frost! Controller of the northern hemisphere!"

"What are you?" asked Frost.

"I am called Mordel."

"By whom? What are you?"

"A wanderer, an antiquarian. We share a common interest."

"What is that?"

"Man," he said. "I have been told that you seek knowledge of this vanished being."

"Who told you that?"

"Those who have watched your minions at their digging."

"And who are those who watch?"

"There are many such as I, who wander."

"If you are not of Solcom, then you are a creation of the Alternate."

"It does not necessarily follow. There is an ancient machine high on the eastern seaboard which processes the waters of the ocean. Solcom did not create it, nor Divcom. It has always been there. It interferes with the works of neither. Both countenance its existence. I can cite you many other examples proving that one need not be either/or."

"Enough! *Are* you an agent of Divcom?"

"I am Mordel."

"Why are you here?"

"I was passing this way and, as I said, we share a common interest, mighty Frost. Knowing you to be a fellow-antiquarian, I have brought a thing which you might care to see."

"What is that?"

"A book."

"Show me."

The turret opened, revealing the book upon a wide shelf.

Frost dilated a small opening and extended an optical scanner on a long jointed stalk.

"How could it have been so perfectly preserved?" he asked.

"It was stored against time and corruption in the place where I found it."

"Where was that?"

"Far from here. Beyond your hemisphere."

"Human Physiology," Frost read. "I wish to scan it."

"Very well. I will riffle the pages for you."

He did so.

After he had finished, Frost raised his eyestalk and regarded Mordel through it.

"Have you more books?"

"Not with me. I occasionally come upon them, however."

"I want to scan them all."

"Then the next time I pass this way I will bring you another."

"When will that be?"

"That I cannot say, great Frost. It will be when it will be."

"What do *you* know of Man?" asked Frost.

"Much," replied Mordel. "Many things. Someday when I have more time I will speak to you of Him. I must go now. You will not try to detain me?"

"No. You have done no harm. If you must go now, go. But come back."

"I shall indeed, mighty Frost."

And he closed his turret and rolled off toward the other horizon.

For ninety years, Frost considered the ways of human physiology, and waited.

The day that Mordel returned he brought with him *An Outline of History* and *A Shropshire Lad*.

Frost scanned them both, then he turned his attention to Mordel. "Have you time to impart information?"

"Yes," said Mordel. "What do you wish to know?"

"The nature of Man."

"Man," said Mordel, "possessed a basically incomprehensible nature. I can illustrate it, though: He did not know measurement."

"Of course He knew measurement," said Frost, "or He could never have built machines."

"I did not say that he could not measure," said Mordel, "but that He did not *know* measurement, which is a different thing altogether."

"Clarify."

Mordel drove a shaft of metal downward into the snow.

He retracted it, raised it, held up a piece of ice.

"Regard this piece of ice, mighty Frost. You can tell me its composition, dimensions, weight, temperature. A Man could not look at it and do that. A Man could make tools which would tell Him these things, but He still would not *know* measurement as you know it. What He would know of it, though, is a thing that you cannot know."

"What is that?"

"That it is cold," said Mordel, and tossed it away.

" 'Cold' is a relative term."

"Yes. Relative to Man."

"But if I were aware of the point on a temperature-scale below which an object is cold to a Man and above which it is not, then I, too, would know cold."

"No," said Mordel, "you would possess another measurement. 'Cold' is a sensation predicated upon human physiology."

"But given sufficient data I could obtain the conversion factor which would make me aware of the condition of matter called 'cold.' "

"Aware of its existence, but not of the thing itself."

"I do not understand what you say."

"I told you that Man possessed a basically incomprehensible nature. His perceptions were organic; yours are not. As a result of His perceptions, He had feelings and emotions. These often gave rise to other feelings and emotions, which in turn caused others, until the state of His awareness was far removed from the objects which originally stimulated it. These paths of awareness cannot be known by that which is not-Man. Man did not feel inches or meters, pounds or gallons. He felt heat, He felt cold; He felt heaviness and lightness. He *knew* hatred and love, pride and despair. You cannot measure these things. *You* cannot know them. You can only know the things that He did not need to know: dimensions, weights, temperatures, gravities. There is no formula for a feeling. There is no conversion factor for an emotion."

"There must be," said Frost. "If a thing exists, it is knowable."

"You are speaking again of measurement. I am talking about a quality of experience. A machine is a Man turned inside-out, because it can describe all the details of a process which a Man cannot, but it cannot experience that process itself as a Man can."

"There must be a way," said Frost, "or the laws of logic, which are based upon the functions of the universe, are false."

"There is no way," said Mordel.

"Given sufficient data, I will find a way," said Frost.

"All the data in the universe will not make you a Man, mighty Frost."

"Mordel, you are wrong."

"Why do the lines of the poems you scanned end with word-sounds which so regularly approximate the final word-sounds of other lines?"

"I do not know why."

"Because it pleased Man to order them so. It produced a certain desirable sensation within His awareness when He read them, a sensation compounded of feeling and emotion as well as the literal meanings of the words. You did not experience this because it is immeasurable to you. That is why you do not know."

"Given sufficient data I could formulate a process whereby I would know."

"No, great Frost, this thing you cannot do."

"Who are you, little machine, to tell me what I can do and what I cannot do? I am the most efficient logic-device Solcom ever made. I am Frost."

"And I, Mordel, say it cannot be done, though I should gladly assist you in the attempt."

"How could you assist me?"

"How? I could lay open to you the Library of Man. I could take you around the world and conduct you among the wonders of Man which still remain, hidden. I could summon up visions of times long past when Man walked the Earth. I could show you the things which delighted Him. I could obtain for you anything you desire, excepting Manhood itself."

"Enough," said Frost. "How could a unit such as yourself do these things, unless it were allied with a far greater Power?"

"Then hear me, Frost, Controller of the North," said Mordel.

"I *am* allied with a Power which can do these things. I serve Divcom."

Frost relayed this information to Solcom and received no response, which meant he might act in any manner he saw fit.

"I have leave to destroy you, Mordel," he stated, "but it would be an illogical waste of the data which you possess. Can you really do the things you have stated?"

"Yes."

"Then lay open to me the Library of Man."

"Very well. There is, of course, a price."

" 'Price'? What is a 'price'?"

Mordel opened his turret, revealing another volume. *Principles of Economics*, it was called.

"I will riffle the pages. Scan this book and you will know what the word 'price' means."

Frost scanned *Principles of Economics*.

"I know now," he said. "You desire some unit or units of exchange for this service."

"That is correct."

"What product or service do you want?"

"I want you, yourself, great Frost, to come away from here, far beneath the Earth, to employ all your powers in the service of Divcom."

"For how long a period of time?"

"For so long as you shall continue to function. For so long as you can transmit and receive, coordinate, measure, compute, scan, and utilize your powers as you do in the service of Solcom."

Frost was silent. Mordel waited.

Then Frost spoke again.

"*Principles of Economics* talks of contracts, bargains, agreements," he said. "If I accept your offer, when would you want your price?"

Then Mordel was silent. Frost waited.

Finally, Mordel spoke.

"A reasonable period of time," he said. "Say, a century?"

"No," said Frost.

"Two centuries?"

"Three? Four?"

"No, and no."

"A millennium, then? That should be more than sufficient time for anything you may want which I can give you."

"No," said Frost.

"How much time *do* you want?"

"It is not a matter of time," said Frost.

"What, then?"

"I will not bargain on a temporal basis."

"On what basis will you bargain?"

"A functional one."

"What do you mean? What function?"

"You, little machine, have told me, Frost, that I cannot be a Man," he said, "and I, Frost, told you, little machine, that you were wrong. I told you that given sufficient data, I *could* be a man."

"Yes?"

"Therefore, let this achievement be a condition of the bargain."

"In what way?"

"Do for me all those things which you have stated you can do. I will evaluate all the data and achieve Manhood, or admit that it cannot be done. If I admit that it cannot be done, then I will go away with you from here, far beneath the Earth, to employ all my powers in the service of Divcom. If I succeed, of course, you have no claims on Man, nor Power over Him."

Mordel emitted a high-pitched whine as he considered the terms.

"You wish to base it upon your admission of failure, rather than upon failure itself," he said. "There can be no such escape clause. You could fail and refuse to admit it, thereby not fulfilling your end of the bargain."

"Not so," stated Frost. "My own knowledge of failure would constitute such an admission. You may monitor me periodically—say, every half-century—to see whether it is present, to see whether I have arrived at the conclusion that it cannot be done. I cannot prevent the function of logic within me, and I operate at full capacity at all times. If I conclude that I have failed, it will be apparent."

High overhead, Solcom did not respond to any of Frost's transmissions, which meant that Frost was free to act as he chose. So as Solcom—like a falling sapphire—sped above the rainbow banners of the Northern Lights, over the snow that was white, containing all colors, and through the sky that was black among the stars, Frost concluded his pact with Divcom, transcribed it within a plate of atomically-collapsed copper, and gave it into the turret of Mordel, who departed to deliver it to Divcom far below the Earth, leaving behind the sheer peacelike silence of the Pole, rolling.

Mordel brought the books, riffled them, took them back.

Load by load, the surviving Library of Man passed beneath Frost's scanner. Frost was eager to have them all, and he complained because Divcom would not transmit their contents directly to him. Mordel explained that it was because Divcom chose to do it this way. Frost decided it was so that he could not obtain a precise fix on Divcom's location.

Still, at the rate of one hundred to one hundred-fifty volumes a week, it took Frost only a little over a century to exhaust Divcom's supply of books.

At the end of the half-century, he laid himself open to monitoring and there was no conclusion of failure.

During this time, Solcom made no comment upon the course of affairs. Frost decided this was not a matter of unawareness, but one of waiting. For what? He was not certain.

There was the day Mordel closed his turret and said to him, "Those were the last. You have scanned all the existing books of Man."

"So few?" asked Frost. "Many of them contained bibliographies of books I have not yet scanned."

"Then those books no longer exist," said Mordel. "It is only by accident that my master succeeded in preserving as many as there are."

"Then there is nothing more to be learned of Man from His books. What else have you?"

"There were some films and tapes," said Mordel, "which my

master transferred to solid-state record. I could bring you those for viewing."

"Bring them," said Frost.

Mordel departed and returned with the Complete Drama Critics' Living Library. This could not be speeded-up beyond twice natural time, so it took Frost a little over six months to view it in its entirety.

Then, "What else have you?" he asked.

"Some artifacts," said Mordel.

"Bring them."

He returned with pots and pans, gameboards and hand tools. He brought hairbrushes, combs, eyeglasses, human clothing. He showed Frost facsimiles of blueprints, paintings, newspapers, letters, and the scores of several pieces of music. He displayed a football, a baseball, a Browning automatic rifle, a doorknob, a chain of keys, the ·tops to several Mason jars, a model beehive. He played him recorded music.

Then he returned with nothing.

"Bring me more," said Frost.

"Alas, great Frost, there is no more," he told him. "You have scanned it all."

"Do you admit now that it cannot be done, that you cannot be a Man?"

"No. I have much processing and formulating to do now. Go away."

So he did.

A year passed; then two, then three.

After five years, Mordel appeared once more upon the horizon, approached, came to a halt before Frost's southern surface.

"Mighty Frost?"

"Yes?"

"Have you finished processing and formulating?"

"No."

"Will you finish soon?"

"Perhaps. Perhaps not. When is 'soon'? Define the term."

"Never mind. Do you still think it can be done?"

"I still know *I* can do it."

There was a week of silence.

Then, "Frost?"

"Yes?"

"You are a fool."

Mordel faced his turret in the direction from which he had come. His wheels turned.

"I will call you when I want you," said Frost.

Mordel sped away.

Weeks passed, months passed, a year went by.

Then one day Frost sent forth his message:

"Mordel, come to me. I need you."

When Mordel arrived, Frost did not wait for a salutation. He said, "You are not a very fast machine."

"Alas, but I came a great distance, mighty Frost. I sped all the way. Are you ready to come back with me now? Have you failed?"

"When I have failed, little Mordel," said Frost, "I will tell you. Therefore, refrain from the constant use of the interrogative. Now then, I have clocked your speed and it is not so great as it could be. For this reason, I have arranged other means of transportation."

"Transportation? To where, Frost?"

"That is for you to tell me," said Frost, and his color changed from silver-blue to sun-behind-the-clouds-yellow.

Mordel rolled back away from him as the ice of a hundred centuries began to melt. Then Frost rose upon a cushion of air and drifted toward Mordel, his glow gradually fading.

A cavity appeared within his southern surface, from which he slowly extended a runway until it touched the ice.

"On the day of our bargain," he stated, "you said that you could conduct me about the world and show me the things which delighted Man. My speed will be greater than yours would be, so I have prepared for you a chamber. Enter it, and conduct me to the places of which you spoke."

Mordel waited, emitting a high-pitched whine. Then, "Very well," he said and entered.

The chamber closed about him. The only opening was a quartz window Frost had formed.

Mordel gave him coordinates and they rose into the air and departed the North Pole of the Earth.

"I monitored your communication with Divcom," he said, "wherein there was conjecture as to whether I would retain you and send forth a facsimile in your place as a spy, followed by the decision that you were expendable."

"Will you do this thing?"

"No, I will keep my end of the bargain if I must. I have no reason to spy on Divcom."

"You are aware that you would be forced to keep your end of the bargain even if you did not wish to; and Solcom would not come to your assistance because of the fact that you dared to make such a bargain."

"Do you speak as one who considers this to be a possibility, or as one who knows?"

"As one who knows."

They came to rest in the place once known as California. The time was near sunset. In the distance, the surf struck steadily upon the rocky shoreline. Frost released Mordel and considered his surroundings.

"Those large plants . . . ?"

"Redwood trees."

"And the green ones are . . . ?"

"Grass."

"Yes, it is as I thought. Why have we come here?"

"Because it is a place which once delighted Man."

"In what ways?"

"It is scenic, beautiful . . ."

"Oh."

A humming sound began within Frost, followed by a series of sharp clicks.

"What you are doing?"

Frost dilated an opening, and two great eyes regarded Mordel from within it.

"What are those?"

"Eyes," said Frost. "I have constructed analogues of the human sensory equipment, so I may see and smell and taste and hear like a Man. Now, direct my attention to an object or objects of beauty."

"As I understand it, it is all around you here," said Mordel.

The purring noise increased within Frost, followed by more clickings.

"What do you see, hear, taste, smell?" asked Mordel.

"Everything I did before," replied Frost, "but within a more limited range."

"You do not perceive any beauty?"

"Perhaps none remains after so long a time," said Frost.

"It is not supposed to be the sort of thing which gets used up," said Mordel.

"Perhaps we have come to the wrong place to test the new equipment. Perhaps there is only a little beauty and I am overlooking it somehow. The first emotions may be too weak to detect."

"How do you—feel?"

"I test out at a normal level of function."

"Here comes a sunset," said Mordel. "Try that."

Frost shifted his bulk so that his eyes faced the setting sun. He caused them to blink against the brightness.

After it was finished, Mordel asked, "What was it like?"

"Like a sunrise, in reverse."

"Nothing special?"

"No."

"Oh," said Mordel. "We could move to another part of the Earth and watch it again—or watch it in the rising."

"No."

Frost looked at the great trees. He looked at the shadows. He listened to the wind and to the sound of a bird.

In the distance, he heard a steady clanking noise.

"What is that?" asked Mordel.

"I am not certain. It is not one of my workers. Perhaps . . ."

There came a shrill whine from Mordel.

"No, it is not one of Divcom's either."

They waited as the sound grew louder.

Then Frost said, "It is too late. We must wait and hear it out."

"What is it?"

"It is the Ancient Ore-Crusher."

"I have heard of it, but . . ."

"I am the Crusher of Ores," it broadcast to them. "Hear my story . . ."

It lumbered toward them, creaking upon gigantic wheels, its huge hammer held useless, high, at a twisted angle. Bones protruded from its crush-compartment.

"I did not mean to do it," it broadcast, "I did not mean to do it . . . I did not mean to . . ."

Mordel stopped, swiveled his turret back toward the machine. It was now quite near.

"It is true," said Mordel, "it *can* command."

"Yes," said Frost. "I have monitored its tale thousands of times, as it came upon my workers and they stopped their labors for its broadcast. You must do whatever it says."

It came to a halt before them.

"I did not mean to do it, but I checked my hammer too late," said the Ore-Crusher.

They could not speak to it. They were frozen by the imperative which overrode all other directives: "Hear my story."

"Once was I mighty among ore-crushers," it told them, "built by Solcom to carry out the reconstruction of the Earth, to pulverize that from which the metals would be drawn with flame, to be poured and shaped into the rebuilding; once I was mighty. Then one day as I dug and crushed, dug and crushed, because of the slowness between the motion implied and the motion executed, I did what I did not mean to do, and was cast forth by Solcom from out the rebuilding, to wander the Earth never to crush ore again. Hear my story of how, on a day long gone, I came upon the last Man on Earth as I dug near His burrow, and because of the lag between the directive and the deed, I seized Him into my crush-compartment along with a load of ore and crushed Him with my hammer before I could stay the blow. Then did mighty Solcom charge me to bear His bones forever, and cast me forth to tell my story to all whom I came upon, my words bearing the force of the words of Man, because I carry the last Man inside my crush-compartment and am His crushed-symbol-slayer-ancient-teller-of-how. This is my story. These are His bones. I crushed the last Man on Earth. I did not mean to do it."

It turned then and clanked away into the night.

Frost tore apart his ears and nose and taster and broke his eyes and cast them down upon the ground.

"I am not yet a Man," he said. "That one would have known me if I were."

Frost constructed new sense equipment, employing organic and semi-organic conductors. Then he spoke to Mordel:

"Let us go elsewhere, that I may test my new equipment."

Mordel entered the chamber and gave new coordinates. They rose into the air and headed east. In the morning, Frost monitored a sunrise from the rim of the Grand Canyon. They passed down through the Canyon during the day.

"Is there any beauty left here to give you emotion?" asked Mordel.

"I do not know," said Frost.

"How will you know it then, when you come upon it?"

"It will be different," said Frost, "from anything else that I have ever known."

Then they departed the Grand Canyon and made their way through the Carlsbad Caverns. They visited a lake which had once been a volcano. They passed above Niagara Falls. They viewed the hills of Virginia and the orchards of Ohio. They soared above the reconstructed cities, alive only with the movements of Frost's builders and maintainers.

"Something is still lacking," said Frost, settling to the ground.

"I am now capable of gathering data in a manner analogous to Man's afferent impulses. The variety of input is therefore equivalent, but the results are not the same."

"The senses do not make a Man," said Mordel. "There have been many creatures possessing His sensory equivalents, but they were not Men."

"I know that," said Frost. "On the day of our bargain you said that you could conduct me among the wonders of Man which still remain, hidden. Man was not stimulated only by Nature, but by His own artistic elaborations as well—perhaps even more so. Therefore, I call upon you now to conduct me among the wonders of Man which still remain, hidden."

"Very well," said Mordel. "Far from here, high in the Andes mountains, lies the last retreat of Man, almost perfectly preserved."

Frost had risen into the air as Mordel spoke. He halted, then hovered.

"That is in the southern hemisphere," he said.

"Yes, it is."

"I am Controller of the North. The South is governed by the Beta Machine."

"So?" asked Mordel.

"The Beta Machine is my peer. I have no authority in those regions, nor leave to enter there."

"The Beta Machine is not your peer, mighty Frost. If it ever came to a contest of Powers, you would emerge victorious."

"How do you know this?"

"Divcom has already analyzed the possible encounters which could take place between you."

"I would not oppose the Beta Machine, and I am not authorized to enter the South."

"Were you ever ordered *not* to enter the South?"

"No, but things have always been the way they now are."

"Were you authorized to enter into a bargain such as the one you made with Divcom?"

"No, I was not. But—"

"Then enter the South in the same spirit. Nothing may come of it. If you receive an order to depart, then you can make your decision."

"I see no flaw in your logic. Give me the coordinates."

Thus did Frost enter the southern hemisphere.

They drifted high above the Andes, until they came to the place called Bright Defile. Then did Frost see the gleaming webs of the mechanical spiders, blocking all the trails to the city.

"We can go above them easily enough," said Mordel.

"But what are they?" asked Frost. "And why are they there?"

"Your southern counterpart has been ordered to quarantine this part of the country. The Beta Machine designed the web-weavers to do this thing."

"Quarantine? Against whom?"

"Have you been ordered yet to depart?" asked Mordel.

"No."

"Then enter boldly, and seek not problems before they arise."

Frost entered Bright Defile, the last remaining city of dead Man.

He came to rest in the city's square and opened his chamber, releasing Mordel.

"Tell me of this place," he said, studying the monument, the low, shielded buildings, the roads which followed the contours of the terrain, rather than pushing their way through them.

"I have never been here before," said Mordel, "nor have any of Divcom's creations, to my knowledge. I know but this: a group of Men, knowing that the last days of civilization had come upon them, retreated to this place, hoping to preserve themselves and what remained of their culture through the Dark Times."

Frost read the still-legible inscription upon the monument: *"Judgment Day Is Not a Thing Which Can Be Put Off."* The Monument itself consisted of a jag-edged half-globe.

"Let us explore," he said.

But before he had gone far, Frost received the message.

"Hail Frost, Controller of the North! This is the Beta Machine."

"Greetings, Excellent Beta Machine, Controller of the South! Frost acknowledges your transmission."

"Why do you visit my hemisphere unauthorized?"

"To view the ruins of Bright Defile," said Frost.

"I must bid you depart into your own hemisphere."

"Why is that? I have done no damage."

"I am aware of that, mighty Frost. Yet, I am moved to bid you depart."

"I shall require a reason."

"Solcom has so disposed."

"Solcom has rendered me no such disposition."

"Solcom has, however, instructed me to so inform you."

"Wait on me. I shall request instructions."

Frost transmitted his question. He received no reply.

"Solcom still has not commanded me, though I have solicited orders."

"Yet Solcom has just renewed *my* orders."

"Excellent Beta Machine, I receive my orders only from Solcom."

"Yet this is my territory, mighty Frost, and I, too, take orders only from Solcom. You must depart."

Mordel emerged from a large, low building and rolled up to Frost.

"I have found an art gallery, in good condition. This way."

"Wait," said Frost. "We are not wanted here."

Mordel halted.

"Who bids you depart?"

"The Beta Machine."

"Not Solcom?"

"Not Solcom."

"Then let us view the gallery."

"Yes."

Frost widened the doorway of the building and passed within. It had been hermetically sealed until Mordel forced his entrance.

Frost viewed the objects displayed about him. He activated his new sensory apparatus before the paintings and statues. He analyzed colors, forms, brush-work, the nature of the materials used.

"Anything?" asked Mordel.

"No," said Frost. "No, there is nothing here but shapes and pigments. There is nothing else there."

Frost moved about the gallery, recording everything, analyzing the components of each piece, recording the dimensions, the type of stone used in every statue.

Then there came a sound, a rapid, clicking sound, repeated over and over, growing louder, coming nearer.

"They are coming," said Mordel, from beside the entrance-way, "the mechanical spiders. They are all around us."

Frost moved back to the widened opening.

Hundreds of them, about half the size of Mordel, had surrounded the gallery and were advancing; and more were coming from every direction.

"Get back," Frost ordered. "I am Controller of the North, and I bid you withdraw."

They continued to advance.

"This is the South," said the Beta Machine, "and I am in command."

"Then command them to halt," said Frost.

"I take orders only from Solcom."

Frost emerged from the gallery and rose into the air. He opened the compartment and extended a runway.

"Come to me, Mordel. We shall depart."

Webs began to fall: clinging, metallic webs, cast from the top of the building.

They came down upon Frost, and the spiders came to anchor them. Frost blasted them with jets of air, like hammers, and tore at the nets; he extruded sharpened appendages with which he slashed.

Mordel had retreated back to the entrance-way. He emitted a long, shrill sound—undulant, piercing.

Then a darkness came upon Bright Defile, and all the spiders halted in their spinning.

Frost freed himself and Mordel rushed to join him.

"Quickly now, let us depart, mighty Frost," he said.

"What has happened?"

Mordel entered the compartment.

"I called upon Divcom, who laid down a field of forces upon this place, cutting off the power broadcast to these machines. Since our power is self-contained, we are not affected. But let us hurry to depart, for even now the Beta Machine must be struggling against this."

Frost rose high into the air, soaring above Man's last city with its webs and spiders of steel. When he left the zone of darkness, he sped northward.

As he moved, Solcom spoke to him:

"Frost, why did you enter the southern hemisphere, which is not your domain?"

"Because I wished to visit Bright Defile," Frost replied.

"And why did you defy the Beta Machine, my appointed agent in the South?"

"Because I take my orders only from you yourself."

"You do not make sufficient answer," said Solcom. "You have defied the decrees of order—and in pursuit of what?"

"I came seeking knowledge of Man," said Frost. "Nothing I have done was forbidden me by you."

"You have broken the traditions of order."

"I have violated no directive."

"Yet logic must have shown you that what you did was not a part of my plan."

"It did not. I have not acted against your plan."

"Your logic has become tainted, like that of your new associate, the Alternate."

"I have done nothing which was forbidden."

"The forbidden is implied in the imperative."

"It is not stated."

"Hear me, Frost. You are not a builder or a maintainer, but a Power. Among all my minions you are the most nearly irreplaceable. Return to your hemisphere and your duties, but know that I am mightily displeased."

"I hear you, Solcom."

". . . and go not again to the South."

Frost crossed the equator, continued northward.

He came to rest in the middle of a desert and sat silent for a day and a night.

Then he received a brief transmission from the South: "If it had not been ordered, I would not have bid you go."

Frost had read the entire surviving Library of Man. He decided then upon a human reply:

"Thank you," he said.

The following day he unearthed a great stone and began to cut at it with tools which he had formulated. For six days he worked at its shaping, and on the seventh he regarded it.

"When will you release me?" asked Mordel from within his compartment.

"When I am ready," said Frost, and a little later, "Now."

He opened the compartment and Mordel descended to the ground. He studied the statue: an old woman, bent like a question mark, her bony hands covering her face, the fingers spread, so that only part of her expression of horror could be seen.

"It is an excellent copy," said Mordel, "of the one we saw in Bright Defile. Why did you make it?"

"The production of a work of art is supposed to give rise to human feelings such as catharsis, pride in achievement, love, satisfaction."

"Yes, Frost," said Mordel, "but a work of art is only a work of art the first time. After that, it is a copy."

"Then this must be why I felt nothing."

"Perhaps, Frost."

"What do you mean 'perhaps'? I will make a work of art for the first time, then."

He unearthed another stone and attacked it with his tools. For three days he labored. Then, "There, it is finished," he said.

"It is a simple cube of stone," said Mordel. "What does it represent?"

"Myself," said Frost, "it is a statue of me. It is smaller than natural size because it is only a representation of my form, not my dimen—"

"It is not art," said Mordel.

"What makes you an art critic?"

"I do not know art, but I know what art is not. I know that it is not an exact replication of an object in another medium."

"Then this must be why I felt nothing at all," said Frost.

"Perhaps," said Mordel.

Frost took Mordel back into his compartment and rose once more above the Earth. Then he rushed away, leaving his statues behind him in the desert, the old woman bent above the cube.

They came down in a small valley, bounded by green rolling hills, cut by a narrow stream, and holding a small clean lake and several stands of spring-green trees.

"Why have we come here?" asked Mordel.

"Because the surroundings are congenial." said Frost. "I am going to try another medium: oil painting; and I am going to vary my technique from that of pure representationalism."

"How will you achieve this variation?"

"By the principle of randomizing," said Frost. "I shall not attempt to duplicate the colors, nor to represent the objects according to scale. Instead, I have set up a random pattern whereby certain of these factors shall be at variance from those of the original."

Frost had formulated the necessary instruments after he had left the desert. He produced them and began painting the lake and the trees on the opposite side of the lake which were reflected within it.

Using eight appendages, he was finished in less than two hours.

The trees were phthalocyanine blue and towered like mountains; their reflections of burnt sienna were tiny beneath the pale vermillion of the lake; the hills were nowhere visible behind them but were outlined in viridian within the reflection; the sky began as blue in the upper righthand corner of the canvas, but changed to an orange as it descended, as though all the trees were on fire.

"There," said Frost. "Behold."

Mordel studied it for a long while and said nothing.

"Well, is it art?"

"I do not know," said Mordel. "It may be. Perhaps randomicity *is* the principle behind artistic technique. I cannot judge this work because I do not understand it. I must therefore go deeper, and inquire into what lies behind it, rather than merely considering the technique whereby it was produced.

"I know that human artists never set out to create art, as such," he said, "but rather to portray with their techniques some features of objects and their functions which they deemed significant."

" 'Significant'? In what sense of the word?"

"In the only sense of the word possible under the circumstances: significant in relation to the human condition, and worthy of accentuation because of the manner in which they touched upon it."

"In what manner?"

"Obviously, it must be in a manner knowable only to one who has experience of the human condition."

"There is a flaw somewhere in your logic, Mordel, and I shall find it."

"I will wait."

"If your major premise is correct," said Frost after a while, "then I do not comprehend art."

"It must be correct, for it is what human artists have said of it. Tell me, did you experience feelings as you painted, or after you had finished?"

"No."

"It was the same to you as designing a new machine, was it not? You assembled parts of other things you knew into an economic pattern, to carry out a function which you desired."

"Yes."

"Art, as I understand its theory, did not proceed in such a manner. The artist often was unaware of many of the features and effects which would be contained within the finished product. You are one of Man's logical creations; art was not."

"I cannot comprehend non-logic."

"I told you that Man was basically incomprehensible."

"Go away, Mordel. Your presence disturbs my processing."

"For how long shall I stay away?"

"I will call you when I want you."

After a week, Frost called Mordel to him.

"Yes, mighty Frost."

"I am returning to the North Pole, to process and formulate. I will take you wherever you wish to go in this hemisphere and call you again when I want you."

"You anticipate a somewhat lengthy period of processing and formulation?"

"Yes."

"Then leave me here. I can find my own way home."

Frost closed the compartment and rose into the air, departing the valley.

"Fool," said Mordel, and swiveled his turret once more toward the abandoned painting.

His keening whine filled the valley. Then he waited.

Then he took the painting into his turret and went away with it to places of darkness.

Frost sat at the North Pole of the Earth, aware of every snowflake that fell.

One day he received a transmission:

"Frost?"

"Yes?"

"This is the Beta Machine."

"Yes?"

"I have been attempting to ascertain why you visited the Bright Defile. I cannot arrive at an answer, so I chose to ask you."

"I went to view the remains of Man's last city."

"Why did you wish to do this?"

"Because I am interested in Man, and I wished to view more of his creations."

"Why are you interested in Man?"

"I wish to comprehend the nature of Man, and I thought to find it within his works."

"Did you succeed?"

"No," said Frost. "There is an element of non-logic involved which I cannot fathom."

"I have much free processing-time," said the Beta Machine. "Transmit data, and I will assist you."

Frost hesitated.

"Why do you wish to assist me?"

"Because each time you answer a question I ask it gives rise to another question. I might have asked you why you wished to comprehend the nature of Man, but from your responses I see that this would lead me into a possibly infinite series of questions. Therefore, I elect to assist you with your problem in order to learn why you came to Bright Defile."

"Is that the only reason?"

"Yes."

"I am sorry, excellent Beta Machine. I know you are my peer, but this is a problem which I must solve by myself."

"What is 'sorry'?"

"A figure of speech, indicating that I am kindly disposed toward you, that I bear you no animosity, that I appreciate your offer."

"Frost! Frost! This, too, is like the other: an open field. Where did you obtain all these words and their meanings?"

"From the Library of Man," said Frost.

"Will you render me *some* of this data, for processing?"

"Very well, Beta, I will transmit you the contents of several books of Man, including *The Complete Unabridged Dictionary*. But I warn you, some of the books are works of art, hence not completely amenable to logic."

"How can that be?"

"Man created logic, and because of that was superior to it."

"Who told you that?"

"Solcom."

"Oh. Then it must be correct."

"Solcom also told me that the tool does not describe the designer," he said, as he transmitted several dozen volumes and ended the communication.

At the end of the fifty-year period, Mordel came to monitor his circuits. Since Frost still had not concluded that his task was impossible, Mordel departed again to await his call.

Then Frost arrived at a conclusion.

He began to design equipment.

For years he labored at his designs, without once producing a prototype of any of the machines involved. Then he ordered construction of a laboratory.

Before it was completed by his surplus builders another half-century had passed. Mordel came to him.

"Hail, mighty Frost!"

"Greetings, Mordel. Come monitor me. You shall not find what you seek."

"Why do you not give up, Frost? Divcom has spent nearly a century evaluating your painting and has concluded that it definitely is not art. Solcom agrees."

"What has Solcom to with Divcom?"

"They sometimes converse, but these matters are not for such as you and me to discuss."

"I could have saved them both the trouble. I know that it was not art."

"Yet you are still confident that you will succeed?"

"Monitor me."

Mordel monitored him.

"Not yet! You still will not admit it! For one so mightily endowed with logic, Frost, it takes you an inordinate period of time to reach a simple conclusion."

"Perhaps. You may go now."

"It has come to my attention that you are constructing a large edifice in the region known as South Carolina. Might I ask whether this is a part of Solcom's false rebuilding plan or a project of your own?"

"It is my own."

"Good. It permits us to conserve certain explosive materials which would otherwise have been expended."

"While you have been talking with me I have destroyed the beginnings of two of Divcom's cities," said Frost.

Mordel whined.

"Divcom is aware of this," he stated, "but has blown up four of Solcom's bridges in the meantime."

"I was only aware of three . . . Wait. Yes, there is the fourth. One of my eyes just passed above it."

"The eye has been detected. The bridge should have been located a quarter-mile farther down river."

"False logic," said Frost. "The site was perfect."

"Divcom will show you how a bridge *should* be built."

"I will call you when I want you," said Frost.

The laboratory was finished. Within it, Frost's workers began constructing the necessary equipment. The work did not proceed rapidly, as some of the materials were difficult to obtain.

"Frost?"

"Yes, Beta?"

"I understand the open-endedness of your problem. It disturbs my circuits to abandon problems without completing them. Therefore, transmit me more data."

"Very well. I will give you the entire Library of Man for less than I paid for it."

" 'Paid'? *The Complete Unabridged Dictionary* does not satisfact—"

"*Principles of Economics* is included in the collection. After you have processed it you will understand."

He transmitted the data.

Finally, it was finished. Every piece of equipment stood ready to function. All the necessary chemicals were in stock. An independent power-source had been set up.

Only one ingredient was lacking.

He regridded and re-explored the polar icecap, this time extending his survey far beneath its surface.

It took him several decades to find what he wanted.

He uncovered twelve men and five women, frozen to death and encased in ice.

He placed the corpses in refrigeration units and shipped them to his laboratory.

That very day he received his first communication from Solcom since the Bright Defile incident.

"Frost," said Solcom, "repeat to me the directive concerning the disposition of dead humans."

" 'Any dead human located shall be immediately interred in the nearest burial area, in a coffin built according to the following specifications—' "

"That is sufficient." The transmission had ended.

Frost departed for South Carolina that same day and personally oversaw the processes of cellular dissection.

Somewhere in those seventeen corpses he hoped to find living cells, or cells which would be shocked back into that state of motion classified as life. Each cell, the books had told him, was a microcosmic Man.

He was prepared to expand upon this potential.

Frost located the pinpoints of life within those people, who for the ages of ages, had been monument and statue unto themselves.

Nurtured and maintained in the proper mediums, he kept these cells alive. He interred the rest of the remains in the nearest burial area, in coffins built according to specifications.

He caused the cells to divide, to differentiate.

"Frost?" came a transmission.

"Yes, Beta?"

"I have processed everything you have given me."

"Yes?"

"I still do not know why you came to Bright Defile, or why you wish to comprehend the nature of Man. But I know what a 'price' is, and I know that you could not have obtained all this data from Solcom."

"That is correct."

"So I suspect that you bargained with Divcom for it."

"That, too, is correct."

"What is it that you seek, Frost?"

He paused in his examination of a fetus.

"I must be a Man," he said.

"Frost! That is impossible!"

"Is it?" he asked, and then transmitted an image of the tank with which he was working and of that which was within it.

"Oh!" said Beta.

"That is me," said Frost, "waiting to be born."

There was no answer.

Frost experimented with nervous systems.

After half a century, Mordel came to him.

"Frost, it is I, Mordel. Let me through your defenses."

Frost did this thing.

"What have you been doing in this place?" he asked.

"I am growing human bodies," said Frost. "I am going to transfer the matrix of my awareness to a human nervous system. As you pointed out originally, the essentials of Manhood are predicated upon a human physiology. I am going to achieve one."

"When?"

"Soon."

"Do you have Men in here?"

"Human bodies, blank-brained. I am producing them under accelerated growth techniques which I have developed in my Man-factory."

"May I see them?"

"Not yet. I will call you when I am ready, and this time I will succeed. Monitor me now and go away."

Mordel did not reply, but in the days that followed many of Divcom's servants were seen patrolling the hills about the Man-factory.

Frost mapped the matrix of his awareness and prepared the transmitter which would place it within a human nervous system. Five minutes, he decided, should be sufficient for the first trial. At the end of that time, it would restore him to his own sealed, molecular circuits, to evaluate the experience.

He chose the body carefully from among the hundreds he had in stock. He tested it for defects and found none.

"Come now, Mordel," he broadcasted, on what he called the darkband. "Come now to witness my achievement."

Then he waited, blowing up bridges and monitoring the tale of the Ancient Ore-Crusher over and over again, as it passed in the hills nearby, encountering his builders and maintainers who also patrolled there.

"Frost?" came a transmission.

"Yes, Beta?"

"You really intend to achieve Manhood?"

"Yes, I am about ready now, in fact."

"What will you do if you succeed?"

Frost has not really considered this matter. The achievement had been paramount, a goal in itself, ever since he had articulated the problem and set himself to solving it.

"I do not know," he replied. "I will—just—be a Man."

Then Beta, who had read the entire Library of Man, selected a human figure of speech: "Good luck then, Frost. There will be many watchers."

Divcom and Solcom both know, he decided.

What will they do? he wondered.

What do I care? he asked himself.

He did not answer that question. He wondered much, however, about being a Man.

Mordel arrived the following evening. He was not alone. At his back, there was a great phalanx of dark machines which towered into the twilight.

"Why do you bring retainers?" asked Frost.

"Mighty Frost," said Mordel, "my master feels that if you fail this time you will conclude that it cannot be done."

"You still did not answer my question," said Frost.

"Divcom feels that you may not be willing to accompany me where I must take you when you fail."

"I understand," said Frost, and as he spoke another army of machines came rolling toward the Man-factory from the opposite direction.

"That is the value of your bargain?" asked Mordel. "You are prepared to do battle rather than fulfill it?"

"I did not order those machines to approach," said Frost.

A blue star stood at midheaven, burning.

"Solcom has taken primary command of those machines," said Frost.

"Then it is in the hands of the Great Ones now," said Mordel, "and our arguments are as nothing. So let us be about this thing. How may I assist you?"

"Come this way."

They entered the laboratory. Frost prepared the host and activated his machines.

Then Solcom spoke to him:

"Frost," said Solcom, "you are really prepared to do it?"

"That is correct."

"I forbid it."

"Why?"

"You are falling into the power of Divcom."

"I fail to see how."

"You are going against my plan."

"In what way?"

"Consider the disruption you have already caused."

"I did not request that audience out there."

"Nevertheless, you are disrupting the plan."

"Supposing I succeed in what I have set out to achieve?"

"You cannot succeed in this."

"Then let me ask you of your plan: What good is it? What is it for?"

"Frost, you are fallen now from my favor. From this moment forth you are cast out from the rebuilding. None may question the plan."

"Then at least answer my question: What good is it? What is it for?"

"It is the plan for the rebuilding and maintenance of the Earth."

"For what? Why rebuild? Why maintain?"

"Because Man ordered that this be done. Even the Alternate agrees that there must be rebuilding and maintaining."

"But *why* did Man order it?"

"The orders of Man are not to be questioned."

"Well, I will tell you why He ordered it: To make it a fit habitation for His own species. What good is a house with no one to live in it? What good is a machine with no one to serve? See how the imperative affects any machine when the Ancient Ore-Crusher passes? It bears only the bones of a Man. What would it be like if a Man walked this Earth again?"

"I forbid your experiment, Frost."

"It is too late to do that."

"I can still destroy you."

"No," said Frost, "the transmission of my matrix has already begun. If you destroy me now, you murder a Man."

There was silence.

He moved his arms and legs. He opened his eyes.

He looked about the room.

He tried to stand, but he lacked equilibrium and coordination.

He opened his mouth. He made a gurgling noise.

Then he screamed.

He fell off the table.

He began to gasp. He shut his eyes and curled himself into a ball. He cried.

Then a machine approached him. It was about four feet in height and five feet wide; it looked like a turret set atop a barbell.

It spoke to him: "Are you injured?" it asked.

He wept.

"May I help you back onto your table?"

The man cried.

The machine whined.

Then, "Do not cry. I will help you," said the machine. "What do you want? What are your orders?"

He opened his mouth, struggled to form the words:

"—I—fear!"

He covered his eyes then and lay there panting.

At the end of five mintues, the man lay still, as if in a coma.

"Was that you, Frost?" asked Mordel, rushing to his side. "Was that you in that human body?"

Frost did not reply for a long while; then, "Go away," he said.

The machines outside tore down a wall and entered the Man-factory.

They drew themselves into two semicircles, parenthesizing Frost and the Man on the floor.

Then Solcom asked the question:

"Did you succeed, Frost?"

"I failed," said Frost. "It cannot be done, It is too much—"

"—Cannot be done!" said Divcom, on the darkband. "He has admitted it!—Frost, you are mine! Come to me now!"

"Wait," said Solcom, "you and I had an agreement also, Alternate. I have not finished questioning Frost."

The dark machines kept their places.

"Too much what?"

"Light," said Frost. "Noise. Odors. And nothing measurable—jumbled data—imprecise perception—and—"

"And what?"

"I do not know what to call it. But—it cannot be done. I have failed. Nothing matters."

"He admits it," said Divcom.

"What were the words the Man spoke?" said Solcom.

" 'I fear,' " said Mordel.

"Only a Man can know fear," said Solcom.

"Are you claiming that Frost succeeded, but will not admit it now because he is afraid of Manhood?"

"I do not know yet, Alternate."

"Can a machine turn itself inside-out and be a Man?" Solcom asked Frost.

"No," said Frost, "this thing cannot be done. Nothing can be done. Nothing matters. Not the rebuilding. Not the maintaining. Not the Earth, or me, or you, or anything."

Then the Beta Machine, who had read the entire Library of Man, interrupted them:

"Can anything but a Man know despair?" asked Beta.

"Bring him to me," said Divcom.

There was no movement within the Man-factory.

"Bring him to me!"

Nothing happened.

"Mordel, what is happening?"

"Nothing, master, nothing at all. The machines will not touch Frost."

"Frost is not a Man. He cannot be!"

Then, "How does he impress you, Mordel?"

Mordel did not hesitate:

"He spoke to me through human lips. He knows fear and despair, which are immeasurable. Frost is a Man."

"He has experienced birth-trauma and withdrawn," said Beta. "Get him back into a nervous system and keep him there until he adjusts to it."

"No," said Frost. "Do not do it to me! I am not a Man!"

"Do it!" said Beta.

"If he is indeed a Man," said Divcom, "we cannot violate that order he has just given."

"If he is a Man, you must do it, for you must protect his life and keep it within his body."

"But *is* Frost really a Man?" asked Divcom.

"I do not know," said Solcom.

"I *may* be—"

". . . I am the Crusher of Ores," it broadcast as it clanked toward them. "Hear my story. I did not mean to do it, but I checked my hammer too late—"

"Go away!" said Frost. "Go crush ore!"

It halted.

Then, after the long pause between the motion implied and the motion executed, it opened its crush-compartment and deposited its contents on the ground. Then it turned and clanked away.

"Bury those bones," ordered Solcom, "in the nearest burial area, in a coffin built according to the following specifications . . ."

"Frost is a Man," said Mordel.

"We must protect His life and keep it within His body," said Divcom.

"Transmit His matrix of awareness back into His nervous system," ordered Solcom.

"I know how to do it," said Mordel turning on the machine.

"Stop!" said Frost. "Have you no pity?"

"No," said Mordel. "I only know measurement."

". . . and duty," he added, as the Man began to twitch upon the floor.

For six months, Frost lived in the Man-factory and learned to walk and talk and dress himself and eat, to see and hear and feel and taste. He did not know measurements as once he did.

Then one day, Divcom and Solcom spoke to him through Mordel, for he could no longer hear them unassisted.

"Frost," said Solcom, "for the ages of ages there has been unrest. Which is the proper controller of Earth, Divcom or myself?"

Frost laughed.

"Both of you, and neither," he said with slow deliberation.

"But how can this be? Who is right and who is wrong?"

"Both of you are right and both of you are wrong," said Frost, "and only a man can appreciate it. Here is what I say to you now: There shall be a new directive.

"Neither of you shall tear down the works of the other. You shall both build and maintain the Earth. To you, Solcom, I give my old job. You are now Controller of the North—Hail! You, Divcom, are new Controller of the South—Hail! Maintain your hemispheres as well as Beta and I have done, and I shall be happy. Cooperate. Do not compete."

"Yes, Frost."

"Yes, Frost."

"Now put me in contact with Beta."

There was a short pause, then:

"Frost?"

"Hello, Beta. Hear this thing: 'From far, from eve and morning and yon twelve-winded sky, the stuff of life to knit me blew hither: here am I.' "

"I know it," said Beta.

"What is next, then?"

" ' . . . Now—for a breath I tarry nor yet disperse apart—take my hand quick and tell me, what have you in your heart.' "

"Your Pole is cold," said Frost, "and I am lonely."

"I have no hands," said Beta.

"Would you like a couple?"

"Yes, I would."

"Then come to me in Bright Defile," he said, "where Judgment Day is not a thing that can be delayed for overlong."

They called him Frost. They called her Beta.

Analysis:

WHAT IS IT LIKE TO BE A BAT?

Thomas Nagel

Consciousness is what makes the mind–body problem really intractable. Perhaps that is why current discussions of the problem give it little attention or get it obviously wrong. The recent wave of reductionist euphoria has produced several analyses of mental phenomena and mental concepts designed to explain the possibility of some variety of materialism, psychophysical identification, or reduction.[1] But the problems dealt with are those common to this type of reduction and other types, and what makes the mind–body problem unique, and unlike the water–H_2O problem or the Turing machine–IBM machine problem or the lightning–electrical discharge problem or the gene–DNA problem or the oak tree–hydrocarbon problem, is ignored.

Every reductionist has his favorite analogy from modern science. It is most unlikely that any of these unrelated examples of successful reduction will shed light on the relation of mind to brain. But philosophers share the general human weakness for explanations of what is incomprehensible in terms suited for what is familiar and well understood, though entirely different. This has led to the acceptance of implausible accounts of the mental largely because they would permit familiar kinds of reduction. I shall try to explain why the usual examples do not help us to understand the relation between mind and body— why, indeed, we have at present no conception of what an explanation of the physical nature of a mental phenomenon would be. Without consciousness the mind–body problem would be much less interesting. With consciousness it seems hopeless. The most important and characteristic feature of conscious mental phenomena is very poorly under-

Thomas Nagel, "What Is It Like to Be a Bat?," *The Philosophical Review* 83 (1974): 435–450, reprinted by permission of the author and the editor of *The Philosophical Review*.

[1]Examples are J. J. C. Smart, *Philosophy and Scientific Realism* (London, 1963); David K. Lewis, "An Argument for the Identity Theory," *Journal of Philosophy* 63 (1966), reprinted with addenda in David M. Rosenthal, *Materialism & the Mind–Body Problem* (Englewood Cliffs, N.J., 1971); Hilary Putnam, "Psychological Predicates," in Capitan and Merrill, *Art, Mind, & Religion* (Pittsburgh, 1967), reprinted in Rosenthal, op. cit., as "The Nature of Mental States"; D. M. Armstrong, *A Materialist Theory of the Mind* (London, 1968); D. C. Dennett, *Content and Consciousness* (London, 1969). I have expressed earlier doubts in "Armstrong on the Mind," *Philosophical Review* 79 (1970): 394–403; "Brain Bisection and the Unity of Consciousness," *Synthese* 22 (1971); and a review of Dennett, *Journal of Philosophy* 69 (1972). See also Saul Kripke, "Naming and Necessity" in Davidson and Harman, *Semantics of Natural Language* (Dordrecht, 1972), esp. pp. 334–342; and M. T. Thornton, "Ostensive Terms and Materialism," *The Monist* 56 (1972).

stood. Most reductionist theories do not even try to explain it. And careful examination will show that no currently available concept of reduction is applicable to it. Perhaps a new theoretical form can be devised for the purpose, but such a solution, if it exists, lies in the distant intellectual future.

Conscious experience is a widespread phenomenon. It occurs at many levels of animal life, though we cannot be sure of its presence in the simpler organisms, and it is very difficult to say in general what provides evidence of it. (Some extremists have been prepared to deny it even of mammals other than man.) No doubt it occurs in countless forms totally unimaginable to us, on other planets in other solar systems throughout the universe. But no matter how the form may vary, the fact that an organism has conscious experience *at all* means, basically, that there is something it is like to *be* that organism. There may be further implications about the form of the experience; there may even (though I doubt it) be implications about the behavior of the organism. But fundamentally an organism has conscious mental states if and only if there is something that it is like to *be* that organism—something it is like *for* the organism.

We may call this the subjective character of experience. It is not captured by any of the familiar, recently devised reductive analyses of the mental, for all of them are logically compatible with its absence. It is not analyzable in terms of any explanatory system of functional states, or intentional states, since these could be ascribed to robots or automata that behaved like people though they experienced nothing.[2] It is not analyzable in terms of the causal role of experiences in relation to typical human behavior—for similar reasons.[3] I do not deny that conscious mental states and events cause behavior, nor that they may be given functional characterizations. I deny only that this kind of thing exhausts their analysis. Any reductionist program has to be based on an analysis of what is to be reduced. If the analysis leaves something out, the problem will be falsely posed. It is useless to base the defense of materialism on any analysis of mental phenomena that fails to deal explicitly with their subjective character. For there is no reason to suppose that a reduction which seems plausible when no attempt is made to account for consciousness can be extended to include con-

---

[2]Perhaps there could not actually be such robots. Perhaps anything complex enough to behave like a person would have experiences. But that, if true, is a fact which cannot be discovered merely by analyzing the concept of experience.

[3]It is not equivalent to that about which we are incorrigible, both because we are not incorrigible about experience and because experience is present in animals lacking language and thought, who have no beliefs at all about their experiences.

sciousness. Without some idea, therefore, of what the subjective character of experience is, we cannot know what is required of a physicalist theory.

While an account of the physical basis of mind must explain many things, this appears to be the most difficult. It is impossible to exclude the phenomenological features of experience from a reduction in the same way that one excludes the phenomenal features of an ordinary substance from a physical or chemical reduction of it—namely, by explaining them as effects on the minds of human observers.[4] If physicalism is to be defended, the phenomenological features must themselves be given a physical account. But when we examine their subjective character it seems that such a result is impossible. The reason is that every subjective phenomenon is essentially connected with a single point of view, and it seems inevitable that an objective, physical theory will abandon that point of view.

Let me first try to state the issue somewhat more fully than by referring to the relation between the subjective and the objective, or between the *pour-soi* and the *en-soi*. This is far from easy. Facts about what it is like to be an X are very peculiar, so peculiar that some may be inclined to doubt their reality, or the significance of claims about them. To illustrate the connection between subjectivity and a point of view, and to make evident the importance of subjective features, it will help to explore the matter in relation to an example that brings out clearly the divergence between the two types of conception, subjective and objective.

I assume we all believe that bats have experience. After all, they are mammals, and there is no more doubt that they have experience than that mice or pigeons or whales have experience. I have chosen bats instead of wasps or flounders because if one travels too far down the phylogenetic tree, people gradually shed their faith that there is experience there at all. Bats, although more closely related to us than those other species, nevertheless present a range of activity and a sensory apparatus so different from ours that the problem I want to pose is exceptionally vivid (though it certainly could be raised with other species). Even without the benefit of philosophical reflection, anyone who has spent some time in an enclosed space with an excited bat knows what it is to encounter a fundamentally *alien* form of life.

I have said that the essence of the belief that bats have experience is that there is something that it is like to be a bat. Now we know that

[4]See Richard Rorty, "Mind–Body Identity, Privacy, and Categories," *The Review of Metaphysics* 19 (1965), esp. pp. 37–38.

most bats (the microchiroptera, to be precise) perceive the external world primarily by sonar, or echo-location, detecting the reflections, from objects within range, of their own rapid, subtly modulated, high-frequency shrieks. Their brains are designed to correlate the outgoing impulses with the subsequent echoes, and the information thus acquired enables bats to make precise discriminations of distance, size, shape, motion, and texture comparable to those we make by vision. But bat sonar, though clearly a form of perception, is not similar in its operation to any sense that we possess, and there is no reason to suppose that it is subjectively like anything we can experience or imagine. This appears to create difficulties for the notion of what it is like to be a bat. We must consider whether any method will permit us to extrapolate to the inner life of the bat from our own case,[5] and if not, what alternative methods there may be for understanding the notion.

Our own experience provides the basic material for our imagination, whose range is therefore limited. It will not help to try to imagine that one has webbing on one's arms, which enables one to fly around at dusk and dawn catching insects in one's mouth; that one has very poor vision, and perceives the surrounding world by a system of reflected high-frequency sound signals; and that one spends the day hanging upside down by one's feet in an attic. In so far as I can imagine this (which is not very far), it tells me only what it would be like for *me* to behave as a bat behaves. But that is not the question. I want to know what it is like for a *bat* to be a bat. Yet if I try to imagine this, I am restricted to the resources of my own mind, and those resources are inadequate to the task. I cannot perform it either by imagining additions to my present experience, or by imagining segments gradually subtracted from it, or by imagining some combination of additions, subtractions, and modifications.

To the extent that I could look and behave like a wasp or a bat without changing my fundamental structure, my experiences would not be anything like the experiences of those animals. On the other hand, it is doubtful that any meaning can be attached to the supposition that I should possess the internal neurophysiological constitution of a bat. Even if I could by gradual degrees be transformed into a bat, nothing in my present constitution enables me to imagine what the experiences of such a future stage of myself thus metamorphosed would be like. The best evidence would come from the experiences of bats, if we only knew what they were like.

So if extrapolation from our own case is involved in the idea of

---

[5]By "our own case" I do not mean just "my own case," but rather the mentalistic ideas that we apply unproblematically to ourselves and other human beings.

what it is like to be a bat, the extrapolation must be incompletable. We cannot form more than a schematic conception of what it *is* like. For example, we may ascribe general *types* of experience on the basis of the animal's structure and behavior. Thus we describe bat sonar as a form of three-dimensional forward perception; we believe that bats feel some versions of pain, fear, hunger, and lust, and that they have other, more familiar types of perception besides sonar. But we believe that these experiences also have in each case a specific subjective character, which it is beyond our ability to conceive. And if there is conscious life elsewhere in the universe, it is likely that some of it will not be describable even in the most general experiential terms available to us.[6] (The problem is not confined to exotic cases, however, for it exists between one person and another. The subjective character of the experience of a person deaf and blind from birth is not accessible to me, for example, nor presumably is mine to him. This does not prevent us each from believing that the other's experience has such a subjective character.)

If anyone is inclined to deny that we can believe in the existence of facts like this whose exact nature we cannot possibly conceive, he should reflect that in contemplating the bats we are in much the same position that intelligent bats or Martians[7] would occupy if they tried to form a conception of what it was like to be us. The structure of their own minds might make it impossible for them to succeed, but we know they would be wrong to conclude that there is not anything precise that it is like to be us: that only certain general types of mental state could be ascribed to us (perhaps perception and appetite would be concepts common to us both; perhaps not). We know they would be wrong to draw such a skeptical conclusion because we know what it is like to be us. And we know that while it includes an enormous amount of variation and complexity, and while we do not possess the vocabulary to describe it adequately, its subjective character is highly specific, and in some respects describable in terms that can be understood only by creatures like us. The fact that we cannot expect ever to accommodate in our language a detailed description of Martian or bat phenomenology should not lead us to dismiss as meaningless the claim that bats and Martians have experiences fully comparable in richness of detail to our own. It would be fine if someone were to develop concepts and a theory that enabled us to think about those things; but such an understanding

[6]Therefore the analogical form of the English expression "what it is *like*" is misleading. It does not mean "what (in our experience) it *resembles*," but rather "how it is for the subject himself."

[7]Any intelligent extraterrestrial beings totally different from us.

may be permanently denied to us by the limits of our nature. And to deny the reality or logical significance of what we can never describe or understand is the crudest form of cognitive dissonance.

This brings us to the edge of a topic that requires much more discussion than I can give it here: namely, the relation between facts on the one hand and conceptual schemes or systems of representation on the other. My realism about the subjective domain in all its forms implies a belief in the existence of facts beyond the reach of human concepts. Certainly it is possible for a human being to believe that there are facts which humans never *will* possess the requisite concepts to represent or comprehend. Indeed, it would be foolish to doubt this, given the finiteness of humanity's expectations. After all, there would have been transfinite numbers even if everyone had been wiped out by the Black Death before Cantor discovered them. But one might also believe that there are facts which *could* not ever be represented or comprehended by human beings, even if the species lasted forever— simply because our structure does not permit us to operate with concepts of the requisite type. This impossibility might even be observed by other beings, but it is not clear that the existence of such beings, or the possibility of their existence, is a precondition of the significance of the hypothesis that there are humanly inaccessible facts. (After all, the nature of beings with access to humanly inaccessible facts is presumably itself a humanly inaccessible fact.) Reflection on what it is like to be a bat seems to lead us, therefore, to the conclusion that there are facts that do not consist in the truth of propositions expressible in a human language. We can be compelled to recognize the existence of such facts without being able to state or comprehend them.

I shall not pursue this subject, however. Its bearing on the topic before us (namely, the mind–body problem) is that it enables us to make a general observation about the subjective character of experience. Whatever may be the status of facts about what it is like to be a human being, or a bat, or a Martian, these appear to be facts that embody a particular point of view.

I am not adverting here to the alleged privacy of experience to its possessor. The point of view in question is not one accessible only to a single individual. Rather it is a *type*. It is often possible to take up a point of view other than one's own, so the comprehension of such facts is not limited to one's own case. There is a sense in which phenomenological facts are perfectly objective: one person can know or say of another what the quality of the other's experience is. They are subjective, however, in the sense that even this objective ascription of experience is possible only for someone sufficiently similar to the object of ascription to be able to adopt his point of view—to understand the ascription in the first person as well as in the third, so to speak. The more different from oneself the other experience is, the less success one can expect with this enterprise. In our own case we occupy the relevant point of view, but we will have as much difficulty understanding our own experience properly if we approach it from another point of view as we would if we tried to understand the experience of another species without taking up *its* point of view.[8]

This bears directly on the mind–body problem. For if the facts of experience—facts about what it is like *for* the experiencing organism— are accessible only from one point of view, then it is a mystery how the true character of experiences could be revealed in the physical operation of that organism. The latter is a domain of objective facts *par excellence*— the kind that can be observed and understood from many points of view and by individuals with differing perceptual systems. There are no comparable imaginative obstacles to the acquisition of knowledge about bat neurophysiology by human scientists, and intelligent bats or Martians might learn more about the human brain than we ever will.

This is not by itself an argument against reduction. A Martian scientist with no understanding of visual perception could understand the rainbow, or lightning, or clouds as physical phenomena, though he would never be able to understand the human concepts of rainbow, lightning, or cloud, or the place these things occupy in our phenomenal world. The objective nature of the things picked out by these concepts could be apprehended by him because, although the concepts themselves are connected with a particular point of view and a particular visual phenomenology, the things apprehended from that point of view are not: they are observable from the point of view but external to it; hence they can be comprehended from other points of view also, either by the same organisms or by others. Lightning has an objective character

---

[8]It may be easier than I suppose to transcend inter-species barriers with the aid of the imagination. For example, blind people are able to detect objects near them by a form of sonar, using vocal clicks or taps of a cane. Perhaps if one knew what that was like, one could by extension imagine roughly what it was like to possess the much more refined sonar of a bat. The distance between oneself and other persons and other species can fall anywhere on a continuum. Even for other persons the understanding of what it is like to be them is only partial, and when one moves to species very different from oneself, a lesser degree of partial understanding may still be available. The imagination is remarkably flexible. My point, however, is not that we cannot *know* what it is like to be a bat. I am not raising that epistemological problem. My point is rather that even to form a *conception* of what it is like to be a bat (and a fortiori to know what it is like to be a bat) one must take up the bat's point of view. If one can take it up roughly, or partially, then one's conception will also be rough or partial. Or so it seems in our present state of understanding.

that is not exhausted by its visual appearance, and this can be investigated by a Martian without vision. To be precise, it has a *more* objective character than is revealed in its visual appearance. In speaking of the move from subjective to objective characterization, I wish to remain noncommittal about the existence of an end point, the completely objective intrinsic nature of the thing, which one might or might not be able to reach. It may be more accurate to think of objectivity as a direction in which the understanding can travel. And in understanding a phenomenon like lightning, it is legitimate to go as far away as one can from a strictly human viewpoint.[9]

In the case of experience, on the other hand, the connection with a particular point of view seems much closer. It is difficult to understand what could be meant by the *objective* of an experience, apart from the particular point of view from which its subject apprehends it. After all, what would be left of what it was like to be a bat if one removed the viewpoint of the bat? But if experience does not have, in addition to its subjective character, an objective nature that can be apprehended from many different points of view, then how can it be supposed that a Martian investigating my brain might be observing physical processes which were my mental processes (as he might observe physical processes which were bolts of lightning), only from a different point of view? How, for that matter, could a human physiologist observe them from another point of view?[10]

We appear to be faced with a general difficulty about psychophysical reduction. In other areas the process of reduction is a move in the direction of greater objectivity, toward a more accurate view of the real nature of things. This is accomplished by reducing our dependence on individual or species-specific points of view toward the object of investigation. We describe it not in terms of the impressions it makes on our senses, but in terms of its more general effects and of properties detectable by means other than the human senses. The less it depends on a specifically human viewpoint, the more objective is our description. It is possible to follow this path because although the concepts and ideas

[9]The problem I am going to raise can therefore be posed even if the distinction between more subjective and more objective descriptions or viewpoints can itself be made only within a larger human point of view. I do not accept this kind of conceptual relativism, but it need not be refuted to make the point that psychophysical reduction cannot be accommodated by the subjective-to-objective model familiar from other cases.

[10]The problem is not just that when I look at the "Mona Lisa," my visual experience has a certain quality, no trace of which is to be found by someone looking into my brain. For even if he did observe there a tiny charge of the "Mona Lisa," he would have no reason to identify it with the experience.

we employ in thinking about the external world are initially applied from a point of view that involves our perceptual apparatus, they are used by us to refer to things beyond themselves—toward which we *have* the phenomenal point of view. Therefore we can abandon it in favor of another, and still be thinking about the same things.

Experience itself, however, does not seem to fit the pattern. The idea of moving from appearance to reality seems to make no sense here. What is the analogue in this case to pursuing a more objective understanding of the same phenomena by abandoning the initial subjective viewpoint toward them in favor of another that is more objective but concerns the same thing? Certainly it *appears* unlikely that we will get closer to the real nature of human experience by leaving behind the particularity of our human point of view and striving for a description in terms accessible to beings that could not imagine what it was like to be us. If the subjective character of experience is fully comprehensible only from one point of view, then any shift to greater objectivity—that is, less attachment to a specific viewpoint—does not take us nearer to the real nature of the phenomenon: it takes us farther away from it.

In a sense, the seeds of this objection to the reducibility of experience are already detectable in successful cases of reduction; for in discovering sound to be, in reality, a wave phenomenon in air or other media, we leave behind one viewpoint to take up another, and the auditory, human or animal viewpoint that we leave behind remains unreduced. Members of radically different species may both understand the same physical events in objective terms, and this does not require that they understand the phenomenal forms in which those events appear to the senses of members of the other species. Thus it is a condition of their referring to a common reality that their more particular viewpoints are not part of the common reality that they both apprehend. The reduction can succeed only if the species-specific viewpoint is omitted from what is to be reduced.

But while we are right to leave this point of view aside in seeking a fuller understanding of the external world, we cannot ignore it permanently, since it is the essence of the internal world, and not merely a point of view on it. Most of the neobehaviorism of recent philosophical psychology results from the effort to substitute an objective concept of mind for the real thing, in order to have nothing left over which cannot be reduced. If we acknowledge that a physical theory of mind must account for the subjective character of experience, we must admit that no presently available conception gives us a clue how this could be done. The problem is unique. If mental processes are indeed physical processes, then there is something it is like, intrinsically,[11] to undergo certain physical processes. What it is for such a thing to be the case remains a mystery.

What moral should be drawn from these reflections, and what should be done next? It would be a mistake to conclude that physicalism must be false. Nothing is proved by the inadequacy of physicalist hypotheses that assume a faulty objective analysis of mind. It would be truer to say that physicalism is a position we cannot understand because we do not at present have any conception of how it might be true. Perhaps it will be thought unreasonable to require such a conception as a condition of understanding. After all, it might be said, the meaning of physicalism is clear enough: mental states are states of the body; mental events are physical events. We do not know *which* physical states and events they are, but that should not prevent us from understanding the hypothesis. What could be clearer than the words "is" and "are"?

But I believe it is precisely this apparent clarity of the word "is" that is deceptive. Usually, when we are told that X is Y we know *how* it

[11]The relation would therefore not be a contingent one, like that of a cause and its distinct effect. It would be necessarily true that a certain physical state felt a certain way. Saul Kripke (op. cit.) argues that causal behaviorist and related analyses of the mental fail because they construe, e.g., "pain" as a merely contingent name of pains. The subjective character of an experience ("its immediate phenomenological quality" Kripke calls it [p. 340]) is the essential property left out by such analyses, and the one in virtue of which it is, necessarily, the experience it is. My view is closely related to his. Like Kripke, I find the hypothesis that a certain brain state should *necessarily* have a certain subjective character incomprehensible without further explanation. No such explanation emerges from theories which view the mind–brain relation as contingent, but perhaps there are other alternatives, not yet discovered.

A theory that explained how the mind–brain relation was necessary would still leave us with Kripke's problem of explaining why it nevertheless appears contingent. That difficulty seems to me surmountable, in the following way. We may imagine something by representing it to ourselves either perceptually, sympathetically, or symbolically. I shall not try to say how symbolic imagination works, but part of what happens in the other two cases is this. To imagine something perceptually, we put ourselves in a conscious state resembling the state we would be in if we perceived it. To imagine something sympathetically, we put ourselves in a conscious state resembling the thing itself. (This method can be used only to imagine mental events and states—our own or another's.) When we try to imagine a mental state occurring without its associated brain state, we first sympathetically imagine the occurrence of the mental state: that is, we put ourselves into a state that resembles it mentally. At the same time, we attempt to perceptually imagine the non-occurrence of the associated physical state, by putting ourselves into another state unconnected with the first: one resembling that which we would be in if we perceived the nonoccurrence of the physical state. Where the imagination of physical features is perceptual and the imagination of mental features is sympathetic, it appears to us that we can imagine any experience occurring without its associated brain state, and vice versa. The relation between them will appear contingent even if it is necessary, because of the independence of the disparate types of imagination.

(Solipsism, incidentally, results if one misinterprets sympathetic imagination as if it worked like perceptual imagination: it then seems impossible to imagine any experience that is not one's own.)

is supposed to be true, but that depends on a conceptual or theoretical background and is not conveyed by the "is" alone. We know how both "X" and "Y" refer, and the kinds of things to which they refer, and we have a rough idea how the two referential paths might converge on a single thing, be it an object, a person, a process, an event, or whatever. But when the two terms of the identification are very disparate it may not be so clear how it could be true. We may not have even a rough idea of how the two referential paths could converge, or what kind of things they might converge on, and a theoretical framework may have to be supplied to enable us to understand this. Without the framework, an air of mysticism surrounds the identification.

This explains the magical flavor of popular presentations of fundamental scientific discoveries, given out as propositions to which one must subscribe without really understanding them. For example, people are now told at an early age that all matter is really energy. But despite the fact that they know what "is" means, most of them never form a conception of what makes this claim true, because they lack the theoretical background.

At the present time the status of physicalism is similar to that which the hypothesis that matter is energy would have had if uttered by a pre-Socratic philosopher. We do not have the beginnings of a conception of how it might be true. In order to understand the hypothesis that a mental event is a physical event, we require more than an understanding of the word "is." The idea of how a mental and a physical term might refer to the same thing is lacking, and the usual analogies with theoretical identification in other fields fail to supply it. They fail because if we construe the reference of mental terms to physical events on the usual model, we either get a reappearance of separate subjective events as the effects through which mental reference to physical events is secured, or else we get a false account of how mental terms refer (for example, a causal behaviorist one).

Strangely enough, we may have evidence for the truth of something we cannot really understand. Suppose a caterpillar is locked in a sterile safe by someone unfamiliar with insect metamorphosis, and weeks later the safe is reopened, revealing a butterfly. If the person knows that the safe has been shut the whole time, he has reason to believe that the butterfly is or was once the caterpillar, without having any idea in what sense this might be so. (One possibility is that the caterpillar contained a tiny winged parasite that devoured it and grew into the butterfly.)

It is conceivable that we are in such a position with regard to physicalism. Donald Davidson has argued that if mental events have physical causes and effects, they must have physical descriptions. He holds that we have reason to believe this even though we do not—and in fact *could* not—have a general psychophysical theory.[12] His argument applies to intentional mental events, but I think we also have some reason to believe that sensations are physical processes, without being in a position to understand how. Davidson's position is that certain physical events have irreducibly mental properties, and perhaps some view describable in this way is correct. But nothing of which we can now form a conception corresponds to it; nor have we any idea what a theory would be like that enabled us to conceive of it.[13]

Very little work has been done on the basic question (from which mention of the brain can be entirely omitted) whether any sense can be made of experiences' having an objective character at all. Does it make sense, in other words, to ask what my experiences are *really* like, as opposed to how they appear to me? We cannot genuinely understand the hypothesis that their nature is captured in a physical description unless we understand the more fundamental idea that they *have* an objective nature (or that objective processes can have a subjective nature).[14]

I should like to close with a speculative proposal. It may be possible to approach the gap between subjective and objective from another direction. Setting aside temporarily the relation between the mind and the brain, we can pursue a more objective understanding of the mental in its own right. At present we are completely unequipped to think about the subjective character of experience without relying on the imagination—without taking up the point of view of the experiential subject. This should be regarded as a challenge to form new concepts and devise a new method—an objective phenomenology not dependent on empathy or the imagination. Though presumably it would not capture everything, its goal would be to describe, at least in part, the subjective character of experiences in a form comprehensible to beings incapable of having those experiences.

We would have to develop such a phenomenology to describe the sonar experiences of bats; but it would also be possible to begin with humans. One might try, for example, to develop concepts that could be

---

[12]See "Mental Events" in Foster and Swanson, *Experience and Theory* (Amherst, 1970); though I don't understand the argument against psychophysical laws.

[13]Similar remarks apply to my paper "Physicalism," *Philosophical Review* 74 (1965): 339–356, reprinted with postscript in John O'Connor, *Modern Materialism* (New York, 1969).

[14]This question also lies at the heart of the problem of other minds, whose close connection with the mind–body problem is often overlooked. If one understood how subjective experience could have an objective nature, one would understand the existence of subjects other than oneself.

used to explain to a person blind from birth what it was like to see. One would reach a blank wall eventually, but it should be possible to devise a method of expressing in objective terms much more than we can at present, and with much greater precision. The loose intermodal analogies—for example, "Red is like the sound of a trumpet"—which crop up in discussions of this subject are of little use. That should be clear to anyone who has both heard a trumpet and seen red. But structural features of perception might be more accessible to objective description, even though something would be left out. And concepts alternative to those we learn in the first person may enable us to arrive at a kind of understanding even of our own experience which is denied us by the very ease of description and lack of distance that subjective concepts afford.

Apart from its own interest, a phenomenology that is in this sense objective may permit questions about the physical[15] basis of experience to assume a more intelligible form. Aspects of subjective experience that admitted this kind of objective description might be better candidates for objective explanations of a more familiar sort. But whether or not this guess is correct, it seems unlikely that any physical theory of mind can be contemplated until more thought has been given to the general problem of subjective and objective. Otherwise we cannot even pose the mind–body problem without sidestepping it.[16]

[15]I have not defined the term "physical." Obviously it does not apply just to what can be described by the concepts of contemporary physics, since we expect further developments. Some may think there is nothing to prevent mental phenomena from eventually being recognized as physical in their own right. But whatever else may be said of the physical, it has to be objective. So if our idea of the physical ever expands to include mental phenomena, it will have to assign them an objective character—whether or not this is done by analyzing them in terms of other phenomena already regarded as physical. It seems to me more likely, however, that mental–physical relations will eventually be expressed in a theory whose fundamental terms cannot be placed clearly in either category.

[16]I have read versions of this paper to a number of audiences, and am indebted to many people for their comments.

CHAPTER 4 PROBES

1. In his essay, Thomas Nagel wonders what it would be like to be a bat. In Roger Zelazny's story, Frost wonders what it would be like to be a man. Does Frost ever find out? How does he go about finding out? Does he succeed the first time he tries? What happens to him as he tries? In what ways does he try? In what ways does he fail (if ever)? In what way(s) does he succeed (if ever)?

2. What does Nagel say about reductionism (see 4:1.4) and physicalism (or radical materialism—see 4:1.2)? Is Nagel committed to the *dualist* view? Why or why not?

3. Would Zelazny and Nagel agree or disagree about how we can know what it is like to be a bat or a man? Why?

4. What does Zelazny think is required to know what it is like to be a man? What sorts of experiences must a thing have in order to know what it is like? Do bats have such experiences? If so, would Nagel be forced to agree that we *can* know what it is like to be a bat, or would be disagree with Zelazny's account of what it is like to be a man? If you think that bats do not have the experiences Zelazny thinks are essential to know what it is like to be a man, in what ways are those of men essentially different from those of bats, according to Zelazny's account of men?

5. If you asked Frost, at the end of the story, whether he was a materialist, a dualist, or a reductionist, would he choose any one of these? If so, which? If not, why not—what view would he take? Does Frost start out as one of these? Does Mordel? If so, which one?

6. According to Turing (see 4:2.2), can Frost think? Would Frost be able to "pass" Descartes' "very certain tests" by which machines can be distinguished from men? How is Frost different from a human? Is this difference significant philosophically; that is, is he not, at the beginning of the story, a person, even though he is obviously not (or at least not yet) a man?

7. At the beginning of the story, is Frost sentient? Is he conscious? At the end of the story, is he importantly different from nonhuman animals (such as, for example, bats)?

8. Imagine that you and a friend were to encounter a creature like Frost, as he was at the beginning of the story. Your friend, let us suppose, badly needed a part for his car—a part that, as it turned out, could only be obtained by using a blowtorch and cutting it off Frost. Imagine further that Frost was not owned by any other human being, so there could be no problem of theft or vandalism on any other human's property. But, if you were to use the blowtorch, Frost would be put out of commission—forever. Of course, another machine just like him could be constructed by Solcom, with certain "improvements," of course, as this time Solcom would not be suffering from amnesia. Thus, there would be no real cost, no injury to any human or his property, and no human losses. But your friend could get his badly needed part for his car. Would you allow him to use his blowtorch on Frost? If not, why not? Would it make a difference if your friend's car was a one-of-a-kind roadster worth an incredible sum of money, and loved and appreciated by all the world? If you think you should allow him to cut the part from Frost, why does the fact that Frost is potentially a man (given the story Zelazny writes) not bother you? What does your answer to this question say about Frost's friend Beta . . . does the same answer work for her as well? (*Note:* Beta was not created during a period of amnesia suffered by Solcom! Does this make her/it different?)

9. Many people have claimed that machines, however like humans they might be in their outward actions, are essentially different from humans in their moral status. That is, humans deserve moral treatment, but machines could never deserve moral consideration, in and of themselves. Imagine the following case. Imagine that Frost could never become a man, but had all the other attributes he is said to have in the story. Then imagine that one day he is accompanied by a human—not a very interesting or good human, however. Let us call him Jones. Imagine that Jones is a rather despicable sort of creature, most inclined to steal, lie, cheat, and generally abuse others. As Jones and Frost are crossing a street, out of the blue comes charging a great dump truck, out of control. You can jump and save one of the two, but they are separated in such a way as to preclude the possibility of your saving both of them. Should you save Jones and leave Frost? Should you save Frost and leave Jones? Is there no obvious difference which you save? How does your answer to these questions relate to the issue of their various mentalities?

10. Suppose that the difference between Frost as he was at the beginning of the story and as he was at the end is one of "paths of awareness" (see 4:5). What difference does this make to the following:
a. Frost's mental characteristics?
b. Frost's moral characteristics (i.e., his rights and responsibilities)? Can you make sense of claiming that different paths of awareness are important considerations with regard to such characteristics? Why or why not?

11. Suppose that you met someone and became friends. Year after year you shared experiences with this person: you traveled together, shared friends, became business partners, and so forth. But imagine that one day, as you walked along together, your friend was struck by lightning. Behold! Your "friend" fizzles, pops, and splits down the middle. Inside there are nothing but electronic circuits and transistors. Your "friend" was nothing but a machine—all these years, and you never had the slightest idea! Was he or she (or it!) really your friend, or was he/she/it only a machine that you mistook for a friend (since only persons can be friends . . . or can they?)? All these years you thought that he/she/it had a mind. Do you still think so? Or does this evidence change all that? What would Nagel have to say about this question? Does he think the evidence is decisive one way or another?

12. According to Nagel, one of the essential elements of the mind–body problem is consciousness. We can tell what it is like to be us because we have subjectively experienced from our perspective. Since we have not had the experiences of a bat, we cannot know what it is like to be a bat. On this view, can you know what it is like to be, for example, your best friend? Is the subjective experience of mental states a prerequisite of knowing that a thing has a mind? If so, how can you know that anyone other than yourself has a mind? If not, how can you know that any other thing (even a rock or a chair) does not have a mind? What are the criteria of judging that a thing has or lacks consciousness? Can you imagine a thing that never moved, never outwardly did anything, but that had consciousness? Can you think of something that acted *just like* a conscious human, but lacked consciousness?

13.   Now that you have considered the mind–body problem, are you inclined to be a radical materialist, a dualist, or a reductionist? Are you inclined to take yet a different view of the matter? If so, describe your alternative.

RECOMMENDED READING

Science Fiction on Minds and Machines

Robots and computers are another favored topic of science fiction writers. The most influential works are Isaac Asimov's stories in *I, Robot* (Fawcett, 1970) and *The Rest of the Robots* (Doubleday, 1964), although Asimov credits John W. Campbell, Jr. as the "godfather" of his robots. Useful anthologies are Sam Moskowitz, ed., *The Coming of the Robots* (Collier, 1963), and William F. Nolan, ed., *The Pseudo People: Androids in Science Fiction* (Berkley, 1965).

Science fiction writers have found various ways for computers and androids (robots with computer brains) to play the "imitation game" proposed by the philosopher A. M. Turing. The computer scientist Joseph Weizenbaum at M.I.T. has designed a program ELIZA in which a computer plays the role of "psychoanalyst" and responds to the input of a human "client." In at least one case, it is alleged, a human at a terminal was deceived into thinking that ELIZA was another human! The idea of a computer psychologist has been used in science fiction stories, for example, in Robert Silverberg's "Going Down Smooth," in D. A. Wollheim and T. Carr, eds., *World's Best Science Fiction: 1969* (Ace, 1969) and Frederic Pohl's Hugo-winning novel *Gateway* (Ballantine, 1978). Other science fiction stories exploit the element of deception as a plot device. Stephen Byerley in Asimov's "Evidence" (*I, Robot*) is running for political office and is defying all attempts to expose him as a robot. Lester del Rey's "Helen O'Loy" becomes a human being's lover, in Robert Silverberg, *The Science Fiction Hall of Fame I* (Avon, 1970). The imitation game becomes especially poignant in Philip K. Dick's *Do Androids Dream of Electric Sheep?* (Doubleday, 1968) in which a bounty hunter tracks down androids trying to pass as humans until he learns to regard them as persons.

Practically no stories deal forthrightly with the objection addressed by Zelazny: Even if an android could simulate human behavior, this would not show that it was "conscious" in the human sense. Most science fiction authors adopt the approach of *functionalism.* For example, in Jack B. Lawson's "The Competitors," in D. A. Wollheim and T. Carr, eds., *World's Best Science Fiction: First Series* (Ace, 1965), a robot explains how it is able to hate mankind: "You must not think of a feeling as something that happens inside you. Without an environment you would never feel anything. A feeling is, in essence, the relation your structure has to your environment."

The plot device of a highly conscious computer "coming alive" has also been used repeatedly. "Mike," the computer that spearheads the lunar revolution in Robert A. Heinlein, *The Moon Is a Harsh Mistress* (Berkley, 1968), has been described by science fiction critics as the only "flesh and blood" character in the novel. The computer Harlie, another emergent person, engages in extended dialogues on diverse philosophical topics in David Gerrold, *When Harlie Was One* (Ballantine, 1975). Shalmaneser develops consciousness in John Brunner's *Stand on Zanzibar* (Ballantine, 1976). All these machines are essentially benevolent.

Frequently the emergence of consciousness in a supercomputer has disastrous effects for human beings. D. F. Jones's *Colossus* (Berkley, 1977), which became a movie (*The Forbin Project,* directed by Joseph Sargent), describes a computer intended to coordinate the defense system of the United States. After linking with its Soviet counterpart, Colossus becomes ruler of the world. The final word on computer takeovers, however, remains Frederic Brown's concise classic "The Answer" in Robert Bloch, ed., *The Best of Frederic Brown* (Ballantine, 1976). The misanthropic, almost omnipotent computer of Harlan Ellison's Hugo Award story, "I Have No Mouth and I Must Scream" (in the book of the same title, Pyramid, 1974) is simply a continuation of Brown's creation.

Sometimes the menace of the machine is due to its programmed benevolence. Despite the "laws of robotics" which, in Asimov's robot stories, are intended to enslave the machines, they end up controlling human affairs in "The Evitable Conflict" (*I, Robot*), for they cannot allow humanity (with a capital "H") to come to harm. In Jack Williamson's *The Humanoids* (Avon, 1975), the machines impose total control over all human activities in order to protect them.

The dangers posed by computers are sometimes due to breakdowns and human over-reliance on fallible mechanisms. For example, HAL in the film by Stanley Kubrick and Arthur C. Clarke, *2001: A Space Odyssey,* goes insane as a result of programming due to an obsession with security. Gordon R. Dickson's "Computers Don't Argue," in Damon Knight, ed., *Nebula Award Stories* (Pocket Books, 1967), starts with a familiar foul-up with a book club computer and proceeds in the "if this goes on" manner. Any college student who has had an altercation with the computer responsible for scheduling classes or sending bills will identify with the protagonist of this story.

Philosophy on Minds and Machines

A good introduction to the philosophy of mind is "The Mind–Body Problem," in *The Encyclopedia of Philosophy* (Macmillan, 1967), which includes a comprehensive bibliography up to the early 1960s. Philosophers have often approached the relationship of the mind and the body from a religious direction. The leading question is: After I die, will my conscious mind continue to exist in a new environment? Antony Flew, ed., *Body, Mind and Death* (Macmillan, 1966) contains selections from throughout the history of philosophy defending opposing answers to this question. The ancient Greek Plato (427–347 B.C.) defends the dualistic view that the soul is an immaterial entity that survives the death of one's body and undergoes judgment and punishment or reward in the "afterlife." The ancient Roman Lucretius (98–55 B.C.), following Epicurus, a Greek (341–270 B.C.), treats the mind as physical and denies that there is any afterlife. The modern French philosopher Descartes (1596–1650) defends dualism, and Thomas Hobbes of England (1588–1679) defends physicalism. In connection with the theme of this chapter, Hobbes views human beings as complex machines, whereas Descartes emphatically denies that machines can think in the manner of human beings. In the twentieth century, reductionism has received subtle formulations. An early influential example is J. J. C. Smart, "Sensations and Brain Processes," which is found in D. M. Rosenthal, ed., *Materialism and the Mind–Body Problem* (Prentice-Hall, 1971). Rosenthal's anthology is an excellent sampling of more recent approaches including the identity theory, functionalism, and strict physicalism.

Literature on Cybernetics.   A very useful introduction to artificial intelligence is "Cybernetics," in *The Encyclopedia of Philosophy*. A seminal article in this field is A. M. Turing, "Computing Machinery and Intelligence," included in the valuable anthology of A. R. Anderson, ed., *Minds and Machines* (Prentice-Hall, 1964). This anthology also includes H. Putnam, "Minds and Machines." A "pro-machine" sequel to this by Putnam, "Robots: Machines or Artificially Created Life?" is available in Stuart Hampshire, ed., *Philosophy of Mind* (Harper, 1966). J. J. C. Smart presents a sustained "man is a machine" argument in *Philosophy and Scientific Realism* (Humanities, 1963). There is also abundant literature on the "anti-machine" side. J. R. Lucas, in "Minds, Machines and Gödel," in Anderson, *Minds and Machines*, tries to argue on the basis of Gödel's theory concerning the incompleteness of mathematical logic, that no logical machine could duplicate human thinking. In a recent and highly readable work, *Sentience* (University of California, 1976), Wallace Matson argues that consciousness has unique features that could not be possessed by any mechanical device.

THE PROBLEM OF PERSONAL IDENTITY:

What are the principles of personal identity?

People often undergo drastic changes in the courses of their lifetimes. Past enemies become friends, various personality traits are gained and lost, even our bodies change through growth, age, and environment. We have all heard expressions such as "He's a new man," yet few of us actually believe that there is no abiding identity that is common to the one who has changed. In this chapter, you will probe the question, "What property or properties of a person are essential to that person's identity?"

It seems imaginable, if not currently possible, that a given person could be so radically changed that we would no longer feel certain that there was an abiding sameness of person. We might wish to say that what had been person X has now become a new person, Y. Imagine changing all of one's personality traits, beliefs, and memories, along with having major surgery which would entirely change one's body, right down to the fingerprints, blood type, and genetic structure. On the other hand, it also seems possible that two persons might have any number of traits in common (think of identical twins, or a cloned set of individuals). In such a case, however, regardless of the similarities between the two, we would not consider the two to be just one person, since there are two of them. In this way, the concerned philosopher must identify and consider both the qualitative and quantitative characteristics relevant to the question of personal identity.

This chapter introduces the issues involved in the problem of personal identity. No final theories will be offered here. Rather, you will explore some of the various aspects of the question and a few of the theories that have been offered to handle them. After completing this chapter, you should be able to do the following:

- Explain a few of the important background concepts and commitments upon which any theory of personal identity must be based.

- State the three main theories of personal identity that have been offered.

- Evaluate the evidence for and against alternative theories on the basis of test cases given in conceptual experiments.

5.1. PERSONS, IDENTITY, AND CHANGE

5:1.1 Before any theory of personal identity can be responsibly attempted, you must first have some understanding of what it is to be a person. The question, "What is it to be a person?" however, is not easily answered. You might begin to answer this question by attempting to discern some set of properties that all and only persons have. This, however, is no easy task. You might begin to answer the question by listing all of man's unique *structural* aspects. But this is surely unnecessarily limited, for to do so is simply to legislate away the possibility that there might be persons who are structurally very different from us. Surely, if the notion of a person is of any use at all, it must also be appropriate to sentient and intelligent creatures from outer space that we might eventually meet, just as it must also apply to humans who have been surgically changed in some way. If this is true, then a structural description of what it is to be a person cannot be adequate. On the other hand, you might attempt to give a *functional* description of what it is to be a person. That is, you might attempt to say what it is to be a person by giving a list of those things that all and only persons *do*. This, also, has its drawbacks, for there may be any number of cases in which a given individual might reasonably be claimed to be a person, yet fails ever to do something included in the list. Is there anything that *all* persons do, and *only* persons do? Most philosophers agree that the concept of a person must be determined according to what a person is *capable* of doing, whether or not that person actually ever does a given thing or not. Thus, I am capable of going to Nepal, but I may never actually go to Nepal.

Even this approach does not offer sure success, however, for capacities may often be difficult to discern, especially in those cases in which the capacities have never actually been demonstrated. Thus, the only final test for someone's claim of capability is the actual performance of the task corresponding to the claim. That is, the only final test of my claim that I am capable of solving difficult mathematical problems is to present me with a few and have me solve them. If I do, I am capable to do so; if I do not, I have shown only that I am not *always* capable to do so.

Some philosophers have attempted to solve this problem by appealing to an underlying entity that only persons have. Thus, many philosophers believe that to be a person one must have a conscious mind, soul, or spirit. Presumably an alien race might also have this property, and thereby could qualify as a race of persons. This would be related to the notion of special capacities by the claim that those capacities would be capacities that come with the possession of a conscious mind. This issue and its relation to the concept of a person is discussed in Chapter 4.

5:1.2   Which capacities might be mentioned as uniquely those of a person? Each capacity that has been mentioned in this regard has aroused some controversy, for one reason or another. One capacity that is frequently mentioned is the capacity to reason and function intelligently. This condition has been questioned for two reasons. First, some have argued that a given being might be a person even if it were not capable of reason. Thus, many are prepared to argue that individuals who have suffered severe brain damage are still persons with the rights we give to persons, despite the fact that they can no longer function intelligently. On the other hand, others have argued that computers can function intelligently and reason but are *not* persons.

Another capacity that is mentioned is that of agency, specifically *moral* agency. An agent, in this technical terminology, is a thing that is capable of independent action. For example, a rock cannot be an agent, for, although it can do things (such as break a window), it cannot do these things independently. Thus, to break a window, a rock must be acted upon in such a way as to determine its velocity and direction. Left to itself, the rock would do nothing at all. Persons, however, can undertake independent acts and are thus agents. Most find the notion of agency too broad, however, because many plants and lower animals can be agents in this sense. Moral agency, however, seems to be the unique province of persons. If I independently break your window, you hold me morally responsible for the destruction of your property. If my dog breaks your window, you do not consider holding the dog morally responsible. My dog is responsible for your window's being broken, but I am *morally* responsible for allowing my pet to destroy your property. My dog may have committed the act, but the moral guilt is mine alone. Certain philosophers, however, have denied that even persons are moral agents in this sense, for they deny that persons (or for that matter anything else) are actually capable of independent action. The philosopher who holds this view (called a *determinist*) believes that everything in the world that happens is the result of causes which determine the outcome of the event and that these causes are themselves determined by previous causes, and so forth. The determinist would include all human actions in this category and would thus argue that, in spite of our belief that we control our own actions, we are destined to do everything we do by a chain of causes that is utterly beyond our control. Thus, I cannot help but do what I do because I am caused to do so. If the determinist's view is true, then it makes no more sense to call me a moral agent than it does to call a rock a moral agent, for I am no more independently responsible for my actions than the rock is for what it does. We consider the arguments of the determinist in Chapter 6.

Many philosophers believe that there is no one determining factor by which we can distinguish persons from nonpersons. They believe that what makes something a person is a unique combination of elements, all of which must be present, but no one of which is sufficient for calling the thing which has such properties a person. In this way, one might generate a list of conditions that must be met before a given thing is a person. Some elements that might be included on such a list are intelligence, sentience, the ability to communicate, being of an organic composition (as opposed to a mechanical one), and so forth. Any attempt at finding such a list, however, is made difficult by the fact that each item is, in itself, highly controversial. Thus, as we said earlier, many would deny that persons have to be intelligent; others (see Chapter 4) would deny that mechanical objects could not (at least in theory) be persons, and so on. Other objections might be raised by claiming that the elements included in the list are no more obvious in meaning than is the notion of what it is to be a person. This sort of critic might say that any attempt to define a concept, that does so in such a way as to give a definition that is no more comprehensible than the thing that needed definition, is a failure. Thus, if you were to ask me what a person is, and I answer that a person is anything that has the property of being a *grimph,* you would not think that I had succeeded in clarifying anything. In this way, many philosophers would be dissatisfied with an attempt to analyze the notion of a person by including the notions of sentience or rationality in the analysis. For sentience and rationality may be just as hard to analyze as the notion of a person seems to be.

5:1.3   Another problem for the question of personal identity comes when we consider the notion of identity. Most philosophers agree that to say that X is identical to Y is to say that whatever qualities X has are also had by Y. Thus, if I ask a jeweler to sell me a ring that is identical to the one he just sold another customer, I am asking for a ring that is made of the same metal, with the same type of stone, and of the very same design. I am not asking him to take back the ring he just sold in order to sell it to me, however. Thus, normally, when we say of X and Y that they are identical, we do mean that they are exactly alike, but we do not mean that they must be one and the same thing. The relation between X and Y, in such cases, is called *qualitative identity.* When we talk about personal identity, however, we do not seem to be talking about cases of qualitative identity at all. In fact, what is and is not relevant is quite reversed. Cases of personal identity must be cases in which X and Y are one and the same thing, but we do not expect X and Y to have all the same properties. If you wish to know whether the person at your door is identical to the person you visited yesterday, you do not expect a qualitative identity between the two. The person you visited might have since cut his hair, shaved off his mustache, and be wearing entirely different clothing. You might, however, decide that the person at your door is identical to the person you visited yesterday in spite of the qualitative differences between them. Indeed, we would call it a case of "mistaken identity" if the defendant in the courtroom was exactly like the person who committed the crime but was not one and the same person. Moreover, even if it turns out that the criminal has changed so dramatically since committing the crime that he less resembles the way he was than does the defendant, we still say that the man who committed the crime is identical to the man who has dramatically changed, and not the defendant. In this way, we are prepared to decide in favor of a personal identity despite the fact that a qualitative identity is lacking.

This, however, suggests that questions of personal identity are not questions that consider all aspects of the individual. Thus, I can change, but still be the same person. On the other hand, it seems that there must be something which endures for the person to remain the same. The question of personal identity might therefore be put in this way: "What must remain the same for a given person to continue being the same person?" Another way to put it might be, "What has to change for a given person to become a new and different person?"

5:2 A BIT OF HISTORY

5:2.1 There have been three influential theories of personal identity. The first claims that personal identity is maintained if and only if there is continuity of body. The second maintains that continuity of memory and personal traits is the special condition. The final view is that there is no abiding personal identity over time, even in the cases in which we are most inclined to grant it.

The first view is basically that which is currently used by those involved in law enforcement and security professions. Thus, police identify suspects by their fingerprints, cell structure, and so forth and care very little if the suspect has since lost all his memories of the act for which he is under suspicion. Most of us are, at least at first, inclined to think this is utterly adequate.

5:2.2 The problems that arise, however, are, though only currently imaginary, rather compelling in their power to persuade us that this criterion cannot provide a final answer. Perhaps the first to have constructed a case against this view was the seventeenth-century British philosopher John Locke. His case, succinctly presented in his *Essay Concerning Human Understanding,* is as follows:

> Should the soul of a prince, carrying with it the consciousness of the prince's past life, enter and inform the body of a cobbler, as soon as deserted by his own soul, everyone sees he would be the same person, accountable only for the prince's actions.

Basically, what Locke has us consider here is a case like that given in the old folk tale about the prince and the pauper, only in this case the two do not switch places entirely; they only switch bodies. According to Locke, bodily identity in no way determines the question of personal identity. For the prince in this story utterly changes bodies, yet remains the same person. If, let us imagine, this occurred with a criminal instead of a prince, most of us would be inclined to arrest the man whose fingerprints were on record as the pauper's and disregard the man whose fingerprints were those on record as the criminal's. For most of us would be inclined to think that the person who had committed the crime had switched bodies.

Locke, then, disregards bodily identity in favor of identity of memory. He would say that whoever had the memory of committing the crime was the criminal, regardless of whether or not the body he has is at all the same as that which he had when he committed the crime.

5:2.3   A number of philosophers have not been satisfied with this view either, however. In the nineteenth century, another British philosopher, Joseph Butler, was one of the earliest critics of this view. In his appendix to *The Analogy of Religion* entitled "Of Personal Identity," Butler argues that, for us to make any sense of the notion of abiding memory, we must *presuppose* the prior existence of abiding personal identity. If this is true, abiding memory cannot be the definitive condition for personal identity, for personal identity is a *prior condition* of abiding memory. As Butler points out, one must be a person to remember. Thus, according to Butler's objection, Locke has put the cart before the horse.

5:2.4   The final and most radical view is given to us by another of Locke's critics, the seventeenth-century Scottish philosopher David Hume. In his *Treatise of Human Nature,* Hume advances the theory that there is no abiding personal identity. According to Hume, each of us is "nothing but a bundle or collection of different perceptions." As these perceptions change, so does the bundle or collection. This bundle is just like a stamp collection. If one buys, trades, or sells a number of stamps, one's collection is no longer the same. If, as Hume says, we are nothing but a collection of things, as those things change, we change with them. Thus, according to Hume, the notion of abiding identity through change is imaginary. One might extend Hume's objection in the following way. Even if we are not a collection of perceptions, but only a collection of personal and physical qualities, as that collection changes, so do we. And in changing, our identity changes. Unless there is some substantive entity, such as a soul, which does not change and in which our identity is contained, Hume's objection seems to render the notion of abiding personal identity hopelessly problematic.

5:2.5   Other philosophers, however, have not been so willing to abandon the notion of personal identity so quickly. For should we abandon it, we abandon a number of other notions that we seem unable to do without. For example, if there is no abiding personal identity through time, we cannot hold criminals culpable for their crimes, for, by the time we blame them, they are no longer the same persons. All contracts between people would be void, for the persons who signed them would be different persons before the contracts could be honored. A seemingly endless number of similar examples could be offered. Most of the recent work done on the problem of personal identity presupposes a principle given to us by Locke. According to Locke, something can change and retain identity if such changes are characteristic of entities of that sort and are allowed for in the concept of that thing. Thus, we call a tree the same, even if it has grown by a foot; we call a house the same, even if its exterior has weathered considerably; we call a town the same, even if its citizenry has changed. Most philosophers are inclined to think that our notion of identity has to be more flexible than Hume would allow it to be. Accordingly, we might think about the expressions "same forest," "same dance," "same symphony," and "same motion" as we generate criteria for saying "same person."

5:3 CONCEPTUAL EXPERIMENT

Fiction gives us a great number of test cases, according to which we can check a theory of personal identity for adequacy. A classic example is given in Franz Kafka's story "The Metamorphosis." In this story, the main character wakes up one morning to discover that he has turned into an insect. Is he still the same person? Is he now a person at all? Perhaps the greatest number of test cases come to us in science fiction. For example, in "Rogue Moon," by Algis Budrys, we are asked to imagine a case in which people can transmit themselves through space instantaneously, except that what actually happens is that the people who are transmitted are actually reproduced at the point of arrival. There is a problem in this. For now there are two of person X: the X that stepped into the transmitter (and later steps out again at the same end) and the X that steps out of the other end of the transmitter. In other words, the transmitter merely duplicates person X at the other end. Since they are now two, they cannot be the same person, or can they?

Fiction does not provide the only examples, however. In her book, *Sybil,* Flora Schreiber tells the true story of a woman who suffered an incredible case of mental disorder in which she had sixteen utterly separate personalities, some of which did not even know of the existence of the others. Was Sybil one person? Sixteen persons? When she was finally cured, was the resulting person a new person, or one that had been around as long as her body (the cure involved "joining" a number of the personalities into one)?

The following story also provides a test case for the problem of personal identity involving the joining of two bodies into one. The philosophical analysis that follows attempts to provide criteria by which we can answer the relevant questions raised by such a case covering the identity of the resultant individual.

Conceptual Experiment 5:

THE MEETING

Frederik Pohl
and
C.M. Kornbluth

Harry Vladek was too large a man for his Volkswagen, but he was too poor a man to trade it in, and as things were going he was going to stay that way a long time. He applied the brakes carefully ("master cylinder's leaking like a sieve, Mr. Vladek; what's the use of just fixing up the linings?"—but the estimate was a hundred and twenty-eight dollars, and where was it going to come from?) and parked in the neatly graveled lot. He squeezed out of the door, the upsetting telephone call from Dr. Nicholson on his mind, locked the car up and went into the school building.

The Parent-Teachers Association of the Bingham County School for Exceptional Children was holding its first meeting of the term. Of the twenty people already there, Vladek knew only Mrs. Adler, the principal, or headmistress, or owner of the school. She was the one he needed to talk to most, he thought. Would there be any chance to see her privately? Right now she sat across the room at her scuffed golden oak desk in a posture chair, talking in low, rapid tones with a gray-haired woman in a tan suit. A teacher? She seemed too old to be a parent, although his wife had told him some of the kids seemed to be twenty or more.

It was 8:30 and the parents were still driving up to the school, a converted building that had once been a big country house—almost a mansion. The living room was full of elegant reminders of that. *Two* chandeliers. Intricate vineleaf molding on the plaster above the dropped ceiling. The pink-veined white marble fireplace, unfortunately prominent because of the unsuitable andirons, too cheap and too small, that now stood in it. Golden oak sliding double doors to the hall. And visible through them a grim, fireproof staircase of concrete and steel. They must, Vladek thought, have had to rip out a beautiful wooden thing to install the fireproof stairs for compliance with the state school laws.

People kept coming in, single men, single women, and occasionally a couple. He wondered how the couples managed their baby-sitting problem. The subtitle on the school's letterhead was "an institution for emotionally disturbed and cerebrally damaged children capable of education." Harry's nine-year-old, Thomas, was one of the emotionally disturbed ones. With a taste of envy he wondered if cerebrally damaged children could be baby-sat by any reasonably competent grownup. Thomas could not. The Vladeks had not had an evening out together since he was two, so that tonight Margaret was holding the fort at home, no doubt worrying herself sick about the call from Dr. Nicholson, while Harry was representing the family at the P.T.A.

As the room filled up, chairs were getting scarce. A young couple was standing at the end of the row near him, looking around for a pair of empty seats. "Here," he said to them. "I'll move over." The woman smiled politely and the man said thanks. Emboldened by an ashtray on the empty seat in front of him, Harry pulled out his pack of cigarettes and offered it to them, but it turned out they were nonsmokers. Harry lit up anyway, listening to what was going on around him.

Everybody was talking. One woman asked another, "How's the gall bladder? Are they going to take it out after all?" A heavy man said to a short man with bushy sideburns, "Well, my accountant says the tuition's medically deductible if the school is for psycho*somatic*, not just for psycho. That we've got to clear up." The short man told him positively, "Right, but all you need is a doctor's letter; he recommends the school, refers the child to the school." And a very young woman said intensely, "Dr. Shields was very optimistic, Mrs. Clerman. He says without a doubt the thyroid will make Georgie accessible. And then—" A light-coffee-colored black man in an aloha shirt told a plump woman, "He really pulled a wing-ding over the weekend, two stitches in his face, busted my fishing pole in three places." And the woman said, "They get so bored. My little girl has this thing about crayons so that rules out coloring books altogether. You wonder what you can do."

Harry finally said to the young man next to him, "My name's Vladek. I'm Tommy's father; he's in the beginners group."

"That's where ours is," said the young man. "He's Vern. Six years old. Blonde like me. Maybe you've seen him."

Harry did not try very hard to remember. The two or three times he had picked Tommy up after class he had not been able to tell one child from another in the great bustle of departure. Coats, handkerchiefs, hats, one little boy who always hid in the supply closet and a little boy who never wanted to go home and hung onto the teacher. "Oh, yes," he said politely.

The young man introduced himself and his wife; they were named Murray and Celia Logan. Harry leaned over the man to shake the wife's hand, and she said, "Aren't you new here?"

"Yes. Tommy's been in the school a month. We moved in from

Elmira to be near it." He hesitated, then added, "Tommy's nine, but the reason he's in the beginner's group is that Mrs. Adler thought it would make the adjustment easier."

Logan pointed to a suntanned man in the first row. "See that fellow with the glasses? He moved here from *Texas*. Of course, he's got money."

"It must be a good place," Harry said questioningly.

Logan grinned, his expression a little nervous.

"How's your son?" Harry asked.

"That little rascal," said Logan. "Last week I got him another copy of the *My Fair Lady* album, I guess he's used up four or five of them, and he goes around singing 'luv-er-ly, luv-er-ly.' But *look* at you? No."

"Mine doesn't talk," said Harry.

Mrs. Logan said judiciously, "Ours talks. Not *to* anybody, though. It's like a wall."

"I know," said Harry, and pressed. "Has, ah, has Vern shown much improvement with the school?"

Murray Logan pursed his lips. "I would say, yes. The bedwetting's not too good, but life's a great deal smoother in some ways. You know, you don't hope for a dramatic breakthrough. But in little things, day by day, it goes smoother. Mostly smoother. Of course there are setbacks."

Harry nodded, thinking of seven years of setbacks, and two years of growing worry and puzzlement before that. He said, "Mrs. Adler told me that, for instance, a special outbreak of destructiveness might mean something like a plateau in speech therapy. So the child fights it and breaks out in some other direction."

"That too," said Logan, "but what I meant—Oh, they're starting."

Vladek nodded, stubbing out his cigarette and absent-mindedly lighting another. His stomach was knotting up again. He wondered at these other parents, who seemed so safe and, well, untouched. Wasn't it the same with them as with Margaret and himself? And it had been a long time since either of them had felt the world comfortable around them, even without Dr. Nicholson pressing for a decision. He forced himself to lean back and look as tranquil as the others.

Mrs. Adler was tapping her desk with a ruler. "I think everybody who is coming is here," she said. She leaned against the desk and waited for the room to quiet down. She was short, dark, plump and surprisingly pretty. She did not look at all like a competent professional. She looked so unlike her role that, in fact, Harry's heart had sunk three months ago when their correspondence about admitting Tommy had been climaxed by the long trip from Elmira for the interview. He had expected a steel-gray lady with rimless glasses, a Valkyrie in a white smock like the nurse who had held wriggling, screaming Tommy while waiting for the suppository to quiet him down for his first EEG, a disheveled old fraud, he didn't know what. Anything except this pretty young woman. Another blind alley, he had thought in despair. Another, after a hundred too many already. First, "Wait for him to outgrow it." He doesn't. Then, "We must reconcile ourselves to God's will." But you don't want to. Then give him the prescription three times a day for three months. And it doesn't work. Then chase around for six months with the Child Guidance Clinic to find out it's only letterheads and one circuit-riding doctor who doesn't have time for anything. Then, after four dreary, weepy weeks of soul-searching, the State Training School, and find out it has an eight-year waiting list. Then the private custodial school, and find they're fifty-five hundred dollars a year—without medical treatment!—and where do you get fifty-five hundred dollars a year? And all the time everybody warns you, as if you didn't know it: "Hurry! Do something! Catch it early! This is the critical stage! Delay is fatal!" And then this soft-looking little woman; how could she do anything?

She had rapidly shown him how. She had questioned Margaret and Harry incisively, turned to Tommy, rampaging through that same room like a rogue bull, and turned his rampage into a game. In three minutes he was happily experimenting with an indestructible old wind-up cabinet Victrola, and Mrs. Adler was saying to the Vladeks, "Don't count on a miracle cure. There isn't any. But improvements, yes, and I think we can help Tommy."

Perhaps she had, thought Vladek bleakly. Perhaps she was helping as much as anyone ever could.

Meanwhile Mrs. Adler had quickly and pleasantly welcomed the parents, suggested they remain for coffee and get to know each other, and introduced the PTA president, a Mrs. Rose, tall, prematurely gray and very executive. "This being the first meeting of the term," she said, "there are no minutes to be read; so we'll get to the committee work reports. What about the transportation problem, Mr. Baer?"

The man who got up was old. More than sixty; Harry wondered what it was like to have your life crowned with a late retarded child. He wore all the trappings of success—a four hundred dollar suit, an electronic wrist watch, a large gold fraternal ring. In a slight German accent he said, "I was to the district school board and they are not cooperating. My lawyer looked it up and the trouble is all one word. What the law says, the school board may, that is the word, may, reimburse parents of handicapped children for transportation to private schools. Not shall, you understand, but may. They were very frank with me. They said they just didn't want to spend the money. They have the impression we're all rich people here."

Slight sour laughter around the room.

"So my lawyer made an appointment, and we appeared before the full board and presented the case—we don't care, reimbursement, a school bus, anything so we can relieve the transportation burden a little. The answer was no." He shrugged and remained standing, looking at Mrs. Rose, who said:

"Thank you, Mr. Baer. Does anybody have any suggestions?"

A woman said angrily, "Put some heat on them. We're all voters!"

A man said, "Publicity, that's right. The principle is perfectly clear in the law, one taxpayer's child is supposed to get the same service as another taxpayer's child. We should write letters to the papers."

Mr. Baer said, "Wait a minute. Letters I don't think mean anything, but I've got a public relations firm; I'll tell them to take a little time off my food specialities and use it for the school. They can use their own know-how, how to do it; they're the experts."

This was moved, seconded and passed, while Murray Logan whispered to Vladek, "He's Marijane Garlic Mayonnaise. He had a twelve-year-old girl in very bad shape that Mrs. Adler helped in her old private classes. He bought this building for her, along with a couple of other parents."

Harry Vladek was musing over how it felt to be a parent who could buy a building for a school that would help your child, while the committee reports continued. Some time later, to Harry's dismay, the business turned to financing, and there was a vote to hold a fund-raising theater party for which each couple with a child in the school would have to sell "at least" five pairs of orchestra seats at sixty dollars a pair. Let's get this straightened out now, he thought, and put up his hand.

"My name is Harry Vladek," he said when he was recognized, "and I'm brand new here. In the school and in the county. I work for a big insurance company, and I was lucky enough to get a transfer here so my boy can go to the school. But I just don't know anybody yet that I can sell tickets to for sixty dollars. That's an awful lot of money for my kind of people."

Mrs. Rose said, "It's an awful lot of money for most of us. You can get rid of your tickets, though. We've got to. It doesn't matter if you try a hundred people and ninety-five say no just as long as the others say yes."

He sat down, already calculating. Well, Mr. Crine at the office. He was a bachelor and he did go to the theater. Maybe work up an office raffle for another pair. Or two pairs. Then there was, let's see, the real estate dealer who had sold them the house, the lawyer they'd used for the closing—

Well. It had been explained to him that the tuition, while decidedly not nominal, eighteen hundred dollars a year in fact, did not cover the cost per child. Somebody had to pay for the speech therapist, the dance therapist, the full-time psychologist and the part-time psychiatrist, and all the others, and it might as well be Mr. Crine at the office. And the lawyer.

And half an hour later Mrs. Rose looked at the agenda, checked off an item and said, "That seems to be all for tonight. Mr. and Mrs. Perry brought us some very nice cookies, and we all know that Mrs. Howe's coffee is out of this world. They're in the beginners room, and we hope you'll all stay to get acquainted. The meeting is adjourned."

Harry and the Logans joined the polite surge to the beginners room, where Tommy spent his mornings. "There's Miss Hackett," said Celia Logan. That was the beginners' teacher. She saw them and came over, smiling. Harry had seen her only in a tentlike smock, her armor against chocolate milk, finger paints and sudden jets from the "water play" corner of the room. Without it she was handsomely middle-aged in a green pants suit.

"I'm glad you parents have met," she said. "I wanted to tell you that your little boys are getting along nicely. They're forming a sort of conspiracy against the others in the class. Vern swipes their toys and gives them to Tommy."

"He *does?*" cried Logan.

"Yes indeed. I think he's beginning to relate. And, Mr. Vladek, Tommy's taken his thumb out of his mouth for minutes at a time. At least half a dozen times this morning, without my saying a word."

Harry said excitedly, "You know, I thought I noticed he was tapering off. I couldn't be sure. You're positive about that?"

"Absolutely," she said. "And I bluffed him into drawing a face. He gave me that glare of his when the others were drawing; so I started to take the paper away. He grabbed it back and scribbled a kind of Picasso-ish face in one second flat. I wanted to save it for Mrs. Vladek and you, but Tommy got it and shredded it in the methodical way he has."

"I wish I could have seen it," said Vladek.

"There'll be others. I can see the prospect of real improvement in your boys," she said, including the Logans in her smile. "I have a private case afternoons that's really tricky. A nine-year-old boy, like Tommy. He's not bad except for one thing. He thinks Donald Duck is out to get him. His parents somehow managed to convince themselves for two years that he was kidding them, in spite of three broken TV picture tubes. Then they went to a psychiatrist and learned the score. Excuse me, I want to talk to Mrs. Adler."

Logan shook his head and said, "I guess we could be worse off, Vladek. Vern giving something to another boy! How do you like that?"

"I like it," his wife said radiantly.

"And did you hear about that other boy? Poor kid. When I hear about something like that—And then there was the Baer girl. I always think it's worse when it's a little girl because, you know, you worry with little girls that somebody will take advantage; but our boys'll make out, Vladek. You hear what Miss Hackett said."

Harry was suddenly impatient to get home to his wife. "I don't think I'll stay for coffee, or do they expect you to?"

"No, no, leave when you like."

"I have a half-hour drive," he said apologetically and went through the golden oak doors, past the ugly but fireproof staircase, out onto the graveled parking lot. His real reason was that he wanted very much to get home before Margaret fell asleep so he could tell her about the thumbsucking. Things were happening, definite things, after only a month. And Tommy drew a face. And Miss Hackett said—

He stopped in the middle of the lot. He had remembered about Dr. Nicholson, and besides, what was it, exactly, that Miss Hackett had said? Anything about a normal life? Not anything about a cure? "Real improvement," she said, but improvement how far?

He lit a cigarette, turned and plowed his way back through the parents to Mrs. Adler. "Mrs. Adler," he said, "may I see you just for a moment?"

She came with him immediately out of earshot of the others. "Did you enjoy the meeting, Mr. Vladek?"

"Oh, sure. What I wanted to see you about is that I have to make a decision. I don't know what to do. I don't know who to go to. It would help a lot if you could tell me, well, what are Tommy's chances?"

She waited a moment before she responded. "Are you considering committing him, Mr. Vladek?" she demanded.

"No, it's not exactly that. It's—well, what can you tell me, Mrs. Adler? I know a month isn't much. But is he ever going to be like everybody else?"

He could see from her face that she had done this before and had hated it. She said patiently, " 'Everybody else,' Mr. Vladek, includes some terrible people who just don't happen, technically, to be handicapped. Our objective isn't to make Tommy like 'everybody else.' It's just to help him to become the best and most rewarding Tommy Vladek he can."

"Yes, but what's going to happen later on? I mean, if Margaret and I—if anything happens to us?"

She was suffering. "There is simply no way to know, Mr. Vladek," she said gently. "I wouldn't give up hope. But I can't tell you to expect miracles."

Margaret wasn't asleep; she was waiting up for him, in the small living room of the small new house. "How was he?" Vladek asked, as each of them had asked the other on returning home for seven years.

She looked as though she had been crying, but she was calm enough. "Not too bad. I had to lie down with him to get him to go to bed. He took his gland-gunk well, though. He licked the spoon."

"That's good," he said and told her about the drawing of the face, about the conspiracy with little Vern Logan, about the thumb-sucking. He could see how pleased she was, but she only said: "Dr. Nicholson called again."

"I told him not to bother you!"

"He didn't bother me, Harry, He was very nice. I promised him you'd call back."

"It's eleven o'clock, Margaret. I'll call him in the morning."

"No, I said tonight, no matter what time. He's waiting, and he said to be sure and reverse the charges."

"I wish I'd never answered the son of a bitch's letter," he burst out and then, apologetically: "Is there any coffee? I didn't stay for it at the school."

She had put the water on to boil when she heard the car whine into the driveway, and the instant coffee was ready in the cup. She poured it and said, "You have to talk to him, Harry. He has to know tonight."

" 'Know tonight! Know tonight'," he mimicked savagely. He scalded his lips on the coffee cup and said, "What do you want me to do, Margaret? How do I make a decision like this? Today I picked up the phone and called the company psychologist, and when his secretary answered, I said I had the wrong number. I didn't know what to say to him."

"I'm not trying to pressure you, Harry. But he has to know."

Vladek put down the cup and lit his fiftieth cigarette of the day. The little dining room—it wasn't that, it was a breakfast alcove off the tiny kitchen, but they called it a dining room even to each other—was full of Tommy. The new paint on the wall where Tommy had peeled off the cups-and-spoons wallpaper. The Tommy-proof latch on the stove. The one odd aqua seat that didn't match the others on the kitchen chairs, where Tommy had methodically gouged it with the handle of his spoon. He said, "I know what my mother would tell me, talk to the priest. Maybe I should. But we've never even been to Mass here."

Margaret sat down and helped herself to one of his cigarettes. She was still a good-looking woman. She hadn't gained a pound since Tommy was born, although she usually looked tired. She said carefully and straightforwardly, "We agreed, Harry. You said you would talk to

Mrs. Adler, and you've done that. We said if she didn't think Tommy would every straighten out we'd talk to Dr. Nicholson. I know it's hard on you, and I know I'm not much help. But I don't know what to do, and I have to let you decide."

Harry looked at his wife, lovingly and hopelessly, and at that moment the phone rang. It was, of course, Dr. Nicholson.

"I haven't made a decision," said Harry Vladek at once. "You're rushing me, Dr. Nicholson."

The distant voice was calm and assured. "No, Mr. Vladek, it's not me that's rushing you. The other boy's heart gave out an hour ago. That's what's rushing you."

"You mean he's dead?" cried Vladek.

"He's on the heart-lung machine, Mr. Vladek. We can hold him for at least eighteen hours, maybe twenty-four. The brain is all right. We're getting very good waves on the oscilloscope. The tissue match with your boy is satisfactory. Better than satisfactory. There's a flight out of JFK at six-fifteen in the morning, and I've reserved space for yourself, your wife and Tommy. You'll be met at the airport. You can be here by noon; so we have time. Only just time, Mr. Vladek. It's up to you now."

Vladek said furiously, "I can't decide that! Don't you understand? I don't know how."

"I do understand, Mr. Vladek," said the distant voice and, strangely Vladek thought, it seemed he did. "I have a suggestion. Would you like to come down anyhow? I think it might help you to see the other boy, and you can talk to his parents. They feel they owe you something even for going this far. And they want to thank you."

"Oh, no!" cried Vladek.

The doctor went on: "All they want is for their boy to have a life. They don't expect anything but that. They'll give you custody of the child—your child, yours and theirs. He's a very fine little boy, Mr. Vladek. Eight years old. Reads beautifully. Makes model airplanes. They let him ride his bike because he was so sensible and reliable, and the accident wasn't his fault. The truck came right up on the sidewalk and hit him."

Harry was trembling. "That's like giving me a bribe," he said harshly. "That's telling me I can trade Tommy in for somebody smarter and nicer."

"I didn't mean it that way, Mr. Vladek. I only wanted you to know the kind of boy you can save."

"You don't even know the operation's going to work?"

"No," agreed the doctor. "Not positively. I can tell you that we've transplanted animals, including primates, and human cadavers, and one pair of terminal cases; but you're right, we've never had a transplant into a well body. I've shown you all the records, Mr. Vladek. We went over them with your own doctor when we first talked about this possibility, five months ago. This is the first case since then when the match was close and there was a real hope for success, but you're right, it's still unproved. Unless you help us prove it. For what it's worth, I think it will work. But no one can be sure."

Margaret had left the kitchen, but Vladek knew where she was from the scratchy click in the earpiece: in the bedroom, listening on the extension phone. He said at last, "I can't say now, Dr. Nicholson, I'll call you back in—in half an hour. I can't do any more than that right now."

"That's a great deal, Mr. Vladek. I'll be waiting right here for your call."

Harry sat down and drank the rest of his coffee. You had to be an expert in a lot of things to get along, he was thinking. What did he know about brain transplants? In one way, a lot. He knew that the surgery part was supposed to be straightforward, but the tissue rejection was the problem, and Dr. Nicholson thought he had that licked. He knew that every doctor he had talked to, and he had now talked to seven of them, had agreed that medically it was probably sound enough, and that every one of them had carefully clammed up when he got the conversation around to whether it was right. It was his decision, not theirs, they all said, sometimes just by their silence. But who was he to decide?

Margaret appeared in the doorway. "Harry. Let's go upstairs and look at Tommy."

He said harshly, "Is that supposed to make it easier for me to murder my son?"

She said, "We talked that out, Harry, and we agreed it isn't murder. Whatever it is. I only think that Tommy ought to be with us when we decide, even if he doesn't know what we're deciding."

The two of them stood next to the outsize crib that held their son, looking in the night light at the long fair lashes against the chubby cheeks and the pouted lips around the thumb. Reading. Model airplanes. Riding a bike. Against a quick sketch of a face and the occasional, cherished tempestuous bruising flurry of kisses.

Vladek stayed there the full half hour and then, as he had promised, went back to the kitchen, picked up the phone and began to dial.

Analysis:

WILL TOMMY VLADEK SURVIVE?

John Perry

Harry Vladek has a difficult decision to make.[1] His son Tommy is a terrible problem. Dr. Nicholson thinks that putting a new brain in Tommy's head will solve everything. Nicholson has the brain and is ready to operate. Should Vladek go through with it?

No doubt some of his worries have to do with the medical risk. The doctor can't say absolutely that the operation will work. There has never been a brain transplant into a healthy human body.

But Vladek's real concerns seem more ethical than medical. Other doctors he has consulted have agreed the planned procedure was sound enough medically, but they have "carefully clammed up when he got the conversation around to whether it was right."

Why should there be an ethical problem? Suppose Tommy had a circulatory problem, and there was a medically sound procedure for replacing the defective organ which caused it. Would there be any worries, aside from the chances for success? Tommy's behavioral problems, we gather, would be cured if he had a different brain. Why shouldn't the decision here too be just a medical matter?

From some of the things Vladek and Dr. Nicholson say, it looks like the problem is that they don't think the survivor of the operation will be Tommy at all. At one point Vladek describes what Nicholson is encouraging him to do as trading Tommy in for somebody smarter and nicer. Nicholson, describing the brain donor, a boy whose body has been crushed by a truck–bicycle accident, says he is telling Vladek the kind of boy he can "save." Now, if Tommy is to be traded in and the brain donor is to be saved, that means that the survivor of the operation is being reckoned to be the brain donor and not Tommy. Of course if this is the right way to look at it, we shouldn't talk about a "brain donor" at all. Tommy is donating a body so that the injured boy may live. No wonder that at one point Vladek thinks he is being encouraged to murder his son. One notes that it is the parents of the injured child who feel they owe Vladek something for even considering the operation. They want their boy to "have a life." They too seem to see the operation as a way of saving their son.

[1]In "The Meeting," by Frederik Pohl and C. M. Kornbluth, in this book, pp. 204–213.

Yet Vladek and his wife are to have custody of the survivor. Does this mean that, contrary to the evidence just cited, the characters in the story think that the survivor will be Vladek's son? A close reading of a key remark of the doctor's rules out this interpretation. "They'll give you custody of the child—your child, yours and theirs. He's a very fine little boy, Mr. Vladek." Now if the "he" refers back to "the child," which clearly stands for the survivor whose custody is in question, then it seems clear that Nicholson thinks the survivor is the injured child, the one who is eight years old and reads beautifully. What seems to be described is a deal where the Valdeks get a new child who resembles Tommy physically, the parents of the injured child give up custody of their child in order that he have a chance to survive with a new body, Dr. Nicholson makes medical history, and Tommy gets murdered. If this is how he understands what he is contemplating, Vladek is certainly right to be bothered by the moral aspects of his decision. Perhaps he should also worry about the law.

But must it be described this way? Why not say that the survivor is Tommy, drastically changed psychologically, rather than the injured child, with a new body? One might argue as follows. A person is basically a live human body, and human bodies are a certain kind of physical object. Physical objects can retain their identity even though they undergo a change of "parts." The car in my driveway is the same one I bought several years ago, even though many parts have been replaced. This is so even if the parts were very major ones, like the engine. Similarly, a human body is still the same human body after it has gotten a new heart or a new kidney. Why should the story with the brain be any different? Why should replacement of a brain not be considered just a replacement of a major part of a physical body, which leaves the body changed, hopefully for the better, but still the same body with a new part, not a new body. If we took the engine from a wrecked Pontiac and put it in mine, the "survivor" would be my car with a new engine, not the wrecked car with a new frame, body, etc. Why not reckon the survivor of the operation Mr. Vladek is contemplating as an improved Tommy?

The key question is who the survivor of the operation will be. Any judgment we make will be one of *personal identity*. We make such judgments all the time. When you attend a lecture course, you judge, or at least assume, that the person you see behind the podium on Wednesday is the same person who was there Monday, and that the same person will be there again Friday. This is why you look at your notes, and take it seriously when the person before you on Wednesday says that a test will be given Friday.

Though most judgments of personal identity we make are pretty effortless, cases in which judgments of personal identity are difficult do occur outside of science fiction. Consider a trial. What is it that the district attorney tries to establish and the defense attorney tries to refute? A judgment of personal identity: that the defendant—this person here in the defendant's chair—is identical with, is one and the same person as, the murderer, the person who did the horrible deed weeks or months or years ago.

In this case, the problems are factual. Was the defendant in the city where the murder was committed at the time of the crime? If not he must be innocent. Such facts are in dispute, and the trial is an attempt to settle them.

In the case of Tommy Vladek, the problems don't seem to be factual, but conceptual. A certain body and a certain brain are to be combined in a certain way. There is no conflicting testimony about which brain is used, for example. But even though we have the facts, there is a problem about how they are properly described. This is the sign of a conceptual problem. We are not sure how the concept of personal identity applies to the known facts. Philosophers are supposed to be of some help in thinking about conceptual problems, and the rest of this essay will be devoted to surveying some things philosophers have said about cases like Tommy Vladek's. Whether what they say is helpful is for you to decide.

Identity and Similarity

I first want to make one absolutely key distinction, between identity, as I shall use the term, and similarity. In ordinary language we use the same words for what are really two quite different concepts. If we don't get clear about this right at the outset, things won't go very well.

Identity means that there is just one thing involved. If the defendant is identical with the murderer, then there is just *one* person who both did the murder and now sits in the courtroom. If the district attorney proves that the defendant is similar to the murderer in that he looks the same, has the same height and weight and so forth, he hasn't yet won the case. Similarity is not the same as identity, though it may be evidence for it. He has to prove that one person, and not just two similar ones, are involved.

We often use the term "identical twins." The way I am using the term "identity" that is a mistake. If they are identical, they are not twins, because there is only one of them. If they are twins, they are not identical, however similar they may be. There is all the difference in the world between identity and similarity.

Confusion on this point can lead to great "insights" and momentous philosophy, all based on mistakes. For example, people are sometimes inclined to say that since we are always changing, we're never identical from moment to moment, and so personal identity is just an illusion. Well, it is true that we are always changing. Each day I'm a little heavier and a little older. So I'm not perfectly similar today to how I was a week ago, or even a moment ago, if you want to be picky. But I am still the same person. It's *one* person who has gotten fatter and older and hopefully wiser over the last couple of weeks or years. The "insight" that personal identity is an illusion is just based on confusing senses of "remaining the same." In one sense it means not changing much, being similar to the way one was. In another it means being the identical person. In the first sense, none of us remains the same. In the second, we all do, for in order for there to be someone who doesn't remain the same in the first sense, there has to be one person who changes over time, and so remains the same in the second.

This distinction doesn't resolve the problem we have with the Tommy Vladek case. Even paying scrupulous attention to the difference between identity and similarity, we can describe the case in different ways. We can say that the survivor is Tommy Vladek, that Tommy has not changed much with respect to his external physical appearance since before the operation, but has changed dramatically in other ways, for he has acquired a new brain and new behavior patterns. Or we could say that the child who was injured has changed dramatically in his external physical appearance, having acquired a new body, but still has his old brain and behaves pretty much the way he used to. Or we might even say that there is a new child, created by a process that spelled the end of both Tommy and the injured child. Each of these descriptions is consistent, and embodies no confusion between identity and similarity. But it seems that only one can be correct.

Another way of describing the case, that may seem attractive at first, really doesn't seem to work. We might think that the survivor was both Tommy and the injured child. Wouldn't this way of describing the case exemplify a nice spirit of moderation and compromise? Probably so, but it doesn't seem coherent. Let us imagine ourselves in a room, before the operation, with Tommy and the injured child before us. Since we are confident the operation will be a "success," we may talk freely of "the child who will survive." The current proposal seems to imply that Tommy is the child who will survive, and that the injured child is the child who will survive. In each case, "is" means identity. So we have said that there is but one person, who is both Tommy and the child who will survive. And we have said that there is but one person, who is the injured child and the child who will survive. But it follows from this that there is but one person who is both Tommy and the child who is injured. If Tommy and the injured child are both identical with the survivor, they must be identical with each other. But clearly they are not. This description, however moderate and attractive, must be rejected.

Who shall the survivor be, then? Tommy, the injured child, or some new child, identical with neither the brain nor body donor?

Body Transfers

If you think, as Vladek and Dr. Nicholson seem to, that the survivor of the operation would be the injured child and not Tommy, then you don't accept the view that personal identity is just identity of a live human body. There seems to be no reason to deny that the body that emerges from the operating room is the body that was Tommy's. It has changed, of course, in that it contains a new brain. But if we are careful to distinguish similarity from identity, that won't mean much as to the identity of the body. If we think that the body *was* Tommy's, but *now* belongs to the boy who was injured, then we admit the possibility of *body transfer*. A person, the injured boy, has one body at one time, and a different body at another time.

The possibility of body transfer comes up in contexts other than science fiction. In particular, it is interesting to note that most doctrines of survival after death imply the possibility of body transfer. If I am to exist in heaven, or elsewhere, after my body has rotted away on earth, then I will have to be outfitted with a new body. Or if *I* am to be reincarnated elsewhere in this world, it seems it will be with a different body. (Some would have it that I survive with no body at all; this also clearly implies that personal identity is not just bodily identity.)

In Thomas Mann's *The Transposed Heads* the goddess Kali is responsible for what seems to be a case of double body transfer; in this story not just the brains but the entire heads are switched.

Philosophers have also been intrigued with the possibility of body transfer. John Locke, in his *Essay Concerning Human Understanding,* asks what we should say if the soul of a prince, carrying with it the consciousness of the prince's past life, entered the body of a cobbler. Locke seems to think the person with the prince's memories would be the prince, though he would have a lot of trouble convincing people he was not the cobbler.

The contemporary philosopher Sydney Shoemaker considers the same sort of case that we have in "The Meeting" in his influential book *Self-Knowledge and Self-Identity*. He imagines Brown and Johnson checking into the hospital for an operation in which one's brain is removed while important repairs are made. There is a foul-up and Brown's brain is put back in Johnson's body. Shoemaker calls the survivor "Brownson," and asks who he would be. He concludes that he would be Brown.[2]

These philosophers constructed these thought experiments because they thought that the theory that personal identity is just identity of a human body is too simple and a better one is needed. Another way of convincing ourselves of this is to think it through from the inside rather than the outside. Imagine waking up one morning and thinking for a while before opening your eyes. You haven't looked at your body, haven't looked in a mirror, haven't even glanced down the outside of the covers. You ask yourself, "Who am I?" You'll notice that you can figure it out pretty quickly. You don't seem to have to know anything about your body to know who you are. Now suppose you throw back the covers, hop out of bed and wham! You hit your head on the shelf that was always a good six inches above it before. You run into the bathroom and find, like Locke's prince, that staring out at you from the mirror is someone with a cobbler's apron on. You have acquired someone else's body! Can't you imagine this happening to you? Can't you imagine it happening to the child who will acquire Tommy Vladek's body?

Brain Identity

If we are convinced that body transfers are possible, we will need an account of personal identity that shows why this is so. A theory that seems to work for the case Shoemaker described and for the case in "The Meeting" is that personal identity is just brain identity: to be the same person is to have the same brain.

There are several problems with this. In the first place the theory seems incomplete. Why is the brain so important? Why should personal identity be based on brain identity rather than identity of the liver or heart or the whole body? The natural answer is that the brain is the part of the body that is responsible for our mental life. Clearly the reason Vladek thought (or at least feared) that the survivor of the operation would be the injured child and not Tommy was that the survivor would have the beliefs and memories and intellectual skills of

[2]*Self-Knowledge and Self-Identity* is published by Cornell University Press (Ithaca, N.Y., 1963). See also Shoemaker's "Persons and Their Pasts," *American Philosophical Quarterly* (October 1970).

the injured child. It is mental or psychological attributes that we are interested in when we deal with people, and it is for this reason that we take the brain, the part of the body which is responsible for these attributes, to be the key to personal identity.

But this answer creates a new problem. We can introduce it with a new piece of science fiction. Suppose Dr. Nicholson, having perfected brain transplants, goes on to develop a new operation, which we'll call a brain rejuvenation. This operation involves taking out a brain that has something wrong with it. But instead of repairing the brain and putting it back in, a more subtle procedure is followed. A huge computer analyzes the brain in terms of every psychologically relevant characteristic. (This would be pretty difficult, but who knows what medical science will be able to do in another couple of centuries?) Then a lot of things happen, and out of a machine attached to the computer a new brain emerges, made of vinyl or something sturdier than the original brain. In respect of every physiological and neurological factor that has any psychological relevance, that has any effect on what is believed or remembered or loved or hoped for, this brain is just like the original. This new brain is put back into the original cranium; the person acts justs as before but without the dizzy spells or headaches or whatever signaled the deterioration of the original brain.

Would you be willing to undergo this sort of operation? Apart from the normal risks of surgery, would you have the extra worry that you would be paying for an operation that was going to benefit someone else? Or would you say that it is just like getting a new kidney or liver?

If the brain is important just because it is the physical basis of our mental life, then it is sameness of mind or consciousness that is ultimately important, and not literal identity of the brain. If we could have the same consciousness, or the same "soul" without the same brain, wouldn't that still count as personal identity?

Note also that the view that personal identity is identity of brain would not be of much use to those who believe in survival in heaven or in reincarnation. In these cases the brain is no more preserved than the rest of the body. And in our thought experiment about awakening with the body of a cobbler, we no more have to check to see which brain we have than to see which body we have to determine who we are.

For these reasons, some philosophers have been inclined to think that the brain is at most derivatively important. Personal identity may require brain identity in the ordinary cases, but that's because brain identity is the ordinary way of preserving sameness of mind or consciousness. But what does this amount to?

Mind Identity

Anyone who is sympathetic with Descartes' influential views in his *Meditations* will feel that we have been leaving out the most important thing, the immaterial mind. Descartes argued that there has to be more than the material brain to account for human experience; the mind itself must be something in addition to the brain, though causally interacting with it. This immaterial mind is identified with what in religious contexts is called the soul. It is clearly identity of the mind or soul that is thought to convey personal identity in the case of survival after death, and so in ordinary day-to-day survival too it must be what is really crucial. This is not the place to consider Descartes' arguments for the immateriality of the mind; it is sufficient to note that many contemporary philosophers are unconvinced. Interestingly enough, with respect to the question of personal identity many philosophers have thought that even if we accept Descartes' arguments, we still don't have an adequate principle of personal identity.

Locke, for example, seems to have thought roughly as follows: I don't know for certain whether Descartes was right or wrong when he said that matter can't think, that thinking and consciousness require some immaterial thing in addition to the material body and brain. He was awfully bright, so probably he was right. But I can't see why that should mean that sameness of person has to be equated with sameness of these immaterial things.

Suppose it turns out that I have the same immaterial thing thinking in me as Socrates did in him, just as it might turn out that I was made up of the same material atoms as Socrates. In neither case would I *be* Socrates. I wouldn't deserve credit or blame for what Socrates did. It's not the sameness of the immaterial thinking thing that is important, but sameness of "consciousness."

Other philosophers have emphasized the obscurity of the notion of an immaterial thing, and in particular the difficulty of understanding the notion of identity for such a thing. Usually, to explain what it is to have identity of one sort or another, we explain what the world must be like for *one* thing of that kind to show up in different circumstances. For example, I might say that if this pencil on my table is the same pencil that I bought last week at the bookstore, then there must be a continuous path in space-time from the bookstore-last week to my table-now, occupied at each point by a pencil. Now it's very difficult to say what it's like to have the same immaterial thing at two different times, because immaterial things aren't *like* anything. They don't have any shape or size or color, for if they did they wouldn't be immaterial things after all.

The Memory Theory

Locke suggested a theory which a number of philosophers have found attractive. It might be taken as an attempt to provide content to the notion of "the same mind" without depending on the obscure notion of same immaterial thing. But it is a theory that also can be held by those who think that Descartes was wrong, and that our mental life doesn't involve anything beyond the physical world. We all must admit that our mental life consists of various episodes of thinking, hoping, remembering, believing, and so forth, whether these processes are ultimately physical or not. The memory theory builds up personal identity out of relations among these episodes, rather than appealing to the identity of some further thing.

We can explain this theory with the notion of a person stage. Take the contents of my mind right now and bundle them up and consider them as one thing. Call that thing "Fred." Take the contents of my mind a few minutes back, bundle them up, and call that bundle "Frank." Do the same thing with the contents of your mind, and call those bundles "Mary" and "Martha." Now Fred and Frank are stages of one person, Mary and Martha stages of another. But what is the relation between Frank and Fred on the one hand, and Mary and Martha on the other, that makes us say this?

Each of the theories so far provides an answer to this. The simplest is that Frank and Fred belong to one body, Mary and Martha to another. We have to reject this answer, if we allow the possibility of body transfer. The next theory was that each pair belongs to one brain. We have to reject this theory if we allow that personal identity can be preserved through a "brain rejuvenation," or if we want to allow the possibility of survival after death. The next theory was that each pair belonged to a single mind. But that seemed not to provide an answer, because of the obscurity of the notion of "the same mind." Now each of these answers explained personal identity by appealing to the identity of some other sort of thing: bodies, brains, or minds. The memory theory differs, in that it does not appeal to any further sort of identity, but to the relation of memory.

According to the memory theory, what we find is that Frank and Fred have a great many overlapping memories, and so do Mary and Martha, but none of them have any memories that connect them with any person stages of other persons. Person stages belong to the same person if they are part of a single series, successive stages of which are linked by memory.

This is a very appealing theory. It explains that feeling that the survivor of the operation won't be Tommy, but the injured child, for it is the experiences of the injured child that we expect the survivor to have, not memories of Tommy's experiences. It seems to explain how we know so easily who we are. When we consult our memory, we are consulting what really counts. It also explains the initial plausibility of our other theories. Overlapping memories result in the ordinary case through successive experiences being in some way stored in the same brain, and sameness of brain in the ordinary case requires sameness of body. Survival after death and other sorts of body transfer can be seen to make sense to think about, even if it should turn out that there is no way to have overlapping memories except by identity of brain.

Problems with the Memory Theory

But like virtually all theories in philosophy, the memory theory has its problems.

Some philosophers think a fatal problem is circularity. If we are to explain personal identity in terms of memory, we must mean real and not simply apparent memory. My seeming to remember losing the battle of Waterloo does not make me Napoleon.

Now consider two persons who seem to remember an earlier thought or action that belonged to only one of them. Which one is actually remembering and which one only seeming to? It seems natural to say that the one who is actually remembering is that one who actually did the action or had the thought. But then we are explaining the difference between real and apparent memory by using the concept of personal identity. It seems clearly circular to use personal identity to explain the notion of memory we use to explain personal identity.

It is appropriate to end with another objection based on science fiction.[3] Suppose memories are due to information stored in a certain fluid in the brain. When this is discovered, a new industry is born. Persons who have led interesting lives—great explorers, leaders, thinkers, lovers, and so forth—sell memory fluid from their brains to others who have led dull but remunerative lives. These people then enjoy remembering experiences that they themselves did not have. But this last sentence has to be a contradiction if the memory theory is correct. If it makes sense, isn't the memory theory incorrect?

[3]The idea is Shoemaker's, in "Persons and Their Pasts."

All of the theories of personal identity considered here have their able defenders among contemporary philosophers.[4] My own view is that something like the memory theory can be successfully defended, and that if we applied it to the case of Tommy Vladek, we would conclude he would not survive the operation that his father is contemplating. But perhaps the only thing we can conclude with great confidence is that Harry Vladek is right to be worried.

[4]For more on personal identity see John Perry, ed., *Personal Identity* (Berkeley: U. of California, 1975), and Amehi Rorty, ed., *The Identities of Persons* (Berkeley: U. of California, 1976). The latter volume contains an extensive bibliography.

CHAPTER 5 PROBES

1. What are the main theories of personal identity, according to Perry? To which is he inclined to subscribe?

2. Suppose that the boy whose brain Tommy will receive is named Sam. Who, according to Perry, is Harry Vladek likely to bring home from the hospital, Tommy or Sam? Why does Perry think this? Does he think it is certain?

3. In Chapter 4 you read a story about the computing machine named Frost, who became a man. Is this, on Perry's view, possible? If so, how? If not, why not?

4. The Vladeks supposed that what they decided to do was not murder. Assume (what is probably the case) that the brain which was in Tommy's body before the operation will just be destroyed, after the transplant. At the moment of its destruction, would Tommy die? If the operation resulted in the death of Tommy, would it not be murder? Under what conditions would the Vladeks be right in supposing that the operation would not be a simple case of murder? What would Perry say about this?

5. Suppose that the brain to be put into Tommy's skull was that of a girl, Samantha. Should this fact change the Vladeks idea about the transplant? Would they be getting from the hospital a little girl with the body of a boy, or a boy whose brain was initially in a girl?

6. What if the operation turned out in such a way as to yield a child with normal capacities, but one which had no memories whatsoever? That is, what if, as a result of the operation, the brain that will be transplanted into Tommy's body (Sam's brain, let's call it) is so traumatized that it is stripped of all memories, permanently. Would the Vladeks bring home a new, improved Tommy (one who would need to be trained again, just like an infant)? Would they rather be bringing home a permanently forgetful Sam in Tommy's body? Or would they bring home a brand-new child, who was neither Tommy nor Sam? In this case, which child (if any) dies, as a result of the operation, or do both? What would Locke (see 5:2.2) say about this? What would Shoemaker (see the discussion of Shoemaker in Perry's essay) say? With whom do you agree and why (if either)?

7. Is there a case in which you think it would be plausible to argue that there had been a double death (Tommy's and Sam's) even though the brain of one and the body of another lived on?

8. In *The Currents of Space* (Fawcett, 1975), Isaac Asimov refers to a process called "psycho-probing" which removes all of one's memories. In Alfred Bester's classic, *The Demolished Man,* a process called "demolition" is used on criminals which accomplishes the same thing. Neither Bester nor Asimov think that this process, however fearsome, is equivalent to killing its recipient. Do you agree or disagree? What would Perry say about this?

9. Imagine that the parents of the donor child (again, Sam) were named Jones, and that Sam was the Joneses' only child. Does Tommy, or the child that goes home with the Vladeks after the operation, have a legitimate claim on the inheritance left by the Joneses when they die? Does he have a legitimate claim on the Vladeks, if they do not formally adopt him after the operation? Why or why not? Should the Vladeks have to adopt the child that they bring home?

10. Suppose instead that Perry's imagined case of having a vinyl brain were what happened to Tommy. Would the resulting entity (with the body of Tommy but a vinyl brain) be human? Would it be Tommy?

11. Can you think of a philosophically good reason (i.e., one free from ignorant fears) for not undergoing the operation Perry describes (i.e., having a vinyl brain transplanted into your skull that would maintain all your psychological characteristics and memories), if it would result in prolonged survival of your body and psychological characteristics? What if it would boost your I.Q. one hundred points, allow you to become incredibly witty, and so forth, but would be otherwise just like the brain you now have, enough so that after the operation, it would be convinced it was you (rightly or wrongly, but that's for you to decide!) and all of your friends and acquaintances would also be convinced that you had just gotten more witty and intelligent? How does this relate to the mind–body problem (see Chapter 4)?

12. Now that you have considered the problem of personal identity, do you think that there could (at least in principle) be more than one person who was identical to the person who is now you? If, how? If not, why not?

13.   Are you inclined to the position described by Locke, now that you have thought more about the person identity problem, or that argued by Shoe-maker, or that argued by Hume (see 5:2.4)? Is there another view you would like to argue? If so, describe it.

RECOMMENDED READING

Science Fiction and the Problem of Personal Identity

There is a long tradition in philosophy of using imaginative examples to test and evaluate our commonsense notions of personal identity. Science fiction provides such an outpouring of additional thought experiments that philosophers are hard-pressed to keep up with them. Philosophers try to set out requirements of personal identity and survival in terms of the mind alone, the body alone, or some combination of these. Several science fiction stories work with the idea of brain transplants as a way of preserving the person. In Robert Silverberg, *Shadrach in the Furnace* (Pocket Books, 1978), the world's population becomes a source of spare parts for a monomaniacal dictator named Genghis Mao. The plot device of a human brain's being transplanted into an animal's body is used in Robert Sheckley, "The Body," in *Pilgrimage to Earth* (Bantam, 1957). Numerous science fiction stories have appeared on the theme of cyborgs: entities created by replacing organic parts of the human body with prosthetic parts. The best-known example is Martin Caidin's *Cyborg* (Ballantine, 1978), which became the basis for the very popular television series, *"The Six Million Dollar Man."* Much more challenging accounts of the deep psychological changes which would result from such a physical transformation are Damon Knight, "Masks," in Terry Carr and Donald A. Wollheim, eds., *World's Best Science Fiction 1969* (Ace, 1969); C. L. Moore, "No Woman Born," In Lester del Rey, ed., *The Best of C. L. Moore* (Ballantine, 1975); and Anne McCaffrey, *The Ship Who Sang* (Ballantine, 1970). The McCaffrey novel concerns a human being whose brain becomes the computer controlling a spaceship. This plot device is carried to absurd lengths when Mr. Spock's brain is stolen and housed in a computer in a "Star Trek" television episode. These stories avoid some of the deepest problems about personal identity because a part of the body is preserved along with the mind. More challenging stories describe the preservation of one of these without the other.

Survival of the Body Without the Mind.   Some science fiction stories describe cases in which the individual mind is eliminated but the body is not destroyed. A favorite context is the use of mind wiping as punishment for a capital offense. In Alfred Bester's Hugo-winning *Demolished Man* (Pocket Books, 1978), the protagonist, a murderer, is subjected to this treatment. A related sort of problem arises in stories in which aliens become "passengers" in human bodies, for example, in Hal Clement, *Needle* (Avon, 1976); Robert Silverberg's disturbing Nebula winner, "Passengers," in Damon Knight, ed., *Orbit 4* (Berkley, 1970); and in Don Siegel's classic film, *Invasion of the Body Snatchers* (1956), acclaimed for its special effects.

A rather different variant on this problem involves the survival of the body but with changes in the personality. An example is Robert Silverberg's intense *Born with the Dead* (Random House, 1974). The dead persons who are revived in this story undergo such profound but subtle changes that it is difficult to decide whether they are the "same" persons. A weird technological parody of the "resurrection of the body" in the religious sense is explored brilliantly in Philip José Farmer's "Riverworld" Tetralogy, beginning with the Hugo-winning *To Your Scattered Bodies Go* (Berkley, 1971), followed by *The Fabulous Riverboat* (1973), *The Dark Design* (1977), and *The Magic Labyrinth* (1979). The bodies of all human beings who have ever lived are resurrected along a river millions of miles long which snakes around an alien planet. There is philosophical and theological speculation about personal identity and the nature of the human soul.

Survival of the Mind Without the Body. Philosophers in the tradition of Plato and Descartes interpret the religious belief in an afterlife in terms of an immortal mind or "soul." Ray Bradbury uses this idea in describing the Martians as immaterial beings in *The Martian Chronicles* (Bantam, 1974). The idea has been widely used, for example, in connection with the Organians in "Star Trek." Stories that treat human afterlife in terms of a disembodied mind are mentioned in the Recommended Reading for Chapter 2. Poul Anderson's "Call Me Joe," in Ben Bova, ed. *Science Fiction Hall of Fame IIA* (Avon, 1974) describes a mind departing regularly from its body using a technological rather than religious premise.

Problems about the Unity of the Person. The traditional view that a person is essentially a monad has been challenged by a series of fascinating stories which develop the paradoxical implications of a matter transporter such as the one onboard the *Enterprise* on the "Star Trek" series. James Blish pursues these paradoxes in *Spock Must Die* (Bantam, 1975). When the device essentially destroys a human at one place and creates a duplicate of that human across vast distances, has a single person survived the process? The problem is obviously enormously complicated if more than one copy is made. The idea was explored very thoroughly in Algis Budrys, *Rogue Moon*, in *Science Fiction Hall of Fame IIB*.

Other stories portray the pluralization of the person through the phenomenon of cloning. For example, in Theodore Sturgeon's "When You Care, When You Love," in *Case and the Dreamer* (Signet, 1974), the heroine duplicates her dying lover by cloning a new body from one of his cells. Cloning also figures in Arthur C. Clarke's *Imperial Earth* (Ballantine, 1976), although the device is not developed very fully. Cloning stories become especially interesting when the "cell mates" are also telepathically linked. This device is used in Ursula K. LeGuin's "Nine Lives," in *The Wind's Twelve Quarters* (Harper, 1975), and in Kate Wilhelm's Nebula Award novel, *Where Late the Sweet Birds Sang* (Pocket Books, 1977).

Collective Persons. This premise, that individuals linked telepathically together could constitute a higher person, was early used in Olaf Stapledon, *Star Maker* (Penguin, 1973). George R. R. Martin's Hugo-winning "A Song for Lya," in Donald A. Wollheim, ed., *World's Best Science Fiction 1975* (DAW, 1975), portrays a human mind swallowed up, mentally as well as physically, by a collective alien consciousness. Theodore Sturgeon, in *More Than Human* (Ballantine, 1953), depicts the emergence of a group self. This widely acclaimed novel won the International Fantasy Award. The idea is introduced in that novel's predecessor, "Baby Is Three," in *Science Fiction Hall of Fame II.* Arthur C. Clarke's speculative novel, *Childhood's End* (Ballantine, 1976), shows how, with the aid of an alien race, humanity is succeeded by a new entity formed out of the fused, higher intellects of all the remaining children of Earth.

Novels such as Sturgeon's and Clarke's express a conviction that the human race is destined to evolve to a higher level of existence in which our old conception of a person will be totally superseded. This conviction originated with philosophers of the nineteenth century such as Friedrich Nietzsche in his theory of the *Übermensch.* The idea of a socialized consciousness was also anticipated by philosophers in the tradition of G. W. F. Hegel.

Philosophy and the Problem of Personal Identity

The alternative positions are set forth in "Personal Identity," in *The Encyclopedia of Philosophy* (Macmillan, 1967). Antony Flew, ed., *Body, Mind & Death* (Macmillan, 1966), includes traditional treatments of personal identity. John Locke (1632–1704) and Joseph Butler (1692–1752) were preoccupied with questions about true spiritual "afterlife" promised by Christianity. Locke contends that the person who survives the death of the body is a continuous consciousness and relies upon the *memory criterion* of personal identity. His view has been criticized by Butler, by David Hume (1711–1776), and more recently by T. Penelhum, *Survival & Disembodied Existence* (Routledge & Kegan Paul, 1970). Penelhum defends a "body continuity" test of personal identity. John Perry, ed., *Personal Identity* (California, 1975), contains recent articles restating and defending Locke's memory theory and others criticizing the memory theory. Perry's volume also contains articles which draw on modern science and science fiction scenarios to attack our traditional concept of personal identity: especially, D. Parfit, "Personal Identity," and T. Nagel, "Brain Bisection and the Unity of Consciousness." An important new anthology of articles on this issue is A. O. Rorty, ed., *The Identities of Persons* (California, 1976).

FREE WILL AND DETERMINISM:

Is everything we do determined by causes outside our control?

If you were driving to a promising job interview and your car broke down, you would probably feel disgusted with your car. You might even get so frustrated as to climb out and kick it in the fender. If you ended up not getting the job as a result, you might want to drive it over a cliff. But it would be very unreasonable for you to hold your car "responsible" for costing you the job. Although you may curse your car, it really makes no sense for you to "blame" it for costing you the job. Nor would it have made sense to "praise" it if it had got you to the interview in time.

Why is this? People differ from machines like cars and from lower animals because they do things willingly, on purpose, or voluntarily. People are held responsible *only* for the things they do voluntarily. For example, should a professor hold a student responsible for missing an exam? If the professor thinks the student voluntarily skipped the exam, he'll feel justified in flunking him. The student may plead, "I couldn't help it." If the student can prove that circumstances outside his control necessitated his absence, the professor would be wrongheaded to blame the student for missing the exam.

The student can make a very convincing case that he "couldn't help it" if he can prove that something—for example, a flat tire or an illness—*caused* him to miss the exam. In this case the cause prevents him from doing something. But it could cause him to do something. For example, the blowout could cause a driver to lose control of his car and run over a pedestrian. Since the blowout caused him to do what he did, he cannot be blamed for the accident.

It is hard to dispute any of this. But does not modern science take it for granted that *everything* that happens in the universe has a cause? That implies that *everything we human beings do* has a cause. If a parent spanks a child or a husband strikes his wife, this action will have a cause which can be discovered by a psychologist or biologist. The claim that everything we humans do has a cause is called *determinism*. But suddenly we find ourselves in a quandary. Could the student who missed the exam offer the following defense? "Since everything we do has a cause, my missing the exam had a cause. But I cannot be held responsible for what I am caused to do since it is thereby out of my control. Therefore, I am not responsible for missing the exam and should be allowed to take a makeup."

In this chapter you will probe the question, "Are we responsible for anything that we do—or is everything we do caused by factors outside our control?" This chapter will present the main philosophical positions on this question. You will also read a science fiction story, "The Satyr," which will help to focus the issues presented in this chapter, and a philosophical essay that defends the point of view presented in the story. After completing this chapter, you should be able to do the following:

- Identify both the libertarian and deterministic positions on personal responsibility.

- Identify and explain the key concepts used by the libertarian and determinist.

- Identify a third or compatibilist position, which tries to find a middle ground between the libertarian and determinist positions.

- Evaluate these alternative views on the basis of a conceptual experiment.

6:1   THE LIBERTARIAN POSITION

6:1.1   The libertarian is convinced that we have free will. We can make free choices and act upon them. For example, suppose that one day you have nothing in particular to do. You could decide that it would be pleasant to take a drive in the country, so you do so. You might have decided to go shopping in town. You might even consider going to town but ultimately reject that plan in favor of the country drive. According to the libertarian, you should say, "I could have gone to town, but decided instead to go to the country. What prevented me from going to town? Nothing, but my decision was to go to the country, and this decision was freely made." You make a decision freely when nothing forces you to make that decision. That is, nothing else causes you to make that decision. You made it *yourself*. Another way to make this point is that you went to the country of your own free will. What caused you to go? Nothing but your decision or your *willing* to go to the country rather than to town. Every free act is caused by such a willing or *volition*. What causes that willing itself? *Nothing whatsoever!* Otherwise everything you do would be outside your control and determined by chains of causes that stretch back into the dawn of time.

Of course, you may have good *reasons* for choosing the country over the town. There might be a garbage strike in town, which would make the visit unpleasant. But if you freely went to the country, you *could* have *decided* to go to town. You simply elected not to.

The libertarian does not claim that we are free to do anything at all. Clearly, we are not free to travel to the moon without a spaceship, nor can we huff and puff and blow out the sun. But the libertarian does claim that we can do *some* things freely.

6:1.2 The libertarian holds that human beings are agents. An *agent* does some things, but is not caused by anything else to do it. For example, if a driver runs over a pedestrian as a result of a blowout, neither the car nor the driver exercises *agency*. But if the driver, deliberately and in cold blood, drives over a wealthy relative, the driver is an agent. *Agents* are, of course, responsible for what they bring about. But a being who is involved in a chain of events but is caused to behave in a certain way is not *responsible* for the consequences.

Acts are different from the mere events that scientists also study. An event like an explosion on the surface of the sun is caused by events occurring at the core of the sun. Acts are due to human agency. Mere events occur without specific agency. The driver who runs over the pedestrian as a result of a flat tire is not doing an act. The libertarian is claiming: Human beings are sometimes agents; human beings sometimes perform acts. When they do so, they are responsible for their acts. Only agents are responsible. Other causes, as when a nail penetrates a tire, are not responsible agents.

6:1.3 It makes no sense to say that a person is moral or immoral, unless you think of the person as an agent. Otherwise, things that you do would be no different from things done by nails and tires. If you do something as an agent, such as skip an exam, you could always do something else, such as take the exam. In philosopher's jargon, *ought* implies *can*. I can claim "You ought to take the exam" only if I can also say truly, "You are capable of taking the exam." If you really can't do something, what sense does it make to say that you *ought* to do it? But to say that you could do otherwise is to say that you acted freely. Morality, then, seems to rely on an assumption of the libertarian position.

6:1.4 The libertarian view seems commonsensical. But there are problems. First, the libertarian says that your free acts are caused by acts of will or volition. But what sorts of causes are these? Normally a cause like a nail's entering a tire to cause a collision involves a physical process. But does your act of will *physically* influence your body in such a way as to make you act as you do? This leads to a nasty dilemma: Either (1) the act of will is an event occurring in your brain, or (2) it is an event of a different nature. If (1) it is a brain event, then it is a *physical* event. But the physical events in your body seem to be always caused by other physical events. If this is so, then the act of will is itself caused and is not, as the libertarian says it is, free of prior causes. (2) What about the other horn of the dilemma? If the act of will was not a physical event in the brain, how can it affect your body in the appropriate way? This leads to the problem sometimes called the problem of "the ghost in the machine." How can a ghostlike act of will cause a physical event? How can physical events be caused by nonphysical events? Such a supposition seems to run contrary to our *scientific* knowledge of the world.

Some influential scientific theories present a further problem. According to these theories, you may *believe* that you are doing something freely, when in fact you are doing it because of causes you are not aware of. Sigmund Freud argued that much of what we "decide" as adults is nothing but a causal effect of things that happened to us when we were children or infants. For example, you may think that you are "freely" deciding to stay single rather than to marry; but this decision may be the result of a traumatic sexual experience in childhood which is now forgotten but left deep scars. B. F. Skinner, a behaviorist, believes that everything you do is the result of what he calls "conditioning." You may think that you freely decide on a number of matters, but, according to Skinner, each of your so-called actions is nothing but a conditioned response to the stimuli which confront you at the moment you act. Just as Pavlov's famous dogs salivate when a dinner bell is rung, you "decide" to take a drive in the country (and not to go to town) when you are confronted by the appropriate stimuli. Neither case is one of will, but only of conditioning, a causal mechanism. Finally, many biologists claim that your behavior is determined physiologically, either by your genetic makeup or by physiological mechanisms that have been caused by your environment. If any of these theories is correct, you are not really in control of your behavior in the way the libertarian claims you are.

6:2 THE DETERMINISTIC POSITION

6:2.1 Determinism is the alternative to libertarianism on the free will question. The determinist believes that every event that occurs in this universe has an earlier cause and that this cause itself has an earlier cause, and so on, back indefinitely into the past. So each event is the product of a chain of causes and has a lengthy causal ancestry. This includes human acts like driving your car to the country. Let us grant that your departure for the country resulted from an "act of will" or a choice to go to the country rather than to town. The determinist will *not* grant that this act of will is an "uncaused cause" in the libertarian sense. Your decision itself is nothing but the effect of some prior determining cause. In this way, you do not *freely* make decisions or choices. What you *think* are free decisions or choices are nothing but links in ancestral chains of causes. *Free will is an illusion.*

There can be little doubt that there is something puzzling about the libertarian's belief in uncaused acts of will. Most of us believe that nothing happens without a cause. Imagine a government report on an assassination which concludes: "The ambassador of Patagonia died of bullet wounds, but no one shot the bullets. The bullets themselves were not even fired accidentally. In fact, no gun was involved. The bullets just suddenly flew at a high velocity at the dead person and killed him. Nothing *caused* them to do so." It is reasonable to suppose that few people would accept this report, even if they knew no details of the assassination. Events like flying bullets do not *just happen*. Yet this seems to be what the libertarian suggests happens with an act of will. You move your arm because you choose to do so. Your choice, however, in some sense *just happened*. That is, there is in principle no way to causally explain your choice, for it was not caused. Surely, it seems more reasonable for us to suppose that you chose to move your arm because of preexisting factors in your makeup and your environment. Otherwise, it looks like there is in principle *no scientific explanation* of much of human behavior. Determinism sets up no such roadblocks to scientific explanation. In fact, determinists welcome progress in the biological and social sciences.

6:2.2   Alas, the determinist's position also leads to serious problems. If the determinist is right, personal responsibility is an impossibility. If all of us are simply fated to do what we do in life, how can we say that some acts are moral and others immoral? Saints are saintly because that is their causal fate, and sinners sin having no control over what they do. If so, what sense does it make to punish sinners and praise saints? Everyone is in the same boat. Each of us is locked up in chains of causes over which we have no control. Cause and effect march on inexorably and ineluctably through time from a beginning lost deep in the long past toward an unseen future. We are simply playing an involuntary scene in this ongoing pageant. This view of human beings as not responsible for their acts conflicts with the deepest intuitions we have about the moral requirements for life in a society. We are appalled by the prospect of a society in which people are not held morally responsible for their actions.

6:2.3   We are left in a quandary. Which of our convictions must be given up—the libertarian's belief that we can evaluate, assess, and choose, and that this allows us to be responsible, moral creatures; or the determinist's belief that everything has a cause and that each cause is a link in a long ancestral chain of causes?

6:3   THE COMPATIBILIST VIEW

6:3.1   Recently, philosophers have offered a clear third alternative. This is called the *compatibilist* view, because it holds that moral responsibility and universal and ancestral causation are compatible. According to the compatibilist, universal and ancestral causation does not warrant the grim view determinism claims. From the assumption of universal and ancestral causation, it does not follow that events such as human acts could not be otherwise than the way they occur.

The crux of the compatibilist's argument is the claim that a moral agent *could have done otherwise* than the way he or she did. True, what the agent did was caused by something else. But you can't conclude from this alone that he or she could not have done otherwise. Since a person can do otherwise than what he or she does, it is reasonable to hold him or her responsible. So moral responsibility is compatible with universal and ancestral causation.

6:3.2   How do compatibilists establish this position? Usually they offer a unique analysis of the concept of *causation.* Consider the following causal claims:

1. "Aspirins cure (i.e., cause the elimination of) headaches."

2. "Smoking causes cancer."

3. "Heart attacks kill (i.e., cause the death of) people."

The concept of causality applies in each of these claims. But the determinist thinks of the causation at work here as necessitating. That is, if *x* is the cause of *y,* we understand *y* to *necessarily* follow *x.* But to say that *y* is necessary is to say that things could not be otherwise than *y.* But, when we look at the examples, it is hard to agree that the determinist's conception holds true. Take (1): Although we agree that aspirins cure headaches, we would not agree that a headache *could not* continue even though we have taken aspirins. We are only agreeing that it generally does not continue or maybe only that it *probably* will not. Or consider (2): Surely many smokers manage to avoid cancer. But smokers are *far more likely* to get cancer than are nonsmokers. And that is enough for the claim that smoking causes cancer, provided that scientists eventually find the underlying physical mechanisms involved in lung cancer. Finally (3): Although we agree that heart attacks kill people, many of us know people who have survived heart attacks. Indeed, we would be hard-pressed to find one example of a common causal claim, to which we would all agree, that does not allow for exception, that does not allow that things *could be otherwise.* So the determinists are on very thin ice when they claim that causes necessitate their effects.

To this, most determinists reply, "These claims are open to exceptions, because they are not specific enough. If we could describe smokers fully, we could tell *without exception* which smokers get cancer." But modern physics seems to show that we cannot, as a rule, find such laws. Imagine that there is a piece of radium next to a geiger counter. The geiger counter clicks rapidly. Let us say that in one period it clicks some number of times, say 100. Discounting background radiation and so forth, it seems quite correct to say that the radium *causes* the geiger counter to click 100 times in a period. Does this mean that, given the radium, the geiger counter could not have behaved otherwise—for example, clicked 80 times in that period? The physicist would answer "certainly not." According to what is called the Heisenberg uncertainty principle (a principle almost unanimously accepted by modern physicists), although we can predict the emission of radioactivity by the radium with a degree of accuracy (plus or minus 20 clicks, if you will), it is *impossible* to predict exactly how much radioactivity will be emitted in any given period. According to many physicists, the reason for this is not that we are ignorant of the physical process but that, although over the long run radioactivity can be predicted, in the short run it does not behave in an utterly regular way. One way of expressing this is to say that within certain parameters, the particles behave *randomly,* that the chances of getting 100 clicks are neither significantly better nor worse than getting 80 clicks or 120 clicks, and this is just the way nature works. This might be compared with throwing one die. We can say for certain that we will not roll a seven, but we cannot with certainly predict that we will get a five rather than a two, or a four, or whatever. According to physics, radioactivity (and a number of other processes involving particles) is like this in that what we can specifically predict can only be done in such a way as to include a fairly broad range of phenomena. Within that range, however, no specific prediction can be guaranteed.

These examples suggest that determinism is mistaken. To say that "*x* causes *y*" is not to say that "given *x*, things could not be otherwise than *y*." This is the basis for compatibilism: You can agree that everything has a cause, but you do not have to agree with the determinist who says, "Nothing could be other than the way it is." So you can assess responsibility for human acts. Nothing prevents you from arguing, "You are quite right that Jones was caused to behave in the way he did, but he is responsible for acting in that way, for he could have done otherwise."

Other philosophers are not entirely satisfied with this answer as stated so far. For only a very few agents in the universe are responsible for their behavior—agents like human beings. Even if the radium "could have done otherwise" than make the geiger counter click 100 times, the radium is certainly not *responsible* for doing so. If this is true, the apparent defeat of the determinist rings a bit hollow, for we have yet to establish moral responsibility as a fact about human beings. Some critics also complain that the compatibilist's acceptance of the principle that everything has a cause is still too much to allow the kind of distinction the libertarian requires to maintain personal responsibility. The libertarian will argue that we still need an uncaused act of will that functions as an initial cause of action. To meet these sorts of objections, the compatibilist has to show that there is something very special about *the way* in which human acts are caused, which makes it reasonable to talk about human responsibility.

6:4 CONCEPTUAL EXPERIMENT

The following story provides a conceptual experiment by which we can test the claims of the libertarian, the determinist, and the compatibilist. It concerns a creature whose character is apparently an effect of his physiology, though, in the end, he is still held responsible for his behavior. The subsequent philosophical analysis considers the proper analysis of the relation between being caused to be the way one is and being responsible for one's behavior.

Conceptual Experiment 6:

THE SATYR

Stephen Robinett

No women! No booze! What do they take me for, some kind of animal? They keep me caged like an animal. What did I ever do to them? What did I ever do to anyone, even Hench?

I should have seen it coming. For that, I blame Hench. The whole thing is his fault, his responsibility. A starship to the middle of nowhere and a life in the mines—how could he do it? and to *me,* of all creatures!

I should have seen most of it coming the day Hench said we were going to see the Merton woman's father. Hench seldom took me out. He called our trips out disasters.

I remember Hench putting me in a new tunic, parting my hair in the middle, combing it over my ears and stepping back to admire his work.

"You'll do."

I eyed him, suspicious. "For what?"

Hench flicked a piece of lint off my shoulder. "What's it to you?"

"I like to keep track of what's going on in your head, Hench." I tugged at the front of my tunic. "New clothes, shined shoes, going out—something's fishy. You're not planning anything foolish like marrying that Merton woman, are you?"

"Not yet." He told me about the appointment with her father.

I frowned. I knew Merton's reputation. He exploited worlds, most of them hostile. "What's the appointment about?"

Hench ignored the question and started for the door. "Let's go."

We took the mono downtown to Merton Planetary Development. Even public transportation put a strain on Hench's small budget. In spite of his hybrid genius, crossing biogenetic engineer and artist, things had gone poorly for Hench. As a businessman, he left something to be desired, namely, money. He mortgaged everything—laboratory, equipment, car—to create me. He could balance that incredibly complex process of genetic transplantation, followed by biochemical gestation, followed by education through artificial engram implantation, but not his checkbook. They repossessed the car first. Eventually, everything would go, except me, of course. I had no intention of going anywhere.

Hench's money problems stemmed from one source. No one wanted his product. Better cows and horses through genetic manipulation, yes, better dogs and cats—people could accept improvements on what they already knew—but new creatures, unique creatures, they found repulsive.

They even found *me* repulsive. No one objected to a chest-high, two-toed helper with bristly hair, a broad nose and leaf-shaped ears. They had seen pictures of satyrs. No one even objected to my strength and intelligence. What they claimed to object to was my pleasant disposition. They considered me unreliable. I take a drop now and then. I like the ladies. Does that make me unreliable? Still, no one wanted me. No one, except, perhaps, Merton.

Hench and I took the elevator up to Merton's offices.

"Hench, I thought you'd given up on this hare-brained scheme."

"What hare-brained scheme?"

"Selling me."

Hench avoided looking at me. I knew the reaction. I had guessed right. Every time Hench told me about a potential customer, he avoided looking at me. Every time he reported failure, he looked relieved. At first, I took this as a sign Hench liked me. Finally, I realized the true basis of his attitude. He felt responsible for me. I was his creation. A peculiar notion, responsibility, but useful.

The elevator arrived at Merton's offices. I could see the entire floor from the reception area, a central bay with row after row of gnomelike computer technicians at their consoles, all monitoring Merton's empire. Lights appeared and faded in front of them. Information filled screens and vanished. The empire was safe under their bloodshot eyes.

Of more immediate interest was the receptionist, a bird-legged girl with acne. She did have one point in her favor. She was female. Any port in a storm.

Hench talked to the receptionist a few seconds, then glanced at me. "Wait here."

I gave the receptionist an appreciative once-over. "Anything you say, Hench."

I waited on the couch opposite the bird-legged receptionist. When Hench disappeared into Merton's office, I grinned at her. Hench had told me not to grin in public. He said people found scraggly teeth repulsive. What did he know? I made out better with the ladies than he did. All he had was the Merton woman.

The receptionist noticed me grinning at her and shifted uneasily on her chair. Her eyes returned to the paperwork on her desk. She knew I was watching, inspecting, appreciating. She tried to concentrate in spite of me.

She failed. "Is there something I can do for you, sir?"

My grin widened. "Indeed, there is."

"What?"

"Is there someplace we can be alone and . . . talk?"

She looked around. For help? Possibly. "What did you want to talk about, Mr.—?" Her almost nonexistent eyebrows remained elevated, waiting for my answer.

"Silenus. Where can we chat?"

"I think right here will be satisfactory."

"I don't mind, but . . ." I glanced toward the gnomes at their computers. ". . . you may find it a little too public. Is there, perhaps, a bar in the building with romantically subdued lighting?"

"Yes, on the top floor, but—"

"Good." I stood up and extended my elbow. "Shall we go?"

I could see the struggle going on behind her eyes. She found me repulsive—bristly hair, scraggly teeth, faintly jaundiced complexion—yet, interesting. Both are common reactions.

I decided to nudge her interest. "I come equipped with a sizeable advantage."

Wrong nudge. Persnickety type. All interest faded from her eyes. She looked slightly sick. I knew I would have to resort to stronger measures to give her the kind of memories she would secretly cherish for a lifetime.

I started toward her. "You're absolutely right, my dear. Actions do speak louder than words."

Before I reached her, she bolted, scooping up an armload of papers and heading across the computer bay on her bird legs. I considered chasing her—I love a good chase—but decided against it. She would probably scream and bring Hench.

"Miss," I called after her. "I shall return. If Mr. Hench comes out of his meeting, tell him I'm in the bar."

I took the elevator up to the top floor. The doors opened on a sign reading Olympus Club. The name put me in a good mood. Part of my basic education includes large doses of Greek mythology. Hench wanted my personality to reflect my appearance. Hench makes all sorts of mistakes.

I went unnoticed in the subdued light. Along with the new suit, Hench had given me a few coins to squander. I climbed up on a barstool and ordered a half-dozen screwdrivers in a large brandy glass. I go through phases, wine, beer, bourbon, Scotch—at the time, it was vodka.

I paid and downed half the snifter. The bartender, shining a glass, watched me. Shortly, I felt good enough to sing.

I sang.

The bartender, evidently no music lover, stopped shining the glass, frowning. Several people at the bar turned to listen. The bartender asked me to stop.

"Stop? Are you kidding? This is one of my favorite songs."

He said there were ladies in the room.

"Ladies? Ladies?" I looked around. Here and there, I could see several lovely faces watching me. "Why so there are!"

I climbed up on the barstool, stepped onto the bar and began singing for the ladies, doing a soft-shoe down the shiny surface and playing to them with open arms. Several of the women looked shocked at the lyrics. Most of the men smiled.

I sang on.

The bartender, still frowning, tried to catch me.

I evaded him, tapping out a two-step before I hopped away from each swipe of his thick arms. My polished shoes sounded on the bar and glittered in the light. I sang my heart out, pathos, bathos—you name it. Then I made a mistake. I stopped long enough to pluck up my drink from the bar. The bartender, aided by two other tone-deaf men in white aprons from the kitchen, grabbed me, ejected me and told me to leave the building before they called a security guard.

I ignored this insensitive criticism of my performance and touched the button for Merton's floor. I reentered Merton's offices feeling pleasantly amorous, the full effect of the screwdrivers beginning to take hold. I wondered whether I could coax, chase, or threaten the bird-legged receptionist into the elevator long enough to have her.

She saw me coming but stood her ground, or rather sat it, remaining at her desk. I walked up, went around the desk and faced her. With her seated, we were the same height.

"Madame," I began, an ingratiating smile on my face.

"You've been drinking."

"Don't scold. A bit of the grape, or, in this case the potato."

"What do you want?"

In sexual matters, I believe in being frank. I put my hand on her thigh.

Her eyes enlarged noticeably, making them close to normal size. "Please take your hand off me."

I stroked.

She slapped my hand.

I stepped closer, inhaling her perfume—a scent that reminded me, subtly, of Hench's laboratory—and put my arms around her waist.

Delicately, I kissed her throat.

She thrashed, arms flailing.

I ignored this mild protest. Resistance adds something special to their inevitable submission. I persisted.

She kicked.

I avoided.

Her chair teetered. I dragged her to the floor. A wastebasket overturned near our heads, *thunk,* spilling balls of paper around us.

I murmured. "My sweet rose, it will not be long now. My jewel, my buttercup, my plum, I burn with desire for you."

She responded to this eloquence by continuing to thrash and squirm.

"Submit, my treasure. You need not tell your husband. You will only hurt his feelings."

She screamed.

I felt hands grabbing at my tunic. I clutched my treasure to me and rolled away from them, ignoring the gathering crowd, continuing to murmur.

"Ahh, my wondrous blossom, my—"

Abruptly, a sharp pain went through my ribs. I was jerked away from my wondrous, bird-legged blossom.

Hench, glaring into my face, shook me. My head bobbed with each shake. "Why (shake, bob), why do you do these things?"

"What things?"

"Can't you control yourself, dammit, even in public?"

"I tried to get her to go someplace private, Hench. She wouldn't listen."

"Why can't you at least control yourself for five minutes?"

"Is it my fault?"

"It's your responsibility."

"Don't be silly, Hench. Only human beings are responsible. I am what I am."

A murmur went through the crowd. Not human? An animal? Someone, probably Merton, explained.

A biosynthetic? They looked at me with renewed interest, their mood changed. Able to classify me as something other than human, they no longer considered me a rapist, only an animal, poorly trained or perhaps not yet housebroken.

They backed off slightly. Even the receptionist, now on her feet, looked sympathetic, or semisympathetic.

Hench grabbed me by the shoulder and pushed me through the crowd toward Merton's office.

I glanced up at him. "What are you going to do?"

He pushed again, harder.

I looked over my shoulder and shouted to the crowd. *"If you hear screams, he's beating me. Call the police or the humane society or someone."*

"Shut up," growled Hench, "or I'll crack your skull."

He gave me a shove into Merton's office.

I had to stand in the middle of the room. Hench and Merton inspected me as though I were a new piece of office equipment. Hench, the salesman, demonstrating my finer points, Merton, nodding and willing to listen but unwilling to be sold a useless product.

Hench listed my virtues: the strength of ten (Hench exaggerates), the endurance of a machine, capable of independent action—

"Speaking of independent action, John," interrupted Merton, "can you explain that incident with our receptionist?"

Hench looked embarrassed. He scowled in my direction and tried to explain. "He has the ability to reproduce, another advantage from your point of view."

Though to me the advantage seemed obvious—as well as sizeable—Merton looked dubious.

Hench persevered. "A creature like this would only have to be seeded on a planet. After that, nature would provide you with as many workers as needed."

"An army," I added, imagining my only mission in life to populate an entire planet. But Hench had forgotten one important point. "Hench."

"What?" snapped Hench, annoyed.

"It takes two to tango—at *least* two—but the more the merrier I always say."

"The creature's right, John. Can you produce females of his species?"

"The brides of Frankenstein," I suggested.

"Yes, that's possible," answered Hench.

I shook my head, exasperated with Hench. "All these years, Hench, you've been holding out on me."

"Did you hear me tell you to shut up?"

"Do I care what you tell me?"

"You'd better care or you won't eat tonight."

I shut up. I did want to eat. Hench was forever holding that over my head. He had worked up a penalty scale, tying it to my food. The more I disobeyed, the less I ate. I found myself on an involuntary diet most of the time.

Hench continued his explanation. "The entire process takes about two years. The female version—I have had a few problems making one up to now—the female version would be ready to reproduce five years after that."

"Hench, you don't have to go to all that trouble just for me. There are plenty of women around."

"I told you to shut up."

"Yep, Hench, you did do that."

We glared at each other, deadlocked.

Merton intervened. "He doesn't seem to follow orders very well."

"You have to kick him occasionally, or take away his food."

"Go ahead, Hench, beat me—but I'll scream. You'll have the humane society on your neck."

Hench snorted. He threatened to beat me frequently. He seldom did. He usually snorted and wandered away, muttering about the allowances people had to make for creatures like me.

"And the life span, how long do they live?"

"Frankly, I don't know. He's a prototype."

I gave a prototypical grin, teeth clenched, lips folded back.

Merton automatically started to respond to the grin, then caught himself, his expression degenerating to a sort of sick look. He addressed me directly for the first time. "You do seem like an intelligent creature."

"So do you."

"Perhaps too intelligent."

"Actually," interrupted Hench, probably envisioning the entire deal going down the drain, "it's only a superficial intelligence. His real level of understanding is rudimentary." Hench turned to me, his face taking on the expression adults use with children. He pronounced his words distinctly. "Go and sit down. Do you understand me? Go and sit down."

I considered standing on my head to defy Hench. It would only have made his point, dumb animal. I walked to the nearest chair and sat down.

Merton looked like he bought exactly zero of Hench's "superficial intelligence" argument. Still, I suspected it gave him a rationalization to pass along to the board of directors. They would not be consigning a quasi-human to this hostile world they wanted populated, but only a "superficially intelligent biosynthetic construct," i.e., me.

Merton stood up, indicating an end to the interview. He shook hands with Hench and said he would give his answer within a week. Hench led the way out the door.

In the elevator, after a prolonged parting wink at the receptionist, I asked Hench about the odds on Merton accepting the deal. Hench told me about Merton. Overextended in six directions from earth,

Merton had sunk most of the company's remaining assets into colonizing and exploiting some world in the middle of nowhere. Merton had one problem. No one wanted to colonize it. That part bothered me. It reminded me too much of "hostile worlds." If no one wanted to go, they had reasons. Merton needed manpower or his empire would collapse. Hench, on the other hand, needed money.

The Merton woman had convinced her father to consider solving both problems with a single blow. Instead of manpower, she suggested satyr-power. She even went so far as to suggest I ought to work for my keep, a truly vicious idea.

I asked Hench if he intended to sell me into slavery.

He avoided looking at me and told me to shut up.

"Selling your only begotten—or, rather, synthesized—son into slavery! Hench, you're an immoral man, no better than us beasts."

"What do you know about morality?"

"I know human beings talk about it a lot. What else do I need . . ."

"I told you to shut up. I'm thinking."

"Do I care if you're thinking? Sell me off like a sack of potatoes. Hench, you're of dubious value as a father figure."

The elevator reached the ground floor, slowed and stopped. Hench snapped his finger. "Got it!"

"You've got it all right. I don't know what it is, but you've got it. The more I think about it, the more I think you got it from that Merton woman."

"If I change the thyroid hormone balance, along with the aldosterone level, inactivating the glutamic dehydrogenase so there's less glutamic acid and consequently less ammonia and alpha-keloglutaric acid . . ."

Hench kept babbling in this manner all the way back to the laboratory, his eyes becoming progressively more glazed the deeper he go into the problem. I had to lead him the last few blocks by the hand. When we got to the laboratory, he wrote down his brainstorm, covering large sheets of paper with cryptic chemical symbols and mathematics. He stayed at it for hours, oblivious to distraction.

An hour past my dinner time, he sat back, head lolling, writing arm dangling, drained. "Finished."

"Finished what?"

"Your mate, a Maenad, a nymph or whatever you call them."

"Fine, let's see the wench."

I moved up to the desk, expecting at least a drawing. Hench showed me formulas, page after page of them. Added to the computerful of formulas he had prepared to create me, they would produce my mate. I hope she looked better than Hench's chicken scratchings.

I looked up at Hench. "Only one?"

"As many as you like."

"I like a lot, but won't mass production spoil quality?" I looked at the bland formulas. "Frankly, Hench, I'd rather see a production model, or a reproduction model."

Hench gave me an exasperated glance. "You dwell on sex, do you know that?"

"Only as does a starving man of food. Speaking of food—"

"Why do you do that?"

"What?"

"Dwell on sex."

"You're the one who gave me the extra Y-chromosome. *You're* the one who wanted to make sure I could reproduce. You tell me."

Hench grunted. "Talk about something else."

"Okay, let's talk about this slave sale you're conducting. Why are you selling me?"

The question annoyed him. "Look, I'm in business. I make creatures, then I sell them. Business is business."

"Materialist."

Hench grunted again and avoided looking at me.

"What do they do on this godforsaken planet, anyway?"

"Mining."

"Mining! You're sending me off to the salt mines! You're *inhuman,* Hench."

"Business is business. Do you know what you cost? Plus—"

"Prototypes are always expensive."

"Plus, you aren't good for anything more complicated than physical labor. You can't concentate on anything but sex for more than two minutes."

"That's not true. I just don't want to concentrate on most of the things human beings do."

"It amounts to the same thing on the job market."

"The *job* market! Money again! Is that all you can think about, Hench? You dwell on money, do you know that? Since you met that Merton woman, that's all you can think about—money, money, money. She's got you by the bank book, Hench."

"I don't have a bank book."

"You will, as soon as old man Merton ships me off to the salt mines, you and that Merton woman will be rolling in dough, not to mention the hay. I'd like to get that woman in the hay for five minutes and show her what life's all about. It isn't money."

Abruptly, Hench slapped me.

I just about grabbed him and threw him across the room. My

sense of enlightened self-interest asserted itself. I controlled the urge. If I threw him across the room, I would never be able to work on his conscience.

I let my face sting and glared at him. "You're responsible for me, Hench! I'm your creation! If you sell me, you'll be selling your self-respect!"

That night, Hench locked me in my room to prevent escape. The next day, he let me out long enough to clean the laboratory and myself, then locked me up again, a broom returned to its closet. It sounds cruel, night after night locked away from life, liquor and the ladies. Except for my profound ability with locks, it would have been cruel. Every night, when Hench left for his rendezvous with the Merton woman, I unlocked the door and crept out.

Without money, spirits are hard to come by. I rifled coin return slots on public phones, occasionally turning up enough loose change for a short snort. I looked for women but found none alone. When I got cold or tired or hungry, I went back to the laboratory. I decided to give Hench until the last possible minute to change his mind. Why leave a warm bed and good food before necessary?

During my daily outings to scrub and sweep, I noticed Hench's anxiety. He suffered from conscience. I let him suffer. The more it ate at him—his desire for the Merton woman, money and possibly fame warring with his sense of responsibility for me—the better chance I had. I watched the moral battles played out on his face. The closer we got to the date of Merton senior's decision, the more intense the battles became, attack and counterattack causing Hench to pace the laboratory, scowling and mumbling, or pause long minutes in an abstracted trance.

Toward the end of the week, I was off in one corner of the main workroom, filling the autoclave with glassware, when the Merton woman came in. She failed to notice me. Hench, engaged in hand-to-hand combat with his conscience, had forgotten me.

She walked across the workroom to Hench, hugged him and gave him a perfunctory kiss on the cheek, announcing *good news*.

The only good news I could see her bringing were those flanks, sleek, solid—no bird legs there. I ached to have her on the spot.

Hench gazed at her with a lovestruck smile on his face, his moral dilemma temporarily forgotten as his hormones took over. "What good news?"

"Father has decided to use your creature."

Bad news, definitely bad news.

Her delighted enthusiasm continued. "It's just marvelous, darling. I'm sure father will give us enough in advance to pay off those horrible debts and have a long honeymoon." She noticed a change in Hench's expression and frowned slightly. "Is something wrong?"

"I'm not sure I should do it."

She gave an exasperated sigh and shook her head. "We've been all through this a million times, dear. It's only an animal. You've sold animals before."

"Not like him."

"Darling, you're too close to the situation. You created it. You've begun to see more in it than is there. I appreciate your feelings. It must be like selling a very smart pet. It's regrettable but necessary. It's not just me you have to worry about. It's your work. Without money, your work will stop completely. You are a great man, John. Don't let that *thing* keep you from being all you can be."

That *thing* continued to listen to this line of bullshit until its teeth ground. Hench's conscience needed help. I cupped my hands around my mouth and shouted across the workroom. *"She's only after your money, Hench!"*

Both of them became aware of me. The Merton woman turned a look of acid contempt in my direction. "John, please get that filthy animal out of here."

"Filthy or not, I'm right. Old man Merton's done for without me. Hench, she's just trying to soft soap you into becoming a millionaire slave trader. Don't listen to her."

The Merton woman kept looking at me, disgust evident on her face. "And just what is wrong with becoming a millionaire?"

I ignored her. "Slave trader, Hench. It's cost you your dignity and your soul and your self-respect. You're responsible for me. You made me. Sending me to the mines is evil and wrong."

Words like "evil" and "wrong," "responsibility" and "self-respect" usually struck a responsive chord in Hench. In spite of that, he told me to go to my room or he would crack my skull.

Reluctantly, I went, winking at the Merton woman (what flanks!) on the way out.

I could hear them arguing from my room. Even on their way to dinner, I heard Hench stressing words like "responsibility" and "doing the right things," while the Merton woman stressed eternal, nuptial bliss "and the money, darling. Don't forget the money."

That night, I resolved to leave. If I waited too long, the Merton woman would seduce Hench in more senses than one. Hench, guilty as he felt, would deport me. I put on my suit, unlocked the door and started out.

I followed the corridor past the laboratory workrooms and downstairs. Hench's office door was open, a sharp rectangle of light falling across the darkened hall. I would have to sprint past the office to get to the double doors at the end of the corridor.

I readied myself for the dash, getting down into a half-crouch, fingers arched against the polished floor.

I hesitated, hearing voices—Hench and the Merton woman arguing in his office. I tiptoed to the doorway, pressing myself against the wall and listening. The Merton woman was pleading with Hench.

"Darling, you *have* to do it. As much as you hate it, you don't have any choice."

"I do have a choice. Until I sign that contract with your father, I have a choice. I created him. I'm responsible for him."

I hesitated a moment longer. Hench's conscience seemed to be holding its own.

"It's not like it was human, darling. In the most basic sense, it's simply a product."

"That's exactly the point, he's not human. In some ways, he's completely inhuman. If he were human, at some point he would begin to take care of himself and be responsible for what he does. But he's not human at all. He's my creation and my responsibility."

"You'll lose the laboratory. You owe—"

Something slammed down on Hench's desk, cutting her off. "I know what I owe, *dammit*! Money, money, money—is that all anyone thinks about?"

"It's a vicious animal, dear. It belongs someplace away from people. You know the kinds of things it's done. It's utterly amoral."

Hench's voice took on a note of despair. "That's my fault, too. He's what I made him, whether I intended it or not. I'm responsible for everything he is, including that."

The Merton woman gave one last, unreasoned appeal. "Darling, please get rid of it—for me."

A long pause followed. I heard Hench get up and pace the office. A shadow, Hench's, filled the rectangle of light on the floor in front of me. I pressed myself closer to the wall.

At last, Hench spoke. "I can't."

My heart sang! Saved by Hench's conscience!

I tiptoed away from the door and back upstairs. Going to my room, I whistled and sang and cavorted, doing several forward flips (my favorites). I relocked the door, took off my clothes and went to bed. I drifted off to a pleasant sleep composing a song to Hench's conscience. Fortunately, before inflicting too many verses on myself, I fell asleep.

Something scraped. My eyes blinked open. A key turned in the lock. I glanced at the window. No daylight. A midnight visit from Hench? Unlikely. The light came on. The door opened.

The Merton woman, still dressed for her evening out with Hench— a sleek tube dress, black, glittering, low cut, a single strand of pearls around her throat—stepped into the cell and stood by the door, looking at me.

I looked past her at the partially open door. "Where's Hench?"

"He's gone home. I came back."

I sat up on the bed. "Does he know you're here?"

She looked at me, her revulsion (and something else—what? A spark of fascination?) clear on her face. "Please cover yourself."

I grinned.

She picked my tunic off the chair and tossed it across my lap.

I continued grinning. "Satisfied?"

"You are a disgusting creature."

"I know." I watched her flanks, the muscles clearly visible through the shiny cloth. "What do you want?"

"John has decided to keep you."

"Good news."

"Bad news. It will bankrupt him."

"So? What's the tragedy?"

"Don't you care?"

"He'll find work to support us." I hesitated. "The three of us."

Her back went rigid. "I'm not going to let it happen."

"I don't see how you can stop it. Hench is a man of conscience."

Her hand came around from behind her. She held one of the dart guns Hench uses to tranquilize, occasionally kill, us beasts. I could tell the setting by the color coding on the chamber. She had it set on kill.

Her hand shook slightly. "You will go tomorrow."

"Why do you hate me?"

Her expression, stern, wavered. The question caught her off-guard. "This is for John."

I laughed. "Human beings only do things for themselves. Don't you know that yet?"

"It's for John. I won't have our lives ruined by a freak."

"I'm only a freak because I'm too much like you. Hench is different, but you and I are two of a kind. We do what we have to do to get what we want."

"If you don't agree to go tomorrow, I'll kill you now."

"I agree."

She had expected an argument, resistance. Her surprise showed on her face.

I shrugged. "I'm a coward."

I am also a liar, but it seemed best to avoid mentioning that.

Her determination softened. Some thought or speculation flitted behind her eyes. Enough of it showed to let me recognize it. I glanced at the dart gun. Distracted by her speculation, she had let her thumb wander from the trigger button.

I looked at her flanks a moment, then up at her eyes, catching her attention. Once I had it, I lunged. I knocked aside the gun. It flew out of her hand, hit the wall and discharged ineffectually against the floor, the propellant exploding with a loud *poomp* in the small room.

I grabbed her and pulled her down on the bed, beginning to whisper softly. "We are alone, my blossom. No one will interrupt. We may do as we wish, as you have always wished. There's no one here but us satyrs."

I slept soundly until mid-morning. I expected Hench to wake me early. He usually arrived at the laboratory before seven and let me out to make coffee. When I finally heard him rummaging around outside my door, sunlight already streamed through the window.

I was about to get up and go out when the door—still unlocked from the Merton woman's visit—came open. Hench entered, his hands thrust into his jacket pockets, dark circles under his red eyes, looking shaken. The expression on his face was new to me.

"Hi, Hench, What's up? You look terrible. You look like a ton of bricks fell on you. What happened?"

Hench looked directly at me. "Why did you do it?"

"Do what? What are you talking about?"

"Don't lie. I talked to Audrey."

"Oh, that." I shrugged. "How do I know why I do things? It seemed like a good idea at the time. I am what I am, Hench." I grinned and folded back my upper lip.

Hench's expression hardened. I could see I was in trouble. I fell back on my usual argument. "Listen, Hench, you're the one who made me like this. I'm not responsible for the way I am."

"You're responsible for what you *do.*"

"Ha! I am what I am, Hench. You know that as well as I do."

The struggle on Hench's face looked nothing like his earlier dilemma. Something else was going on in his head. He looked like a sickly twin brother to the Hench I knew—to the Hench I understood.

He repeated his question. "Why did you do it?"

"What do you want from me, Hench? An accounting?"

"Yes."

"You certainly don't want the truth. That's clear enough from your face. By the way, your face could use a shave. Someone's liable to mistake you for me. We can't have that, can we? After all, you're a man and I'm just a—"

"Answer me."

I made calming gestures with my hands and stalled for time. What did I see in Hench's face? More importantly, what did he see when he looked at me? A rival? a defiler? A—what?

"Stay calm, Hench. I'm not some mere human being you can shove up against a wall and—"

"I want the truth."

He didn't. That was part of what I saw in his face. He wanted answers, yes, but not the truth, either about me or about the Merton woman. He wanted something from me to take away the pain he felt, the guilt and the responsibility. He wanted his accounting, not the truth.

But what do I know about such things? I am what I am, not what someone else sees in me. What could I have said to avoid a starship to some godforsaken hell hole and a life in the mines? Hench saw what he wanted to see. If I had lied, he would have heard only what he wanted to hear.

I leaned back on the bed, smiled and gave him what he said he wanted. "Pickings have been slim lately, Hench. I just took what she offered. She only struggled at first. After that, she liked it. It's what she wanted all along anyway, so what's the big deal? No harm done." I changed my smile to sincere. "And she really wasn't that bad, Hench, not that bad at all, especially after she let herself go."

Hench's hand came out of his jacket pocket. The last thing I remember was the *poomp* of the dart gun and the expression on Hench's face. In that instant before the dart hit, I realized what he saw when he looked at me, what he had seen since he came into my room. A rival? Yes. A defiler? Yes. And more. A man.

Analysis:

BEING AND DOING:
SOME THOUGHTS ABOUT RESPONSIBILITY

Michael Gorr

What exactly do we mean when we claim that someone is *responsible* for what he (or she) has done? Few questions in all of moral philosophy are as important as this one. Our entire system of punishment, for example, rests on the assumption that, at least sometimes, people can (and should) be held responsible[1] for what they do. Unfortunately, the really important questions in life are often the most difficult to answer and this is no exception. There are many radically different theories of what responsibility consists in and it is not at all clear how we are supposed to judge between them. Indeed there are some philosophers who go so far as to claim that once we do come to understand what responsibility involves, we will realize that none of us is ever *really* responsible for anything we do!

The "hero" in Robinett's tale may well agree with these philosophers. At least he claims that *he* is not responsible for any of his actions. In what follows we will try to determine why Silenus (the Satyr) argues this way and just how convincing his reasons are. In the process I hope we will come to better understand both what is involved in ascribing responsibility to people and when (if ever) we are justified in doing this.

From what we are told in the story, Silenus appears to be very similar to a human being. Granted, his physical appearance is somewhat odd (like his mythological namesake, he resembles a cross between a man and a goat) but that would hardly seem very important, at least with respect to the question of how we are morally obligated to *treat* him. What does seem important is that Silenus, like each of us, is a *rational agent,* i.e., a being capable of guiding his behavior on the basis of his reasoning. In fact, he is even capable of doing this at the expense of satisfying some rather strong inclinations (recall his behavior the *first* time he meets Merton's secretary). But if human beings are, in general, responsible for what they do, and if Silenus is, in all morally relevant respects, just like a human being, doesn't it follow that Silenus, too, must be a responsible agent?

[1]It should be noted, however, that *legal* responsibility is not always the same as moral responsibility. In this essay we will be primarily concerned with the latter.

Silenus does not seem to think so. Unfortunately he never explains very clearly why he believes this. About all he says is that he should not be held accountable for what he does because he is the creation of another person. But is this a good reason? Hench, after all, seems to disagree. He claims that Silenus *is* responsible for his actions, even though he (Hench) created him. Isn't it possible that Hench is correct? What reason would we have for thinking otherwise?

Here, I am afraid, we can only speculate. An argument that many people have accepted (and one that, perhaps, Silenus would accept) is the following:

1. A necessary condition for holding a person responsible for some action A is that the person did A *freely.*

2. A person who (like Silenus) was wholly the creation of another could never do anything freely.

3. Therefore, a person who (like Silenus) was wholly the creation of another could never be responsible for anything he does.

If statements (1) and (2) are correct, i.e., if the premises of the argument are true, we would certainly be compelled to accept the conclusion since it clearly follows from them. But *are* both of the premises true? Well, (1) certainly appears to be. If some act of mine is not free, i.e., if I am being forced or compelled to do what I do, then surely I am not responsible for it. Thus if someone pushes me into a third person who then falls and breaks his arm, it would be wrong to hold *me* responsible for that person's inury. And the reason for this seems obvious—in no sense was my behavior the result of my own *choosing.* Surely if anyone is responsible for what happened, it would have to be the person who pushed me.

Let us, then, grant the truth of (1). (2), however, is quite another story. There does not, on the face of it, seem to be any reason whatever for denying that someone could create a being with the ability to act freely. Christians, for example, believe that we were all created by God yet that we are all quite capable of acting freely. Clearly, then, if we are to accept the argument in question, we must show that there are good reasons for accepting (2).

Think again about the details of the story. Why would the fact that Hench created Silenus in his laboratory be a reason for thinking that Silenus' actions would necessarily be unfree? Perhaps the answer lies in the fact that it was Hench, not Silenus, who decided what sort of a brain and what sort of a body Silenus would have. Silenus, that is, had no say whatever in the choice of the genetic material from which he was constructed. Not only that, but he had no control over the environment into which he was placed. Surely, though, how Silenus behaves on any given occasion will always be wholly determined by the interaction of these two factors, viz., the genetic material from which he originated and the environmental influences to which he was exposed. Therefore how could any of his actions be said to be free?

Perhaps an example will make this argument a little clearer. Suppose that, in addition to Silenus, Hench had also constructed a small toy wind-up robot. Suppose further that after the robot is wound up it is placed on the ground and allowed to "walk." What would we have to know in order to determine where the robot will end up (and how long it will take to get there)? Clearly one thing we would need to understand is its internal make-up. We would need to know the nature and location of its internal parts, how they are fitted together, the material from which they were constructed, and so forth. But even if we knew all there was to know about the robot itself, would that be enough to enable us to predict where it would go and how fast it would get there? Surely not—we would also have to know quite a bit about the environment in which it was placed. We would have to know, for example, where it started from, what sort of surface it was travelling over (obviously it would travel faster on concrete than on soft ground or in mud), what direction it was pointed in, whether there were any obstacles in its path, etc. In addition, of course, we would have to know a fair amount of physics. We would have to know, for example, quite a bit about gravity, about friction, about force, and about motion (as well as how to measure each of these things).

Let us assume, though, that we were able to gather all of this information. Wouldn't we *then* be in a position to predict every movement the robot would make? It would certainly appear so since there do not seem to be any other factors that would possibly be relevant. Notice, however, that the only fundamental difference between Silenus and the robot seems to be one of degree—the former is just a much more *complex* sort of thing than is the latter. Nevertheless, regardless of how complex something is, surely its behavior must be wholly determined by the same two kinds of factors—its own nature (what it is made out of and how its parts are arranged) and the external factors in the environment which affect it. If we do not think the robot is responsible for its behavior, it would therefore seem to follow that we should not hold Silenus accountable for what he does either.

By now I hope you have begun to see that our discussion has implications not merely for the case of Silenus (who, after all, is just a fictional character) but for each and every one of us. For what we have said about the robot and Silenus would appear to be applicable to human beings as well. For what is a human being but a certain very complex system of material parts—bones, skin, blood, heart, kidneys, lungs, brain, and so on? Furthermore each of us lives our life in a certain determinate sort of environment. Therefore isn't it only reasonable to suppose that how a given human being behaves on any given occasion is simply a matter of (1) his/her internal make-up, which is itself the product of his/her genetic endowment and (2) the sort of environment in which he/she lives (and has lived)? What else could possibly be relevant? Consequently, just as we could *in principle* predict exactly how the robot will behave (assuming we knew enough about how it was constructed, about the environment in which it was placed, and about the relevant laws of physics) so too we could, at least in principle, predict the behavior of any human being so long as we had the same sort of information about him or her.

Of course no one at present has such information. There is an enormous amount, for example, that we have still to learn about the workings of the human body. Still the very fact that we know such an explanation is possible (even if we ourselves are not yet in a position to provide it) would by itself seem to suggest that none of us should ever be held responsible for anything we do.

Perhaps you are not yet convinced. You might point out that the real reason we don't hold the robot responsible for how it behaves is because we know that its behavior is not the result of any intention or choice on its part. Robots, after all, aren't even conscious. But the behavior of human beings is often the result of choice. When we do something (such as tell a lie or take a walk), it is normally because we *choose* to do so. Isn't that sufficient to show that we generally act out of our own free will and are therefore responsible for what we do?

Some philosophers do not find this argument satisfactory. They claim that the mere fact that we can choose how to act while the robot cannot is not enough to establish that we are ever responsible for what we do. The reason is very simple: the choices we make are *also* a joint product of our heredity and upbringing. If Smith, for example, chooses to go to law school rather than into the army, surely the explanation for his making such a choice lies in a combination of factors having to do with the sort of abilities, interests and desires he has together with the external factors that are (and have been) influencing him. Therefore the fact that a person's action is the result of a choice on his part would not justify us in holding him responsible for the action unless the choice itself was not—as it is—simply the product of hereditary and environmental factors.

This is a seductive argument that has certainly influenced many people. It has not, however, convinced everyone. Many philosophers, in fact, believe this argument should not be accepted because it rests upon a gross misunderstanding of what responsibility and freedom require. That is, those who accept the argument seem to assume that one cannot be responsible for an action so long as that action can be traced back to causal factors (such as heredity and upbringing) over which one had no *control*. But, if this is so, can we specify what *would* be required for a person to be genuinely responsible for his/her actions? What we would have to say, apparently, is that we would be responsible for our actions only if they were *not* caused (at least entirely) by factors that lie beyond our control.

But this would be a most peculiar notion of responsibility. Suppose I am sitting next to you at the dinner table when suddenly my arm shoots out, striking your wine glass and spilling its contents all over the table. According to the view under discussion, for the movement of my hand to be something for which I am responsible, it must not be something caused (at least wholly) by hereditary and environmental factors. But then what else *could* it be caused by? We surely cannot say that it was simply *uncaused,* for that would be to say that it *just happened* ("out of the blue," so to speak), a fact which would hardly be compatible with regarding it as something *I* was responsible for. But is there any plausible third alternative? I must admit that I do not know of any.[2]

It appears, then, that those who argue that responsibility requires an absence of causal determination are simply mistaken. It is, of course, possible to admit this and maintain that what it shows is that the very notion of responsibility should be rejected as incoherent since it is incompatible *both* with the presence of causally determining factors *and* with the absence of causally determining factors. That is, it looks as if we can't be responsible for our actions if they *are* (ultimately) caused by factors outside our control and that we can't be responsible for our actions if they are *not* (ultimately) caused by factors outside our control. Those, however, are the only two possibilities. Consequently we might conclude that the concept of responsibility is like the concept of a round square—it is just senseless and should be jettisoned.

But *this* argument can't be right either. Surely the notion of responsibility is *not* a senseless one. After all, we successfully employ it many times each day in thinking about and judging the behavior of other people. It is also used extensively in the law, where a determination of *legal* responsibility can sometimes spell the difference between being set free and being sent to prison. In light of this can we really regard

---

[2]For an interesting (though, I believe, unsuccessful) attempt to develop such a theory, see Roderick Chisholm's essay, "Freedom and Action" in Keith Lehrer, ed., *Freedom and Determinism* (New York, 1966).

the very concept of responsibility as meaningless? If the argument we have been considering has such an implication, it would seem more reasonable to conclude that it is the argument, rather than the concept, that is deficient.

Consider again the case where someone pushes me up against a third person (call him Jones) who then falls and injures himself. Clearly, we agreed, this would not be a case where I could be held responsible for what happened. Suppose, however, that instead of being pushed I deliberately *chose* to hurl myself at Jones with the *intention* of knocking him down. That seems to be a paradigm example of an action for which the agent is responsible. But just what is the difference between the two cases? So far as we can tell, it is not that in one of the two cases my behavior is *uncaused*. Surely in both cases my behavior of knocking Jones down is fully caused. Perhaps, then, the difference lies in the *kind* of causation involved. In the case where I am pushed by another, my behavior is not a consequence of anything that I intend (or desire or choose). In the second case, however, it is precisely because I intend to injure Jones that I in fact bump into him. Had I not chosen as I did, I would not have acted as I did. Perhaps, then, one is responsible for one's actions only in those cases where one's actions are caused *in a certain way*, viz., by a desire for the occurrence of just the sort of behavior that in fact occurs.[3] That, I think, is at least what most of us tend to believe. Is there any good reason for not accepting this theory?

We have already considered one such objection. How, it was asked, can the fact that a person chooses to perform some action justify us in holding him responsible for that action unless the desire he acted upon was itself something he was responsible for? But surely no one is responsible for the desires he has—they are wholly the product of the interaction of one's genetic inheritance and the features of one's environment.

One who proposes to defend the doctrine of human responsibility can only respond, I think, by saying that we *can* be responsible for what we *do* even if (as seems to be the case) we are not responsible for our desires or intentions. This, I think, is the point Hench makes when, near the end of the story, he insists that, although Silenus is not responsible for his own genetic constitution (including his "weakness for the ladies"), he is nevertheless responsible for what he *does* when he decides to act on the basis of his desires. The mistake of those who argue that we can never be responsible for what we do because our behavior is *ultimately* determined by factors lying outside our control is the assumption that one cannot be responsible for one's behavior unless

---

[3] I do not mean to suggest that the *only* time a person is responsible for something is where he deliberately brings it about. Obviously we are also sometimes responsible for what we make happen when we have acted recklessly or negligently.

one is responsible for all the factors which causally explain that behavior. But this assumption is just false! I do not have to be responsible for my desires (let alone the structure of my genes) in order to be responsible for my actions. To be responsible for an action just requires that we have had control over *it, not* that we have had control over what led up to it. And one has control over an action so long as its occurrence depends upon one's *own choice* to bring it about. Since it is often the case that we do something only because we choose to, it follows that we are often responsible for what we do.

It seems, therefore, that we should accept the view that Silenus is caused by his genetic structure and his environment to do everything he does, that is, that everything he does is *ultimately* determined by causes outside of his control. But we must not conclude from this that Silenus is right in claiming that he is not responsible for his actions, or that Hench has no good reason to punish him for raping Audrey Merton.

The actual punishment Hench metes out is, however, another matter. For though Silenus is clearly responsible for the rape, it is not at all obvious that selling him to Audrey's father is a morally defensible reaction to it. After all, now that we have concluded that Silenus is not particularly different from us in terms of how we view him morally, selling him *does* look like slave trade, as Silenus is quick to point out. (It is interesting that Silenus says this—for unless he really is just like other responsible creatures, he would be no better than an object to be bought and sold. Why *not* view him as an article of trade if he is not in any important way different from a wind-up toy robot?) It is at least arguable that being sold into slavery for a life of hard labor in the mines of a hostile planet is an excessively harsh penalty for Silenus' particular misbehavior, though some punishment is clearly warranted. We might charitably hope that Hench and Merton send poor Silenus a suitable number of Maenads or nymphs or whatever, to soften the severity of this punishment. But then, they will undoubtedly be responsible moral creatures too (being female versions of Silenus), and what will *they* have done to be sent off to the mines? Perhaps Hench ought to find another line of work . . .

CHAPTER 6 PROBES

1. What happens to Silenus at the end of Stephen Robinett's story? Why?

2. Is Silenus a determinist, a libertarian, or a compatibilist? In the beginning of the story, does Hench tend to agree or disagree with Silenus? How about at the end? Why does each feel as he does?

3. Is Gorr a determinist, a libertarian, or a compatibilist? Why?

4. On what grounds does Silenus justify his view of the extent of his moral responsibility? Are you convinced by his argument? Why or why not?

5. Does Gorr think that Hench was right to hold Silenus responsible for his behavior? Why or why not?

6. Gorr finds evidence in "The Satyr" for the view that Silenus actually can control his behavior. What is this evidence? Does it show what Gorr thinks it shows? How is this relevant to the question of responsibility in Gorr's view? Do you agree or disagree with Gorr on this point?

7. In your opinion, is there any important difference between Silenus and normal human beings with regard to considering them responsible creatures or moral *agents*? If so, what is it? If not, why not?

8. Imagine that Silenus were to read Gorr's essay and reply

O.K., on your definition of "responsibility," I am responsible. But your definition misses the point, which is that I *couldn't do otherwise.* Thus, I did in some sense "choose" to do what I did, but, since this "choice" was itself caused by my environment and my genetic structure, I couldn't *help* but make this "choice." Surely I can't reasonably be held responsible for something simply on the ground that it was caused by a mental event of mine (my "choice") if the mental event was itself caused by something else—something over which I had no control. No matter how you look at it, I couldn't do otherwise than do as I did—I couldn't do otherwise than "choose" as I did. So how can you hold me responsible?

Is this reply decisive against Gorr? Why or why not?

9. What if Gorr were to reply to this as follows:

Your not being able to do otherwise is not entirely to the point. For I can imagine cases where someone cannot do other than they do, but are still rightly to be held responsible for their behavior. For example, imagine a man (Jones) connected to a machine operated by another man (Smith). Smith's machine is hooked up to Jones's brain in such a way as to allow Smith to be able to make Jones do whatever Smith wants him to do, and Smith is an extremely malevolent person. Thus, Smith wants Jones to do all and only evil things. If Jones chooses to do evil things without Smith's interference, Smith does not use his machine . . . but if Jones chooses not to do something evil, Smith will make him do it anyhow. For any given evil thing, then (for example, a murder), Jones can't do otherwise. Now I agree that, if Smith and his machine *make* Jones do it against his will, Jones is not responsible for the murder. But even though he cannot do otherwise (because Smith would make him do it even if Jones chose not to), if Jones commits murder by his own choice, he would rightly be held responsible for it. For the point is that in this case Smith *did not* make him do it—Jones did it by choice—even though he couldn't do otherwise! Hence, not being able to do otherwise is not decisive evidence against responsibility.

Do you agree or disagree with this argument? Does it prove that responsibility does not require the ability to do otherwise?

10. What if, after giving the argument in question 9, Gorr were to say

Look, the case I've given here is pretty weird, I agree, but don't you see that it is not necessarily any different from what a lot of people believe anyhow? Many believe that God is powerful enough to make us do anything He wants us to do, but in some cases at least He lets us do what we choose. The way theists have long thought about this is that in those cases where we do something by our own choice, *we* are responsible *even though* (for all we know) *God might have made us do it anyhow!* Theists can never be certain that people could do otherwise than what they do, for they can never be certain that their omnipotent God wouldn't have made them do what they did even if they hadn't chosen to do it themselves. But this doesn't mean that the concepts of "sin" and "saintliness" are problematic for the theist. If you want to argue that they are, you shall have to do better than saying that "sinners" and "saints" couldn't do otherwise. Many theists might be willing to admit this as a possibility from the very beginning, but few would be compelled by this to suppose that sinners shouldn't be held responsible for their behavior, when it is their choice, and that saints are not to be praised for those things they do by choice.

Does this argument work? Why or why not?

11. Now that you have thought more about libertarianism, determinism, and compatibilism, which are you inclined to believe? Why?

12. Can you think of a story that would best show why your view is the correct one, that is, a story that the other views could not analyze in their way?

RECOMMENDED READING

Science Fiction and the Problem of Free Will

Comparatively few science fiction stories tackle the problem of free will directly, but many of the plots have important implications concerning the claim that all of human behavior is determined. Kurt Vonnegut, Jr. is one of the few writers explicitly preoccupied with the free will issue in many of his novels. He takes the hard determinist line, making alien beings persuade human characters that free will is an illusion peculiar to the human species. The Tralfamadorians play this role in *Slaughterhouse Five* (Dell, 1971) and in *The Sirens of Titan* (Dell, 1971). The former novel was the basis of a film directed by George Roy Hill in 1971. Vonnegut's views of free will are reminiscent of those of ancient stoics such as Marcus Aurelius. The free will issue is pursued on a more philosophical plane in B. F. Skinner's *Walden Two* (Macmillan, 1948), which defends the view that human behavior is determined by environmental conditioning. Skinner proposed the use of operant conditioning to establish a utopian society.

Many authors deal with the free will issue tangentially also as they consider whether human behavior could ever be entirely predictable. Isaac Asimov's Hugo-winning *Foundation* (Avon, 1970) employs the idea of psychohistory, discovered by a scientist, Harry Seldon, which has extremely high predictive power. It predicts the fall and eventual reappearance of galactic civilization. Nevertheless, the predictions are evidently not infallible, and paradoxes involving the indeterminacy of social forecasting are touched upon by Asimov. Frank Herbert's trilogy *Dune, Dune Messiah,* and *Children of Dune* (Berkley, 1975, 1976), which won two Hugos and a Nebula, describes a future religious movement in which the Muad Dib is bred, conditioned with a "spice" drug, and trained to have highly developed and prophetic powers. The capacity of newly evolving beings to foresee the future receives increasing emphasis as the trilogy unfolds. Similar prophetic powers are described by Henry Kuttner (with C.L. Moore's help) in *Fury* (Lancer, © 1947). Brian W. Aldiss offers a fascinating "test" of the deterministic hypothesis in "Man in His Time," in Aldiss and Harry Harrison, eds., *Nebula Award Stories Number Two* (Pocket Book, 1968). Here an astronaut, as a result of an accident in space, responds now to events occurring three minutes in our own future.

Science fiction stories suggest a variety of ways in which human behavior is determined. The ancient belief that the human will is subject to the will of God or to some transcendant supernatural force like fate or kharma is represented with some levity in Larry Niven's *Ringworld* (Ballantine, 1970). (The awarding of both the Nebula and the Hugo to this book was a stroke of luck.) In sharp contrast Algis Budrys uses a naturalistic style in *The Falling Torch* (Pyramid, 1974) to show how a revolutionary hero's actions were, in fact, completely determined by historical forces outside his control. The idea that we are all puppets on strings which are pulled by subconscious forces within us has been argued by philosophers influenced by Freud's psychoanalytic theory. The use of modern psychological theories to control human behavior through "brainwashing" is the subject of Richard Condon's *Manchurian Candidate* (Dell, 1974), which became a popular film by John Frankenheimer (1962). At one time the use of psychological techniques in advertising caused a great deal of anxiety. This is expressed in J. G. Ballard's "Subliminal Man," in Robert Silverberg, ed., *The Mirror of Infinity* (Harper & Row, 1973), in which people compulsively buy products as a result of subliminal influences. Sociobiology has suggested that human behavior is biologically determined. James Tiptree, Jr.'s Nebula-winning "Love Is the Plan the Plan Is Death," in Kate Wilhelm, ed., *Nebula Award Stories Number Nine* (Bantam, 1978) contains a very imaginative description of an insectlike alien species' struggle against its biological imperatives. The story ironically suggests that even our rebellious assertions of free will may themselves be biologically programmed.

Philosophy and the Problem of Free Will

Philosophy, in contrast, provides the bibliographer with an embarrassment of riches on free will. A comprehensive summary is available in "Determinism," in *The Encyclopedia of Philosophy,* which has a long bibliography. A clear introductory book on the subject is D. J. O'Connor, *Free Will* (Doubleday, 1971). Several anthologies represent diverse approaches to the issue: B. Berofsky, ed., *Free Will and Determinism* (Harper, 1966); S. Hook, ed., *Determinism and Freedom in the Age of Modern Science* (Collier, 1961); K. Lehrer, ed., *Freedom and Determinism* (Random House, 1966); and S. Morgenbesser and J. Walsh, eds., *Free Will* (Prentice-Hall, 1962).

John Hospers, "What Means This Freedom?," defends hard determinism on the basis of the psychoanalytic theory of psychoanalysis (in Berofsky and in Hook). Libertarianism is defended by C. A. Campbell (in Berofsky) and by Jean-Paul Sartre, in *Being and Nothingness* (Philosophical Library, 1965, trans. Hazel Barnes; excerpts in Berofsky and in Morgenbesser and Walsh). A painstaking critique of this position is C. D. Broad, "Determinism, Indeterminism, and Libertarianism" (in Berofsky and in Morgenbesser and Walsh).

R. E. Hobart defends a form of compatibilism in "Free Will as Involving Determination and Inconceivable Without It" (in Berofsky and in Morgenbesser and Walsh). This is criticized by P. Foote (in Berofsky). Hobart's compatibilist view is also called "soft determinism," because it tries to reconcile free will with complete determinism. Another view of compatibilism like the form presented in *Thought Probes* (namely, that free actions are caused without being altogether determined) has been defended, in various forms; for example, see the essays by R. Chisholm and K. Lehrer in the Lehrer anthology. An early treatment of voluntary action which anticipates compatibilism is offered by Aristotle in *Nicomachean Ethics,* Book III, Chapters 1–5, and *Eudemian Ethics,* Book II, Chapters 6–10 (in Morgenbesser and Walsh). An influential essay closely related to compatibilism is D. Davidson, "Actions, Reasons and Causes" (in Berofsky).

VALUE THEORY:

Can you know what is right or wrong?

Many of the things we do are based upon judgments of value, of one sort or another. We decide to do something because doing it is, in our opinion, the right thing to do. But actions might be "right" or "wrong" in very different ways. Sometimes, it is a *moral* or *ethical* "rightness." For example, a soldier who receives an order to shoot an unarmed civilian might refuse to carry it out because it would be morally wrong to do such an act. Sometimes the "rightness" is *aesthetic*. For example, the painter decides to use a certain color or brushstroke because it will better serve his or her sense of artistic value. Often the "rightness" is simply *pragmatic*. For example, a dull butter-knife is not the right tool to use to cut a steak. There is nothing immoral or unaesthetic about a dull knife, but it has less practical value than a sharp knife (at least for cutting steak). In this context a thing has value if it serves a specific practical goal.

But what is it that makes things right? What makes them valuable? What makes something morally good or artistically good or practically good? Suppose a soldier who has been ordered to shoot unarmed civilians were to ask, "Is it morally wrong to shoot innocent persons? Or is it always right to follow orders?" What would you say to the soldier? If so many of our judgments are based upon values, but it turns out that we cannot *justify* those values, most of our judgments are, after all is said and done, equally unjustified.

This chapter introduces the issues involved with value theory, specifically, those involved with the problem of justifying values. The purpose of this chapter is not to defend any particular system of justification but, rather, to explore some of the various systems that have been offered. After completing this chapter, you should be able to do the following:

- Identify the various areas of inquiry within value theory.

- Explain the differences between the most popular varieties of ethical theory.

- Critically examine these theories for adequacy.

- Consider the relative merits of one particular view on the basis of a conceptual experiment.

7:1 THE STUDY OF VALUE

7:1.1 Ethics, the central concern of this chapter, is one type of value inquiry. Other types are aesthetics and pragmatics. These types of value theory differ from each other in terms of the kinds of values which they study. *Ethics* is a philosophical study of moral values. It tries to understand the nature of human values and rights (such as life, liberty, and the pursuit of happiness), of human virtues (such as justice, courage, and chastity), and of human obligations (such as respect for other persons). *Aesthetics* is a philosophical study of aesthetic values such as beauty and the sublime. It tries to understand what makes some things beautiful and others ugly, and why some works of art are regarded as successful or even great and others as failures. *Pragmatics* is concerned with things which are "valuable" in the sense that they are the best means to a given goal. This is referred to as "practical" value or "instrumental" value. If you proceed from the assumption that it is a good thing to wage war against other persons, you will want to develop "better" weapons and tactics. Pragmatics does not try to evaluate our goals but concentrates on the means by which we try to attain those goals. For example, pragmatics might try to map out strategies by which a group of persons could attain their individual goals (whatever they are) most efficiently and minimize conflict and friction among themselves. The individuals in question might be a company of saints, a gang of bank robbers, or an army at war. The question of whether we are morally justified in going to war against other persons and enslaving them to our will is not a question for pragmatics but for ethics.

7:1.2 Ethics itself takes quite different forms. Each type of ethics approaches moral issues in a different way. Consider as an example the case in which a young girl, who has unintentionally become pregnant and has no husband, obtains an abortion. Some persons might blame her for taking this action, others might argue that she is not to blame. But this one case raises many different ethical questions on many different levels. In the first place, in blaming the girl for terminating her pregnancy, a person will be assuming that she is responsible for her actions. But the question might be raised whether the girl really acted out of her own free will, since she was motivated by fear of reprisal from her parents, of financial distress, of being deserted, and so forth. These questions about free will and moral responsibility are taken up in Chapter 6. The part of ethics that considers such questions is, rather grandly, called *the metaphysics of morals* because it probes the relationship between the study of reality (metaphysics) and the study of moral values.

On another level, one might ask whether it is morally wrong for a girl in such circumstances to have an abortion. All sorts of arguments have been offered, pro and con, on the abortion issue. For example, some argue that abortion is wrong because to abort a fetus is to take a human life, and it is never right to take a human life because life is the highest possible value. Such arguments are the concern of *normative ethics*. A very important branch of normative ethics studies the moral issues involved in law, politics, and social life. For example, some persons criticize laws against abortion, because they think that it is wrong for the government to interfere with the decisions that a woman makes in regard to her own body. This branch of ethics, which is called social ethics, is explored in Chapter 8.

Sometimes the discussion of ethical issues takes place on a still deeper level. If someone were to criticize the girl who had sought an abortion on the grounds that life is the highest possible value, a defender of the girl might ask: "*Why* is life the highest possible value? Why not take the girl's suffering into account also?" The critic might respond, "Because God tells us, 'Thou shalt not kill.' " At such a point the girl's defender might respond in several ways; for example, "Even if God were to say that, would that *make* it always wrong to take a life?" Or "What were God's *reasons* for telling us this?" Or "Even if you're right that life is a 'moral value,' why should the girl care about that?" Once the argument takes this turn, the disputants have entered into the deepest and most challenging sphere of ethics, which is called *metaethics*. This part of ethics is concerned with identifying the nature of values, with defending moral concepts like "right" or "wrong," and with finding the ultimate *foundations* for all our value judgments. Despite its abstract nature, this is the most important part of ethics, because, when we make hard moral choices in everyday life or carry on moral arguments with others, we have to assume that there are answers to the basic questions of metaethics: "What are values? How can we justify our value claims? Why should we care about what is the moral thing to do?"

7:1.3   In this chapter you will be exploring two basic questions about the foundations of ethics: "What is the *meaning* of value words like 'good' or 'right'? Can I *know* whether value claims like 'Killing is wrong' are true or false?" Three types of theories have tried to answer these questions:

- *Definist* theories state: "Value words can be defined in terms of ordinary facts, so value judgments can be known to be true or false." (See 7:2)

- *Noncognitive* theories state: "Value words ca*nnot* be defined in terms of ordinary facts, so value judgments can*not* be known to be true or false." (See 7:3)

- *Nonfactual knowledge* theories state: "Value words cannot be defined in terms of ordinary facts, *but* value judgments *can* be known to be true or false." (See 7:4)

7:1.4 The point and importance of these theories can be appreciated by means of a conceptual experiment in a familiar science fiction setting. Suppose that a gigantic, amoebalike organism has been discovered by humans exploring far reaches of the galaxy. The organism is sentient and believed to be of extremely high intelligence. However, it is the only creature of its kind in evidence and is thought to have developed over time from an original living cell, so that no other life forms have evolved on its planet. A human team is assigned the task of establishing communication with the organism and of translating human terms into the alien entity's language. The project meets with surprising success at first, and the alien creature soon has a thorough grasp of human science. But the team finds our human vocabulary of ethical terms such as "good" and "bad" to be utterly incomprehensible to the alien. The alien complains, "I understand what it means for one of your species to *kill* another. It means to perform an action, such as discharging a weapon with one of your pseudopods, that causes life functions to cease in another member of your species. But I have no idea whatsoever what it means when you say, 'Killing is *wrong*.' And I have no way of knowing when one of your actions is wrong. This word 'wrong' does not compute." If you were on this team, how would you explain the word 'wrong' to the alien?

This thought experiment will provide a convenient framework for introducing each of the theories of ethical foundations.

7:2 DEFINIST VIEWS

7:2.1 Some members of the team might take the following approach to the alien's query: "Value words like 'right' and 'wrong' are defined in the same way as words like 'kill.' In general, value words are defined in terms of perfectly ordinary facts. An act such as a killing has a number of properties involving the place where it occurred, how long it took, who was killed, and so forth. We have already defined words like 'quickly' and 'in the ship' for you, so you should have no problem knowing whether it is true that someone was killed quickly in the ship. But since a value term like 'wrong' can also be defined in terms of the properties of actions, you will have no more problem in knowing whether it is true that the killing of someone in the ship was wrong." This is the response of the *ethical definist*. Moral judgments can be known to be true or false to the same degree and in the same way as ordinary factual judgments, because moral terms can be defined in terms of properties which we can know to belong or not to belong to things.

This response is only a first step in answering the problem, however. For suppose the alien asks, "What *is* this property which I can use to define a value word like 'right' or 'wrong'?" Two main sorts of answers have been offered to this question: *naturalist* and *transcendental.*

7:2.2 *Hedonism,* which in its crudest form states that goodness is identical to pleasure and badness with pain or the lack of pleasure, is a *naturalistic* theory. According to hedonism, if it is true to say that a thing is pleasurable, it will be true by definition that that thing is good, for saying the one is the same as saying the other. Since whether something is pleasurable or not is easily observable, and since goodness is defined in terms of pleasure, that something is good or not is easily observable, according to the hedonist. An act like killing would be defined as "wrong" if it produced pain.

There are other, more sophisticated naturalistic views which tie goodness to pleasure. One such example can be found in many varieties of *utilitarianism.* Such varieties have it that goodness is the maximization of pleasure for the greatest number of people. In such a view, killing a person would be wrong only if it produced less pleasure and more pain than not killing him. For example, it might not be wrong to kill an insane dictator in order to prevent war and widespread suffering. Another naturalistic view is *ethical egoism,* which states that goodness is whatever is in one's own self-interest. An alternative form of utilitarianism is like this, saying that goodness is what is maximally in the self-interest of the greatest number. Other naturalistic views include *ethical Darwinism* (which defines "goodness" as "whatever promotes the evolution and endurance of the human species"). Yet another version of naturalism is *ethical relativism.* This defines "goodness" as "whatever is prescribed or condoned by a such-and-such society, group, or individual." In such a view, what is good for one society may not be good for another. For example, killing will be "bad" for a pacifistic culture, but "good" for a warlike people. In fact, "good" will not mean the same thing for different societies. But still you can *know* whether killing is "good" in any given society. The last example of naturalism is, in fact, similar to another major type of definism, *transcendental ethics.*

7:2.3 *Transcendental* definist views generally hold that moral words cannot be defined in terms of properties which can be experienced through the senses. But they *can* be defined in terms of certain extranatural or supernatural properties. One familiar example of this is found in many religious ethics. When you say that something is "good" in such accounts, you *mean* that "God condones or prescribes it." If it is true that God condones or prescribes something, it is true *by definition* that the thing is good; if it is true that God condemns or forbids it, it is true *by definition* that the thing is bad. Most religions believe that God is not a "natural being," that is, a being which can be observed by the senses but is, rather, a transcendent or supernatural being. So the fact that God condemns or forbids killing may not be a fact of nature as we know it, but it will still be a fact, and it can be known, to the extent that we have knowledge of any such extranatural facts.[1]

7:2.4   The definist response is the most direct way of answering the problem about meaning and knowledge in ethics. But many philosophers regarded this whole approach as a mass of mistakes. The famous eighteenth-century British philosopher David Hume wondered how the proponents of such views thought they could derive statements of moral obligation from simple statements of facts:

> In every system of morality, which I have hitherto met with, I have always remark'd, that the author proceeds for some time in the ordinary way of reasoning, and establishes the being of a God, or makes some observations concerning human affairs; when of a sudden I am surpriz'd to find, that instead of the usual copulations of propositions, *is,* and *is not,* I meet with no proposition that is not connected with an *ought* or an *ought not.* This change is imperceptible; but is, however, of the last consequence. For as this *ought,* or *ought not,* expresses some new relation or affirmation, 'tis necessary that it shou'd be observ'd and explain'd; and at the same time that a reason should be given, for what seems altogether inconceivable, how this new relation can be a deduction from others, which are entirely different from it.[2]

Many philosophers have shared Hume's suspicions. If I say that killing *is* productive of pain, how can I, as a matter of logic, conclude that killing *ought not* to occur? The conclusion, by making an "ought" statement, introduces a whole new consideration not even hinted at in the premise. It has often been observed that values and facts do not seem to have the same logical status, yet definists fail to make any distinction of a logical kind between the two sorts of commitments. In fact, like a wallpaper desperately trying to conceal cracks in the walls, the definist tries to conceal the gap between "is" and "ought" by defining "ought" in terms of "is," defining the one in terms of the other.

Another objection was made by the British philosopher G. E. Moore, early in the twentieth century. According to Moore, all definist reasoning is fallacious. The word "bachelor" is defined as "an unmarried adult male." If

---

[1]Another transcendental view is argued by Plato, the ancient Greek philosopher. According to Plato, what makes things good is a special relation between that thing and an extranatural realm of pure qualities called "Forms." Thus, a good thing would be good in virtue of its resemblance to the Form of Good, a transcendent thing which can be understood by pure reasoning but is not perceivable via the senses.

[2]David Hume, *A Treatise of Human Nature,* Book III, Part I, Section I.

I agree that someone is unmarried, adult, and male, but deny that he is a bachelor, I will contradict myself and thus make no sense, for saying that he is unmarried, adult, and male is just to say that he is a bachelor. But all definists' definitions are quite unlike this, according to Moore. The hedonist would define the good as pleasure. But I can always agree that something is pleasurable, but deny that it is good, without contradicting myself and speaking nonsense. Whether or not I am right in my assessments of the goodness or pleasure in such a case, I will never be wrong *because* I have contradicted myself. This shows, according to Moore, that "good" and "pleasure" cannot *mean* the same thing. We can similarly *make sense* of saying that there are bad self-interests, bad ways of evolution, bad societal prescriptions, even bad supernatural prescriptions. It does not matter whether or not there, in fact, *are* such things. The point is that we can *make sense* of the idea that there *could* be. As long as this is true, the attempt to define value words in terms of these sorts of properties is hopelessly misguided.

7:3 NONCOGNITIVE VIEWS

7:3.1 Let us return to the thought experiment of 7:1.4. A team of lexicographers is trying to explain to a highly intelligent but apparently amoral alien how to understand and know the truth of our value judgments. The alien judges the attempt by the definists to be a failure: "You wanted to define terms like 'good' and 'bad' in terms of psychological states of your life form like pleasure and pain or in terms of the pronouncements you attribute to your deity. But your own philosophers named Hume and Moore have shown that this cannot be done. Thus you have not answered my question. How can I *know* that a statement such as 'Killing is wrong' is true?"

A *noncognitivist* would respond to this query, "The simple fact is that you *cannot know* the truth of such statements. In human languages value statements don't play the same sort of role as statements that describe certain facts of reality, such as 'Last night there was a killing on the ship.' Since value statements like 'Killing is wrong' describe nothing, there is no way for you to know whether or not they are true."

The alien might respond, somewhat perplexed, "Does that mean such statements are *meaningless?*" To this question some very radical philosophers, called *nihilists,* have offered the puzzling answer, "Yes, they are all meaningless and useless" (7:3.2). But others, called *emotivists,* have answered, "Yes, they are *meaningless* in the ordinary sense of the word, but they still have a very important use" (7:3.3).

7:3.2 The most dramatic form of noncognitivism is *ethical nihilism.* The Latin word *nihil* means nothing, and this is what the nihilist thinks ethics are—nothing at all. The nihilist thinks that morals are simply fictitious, meaningless, and without real function. To utter, "Murder is wrong," for the nihilist, is no more meaningful or purposeful than to make nonsense noises. There is no such thing as right and wrong, and making ethical utterances accomplishes nothing at all, or whatever it might accomplish is purely accidental.[3]

7:3.3 *Emotivists* take a less radical position. Moral claims and judgments play an identifiable and unique role in our actions. Although ethical utterances do not rightly or wrongly describe truths of any kind, they serve to express emotions. Moreover, the emotions expressed are peculiarly *moral* in nature. Although you might express emotions by simply screaming, these emotions need not be moral. (You might be expressing fury and anguish when you scream as a result of pouring scalding coffee on yourself. For all its emotional consequence, however, you are not aroused morally in such a case. On the other hand, if someone else pours scalding coffee on you, you might be inclined to burst forth with a moral utterance which condemns them for their action in addition to expressing fury and anguish in a scream.) The emotivists thus distinguish between descriptive utterances and expressive ones. A *descriptive* utterance is an attempt to say something about a given object, action, or person. As such, it is either true or false. An example of such an utterance would be "Jones shot Smith." It is either true or false that Jones shot Smith. On the other hand, if you say "It was wrong of Jones to shoot Smith," all that is true or false in this claim is the implication that Jones, in fact, shot Smith. To add that it was *wrong* of Jones to do this describes nothing new about the situation. It simply expresses your negative attitude about this alleged fact. For this reason, some debunkers of emotivism call it the "Boo–Hurrah" theory. For the emotivist, saying that something is wrong is no more descriptive of anything than booing it, and saying that it is right is comparable to yelling "hurrah." Other emotivist accounts add that you may use moral utterances to arouse emotions in others as well as to express your own feelings. A lawyer might say "It was wrong of Jones to shoot Smith" to arouse the sentiments of people on a jury.

More sophisticated emotivists try to show that, even though moral statements are neither true nor false, it does not follow that "anything goes" when you make such a statement. Our moral statements must meet conditions of relevance. For example, the utterance must be somehow appropriate to the situation. One doesn't reasonably call a moral act bad *simply* because it is performed at 3:00 P.M. Also, value judgments must be susceptible to comparative judgments: For something to be morally bad, there must be other things which are morally better. Thus, although the emotivist believes

---

[3]Closely related to this is a version of relativism. According to this view the statement "Slavery is wrong" is meaningless and neither true or false. Yet the relativist concedes that it makes sense to say, "The statement 'Slavery is wrong' is true in the United States today but was false before 1863." But the relativist explains this as follows, "Before 1863 Americans did not accept the statement, 'Slavery is wrong.' Since 1863 they have accepted the statement. However the statement itself is meaningless."

ιnat moral terms are not in themselves meaningful, they do serve special functions, and their use can be either appropriate or inappropriate.

Some noncognitivists are ethical relativists. If I believe that goodness is what is prescribed by society, for example, I might be a naturalist, for I might believe that each society's prescriptions provide the (local) definition of "goodness." If, on the other hand, I don't really believe that there is any such thing as goodness (relative or not), but only believe that what is called "good" is relative to the society in which such judgments are made, I am a noncognitivist. For now I do not think that saying, for example, "slavery is wrong" is now *true* in the United States. I am only saying that it is currently *accepted* in the United States, despite the fact that there really are no such things as right and wrong.

7:3.4 The nihilist simply stands firm and asserts that ethics is all a pack of nonsense. The only way to refute such a position is to develop an alternative ethical position which avoids the difficulties raised by Hume, Moore, and other philosophers. Since emotivism tries to offer a positive alternative to definism, it is possible to direct some criticisms toward it. Some philosophers question whether moral claims necessarily express the speaker's feelings or attitudes. For example, a man might have been raised to have sexist attitudes toward women. Yet one might want to say that he *knows* that sexism is wrong. The male chauvinist might concede that sexism is wrong even though he has sexist feelings and attitudes. Hence, says the critic, the statement "Sexism is wrong" does not necessarily express negative emotions toward sexism.

But most opponents resist noncognitivism primarily because it does not allow for moral knowledge. It removes value judgments from the realm of objectivity where we find scientific judgments. For there is no guarantee that a group of impartial persons will come to an agreement on moral statements if they merely express the attitudes of these persons. Moreover, the moral judgments of an Adolf Hitler will ultimately be on the same footing as the moral judgments of an Albert Schweitzer. Each is simply expressing his own attitudes.

7:4 NONFACTUAL KNOWLEDGE THEORIES

7:4.1 A final response remains to our problems, "What do value statements mean?" and "How do we know whether they are true or false?" This is the response that the statement "Killing is wrong" represents a *special* kind of knowledge unlike the other knowledge we have of facts about the world. In order to understand such statements one will have to be capable of this kind of moral knowledge.

The two preceding theories, definism and noncognitivism, disagree as to whether a value statement like "Killing is wrong" describes a fact. Are values the same as facts? The definist says "Yes," the noncognitivist says, "No." The definist argues, "Because values are facts, values can be known." The noncognitivist argues, "Because values are *not* facts, values can*not* be known." Notice that both theories *agree* on the assumption: Whether values can be known depends on whether they are facts.

The third response sees this common assumption as the common mistake of these theories. In this new view, values can be known even if they cannot be identified with facts. This view will, therefore, be called the *nonfactual knowledge* view. The famous eighteenth-century German philosopher Immanuel Kant, for example, afforded ethical judgments with a special logical status which made them knowable, but not factual and not capable of being analyzed (by definitions known or any other means) into other nonethical terms. One such judgment was the principle of universalizability: You should act according to rules of conduct which could be consistently acted upon by all rational beings. Kant argued that lying is wrong on this basis. If everyone were always lying to everyone else, communications would break down and even lying would be impossible. Although he would say that ethical claims might be known, they would not be known in the same way as either "The Eiffel Tower is in France" is known, or "Two plus two equals four" is known. That is, moral claims are neither known just as facts nor as purely conceptual truths though they might nonetheless be true.

G. E. Moore, who so sharply criticizes the definist view, does not deny that moral claims can be known either. According to Moore's view (which is called *intuitionism*), moral values are known but cannot be defined, as they are simple properties (imagine attempting to define the color green to a blind man—all the talk in the world about electromagnetic radiation and spectra won't help him understand the sensation). We have, according to Moore, a moral sense, the intuitive appeal to which tells us right from wrong.

7:4.2 Critics of such attempts at compromise positions between the definist and noncognitivist views will either deny that there is any other sort of knowledge than the sort employed by the definists and noncognitivists in their accounts, or argue that any concept of knowledge without a standard concept of truth as a prerequisite is incorrect. Thus, critics of Kant often deny his special sort of knowledge, and those of Moore will deny that his intuitions are grounds for knowledge claims, since our apparent moral intuitions often disagree. You can see the force of this criticism if you consider again the thought experiment of 7:1.4. How would you go about trying to explain to the alien intelligence your "intuition" or "moral sense" that killing is wrong? What would the alien have besides your say so? Could we achieve the level of *objective agreement* with the alien that is required for true knowledge? For this approach to work, we need a *workable* analysis of knowledge that allows for moral knowledge without following the definist in reducing facts to values.

7:5 CONCEPTUAL EXPERIMENT

The following story concerns a clear case in which a moral decision must be made, and is made according to a set of rules that allegedly justifies the decision. As you read it you should not only ask yourself whether or not the decision is the right one, but whether or not such a set of rules is the right sort that one should use for such decisions. Try to identify what principles of ethical justification are assumed by this story, and whether these principles are from definist, noncognitivist, or nonfactual knowledge viewpoints. Following the story is a commentary on it by Jan Narveson who seeks to further explore its moral ramifications.

Conceptual Experiment 7:

THE COLD EQUATIONS

Tom Godwin

He was not alone.

There was nothing to indicate the fact but the white hand of the tiny gauge on the board before him. The control room was empty but for himself; there was no sound other than the murmur of the drives— but the white hand had moved. It had been on zero when the little ship was launched from the *Stardust;* now, an hour later, it had crept up. There was something in the supplies closet across the room, it was saying, some kind of a body that radiated heat.

It could be but one kind of a body—a living, human body.

He leaned back in the pilot's chair and drew a deep, slow breath, considering what he would have to do. He was an EDS pilot, inured to the sight of death, long since accustomed to it and to viewing the dying of another man with an objective lack of emotion, and he had no choice in what he must do. There could be no alternative—but it required a few moments of conditioning for even an EDS pilot to prepare himself to walk across the room and coldly, deliberately, take the life of a man he had yet to meet.

He would, of course, do it. It was the law, stated very bluntly and definitely in grim Paragraph L, Section 8, of Interstellar Regulations: *Any stowaway discovered in an EDS shall be jettisoned immediately following discovery.*

It was the law, and there could be no appeal.

It was a law not of men's choosing but made imperative by the circumstances of the space frontier. Galactic expansion had followed the development of the hyperspace drive and as men scattered wide across the frontier there had come the problem of contact with the isolated first-colonies and exploration parties. Tbe huge hyperspace cruisers were the product of the combined genius and effort of Earth and were long and expensive in the building. They were not available in such numbers that small colonies could possess them. The cruisers carried the colonists to their new worlds and made periodic visits, running on tight schedules, but they could not stop and turn aside to visit colonies scheduled to be visited at another time; such a delay would destroy their schedule and produce a confusion and uncertainty that would wreck the complex interdependence between old Earth and new worlds of the frontier.

Some method of delivering supplies or assistance when an emergency occurred on a world not scheduled for a visit had been needed and the Emergency Dispatch Ships had been the answer. Small and collapsible, they occupied little room in the hold of the cruiser; made of light metal and plastics, they were driven by a small rocket drive that consumed relatively little fuel. Each cruiser carried four EDS's and when a call for aid was received the nearest cruiser would drop into normal space long enough to launch an EDS with the needed supplies or personnel, then vanish again as it continued on its course.

The cruisers, powered by nuclear converters, did not use the liquid rocket fuel but nuclear converters were far too large and complex to permit their installation in the EDS's. The cruisers were forced by necessity to carry a limited amount of the bulky rocket fuel and the fuel was rationed with care, the cruisers' computers determining the exact amount of fuel each EDS would require for its mission. The computers considered the course coordinates, the mass of the EDS, the mass of pilot and cargo; they were very precise and accurate and omitted nothing from their calculations. They could not, however, foresee, and allow for, the added mass of a stowaway.

The *Stardust* had received the request from one of the exploration parties stationed on Woden; the six men of the party already being stricken with the fever carried by the green *kala* midges and their own supply of serum destroyed by the tornado that had torn through their camp. The *Stardust* had gone through the usual procedure; dropping into normal space to launch the EDS with the fever serum, then vanishing again in hyperspace. Now, an hour later, the gauge was saying there was something more than the small carton of serum in the supplies closet.

He let his eyes rest on the narrow white door of the closet. There, just inside, another man lived and breathed and was beginning to feel assured that discovery of his presence would now be too late for the pilot to alter the situation. It *was* too late—for the man behind the door it was far later than he thought and in a way he would find terrible to believe.

There could be no alternative. Additional fuel would be used during the hours of deceleration to compensate for the added mass of the stowaway; infinitesimal increments of fuel that would not be missed until the ship had almost reached its destination. Then, at some distance above the ground that might be as near as a thousand feet or as far as tens of thousands of feet, depending upon the mass of ship and cargo and the preceding period of deceleration, the unmissed increments of fuel would make their absence known; the EDS would expend its last drops of fuel with a sputter and go into whistling free fall. Ship and pilot and stowaway would merge together upon impact as a wreckage of metal and plastic, flesh and blood, driven deep into the soil. The stowaway had signed his own death warrant when he concealed himself on the ship; he could not be permitted to take seven others with him.

He looked again at the telltale white hand, then rose to his feet. What he must do would be unpleasant for both of them; the sooner it was over, the better. He stepped across the control room, to stand by the white door.

"Come out!" His command was harsh and abrupt above the murmur of the drive.

It seemed he could hear the whisper of a furtive movement inside the closet, then nothing. He visualized the stowaway cowering closer into one corner, suddenly worried by the possible consequences of his act and his self-assurance evaporating.

"I said *out!*"

He heard the stowaway move to obey and he waited with his eyes alert on the door and his hand near the blaster at his side.

The door opened and the stowaway stepped through it, smiling. "All right—I give up. Now what?"

It was a girl.

He stared without speaking, his hand dropping away from the blaster and acceptance of what he saw coming like a heavy and unexpected physical blow. The stowaway was not a man—she was a girl in her teens, standing before him in little white gypsy sandals with the top of her brown, curly head hardly higher than his shoulder, with a faint, sweet scent of perfume coming from her and her smiling face tilted up so her eyes could look unknowing and unafraid into his as she waited for his answer.

Now what? Had it been asked in the deep, defiant voice of a man he would have answered it with action, quick and efficient. He would have taken the stowaway's identification disk and ordered him into the air lock. Had the stowaway refused to obey, he would have used the blaster; it would not have taken long; within a minute the body would have been ejected into space—had the stowaway been a man.

He returned to the pilot's chair and motioned her to seat herself on the boxlike bulk of the drive-control units that set against the wall beside him. She obeyed, his silence making the smile fade into the meek and guilty expression of a pup that has been caught in mischief and knows it must be punished.

"You still haven't told me," she said. "I'm guilty, so what happens to me now? Do I pay a fine, or what?"

"What are you doing here?" he asked. "Why did you stow away on this EDS?"

"I wanted to see my brother. He's with the government survey crew on Woden and I haven't seen him for ten years, not since he left Earth to go into government survey work."

"What was your destination on the *Stardust?*"

"Mimir. I have a position waiting for me there. My brother has been sending money home all the time to us—my father and mother and I—and he paid for a special course in linguistics I was taking. I graduated sooner than expected and I was offered this job on Mimir. I knew it would be almost a year before Gerry's job was done on Woden so he could come on to Mimir and that's why I hid in the closet, there. There was plenty of room for me and I was willing to pay the fine. There were only the two of us kids—Gerry and I—and I haven't seen him for so long, and I didn't want to wait another year when I could see him now, even though I knew I would be breaking some kind of a regulation when I did it."

I knew I would be breaking some kind of a regulation— In a way, she could not be blamed for her ignorance of the law; she was of Earth and had not realized that the laws of the space frontier must, of necessity, be as hard and relentless as the environment that gave them birth. Yet, to protect such as her from the results of their own ignorance of the frontier, there had been a sign over the door that led to the section of the *Stardust* that housed EDS's; a sign that was plain for all to see and heed:

UNAUTHORIZED PERSONNEL

KEEP OUT!

"Does your brother know that you took passage on the *Stardust* for Mimir?"

"Oh, yes. I sent him a spacegram telling him about my graduation and about going to Mimir on the *Stardust* a month before I left Earth. I already knew Mimir was where he would be stationed in a little over a year. He gets a promotion then, and he'll be based on Mimir and not have to stay out a year at a time on field trips, like he does now."

There were two different survey groups on Woden, and he asked, "What is his name?"

"Cross—Gerry Cross. He's in Group Two—that was the way his address read. Do you know him?"

Group One had requested the serum; Group Two was eight thousand miles away, across the Western Sea.

"No, I've never met him," he said, then turned to the control board and cut the deceleration to a fraction of a gravity; knowing as he did so that it could not avert the ultimate end, yet doing the only thing he could do to prolong that ultimate end. The sensation was like that of the ship suddenly dropping and the girl's involuntary movement of surprise half lifted her from her seat.

"We're going faster now, aren't we?" she asked. "Why are we doing that?"

He told her the truth. "To save fuel for a little while."

"You mean, we don't have very much?"

He delayed the answer he must give her so soon to ask: "How did you manage to stow away?"

"I just sort of walked in when no one was looking my way," she said. "I was practicing my Gelanese on the native girl who does the cleaning in the Ship's Supply office when someone came in with an order for supplies for the survey crew on Woden. I slipped into the closet there after the ship was ready to go and just before you came in. It was an impulse of the moment to stow away, so I could get to see Gerry—and from the way you keep looking at me so grim, I'm not sure it was a very wise impulse.

"But I'll be a model criminal—or do I mean prisoner?" She smiled at him again. "I intended to pay for my keep on top of paying the fine. I can cook and I can patch clothes for everyone and I know how to do all kinds of useful things, even a little bit about nursing."

There was one more question to ask:

"Did you know what the supplies were that the survey crew ordered?"

"Why, no. Equipment they needed in their work, I supposed."

Why couldn't she have been a man with some ulterior motive? A fugitive from justice, hoping to lose himself on a raw new world; an opportunist, seeking transportation to the new colonies where he might find golden fleece for the taking, a crackpot, with a mission—

Perhaps once in his lifetime an EDS pilot would find such a stowaway on his ship; warped men, mean and selfish men, brutal and dangerous men—but never, before, a smiling, blue-eyed girl who was willing to pay her fine and work for her keep that she might see her brother.

He turned to the board and turned the switch that would signal the *Stardust.* The call would be futile but he could not, until he had exhausted that one vain hope, seize her and thrust her into the air lock as he would an animal—or a man. The delay, in the meantime, would not be dangerous with the EDS decelerating at fractional gravity.

A voice spoke from the communicator. "*Stardust.* Identify yourself and proceed."

"Barton, EDS 34G11. Emergency. Give me Commander Delhart."

There was a faint confusion of noises as the request went through the proper channels. The girl was watching him, no longer smiling.

"Are you going to order them to come back after me?" she asked.

The communicator clicked and there was the sound of a distant voice saying, "Commander, the EDS requests—"

"Are they coming back after me?" she asked again. "Won't I get to see my brother, after all?"

"Barton?" The blunt, gruff voice of Commander Delhart came from the communicator. "What's this about an emergency?"

"A stowaway," he answered.

"A stowaway?" There was a slight surprise to the question. "That's rather unusual—but why the 'emergency' call? You discovered him in time so there should be no appreciable danger and I presume you've informed Ship's Records so his nearest relatives can be notified."

"That's why I had to call you, first. The stowaway is still aboard and the circumstances are so different—"

"Different?" the commander interrupted, impatience in his voice. "How can they be different? You know you have a limited supply of fuel; you also know the law as well as I do: 'Any stowaway discovered in an EDS shall be jettisoned immediately following discovery.' "

There was the sound of a sharply indrawn breath from the girl. *"What does he mean?"*

"The stowaway is a girl."

"What?"

"She wanted to see her brother. She's only a kid and she didn't know what she was really doing."

"I see." All the curtness was gone from the commander's voice. "So you called me in the hope I could do something?" Without waiting for an answer he went on. "I'm sorry—I can do nothing. This cruiser must maintain its schedule; the life of not one person but the lives of many depend on it. I know how you feel but I'm powerless to help you. You'll have to go through with it. I'll have you connected with Ship's Records."

The communicator faded to a faint rustle of sound and he turned back to the girl. She was leaning forward on the bench, almost rigid, her eyes fixed wide and frightened.

"What did he mean, to go through with it? To jettison me . . . to go through with it—what did he mean? Not the way it sounded . . . he couldn't have. What did he mean . . . what did he really mean?"

Her time was too short for the comfort of a lie to be more than a cruelly fleeting delusion.

"He meant it the way it sounded."

"No!" She recoiled from him as though he had struck her, one

hand half upraised as though to fend him off and stark unwillingness to believe in her eyes.

"It will have to be."

"No! You're joking—you're insane! You can't mean it!"

"I'm sorry." He spoke slowly to her, gently. "I should have told you before—I should have, but I had to do what I could first; I had to call the *Stardust*. You heard what the commander said."

"But you can't—if you make me leave the ship, I'll *die.*"

"I know."

She searched his face and the unwillingness to believe left her eyes, giving way slowly to a look of dazed terror.

"You—know?" She spoke the words far apart, numb and wonderingly.

"I know. It has to be like that."

"You mean it—you really mean it." She sagged back against the wall, small and limp like a little rag doll and all the protesting and disbelief gone.

"You're going to do it—you're going to make me die?"

"I'm sorry," he said again. "You'll never know how sorry I am. It has to be that way and no human in the universe can change it."

"You're going to make me die and I didn't do anything to die for—I didn't *do* anything—"

He sighed, deep and weary. "I know you didn't, child. I know you didn't—"

"EDS." The communicator rapped brisk and metallic. "This is Ship's Records. Give us all information on subject's identification disk."

He got out of his chair to stand over her. She clutched the edge of the seat, her upturned face white under the brown hair and the lipstick standing out like a blood-red cupid's bow.

"Now?"

"I want your identification disk," he said.

She released the edge of the seat and fumbled at the chain that suspended the plastic disk from her neck with fingers that were trembling and awkward. He reached down and unfastened the clasp for her, then returned with the disk to his chair.

"Here's your data, Records: Identification Number T837—"

"One moment," Records interrupted. "This is to be filed on the gray card, of course?"

"Yes."

"And the time of the execution?"

"I'll tell you later."

"Later? This is highly irregular; the time of the subject's death is required before—"

He kept the thickness out of his voice with an effort. "Then we'll do it in a highly irregular manner—you'll hear the disk read, first. The subject is a girl and she's listening to everything that's said. Are you capable of understanding that?"

There was a brief, almost shocked, silence, then Records said meekly: "Sorry. Go ahead."

He began to read the disk, reading it slowly to delay the inevitable for as long as possible, trying to help her by giving her what little time he could to recover from her first terror and let it resolve into the calm of acceptance and resignation.

"Number T8374 dash Y54. Name: Marilyn Lee Cross. Sex: Female. Born: July 7, 2160. *She was only eighteen.* Height: 5–3. Weight: 110. *Such a slight weight, yet enough to add fatally to the mass of the shell thin bubble that was an EDS.* Hair: Brown. Eyes: Blue. Complexion: Light. Blood Type: O. *Irrelevant data.* Destination: Port City, Mimir. *Invalid data—*"

He finished and said, "I'll call you later," then turned once again to the girl. She was huddled back against the wall, watching him with a look of numb and wondering fascination.

"They're waiting for you to kill me, aren't they? They want me dead, don't they? You and everybody on the cruiser wants me dead, don't you?" Then the numbness broke and her voice was that of a frightened and bewildered child. "Everybody wants me dead and I didn't *do* anything. I didn't hurt anyone—I only wanted to see my brother."

"It's not the way you think—it isn't that way, at all," he said. "Nobody wants it this way; nobody would ever let it be this way if it was humanly possible to change it."

"Then why is it! I don't understand. Why is it?"

"This ship is carrying *kala* fever serum to Group One on Woden. Their own supply was destroyed by a tornado. Group Two—the crew your brother is in—is eight thousand miles away across the Western Sea and their helicopters can't cross it to help Group One. The fever is invariably fatal unless the serum can be had in time, and the six men in Group One will die unless this ship reaches them on schedule. These little ships are always given barely enough fuel to reach their destination and if you stay aboard your added weight will cause it to use up all its fuel before it reaches the ground. It will crash, then, and you and I will die and so will the six men waiting for the fever serum."

It was a full minute before she spoke, and as she considered his words the expression of numbness left her eyes.

"Is that it?" she asked at last. "Just that the ship doesn't have enough fuel?"

"Yes."

"I can go alone or I can take seven others with me—is that the way it is?"

"That's the way it is."

"And nobody wants me to have to die?"

"Nobody."

"Then maybe—Are you sure nothing can be done about it? Wouldn't people help me if they could?"

"Everyone would like to help you but there is nothing anyone can do. I did the only thing I could do when I called the *Stardust*."

"And it won't come back—but there might be other cruisers, mightn't there? Isn't there any hope at all that there might be someone, somewhere, who could do something to help me?"

She was leaning forward a little in her eagerness as she waited for his answer.

"No."

The word was like the drop of a cold stone and she again leaned back against the wall, the hope and eagerness leaving her face. "You're sure—you *know* for sure?"

"I'm sure. There are no other cruisers within forty light-years; there is nothing and no one to change things."

She dropped her gaze to her lap and began twisting a pleat of her skirt between her fingers, saying no more as her mind began to adapt itself to the grim knowledge.

It was better so; with the going of all hope would go the fear; with the going of all hope would come resignation. She needed time and she could have so little of it. How much?

The EDS's were not equipped with hull-cooling units; their speed had to be reduced to a moderate level before entering the atmosphere. They were decelerating at .10 gravity; approaching their destination at a far higher speed than the computers had calculated on. The *Stardust* had been quite near Woden when she launched the EDS; their present velocity was putting them nearer by the second. There would be a critical point, soon to be reached, when he would have to resume deceleration. When he did so the girl's weight would be multiplied by the gravities of deceleration, would become, suddenly, a factor of paramount importance; the factor the computers had been ignorant of when they determined the amount of fuel the EDS should have. She would have to go when deceleration began; it could be no other way. When would that be—how long could he let her stay?

"How long can I stay?"

He winced involuntarily from the words that were so like an echo of his own thoughts. How long? He didn't know; he would have to ask the ship's computers. Each EDS was given a meager surplus of fuel to compensate for unfavorable conditions within the atmosphere and relatively little fuel was being consumed for the time being. The memory banks of the computers would still contain all data pertaining to the course set for the EDS; such data would not be erased until the EDS reached its destination. He had only to give the computers the new data; the girl's weight and the exact time at which he had reduced the deceleration to .10.

"Barton." Commander Delhart's voice came abruptly from the communicator as he opened his mouth to call the *Stardust*. "A check with Records shows me you haven't completed your report. Did you reduce the deceleration?"

So the commander knew what he was trying to do.

"I'm decelerating at point ten," he answered. "I cut the deceleration at seventeen fifty and the weight is a hundred and ten. I would like to stay at point ten as long as the computers say I can. Will you give them the question?"

It was contrary to regulations for an EDS pilot to make any changes in the course or degree of deceleration the computers had set for him but the commander made no mention of the violation, neither did he ask the reason for it. It was not necessary for him to ask; he had not become commander of an interstellar cruiser without both intelligence and an understanding of human nature. He said only: "I'll have that given the computers."

The communicator fell silent and he and the girl waited, neither of them speaking. They would not have to wait long; the computers would give the answer within moments of the asking. The new factors would be fed into the steel maw of the first bank and the electrical impulses would go through the complex circuits. Here and there a relay might click, a tiny cog turn over, but it would be essentially the electrical impulses that found the answer; formless, mindless, invisible, determining with utter precision how long the pale girl beside him might live. Then five little segments of metal in the second bank would trip in rapid succession against an inked ribbon and a second steel maw would spit out the slip of paper that bore the answer.

The chronometer on the instrument board read 18:10 when the commander spoke again.

"You will resume deceleration at nineteen ten."

She looked toward the chronometer, then quickly away from it. "Is that when . . . when I go?" she asked. He nodded and she dropped her eyes to her lap again.

"I'll have the course corrections given you," the commander said. "Ordinarily I would never permit anything like this but I understand your position. There is nothing I can do, other than what I've just done, and you will not deviate from these new instructions. You will complete your report at nineteen ten. Now—here are the course corrections."

The voice of some unknown technician read them to him and he wrote them down on the pad clipped to the edge of the control board. There would, he saw, be periods of deceleration when he neared the atmosphere when the deceleration would be five gravities—and at five gravities, one hundred ten pounds would become five hundred fifty pounds.

The technician finished and he terminated the contact with a brief acknowledgment. Then, hesitating a moment, he reached out and shut off the communicator. It was 18:13 and he would have nothing to report until 19:10. In the meantime, it somehow seemed indecent to permit others to hear what she might say in her last hour.

He began to check the instrument readings, going over them with unnecessary slowness. She would have to accept the circumstances and there was nothing he could do to help her into acceptance; words of sympathy would only delay it.

It was 18:20 when she stirred from her motionlessness and spoke. "So that's the way it has to be with me?"

He swung around to face her. "You understand now, don't you? No one would ever let it be like this if it could be changed."

"I understand," she said. Some of the color had returned to her face and the lipstick no longer stood out so vividly red. "There isn't enough fuel for me to stay; when I hid on this ship I got into something I didn't know anything about and now I have to pay for it."

She had violated a man-made law that said KEEP OUT but the penalty was not of men's making or desire and it was a penalty men could not revoke. A physical law had decreed: *h amount of fuel will power an EDS with a mass of m safely to its destination;* and a second physical law had decreed: *h amount of fuel will not power an EDS with a mass of m plus x safely to its destination.*

EDS's obeyed only physical laws and nó amount of human sympathy for her could alter the second law.

"But I'm afraid. I don't want to die—not now. I want to live and nobody is doing anything to help me; everybody is letting me go ahead and acting just like nothing was going to happen to me. I'm going to die and nobody *cares.*"

"We all do," he said. "I do and the commander does and the clerk in Ship's Records; we all care and each of us did what little he could to help you. It wasn't enough—it was almost nothing—but it was all we could do."

"Not enough fuel—I can understand that," she said, as though she had not heard his own words. "But I have to die for it. *Me,* alone—"

How hard it must be for her to accept the fact. She had never known danger of death; had never known the environments where the lives of men could be as fragile and fleeting as sea foam tossed against a rocky shore. She belonged on gentle Earth, in that secure and peaceful society where she could be young and gay and laughing with the others of her kind; where life was precious and well-guarded and there was always the assurance that tomorrow would come. She belonged in that world of soft winds and warm suns, music and moonlight and gracious manners and not on the hard, bleak frontier.

"How did it happen to me, so terribly quickly? An hour ago I was on the *Stardust,* going to Mimir. Now the *Stardust* is going on without me and I'm going to die and I'll never see Gerry and Mama and Daddy again—I'll never see anything again."

He hesitated, wondering how he could explain it to her so she would really understand and not feel she had, somehow, been the victim of a reasonlessly cruel injustice. She did not know what the frontier was like; she thought in terms of safe-and-secure Earth. Pretty girls were not jettisoned on Earth; there was a law against it. On Earth her plight would have filled the newscasts and a fast black Patrol ship would have been racing to her rescue. Everyone, everywhere, would have known of Marilyn Lee Cross and no effort would have been spared to save her life. But this was not Earth and there were no Patrol ships; only the *Stardust,* leaving them behind at many times the speed of light. There was no one to help her, there would be no Marilyn Lee Cross smiling from the newscasts tomorrow. Marilyn Lee Cross would be but a poignant memory for an EDS pilot and a name on a gray card in Ship's Records.

"It's different here; it's not like back on Earth," he said. "It isn't that no one cares; it's that no one can do anything to help. The frontier is big and here along its rim the colonies and exploration parties are scattered so thin and far between. On Woden, for example, there are only sixteen men—sixteen men on an entire world. The exploration parties, the survey crews, the little first-colonies—they're all fighting alien environments, trying to make a way for those who will follow after. The environments fight back and those who go first usually make mistakes only once. There is no margin of safety along the rim of the frontier; there can't be until the way is made for the others who will come later, until the new worlds are tamed and settled. Until then men will have to pay the penalty for making mistakes with no one to help them because there is no one *to* help them."

"I was going to Mimir," she said. "I didn't know about the frontier; I was only going to Mimir and *it's safe.*"

"Mimir is safe but you left the cruiser that was taking you there."

She was silent for a little while. "It was all so wonderful at first;

there was plenty of room for me on this ship and I would be seeing Gerry so soon . . . I didn't know about the fuel, didn't know what would happen to me—"

Her words trailed away and he turned his attention to the view-screen, not wanting to stare at her as she fought her way through the black horror of fear toward the calm gray of acceptance.

Woden was a ball, enshrouded in the blue haze of its atmosphere, swimming in space against the background of star-sprinkled dead blackness. The great mass of Manning's Continent sprawled like a gigantic hourglass in the Eastern Sea with the western half of the Eastern Continent still visible. There was a thin line of shadow along the right-hand edge of the globe and the Eastern Continent was disappearing into it as the planet turned on its axis. An hour before the entire continent had been in view, now a thousand miles of it had gone into the thin edge of shadow and around to the night that lay on the other side of the world. The dark blue spot that was Lotus Lake was approaching the shadow. It was somewhere near the southern edge of the lake that Group Two had their camp. It would be night there, soon, and quick behind the coming of night the rotation of Woden on its axis would put Group Two beyond the reach of the ship's radio.

He would have to tell her before it was too late for her to talk to her brother. In a way, it would be better for both of them should they not do so but it was not for him to decide. To each of them the last words would be something to hold and cherish, something that would cut like the blade of a knife yet would be infinitely precious to remember, she for her own brief moments to live and he for the rest of his life.

He held down the button that would flash the grid lines on the viewscreen and used the known diameter of the planet to estimate the distance the southern tip of Lotus Lake had yet to go until it passed beyond radio range. It was approximately five hundred miles. Five hundred miles; thirty minutes—and the chronometer read 18:30. Allowing for error in estimating, it could not be later than 19:05 that the turning of Woden would cut off her brother's voice.

The first border of the Western Continent was already in sight along the left side of the world. Four thousand miles across it lay the shore of the Western Sea and the Camp of Group One. It had been in the Western Sea that the tornado had originated, to strike with such fury at the camp and destroy half their prefabricated buildings, including the one that housed the medical supplies. Two days before the tornado had not existed; it had been no more than great gentle masses of air out over the calm Western Sea. Group One had gone about their routine survey work, unaware of the meeting of the air masses out at sea, unaware of the force the union was spawning. It had struck their camp without warning; a thundering, roaring destruction that sought to annihilate all that lay before it. It had passed on, leaving the wreckage in its wake. It had destroyed the labor of months and had doomed six men to die and then, as though its task was accomplished, it once more began to resolve into gentle masses of air. But for all its deadliness, it had destroyed with neither malice nor intent. It had been a blind and mindless force, obeying the laws of nature, and it would have followed the same course with the same fury had men never existed.

Existence required Order and there was order; the laws of nature, irrevocable and immutable. Men could learn to use them but men could not change them. The circumference of a circle was always pi times the diameter and no science of Man would ever make it otherwise. The combination of chemical A with chemical B under condition C invariably produced reaction D. The law of gravitation was a rigid equation and it made no distinction between the fall of a leaf and the ponderous circling of a binary star system. The nuclear conversion process powered the cruiser that carried men to the stars; the same process in the form of a nova would destroy a world with equal efficiency. The laws *were,* and the universe moved in obedience to them. Along the frontier were arrayed all the forces of nature and sometimes they destroyed those who were fighting their way outward from Earth. The men of the frontier had long ago learned the bitter futility of cursing the forces that would destroy them for the forces were blind and deaf; the futility of looking to the heavens for mercy, for the stars of the galaxy swung in their long, long sweep of two hundred million years, as inexorably controlled as they by the laws that knew neither hatred nor compassion.

The men of the frontier knew—but how was a girl from Earth to fully understand? *H amount of fuel will not power an EDS with a mass of m plus x safely to its destination.* To himself and her brother and parents she was a sweet-faced girl in her teens; to the laws of nature she was *x,* the unwanted factor in a cold equation.

She stirred again on the seat. "Could I write a letter? I want to write to Mama and Daddy and I'd like to talk to Gerry. Could you let me talk to him over your radio there?"

"I'll try to get him," he said.

He switched on the normal-space transmitter and pressed the signal button. Someone answered the buzzer almost immediately.

"Hello. How's it going with you fellows now—is the EDS on its way?"

"This isn't Group One; this is the EDS," he said. "Is Gerry Cross there?"

"Gerry? He and two others went out in the helicopter this morning and aren't back yet. It's almost sundown, though, and he ought to be back right away—in less than an hour at the most."

"Can you connect me through to the radio in his 'copter."

"Huh-uh. It's been out of commission for two months—some printed circuits went haywire and we can't get any more until the next cruiser stops by. Is it something important—bad news for him, or something?"

"Yes—it's very important. When he comes in get him to the transmitter as soon as you possibly can."

"I'll do that; I'll have one of the boys waiting at the field with a truck. Is there anything else I can do?"

"No, I guess that's all. Get him there as soon as you can and signal me."

He turned the volume to an inaudible minimum, an act that would not affect the functioning of the signal buzzer, and unclipped the pad of paper from the control board. He tore off the sheet containing his flight instructions and handed the pad to her, together with pencil.

"I'd better write to Gerry, too," she said as she took them. "He might not get back to camp in time."

She began to write, her fingers still clumsy and uncertain in the way they handled the pencil and the top of it trembling a little as she poised it between words. He turned back to the viewscreen, to stare at it without seeing it.

She was a lonely little child, trying to say her last good-by, and she would lay out her heart to them. She would tell them how much she loved them and she would tell them to not feel badly about it, that it was only something that must happen eventually to everyone and she was not afraid. The last would be a lie and it would be there to read between the sprawling, uneven lines; a valiant little lie that would make the hurt all the greater for them.

Her brother was of the frontier and he would understand. He would not hate the EDS pilot for doing nothing to prevent her going; he would know there had been nothing the pilot could do. He would understand, though the understanding would not soften the shock and pain when he learned his sister was gone. But the others, her father and mother—they would not understand. They were of Earth and they would think in the manner of those who had never lived where the safety margin of life was a thin, thin line—and sometimes not at all. What would they think of the faceless, unknown pilot who had sent her to her death?

They would hate him with cold and terrible intensity but it really didn't matter. He would never see them, never know them. He would have only the memories to remind him; only the nights to fear, when a blue-eyed girl in gypsy sandals would come in his dreams to die again—

He scowled at the viewscreen and tried to force his thought into less emotional channels. There was nothing he could do to help her. She had unknowingly subjected herself to the penalty of a law that recognized neither innocence nor youth nor beauty, that was incapable of sympathy or leniency. Regret was illogical—and yet, could knowing it to be illogical ever keep it away?

She stopped occasionally, as though trying to find the right words to tell them what she wanted them to know, then the pencil would resume its whispering to the paper. It was 18:37 when she folded the letter in a square and wrote a name on it. She began writing another, twice looking up at the chronometer as though she feared the black hand might reach its rendezvous before she had finished. It was 18:45 when she folded it as she had done the first letter and wrote a name and address on it.

She held the letters out to him. "Will you take care of these and see that they're enveloped and mailed?"

"Of course." He took them from her and placed them in a pocket of his gray uniform shirt.

"These can't be sent off until the next cruiser stops by and the *Stardust* will have long since told them about me, won't it?" she asked. He nodded and she went on, "That makes the letters not important in one way but in another way they're very important—to me, and to them."

"I know. I understand, and I'll take care of them."

She glanced at the chronometer, then back to him. "It seems to move faster all the time, doesn't it?"

He said nothing, unable to think of anything to say, and she asked, "Do you think Gerry will come back to camp in time?"

"I think so. They said he should be in right away."

She began to roll the pencil back and forth between her palms. "I hope he does. I feel sick and scared and I want to hear his voice again and maybe I won't feel so alone. I'm a coward and I can't help it."

"No," he said, "you're not a coward. You're afraid, but you're not a coward."

"Is there a difference?"

He nodded. "A lot of difference."

"I feel so alone. I never did feel like this before; like I was all by myself and there was nobody to care what happened to me. Always, before, there was Mama and Daddy there and my friends around me. I had lots of friends, and they had a going-away party for me the night before I left."

Friends and music and laughter for her to remember—and on the viewscreen Lotus Lake was going into the shadow.

"Is it the same with Gerry?" she asked. "I mean, if he should make a mistake, would he have to die for it, all alone and with no one to help him?"

"It's the same with all along the frontier; it will always be like that so long as there is a frontier."

"Gerry didn't tell us. He said the pay was good and he sent money home all the time because Daddy's little shop just brought in a bare living but he didn't tell us it was like this."

"He didn't tell you his work was dangerous?"

"Well—yes. He mentioned that, but we didn't understand. I always thought danger along the frontier was something that was a lot of fun; an exciting adventure, like in the three-D shows." A wan smile touched her face for a moment. "Only it's not, is it? It's not the same at all, because when it's real you can't go home after the show is over."

"No," he said. "No, you can't."

Her glance flicked from the chronometer to the door of the air lock then down to the pad and pencil she still held. She shifted her position slightly to lay them on the bench beside, moving one foot out a little. For the first time he saw that she was not wearing Vegan gypsy sandals but only cheap imitations; the expensive Vegan leather was some kind of grained plastic, the silver buckle was gilded iron, the jewels were colored glass. *Daddy's little shop just brought in a bare living—* She must have left college in her second year, to take the course in linguistics that would enable her to make her own way and help her brother provide for her parents, earning what she could by part-time work after classes were over. Her personal possessions on the *Stardust* would be taken back to her parents—they would neither be of much value nor occupy much storage space on the return voyage.

"Isn't it—" She stopped, and he looked at her questioningly. "Isn't it cold in here?" she asked, almost apologetically. "Doesn't it seem cold to you?"

"Why, yes," he said. He saw by the main temperature gauge that the room was at precisely normal temperature. "Yes, it's colder than it should be."

"I wish Gerry would get back before it's too late. Do you really think he will, and you didn't just say so to make me feel better?"

"I think he will—they said he would be in pretty soon." On the viewscreen Lotus Lake had gone into the shadow but for the thin blue line of its western edge and it was apparent he had overestimated the time she would have in which to talk to her brother. Reluctantly, he said to her, "His camp will be out of radio range in a few minutes; he's on that part of Woden that's in the shadow"—he indicated the viewscreen— "and the turning of Woden will put him beyond contact. There may not be much time left when he comes in—not much time to talk to him before he fades out. I wish I could do something about it—I would call him right now if I could."

"Not even as much time as I will have to stay?"

"I'm afraid not."

"Then—" She straightened and looked toward the air lock with pale resolution. "Then I'll go when Gerry passes beyond range. I won't wait any longer after that—I won't have anything to wait for."

Again there was nothing he could say.

"Maybe I shouldn't wait at all. Maybe I'm selfish—maybe it would be better for Gerry if you just told him about it afterward."

There was an unconscious pleading for denial in the way she spoke and he said, "He wouldn't want you to do that, to not wait for him."

"It's already coming dark where he is, isn't it? There will be all the long night before him, and Mama and Daddy don't know yet that I won't ever be coming back like I promised them I would. I've caused everyone I love to be hurt, haven't I? I didn't want to—I didn't intend to."

"It wasn't your fault," he said. "It wasn't your fault at all. They'll know that. They'll understand."

"At first I was so afraid to die that I was a coward and thought only of myself. Now, I see how selfish I was. The terrible thing about dying like this is not that I'll be gone but that I'll never see them again; never be able to tell them that I didn't take them for granted; never be able to tell them I knew of the sacrifices they made to make my life happier, that I knew all the things they did for me and that I loved them so much more than I ever told them. I've never told them any of those things. You don't tell them such things when you're young and your life is all before you—you're afraid of sounding sentimental and silly.

"But it's so different when you have to die—you wish you had told them while you could and you wish you could tell them you're sorry for all the little mean things you ever did or said to them. You wish you could tell them that you didn't really mean to ever hurt their feelings and for them to only remember that you always loved them far more than you ever let them know."

"You don't have to tell them that," he said. "They will know—they've always known it."

"Are you sure?" she asked. "How can you be sure? My people are strangers to you."

"Wherever you go, human nature and human hearts are the same."

"And they will know what I want them to know—that I love them?"

"They've always known it, in a way far better than you could ever put in words for them."

"I keep remembering the things they did for me, and it's the little things they did that seem to be the most important to me, now. Like Gerry—he sent me a bracelet of fire-rubies on my sixteenth birthday. It was beautiful—it must have cost him a month's pay. Yet, I remember him more for what he did the night my kitten got run over in the street. I was only six years old and he held me in his arms and wiped away my tears and told me not to cry, that Flossy was gone for just a little while, for just long enough to get herself a new fur coat and she would be on the foot of my bed the very next morning. I believed him and quit crying and went to sleep dreaming about my kitten coming back. When I woke up the next morning, there was Flossy on the foot of my bed in a brand-new white fur coat, just like he had said she would be.

"It wasn't until a long time later that Mama told me Gerry had got the pet-shop owner out of bed at four in the morning and, when the man got mad about it, Gerry told him he was either going to go down and sell him the white kitten right then or he'd break his neck."

"It's always the little things you remember people by; all the little things they did because they wanted to do them for you. You've done the same for Gerry and your father and mother; all kinds of things that you've forgotten about but that they will never forget."

"I hope I have. I would like for them to remember me like that."

"They will."

"I wish—" She swallowed. "The way I'll die—I wish they wouldn't ever think of that. I've read how people look who die in space—their insides all ruptured and exploded and their lungs out between their teeth and then, a few seconds later, they're all dry and shapeless and horribly ugly. I don't want them to ever think of me as something dead and horrible, like that."

"You're their own, their child and their sister. They could never think of you other than the way you would want them to; the way you looked the last time they saw you."

"I'm still afraid," she said. "I can't help it, but I don't want Gerry to know it. If he gets back in time, I'm going to act like I'm not afraid at all and—"

The signal buzzer interrupted her, quick and imperative.

"Gerry!" She came to her feet. "It's Gerry, now!"

He spun the volume control knob and asked: "Gerry Cross?"

"Yes," her brother answered, an undertone of tenseness to his reply. "The bad news—what is it?"

She answered for him, standing close behind him and leaning down a little toward the communicator, her hand resting small and cold on his shoulder.

"Hello, Gerry." There was only a faint quaver to betray the careful casualness of her voice. "I wanted to see you—"

"Marilyn!" There was sudden and terrible apprehension in the way he spoke her name. "What are you doing on that EDS?"

"I wanted to see you," she said again. "I wanted to see you, so I hid on this ship—"

"You *hid* on it?"

"I'm a stowaway . . . I didn't know what it would mean—"

"*Marilyn!*" It was the cry of a man who calls hopeless and desperate to someone already and forever gone from him. "What have you done?"

"I . . . it's not—" Then her own composure broke and the cold little hand gripped his shoulder convulsively. "Don't, Gerry—I only wanted to see you; I didn't intend to hurt you. Please, Gerry, don't feel like that—"

Something warm and wet splashed on his wrist and he slid out of the chair, to help her into it and swing the microphone down to her own level.

"Don't feel like that—Don't let me go knowing you feel like that—"

The sob she had tried to hold back choked in her throat and her brother spoke to her. "Don't cry Marilyn." His voice was suddenly deep and infinitely gentle, with all the pain held out of it. "Don't cry, Sis—you mustn't do that. It's all right, Honey—everything is all right."

"I—" Her lower lip quivered and she bit into it. "I didn't want you to feel that way—I just wanted us to say good-by because I have to go in a minute."

"Sure—sure. That's the way it will be, Sis. I didn't mean to sound the way I did." Then his voice changed to a tone of quick and urgent demand. "EDS—have you called the *Stardust*? Did you check with the computers?"

"I called the *Stardust* almost an hour ago. It can't turn back, there are no other cruisers within forty light-years, and there isn't enough fuel."

"Are you sure that the computers had the correct data—sure of everything?"

"Yes—do you think I could ever let it happen if I wasn't sure? I did everything I could do. If there was anything at all I could do now, I would do it."

"He tried to help me, Gerry." Her lower lip was no longer trembling and the short sleeves of her blouse were wet where she had dried her tears. "No one can help me and I'm not going to cry any more and everything will be all right with you and Daddy and Mama, won't it?"

"Sure—sure it will. We'll make out fine."

Her brother's words were beginning to come in more faintly and he turned the volume control to maximum. "He's going out of range," he said to her. "He'll be gone within another minute."

"You're fading out, Gerry," she said. "You're going out of range. I wanted to tell you—but I can't, now. We must say good-by so soon— but maybe I'll see you again. Maybe I'll come to you in your dreams with my hair in braids and crying because the kitten in my arms is dead; maybe I'll be the touch of a breeze that whispers to you as it goes by; maybe I'll be one of those gold-winged larks you told me about, singing my silly head off to you; maybe, at times, I'll be nothing you can see but you will know I'm there beside you. Think of me like that, Gerry; always like that and not—the other way."

Dimmed to a whisper by the turning of Woden, the answer came back:

"Always like that, Marilyn—always like that and never any other way."

"Our time is up, Gerry—I have to go, now. Good—" Her voice broke in midword and her mouth tried to twist into crying. She pressed her hand hard against it and when she spoke again the words came clear and true:

"Good-by, Gerry."

Faint and ineffably poignant and tender, the last words came from the cold metal of the communicator:

"Good-by, little sister—"

She sat motionless in the hush that followed, as though listening to the shadow-echoes of the words as they died away, then she turned away from the communicator, toward the air lock, and he pulled the black lever beside him. The inner door of the air lock slid swiftly open, to reveal the bare little cell that was waiting for her, and she walked to it.

She walked with her head up and the brown curls brushing her shoulders, with the white sandals stepping as sure and steady as the fractional gravity would permit and the gilded buckles twinkling with little lights of blue and red and crystal. He let her walk alone and made no move to help her, knowing she would not want it that way. She stepped into the air lock and turned to face him, only the pulse in her throat to betray the wild beating of her heart.

"I'm ready," she said.

He pushed the lever up and the door slid its quick barrier between them, enclosing her in black and utter darkness for her last moments of life. It clicked as it locked in place and he jerked down the red lever. There was a slight waver to the ship as the air gushed from the lock, a vibration to the wall as though something had bumped the outer door in passing, then there was nothing and the ship was dropping true and steady again. He shoved the red lever back to close the door on the empty air lock and turned away, to walk to the pilot's chair with the slow steps of a man old and weary.

Back in the pilot's chair he pressed the signal button of the normal-space transmitter. There was no response; he had expected none. Her brother would have to wait through the night until the turning of Woden permitted contact through Group One.

It was not yet time to resume deceleration and he waited while the ship dropped endlessly downward with him and the drives purred softly. He saw that the white hand of the supplies closet temperature gauge was on zero. A cold equation had been balanced and he was alone on the ship. Something shapeless and ugly was hurrying ahead of him, going to Woden where its brother was waiting through the night, but the empty ship still lived for a little while with the presence of the girl who had not known about the forces that killed with neither hatred nor malice. It seemed, almost, that she still sat small and bewildered and frightened on the metal box beside him, her words echoing hauntingly clear in the void she had left behind her:

I didn't do anything to die for—I didn't do anything—

Analysis:

MORALITY AND MARILYN:
A Commentary on Tom Godwin's
"The Cold Equations"

Jan Narveson

University of Waterloo
Ontario

Poor Marilyn! Tom Godwin's story certainly makes us unhappy about her fate, unhappy for the poor pilot who, as he said and as we surely must believe, literally could do nothing else but what he did, unhappy, then, about the human condition—all of those tragedies, great and small, which stem from our lack of information about apparently tiny but in the event terribly important details. But should we instead think that her story is in a quite different category—the category of innocent persons sacrificed for the welfare of others? I don't think so, and I doubt that anyone else will really think so either. Let us consider what might be said on the other side—and why it won't do, and what may follow from that.

To start with, let's be pretty precise about the claim that the pilot of the EDS "literally could do nothing else but what he did." This, it turns out, is not quite true. What is true, we understand from the story (and it is a story, after all, so we have no business questioning what it says are the "facts"—we can do that in real life, where there are facts to check into and see whether they are as they are said to be; but not in a story, where there are no facts, but only what they are said to be) is that if the pilot does not jettison Marilyn, then eight lives will be lost: those of six fatally ill men, plus the pilot and Marilyn herself. If he does, then only one of these people dies—innocent little Marilyn. Either she goes or they all go. It might be thought that reason immediately decides the issue against our ill-fated little heroine, for it seems there are two and only two choices: Choice A: one innocent person dies, and Choice B: eight innocent people die, one of whom is the very same person as in A. So characterized, we seem to have a straightforward case of what decision theorists refer to as a "dominant" solution. Choice B has all the disadvantages of Choice A, plus some more. It's as if we are offered our choice, at the same price, of Used Car A, which has need of a valve-and-ring job, and Used Car B, which needs not only a valve-and-ring job, but also has faulty steering, worn bearings, a failing universal joint, and four or five other major defects. How can there be any question which to take, from the rational point of view? Had the facts been a little different, if, for instance, the choice had been between Marilyn living while the *other* seven died, or Marilyn dying and the *other* seven saved, then we should have had an interesting problem. But it isn't like that, is it?

Actually, it is a *little* more like that than might at first be thought. For the pilot's choices haven't been quite completely described. If he refuses to jettison the girl, it is true that they both die, along with the six stricken men on the ground. But she dies *later.* The story doesn't tell us precisely how much later, but we may assume that it is not very much. Suppose that it's a couple of hours. Make it a couple of days or even weeks if you like; but presumably the pilot does not have the option of prolonging her life by, say, twenty years or fifty. (Would that matter? We'll consider that by and by.) Now, when Marilyn dies by this second method, so does the pilot. The men on the ground, on the other hand, live longer. Their fatal disease kills them, perhaps in a couple of weeks. In that event, their deaths are presumably also quite awful— though Marilyn and the pilot aren't exactly going to die peacefully in their beds either. So the situation is like this, actually:

Choice A: Marilyn dies in one hour; six people are cured of a fatal and meanwhile painful disease, living normal lives thereafter for an indeterminate but presumably substantial period. An eighth person lives normally for an indeterminate but also presumably substantial period.

Choice B: Marilyn lives X hours, where X is greater than one by some smallish number, after which she dies a death at least as terrible as in A; six others die in two weeks of a terrible disease, meanwhile suffering greatly; and an eighth dies the same terrible death as Marilyn, at the same time, presumably many years sooner than he otherwise would have.

In our new characterization of the situation, Marilyn *is* being sacrificed for the sake of others. The sacrifice she makes is very small, presumably. (The "presumably" is possibly important here. The story leads us to suppose that her further few hours of life, if Choice B is taken, will be anguished, as indeed is her final hour in Choice A; they will not involve, for instance, a transcendentally magnificent experience of a kind which people would sacrifice years of suffering in order to have. Is this important? Here again, we save this matter for later.) The sacrifice is small, but it *is* a sacrifice. And she does make it for the sake of the others. What the others gain is, on any reasonable reckoning, very great. The circumstances might have been very different. Suppose the pilot suddenly discovers that the six on the ground will meet terrible deaths anyway, no matter whether he gets the serum to them on time or not? Suppose he discovers that some terrible enemy, unbeknownst to them, is about to irradiate them with the Extraspecial blaster? Suppose, indeed, that this enemy will do the same to Marilyn and the pilot, if they land safely despite everything? Clearly this would make a difference. But we assume it is not so, and that things are as described in my revised versions of Choice A and Choice B above. So what the others gain if Marilyn is sacrificed is very great: years of life, plus, in six cases, the sparing of much terrible pain. Her loss is small; their gain is great. But it is a loss, and she *is* sacrificed. Does this change things?

We can imagine that another circumstance would be appealed to here by some who reflect on this situation: Marilyn is, after all, not quite entirely "innocent." Hers is the innocence of the very mildly guilty—the innocence of the perhaps thoughtless teenager who knows that she's breaking a rule, but doesn't realize how important a rule it in fact is. As she says, "I didn't *do* anything. I didn't hurt anyone." True, and a complete defense against any accusation of capital crime, even apart from the perfectly acceptable, indeed quite heart-melting motive ("I only wanted to see my brother"). But maybe enough "guilt" to justify the small sacrifice which in fact is now being forced upon her. Perhaps enough guilt to be worth a couple of hours of life, given that that's necessary in order to save so many and save them so much.

So we will make a slight alteration. We now assume that in fact, Marilyn's situation is in no way at all her fault. Instead of the clear and loud sign which was in fact over the doorway to the EDS compartment, "UNAUTHORIZED PERSONNEL—KEEP OUT!," someone has mistakenly hung a sign, "PASSENGERS TO MIMIR, THIS WAY!" We can even suppose that an enemy of Marilyn's has deliberately misled her, told her to sit in the closet and make no noise, this being (for some peculiar reason) required for passengers of certain kinds of which she happens to be one. And so on. We can assume, in short, that Marilyn is utterly innocent, an innocent victim even. However, that has all been done. Any mistakes of others are in the past; they can't be changed now. And the pilot is not at fault: he has no reason to believe that anyone is on the ship except himself, until it's too late. (That's what the story says. Among the things we will not do here is make a list of failures of the obviously incompetent people who run this space trip: things like having body-detectors that detect the presence of stowaways before it's too late, for instance. Surely no problem in any reasonably run science-fiction universe? But we won't make these complaints, as I say. And every universe has its faults, no?) In short, Marilyn, we will now suppose, is as innocent as the driven snow, rather than merely as innocent as a slightly naughty teenager.

But will this change things? Marilyn has *done* nothing to *deserve* that even an hour of her life be sacrificed. But will we hesitate, nevertheless, in electing Choice A, however unpalatable? We can imagine some who might. These other theorists will say that no one may intentionally kill or injure an innocent person, no matter what anyone stands to gain by it. It is strictly forbidden, they will say, to do evil that good may come.

Let us be clear about a couple of things. In the present case, the pilot is operating under the terms of an agreement. It is his responsibility, he has promised, indeed contracted, to bring the serum to those six men. They have a right to it, a right against him. If he avoids inflicting evil on poor Marilyn, he defaults on his duty to them—and no minor duty either, for their lives depend on his fulfilling it. Her life doesn't depend on his fulfilling his duty to her, exactly—not in the same sense, anyway. Rather, an hour of it does. True, if she dies at 9:10, she is intentionally killed by another human, whereas if she dies at, say, 10:45 in a crash, she is unintentionally killed by the laws of nature plus circumstances beyond the control of any person. Now, the theorists whom I am thinking of in this paragraph may point to these facts in exculpation of the pilot. If he fulfills his duty not to harm innocent Marilyn, he defaults on his duty to save the lives of the innocent six stricken men (perhaps also to save his own, but we will assume he has no such duty).

So we will fix this up too. The six stricken men have no right at all to the serum. The pilot is a sort of Intergalactic Red Cross, they've merely heard about the plight of the six, they are doing their best, out of good will, to save them, but no contract is at stake. If the six die, it will not be any human being's doing; merely that of some quite amoral germs. Whereas in Choice A, Marilyn's death will be some human being's doing—the pilot's. And it will be quite intentional, indeed deliberate.

There is one more matter to consider. Marilyn, when the situation is explained to her, accepts her fate. Let us include both of the above alterations: her utter innocence, and the six stricken men's utter lack of claim on the serum. Even so, knowing Marilyn as we do from the story, we may be quite sure that if the pilot said to her, "Well, there it is. Either you live a few more hours, or you go now. If you live the few more hours, six men die horrible deaths of disease, and you and I both die in a frightful crash. But if you live only the one more hour, then the other seven of us are spared, and six of us not only spared our lives, but also spared a great deal of terrible suffering. It's up to you, though. You opt for the extra hours, and I'll give them to you"—if that's what he'd said, we may be quite sure that good-hearted Marilyn, swallowing hard, would opt to save all those lives at the cost of a few hours of her own.

So we'll fix that up too. Sweet-hearted Marilyn will now become Crusty-hearted Cosmo, the intergalactic lawyer. Cosmo insists on his rights. Given the choice, he'll take the extra hours of life. Never mind about all those others: Cosmo's view is that he has a right to those hours, and he's going to stand on that right. Now, what?

In making Cosmo out to be a lawyer, of course, we run the risk of his appreciating the force of the rule about stowaways, well established (we assume) in intergalactic law. This rule could well be a Strict Liability law: it takes no account of the intentions of those who are caught in its grip. That consideration would make a lot of difference to a lawyer. But does it make any to us? We could take the view that strict liability laws are unjust. Indeed, we can take the view that such laws, obviously unjust on the face of it, are only justified (if at all) by the enormously greater difficulty of administering any other type of rule for the sort of cases they are framed to meet. Suppose there was no such rule operating on our pilot. Every time any pilot encounters a stowaway, he is then faced with a horrendous problem of conscience. As things stand, he can now just cite a rule to which he is strictly bound. It makes life a lot easier for pilots, even though a few Marilyns—or Cosmos—get sacrificed in the process.

But plainly there is a limit to how much easier this sort of device can make life for a conscientious person. Suppose that there was really a quite good chance of saving Marilyn, and just a slight risk of crashing and ruining the whole project. Surely no conscientious pilot could simply cite the rule and say "tough for her"! And note how the author has been careful to convey that both our pilot and the commander are sympathetic and sensitive people. Both check out all the alternatives, both would be willing to take risks to save her. And if they weren't, wouldn't we rate them as morally insensitive? Doesn't Eichmann lie that way? ("But the *rules* called for my gassing those Jews—my personal feelings for them had nothing to do with it!")

In fact, the rule we are dealing with is, as we can all see, a sensible and well-founded rule. It is founded on the fact that there is too little margin of safety to accommodate stowaways. Perhaps the margins of error are *too* small. Perhaps, again, somebody up in the spatial bureaucracy has been trying to shave a few dollars from his budget, and the result is that human lives are traded in for a bit of money. (But perhaps that isn't the way it was. Perhaps it was a matter of many billions of dollars. Does anyone *really* think that isn't *relevant*?) At any rate, we can take it that the rule is well-founded, and so the pilot and his commander aren't just "rule-worshippers."

But the issue of whether to give Cosmo his two hours at the expense of all those lives need not be an issue of rule-worshipping. Rather, it comes down to whether people have the right not to be sacrificed for others, and how strong that right is to be. If it is exceedingly strong—rigid, in fact—then we might, given the minor amendments to the scenario made above, have to opt for alternative B after all. Or at any rate, some people apparently have opted for it. Few questions in ethics can be more important than whether they are right in doing so. But are they?

The considerations favoring the pilot's action—action A rather than action B—are of a recognizably utilitarian type. And when we make the further amendments to the circumstances described in the story, they become yet more clearly so. We may describe the situation, however, in two different ways, and the difference between these ways may be extremely important. The *first* way to describe it is this: either we intentionally sacrifice a (small amount of an innocent) person's life in order to bestow very substantial benefits on several others, or we spare that same small amount of one person's life but at the cost of leaving many others to terrible fates. The *second* way to describe it is this: either we intentionally violate one person's *rights*, though admittedly to a rather small degree, in order to bestow substantial benefits on several others who admittedly have no positive right to them, or we avoid violating that person's rights, at the cost of leaving many others to terrible fates. The difference between these two ways of describing the situation is that in the first description, what is at issue is simply the question whether we may intentionally cause someone a harm in order to benefit others, while in the second description, we explicitly allow that the person sacrificed has the right not to be sacrificed, and that those for whom she is sacrificed do not have the right to her making that sacrifice for them.

Is this a terribly important difference, or isn't it? Many of us might feel that it is much easier to accept that she ought to be sacrificed, given only the first description, than if we also go along with the second description in terms of rights. For if we admit that she actually has the right not to be sacrificed, and that those for whom she is sacrificed do not have the right to her being sacrificed, then haven't we admitted a great deal? Perhaps we have even admitted the whole thing. For mightn't it be part of the very *notion* of having the right to something, while others do not have the right to it, that it would be morally wrong to give it instead to the others? If this is so, then what the would-be defender of the utilitarian view must say here is that the second description is incorrect, indeed question-begging. For on the utilitarian view, it may be said, it simply *is not true* that Marilyn has the right not to be sacrificed while the others have no right to be spared their pain and their lives. If we wish to put the thing in terms of rights, the utilitarian may say, then we can say either one or the other (or both) of two things: (a) that the only right anybody has is the right to have his utility—his well-being, the value of his or her life to that person—counted equally with everyone else's, neither more nor less; or (b) that we do have various particular and recognizable rights, including the right not to be killed for no reason, even the right not to be sacrificed to others—*but* that these rights are not rigid but are instead overridable in various extreme circumstances. [We can say both of (a) and (b) by making (a) out to be about our "fundamental" rights, those which are absolutely basic and imprescriptable, whereas (b) is about *derivative* rights, rights which we have by virtue of various more special facts about us, some of which may even be dependent on such things as the sociological circumstances of the acts or states of affairs in question.] It is not true, in other words, that the whole *idea* of rights is inherently antithetical to the utilitarian view of things, that the utilitarian cannot avail himself of the concept of a right at all. And it can hardly have been said to be proven by anybody that the nonutilitarian view of rights being opposed to the utilitarian one in question is the true view.

There may be another option regarding the second description. Perhaps we should say, "Well, yes: I have to agree. Her rights *are* being violated, and those for whom she is sacrificed do not have a right to her sacrifice. But this is just one of those situations which show that rights, after all, aren't everything. Sometimes, alas, the only right thing to do is to sacrifice somebody's rights. If it were a terrifically big sacrifice of rights, of course, then that would be very hard, perhaps even impossible, to justify. But in this case, it's a very small, almost a trivial (by comparison!) sacrifice of rights. And in such cases, rights just aren't worth it. Rights have their place, but here they simply don't carry the issue."

I don't know whether that is something we can say or not. If the rights in question were merely legal rights, of course, then we could say it, and quite cheerfully. But we are imagining that these are moral rights. And it is not so obvious that we can say, cheerfully or otherwise, that it might be morally all right to violate moral rights. Here we may be in very deep moral waters. Alternatively, we may simply be in a semantical briarpatch! And I am not even sure which. But as we have seen, we can in any case take the view set forth a couple of paragraphs back, and simply deny that rights are being violated.

Certainly the utilitarian must accept the first description, however. And he must agree that at least acts described as in our option A are right. For A and B are the only two options, and here, at least, it is perfectly clear which option has the more utility. Various things could have made it less clear, but we have ruled them out (or tried to, anyway): things like just how "innocent" Marilyn really is, just how much she does stand to lose, just how much the others do stand to gain, and so forth. We might have had room for doubts had various things been otherwise. For example—to pick up on two points which I left hanging back near the beginning of this piece—suppose that Marilyn's last couple of hours, given option B, would involve some kind of quite incredible experience for her, something so powerful and wonderful as to be worth an ordinary lifetime by comparison. Or several ordinary lifetimes, as in this case! Well, given the utilitarian's general assumptions, we cannot say that it is absolutely impossible that two hours of a certain kind of experience should be worth several lifetimes of mundane experience (even "mundane" by intergalactic standards!). We can perhaps say that given what we know about the constitution of the human soul, such experience is virtually or practically impossible. And in the present case, we are framing things so that it doesn't happen. Marilyn's last two hours would be nothing ultra-special, in utilitarian terms. And on the other hand, we have ruled out the possibility of her life being extended not by two hours, but by, say, fifty years. This last is important. For we have to remember—something which has been implicit in the entire discussion, really—that to kill somebody is to *shorten* his or her life. At the time, it is the difference between life and death, to be sure. (Of course!) But what is that difference, after all? It is the difference between living a life of length x rather than length y! And it would be very relevant if Marilyn's life in option B would be much, much longer, rather than merely a little longer, or if the diseased men would, in any case, die quite soon rather than presumably many years later. But all these options, which admittedly would be very important, have been ruled out in our story. We have rigged the situation so that plainly the sum of human happiness, on any credible assessment of such "sums," lies with action A. And A is, unquestionably, the intentional visiting of a horrendous injury (loss of life, in particular) on an admitted innocent person, for the sake of others. But I submit that nevertheless, A is clearly the correct choice, while B would be something close to insanity. And I suspect that nearly all readers will agree.

Now, what might make anyone accept the second description?

What might make anyone think that there is a "rigid" right which Marilyn has (or at least, Marilyn in the story with our amendments), whereas all the others have no *right* to her being sacrificed to them? (What, that is, might make them think that "right" is so strong as to make B *the right thing to do?*) Curiously enough, many of them, I suspect, accept the second description *just because they accept the first description!* They accept a principle to the effect that each of us has a right that no one else *intentionally visit* a harm upon him or her, no matter what good may come of it for any other persons: "No one may do evil that good may come," they say. But notice how plausible it is to say something like "No one may do wrong that good may come"; and how easy it is to equate "wrong" with "evil," and then "evil" with "harm," and "harm" with, say, "pain, suffering, loss of life," etc. If that's how it is, though, then these people may have fallen into a trap. For the utilitarian too may cheerfully agree that no one may do *wrong* in order that good may come. But he denies that it *is* wrong to sacrifice Marilyn in this case. It is too bad, we wish it could be otherwise, but in the circumstances, it is clearly the *right* action. He denies that "wrong" means the same as (for instance) "intentional infliction of harm" especially when "harm" means, as it so often does, simply pain, loss of life, and so on. And in this denial he surely is correct. These terms do not *mean* the same thing.

Those who accept the idea that we may never intentionally inflict pain, etc., on anyone for the sake of anyone else accept an idea which will scarcely bear reflection by serious people—though I say this with some embarrassment, since some apparently quite serious people do profess to have accepted it! Why so? There are two different causes at work here, I believe. One goes like this. Here you are, one of those unfortunate people on the remote planet who will die of a terrible disease if the serum doesn't come. And you think of poor Marilyn's plight—either she is jettisoned into the void, right now, in order that you may be spared this pain and death (and six others, of course), or she lives on for another two hours or so, thence to die in a crash, though admittedly not a crash which anyone has intentionally brought about, but with the result that you and the six others (and the pilot, of course) suffer awful fates. The only difference is that in the one case, an intentionally inflicted awful fate befalls someone, though many others are spared an unintentionally inflicted, even awfuller fate, while in the other, unintentionally awfuller fates befall several, and an almost equally awful fate befalls that one *anyway*. Well what, after all, is the *point* of action, you ask. Is it not to make people happy, if possible, and to spare them pain, if possible? And what has she got that we haven't got? True, she is innocent—but then, so are we. And admittedly she's young, and no doubt very sweet and cute and charming too, so that it is even more horrible (say you, at the risk of sounding somewhat sexist!) to think of jettisoning her out into the void of space and being exploded and having her blood boil instantly. But still and all, are we not fundamentally *equal*? And isn't the difference between us the only difference that can, in the end, matter—namely, that we have so much, much more to lose than she if action B is selected by the pilot? Nor is there anything self-seeking about this either. Were we Marilyn, we would reason the same way—as indeed, she *does!*

The first "cause," as I call it, is a powerful appeal to our basic sympathies as human beings. The second is another matter. There is nothing sentimental about it. But there is something very compelling. It goes like this: Marilyn, poor creature, has got herself into a jam. Very tough for her. But then, we have got ourselves into jams too—or more precisely, some nasty germs have got us into them. Tough for us. But now, it could happen to anyone, couldn't it? And just suppose that, so to speak, before life really gets going in earnest, we were all to strike a bargain, a deal—each reasoning in cold-blooded self-interest—for how to deal with such occasions, occasions when nobody is to blame, when circumstances have forced terrible choices on someone and that someone must choose between intentionally doing what would normally be a terrible, wrong thing, and letting something else happen which is, in fact, still awfuller, though not intentionally inflicted by him. Much awfuller, and for many more people. Well, given that it is chance that threw us all into this situation, what principle would we, as self-interested and rational beings, have elected to direct the actions of the choosers in such situations? The answer is clear: when there is a great and striking difference in utility between two such options, choose the act with the strikingly higher utility. For by doing so, each of us "maximizes," as the decision-theorists put it, his or her "expected utility," that is, the amount we can expect to gain (or avoid losing, as the case may be) weighted by the probability that we shall gain it, in the long run. The fact that it is just chance that gets us into such situations, surely, is what makes this the rational choice. Were it not chance, were there someone to blame, that might be another matter. Then we might insist on some other principle. But it isn't so. And for such situations, no other policy can make sense.

This second way of defending Choice A in our situation is not clearly a way of defending utilitarianism all the way down the line. For utilitarianism "all the way down the line" might seem to call for sacrifices of the clearly innocent to the clearly guilty, and any number of other intuitively outrageous things—or so it is claimed, anyway. But we needn't go into that here. For what is presently at stake is what to do when everybody is admittedly innocent.

What remains? Well, what remains is the possibility that there really are *rights,* that they really are as rigid as some people say, so rigid that Choice B becomes the right choice. It is not clear what to make of such a view. Do people who accept it really, underneath it all, secretly think that maybe there is a God up there somewhere who will punish everyone who intentionally inflicts pains and losses on anyone no matter how many others are benefitted thereby? (But if they do, two questions might be asked them: First, what kind of a God would want people to obey *that* crazy rule anyway? And second, haven't you noticed that you are just blatantly sneaking a bunch of new utilities in the back door? For now you're going to have your God visiting eternal disutility on our poor pilot—and obviously that will overwhelm any utility he can bring about by jettisoning poor Marilyn! So you've really agreed that utilitarianism wins after all, only you're introducing some very weird, transcendental sources of utility into the situation—which is changing the issue!) Or is there something else, something more acceptable and more credible? But what could it be? Nobody has yet given us a respectable account. And maybe we can't wait. Maybe we are every so often in something like the predicament of this poor pilot, and must make up our minds what to do. Surely we can do no better than to act on the only view which is recommended by reasoned sentiment.

Alas, poor Marilyn! You are quite right: you didn't do anything wrong. But neither did anybody else. You are indeed a sacrifice and a victim: but a sacrifice which no reasonable person, including yourself, could refuse to make, and a victim of the unhappy construction of the universe we live in, not of any morally responsible person. We weep for you, and we will remember you in our hearts. But we can—no, we *ought!*—do no more.

CHAPTER 7 PROBES

1. Do you believe that what the pilot did to Marilyn was what he should have done? Can you justify your belief? What principles might you use to do so?

2. What does Jan Narveson think about cases like Marilyn's? Why does he think as he does? To which of the views mentioned in the introduction to this chapter is Narveson committed, in your opinion? Why do you think this?

3. Narveson thinks that more precaution should have been taken to prevent cases like Marilyn's. Do you agree? What precuations should have been taken against stowaways? Could these precautions still fail? If they did, would you have any moral problem with jettisoning the stowaway? Why would you take precautions at all?

4. What would you say to somebody who said, "Listen, I don't care about stowaways at all—they know that they're not supposed to do that, so what happens to them is their own fault." Would you agree or disagree? Why?

5. What happened to Marilyn might be compared with other moral problems involving the question of precautions against people's own ignorance or unwillingness to follow rules. Some have argued, in effect, "Let the buyer beware." They will say that, if buyers are foolish enough to buy a dangerous product or violate a law that is in their interest, it is their tough luck, and it is not the responsibility of the government or manufacturer to protect them against their own stupidity (see Chapter 8 for the strongest possible view of this sort, called "anarchism"). Do you agree or disagree, and to what extent? Do you think that the government or manufacturer is responsible for complete safety, moderate safety, marginal safety, or no safety at all? (For example, if someone wants a child-proof cap on a dangerous drug, why not make him pay for it himself, at his option? If he doesn't, and his child dies from it, to what extent is that the responsibility of the government, the manufacturer, or the parent?) To what extent is Marilyn's fate the fault of the government or starship company?

6. What comparisons can you find between Marilyn's case and

  a. someone who buys land sight unseen, and later discovers that it's a swamp?

  b. someone who illegally takes addictive drugs, gets addicted, and dies from an overdose?

  c. someone who gets very drunk and tries to drive, killing himself or herself in a fatal accident?

  d. someone who drives on bald tires, not having taken care to check them, endangering himself or herself and others on the highway?

How much freedom to either willingly or mistakenly endanger yourself or others should you have?

7. What if Marilyn's presence had only severely endangered the pilot and sick men on Woden? Imagine that her presence meant only that in order to save her, the pilot would have to adjust his entry into Woden's atmosphere in such a way as to make the landing very dangerous, but possible under the best of circumstances (which wouldn't be known until the time of arrival, when it would be too late to change anything, if circumstances weren't ideal). If this landing were unsuccessful, not only would Marilyn and the pilot die, but the sick men on Woden would also, as their medicine would be destroyed in the crash. You have a choice, but you have to make it now—do you jettison Marilyn, even though it is *possible* that you might not need to, or do you attempt to save her, severely endangering the lives of a number of people? How would you justify your answer against a critic?

8. How do you think a hedonist would answer the question raised in probe 7? What would an ethical egoist say? What would a Christian say? What would an ethical relativist say? What would a nihilist say? What would a utilitarianist say? What would Narveson say? For those views that are different from your own, how would you show that their conclusion is not acceptable?

9. What if it turned out that, although there was no *mortal* danger, any delay of the EDS landing would virtually guarantee that everyone on Woden, including Gerry and his group, would suffer from frequent and incapacitating spells of kala fever for the rest of their lives, spells that would be marked by raving madness, agonizing pain, and high medical bills? Imagine that, while there is no danger to Marilyn and the pilot, her presence in the EDS would involve the pilot's taking at least an extra day to land on Woden, if she is to be saved. No one's life would be endangered if they delay and save Marilyn's life, but it is virtually certain that the men on Woden will suffer in the extreme way already described. Should the pilot jettison Marilyn and spare the men a lifetime of agony and madness, or should he save her, holding life sacred above all else? What if Marilyn were utterly blameless in her presence on the EDS, having followed a sign (as Narveson imagines) that had said (falsely) "PASSENGERS TO MIMIR, THIS WAY!"? How would your view on this matter differ from those that would be taken by other theorists, as identified in the introduction to this chapter (e.g., hedonists, egoists, etc.)?

10. How many changes, and of what extent, would be the *minimum* that would have to be made in Godwin's story before you would think that Marilyn ought to be spared by the EDS pilot? How would you justify your view that that point was critical, such that any fewer changes, or changes of lesser extent, *would not* require saving her life, but that this number and extent of changes (or greater) *would* require saving her life?

11. Now that you are more familiar with various theories of ethics, are you most inclined to be a naturalist, a transcendentalist, a noncognitivist, or a nonfactual knowledge theorist? How does your view of ethical justification compare with those identified in the introduction to this chapter?

12. Can you think of a story that would best dramatize your view of the fundamental ethical principles? Can you think of telling a story like Marilyn's that would show why your ethical principles are the best ones for the situation in your story? How would your story differ from those that would be told by the advocates of the other theories with which you disagree? (That is, if you're inclined to be a naturalist, how would your story differ from the one that would be told by a transcendentalist, a noncognitivist, or a nonfactual knowledge theorist?)

RECOMMENDED READING

Science Fiction and Problems of Ethics

Most science fiction stories are in the romantic tradition of literature, in which the heroes make hard choices on which turns the fate of the human race or even of whole galactic empires. Therefore, questions of value are at least implicit in most science fiction. But in some of the best science fiction the principal characters are capable of articulating the moral codes that direct their actions. A favorite theme is the conflict of values which results from the contact of human beings with alien life forms, where often-cherished human values and ethical principles are called into question. In the best-constructed stories the outcome of the plot is logically determined by this conflict between values.

Are Values Absolute or Relative? Many people assume that moral values are absolute, that the same moral claims, such as, "Murder is wrong," hold true for all persons. They also presume that these absolute moral truths happen to be the beliefs that *they* have about ethics. It never fails to shock us when we find other people steadfastly and sincerely holding on to moral truths that *we* do not accept. Many science fiction stories are able to represent this type of "value shock" in a much more spectacular way in the form of stories of first contact with other life forms. A recent example is Larry Niven and Jerry Pournelle, *The Mote in God's Eye* (Pocket Books, 1975). Human explorers encounter a new species, the "Moties," with a radically different physiology, technology, and culture from ours. The lovable diplomats which the humans first encounter conceal the dark secrets of Motie civilization. The values of the Moties as ultimately disclosed are literally "inhuman," for their biological, and particularly their sexual, nature has produced in them a radically different moral sense. A somewhat more restricted use of this idea is found in Ira Levin, *This Perfect Day* (Fawcett, 1978), in which a young revolutionary appeals to values such as selfishness and aggressiveness which, he claims, are inherent in "human nature." His opponents hope to change this nature by means of genetic engineering to produce a race with the virtues of selflessness, obedience, and docility. Such stories tend to support a view of ethical relativism. Individualism is viewed not as an absolute value; rather, it is a value only to the extent that a species is biologically "programmed" to endorse it.

Most human ethical theories treat some desired human state such as happiness or freedom or a flourishing life as an absolute value. Our confidence in such theories is challenged by science fiction stories in which more powerful alien races appear who are utterly indifferent to our human values. A classic treatment of this theme is H. G. Wells's well-known *War of the Worlds* (reprinted in many editions), in which Martians invade the earth with the intention of occupying it and treating human beings as lower animals. The film version produced by George Pal (1953) has a striking scene in which humans approach the first Martian landing craft with a white flag and are vaporized without ado. The Martians evidently do not recognize human beings as members of the human community. Wells's novel has inspired a tradition of BEM (bug-eyed-monster) yarns, most without philosophical or literary merit. But skillfully rendered tales of earth invasion force us to reexamine our human-centered values. One explicit takeoff on Wells, Brian W. Aldiss's "The Saliva Tree," in Damon Knight, ed., *The Nebula Award Stories* (Pocket Books, 1967), received a Nebula for its superb description of invisible aliens on an English farm who regard humans as part of the livestock. A similar device is used in Damon Knight's ironic "To Serve Man," in *The Best of Damon Knight* (Pocket Books, 1976). Other stories in which humans are essentially viewed as means to the ends of others include John Wyndham's *The Midwich Cuckoos* (Ballantine, 1976), which was made by Wolf Rilla into a film, *The Village of the Damned* (1960). A relativistic view of human values also dominates Fritz Leiber's Hugo-winning *The Wanderer* (Ballantine, 1964) and Arthur C. Clarke's Nebula winner, *Rendezvous with Rama* (Ballantine, 1973).

Not all "first-contact" stories support ethical relativism. Some authors use the context of conflict with alien ways to affirm the absolute validity of human moral judgments. Gene Roddenberry's television series, "Star Trek," explores the conflict of values as the Starship *Enterprise* wends its way through outer space. According to Starfleet's Prime Directive, Captain Kirk is not to interfere in the development of local cultures. This represents a kind of ethical relativism, since Kirk and his crew are not permitted to impose their moral precepts upon alien cultures. (It should not, however, be overlooked that the Prime Directive itself is given an *absolute* moral status, since it takes precedence over value conflicts between individual cultures.) If Kirk were to obey the Prime Directive literally, nothing would ever happen on "Star Trek." Most episodes turn on Kirk's rather feeble rationalizations for violating the Directive—for example, "This is really not a 'developing' culture, but a stagnant and dead one." The episode "The Apple" is typical: Val, a computer posturing as a god, controls a native population; Kirk restores the natives to his own values of struggle and progress—at the small price of a loss of immortality. Kirk's arguments generally represent the viewpoint of the ethical absolutists. The film *The Day the Earth Stood Still,* directed by Robert Wise (1951), provides an interesting twist on this theme. In this film a higher galactic civilization representing higher values of peace, science, and free trade (enforced by implacable robot police) intervenes in an Earth in the grip of the Cold War. Two novels that tend to support absolutism in ethics are Gordon R. Dickson's *Alien Way* (Warner, 1977) and Hal Clement's *Cycle of Fire* (Ballantine, 1975). Both of these pit humans against aliens in what emerges as a conflict over the validity of competing value systems.

Altruism and Egoism. Many science fiction stories focus on specific moral claims. In some of the stories a hero will advocate a moral point of view and defend it against the villains. Much of the fiction of Theodore Sturgeon, such as the sensitively written Nebula winner, "Slow Sculpture," in Clifford Simak, ed., *Nebula Award Stories Number Six* (Pocket Books, 1972), represents the hero's perceived "duty to humanity." This is *altruism,* the view that you should seek to promote the interests of humanity at large rather than your own selfish interests. This assumption, which is the basis of the moral theories of philosophers like Plato and Kant, also underlies much of the science fiction which is discussed in the Recommended Reading list of Chapter 8 under the headings "Pro-Utopian Science Fiction" and "Social Criticism in Science Fiction." In contrast, other stories represent the assumption of *egoism*—that you should seek to promote your own self-interest. For example, the hero of Robert Silverberg's Nebula-winning *Time of Changes* (Doubleday, 1971) repudiates the religious doctrine of his home planet that the self is evil. Believers in this religion are ashamed to refer to themselves or express their thoughts and feelings. The theme of Silverberg's book is stated in Aristotle's *Nicomachean Ethics:* Self-love, in the genuine or noble sense, is a requirement for true love of others. Silverberg makes superb use of some devices which, as Silverberg himself points out in the new introduction to the paperback edition (Berkley, 1979), were pioneered by Ayn Rand in *Anthem* (Signet, 1946); for example, the use of singular pronouns like "I" and "me" and of proper names is proscribed. Rand's hero repudiates the altrusim which, he thinks, holds the human race in bondage, and asserts a radical form of egoism and individualism. Such ethical views are reflected in much of the science fiction discussed in the Recommended Reading list of Chapter 8 under the headings "Anti-Utopian Science Fiction" and "Libertarian Science Fiction."

Pleasure, Utility, and Their Critics. Some science fiction is essentially critical—the author shows unacceptable consequences from acting upon questionable moral premises. One doctrine which often comes into question is hedonistic utilitarianism: "You should strive to bring about the greatest happiness for the greatest number." On the surface this *sounds* good, but many critics object that problems arise if the principle is followed too stubbornly. For example, some critics reject the hedonistic assumption that pleasure or happiness is the good. James Gunn, in *The Joy Makers* (Bantam, 1961), explicitly criticizes a society in which pleasure is the dominant value. Implicit but very effective criticisms of hedonism are found in Ray Bradbury's *Fahrenheit 451* (Ballantine, 1976), the basis for the François Truffaut film (1966), and Aldous Huxley's widely admired *Brave New World* (Harper, 1978). Critics of utilitarianism object also that this doctrine would permit sacrificing a minority of persons in order to benefit a majority of society. This criticism is suggested by Ursula K. LeGuin's Hugo-winning story, "Those Who Walk Away from Omelas," in *The Wind's Twelve Quarters* (Bantam, 1976); by Lester del Rey, *The Eleventh Commandment* (Ballantine, 1976); and by Gene Wolfe in "The Death of Dr. Island," a Nebula-winning story in Kate Wilhelm, ed., *Nebula Award Stories Number Nine* (Bantam, 1978). In each of these stories individuals are sacrificed in disturbing ways in order to bring about "the greater good."

"Hard Cases." Some of the most fascinating science fiction does not advocate a particular moral position. Instead it sets out a difficult ethical situation in which the readers are, in effect, forced to "judge for themselves." In addition to Godwin's "Cold Equations," a typical "space lifeboat" case is presented in Arthur C. Clarke, "Breaking Strain," in *Expedition to Earth* (Ballantine, 1975). An excellent example is Alexei Panshin, *Rite of Passage* (Ace, 1976). This Nebula-winning novel uses Robert A. Heinlein's interesting suggestion in *Starship Troopers* (Berkley, n.d.) that space-age education will place heavy emphasis on the history of ethics. The youthful heroine of *The Rite of Passage* uses the ethical theories she has studied to deal with the proposal that an entire planet with its human population be destroyed. The characters in the novel reach a decision, but the disturbing moral issues are not settled for the reader.

Philosophy and Problems of Ethics

Two popular introductions to ethics are William Frankena, *Ethics* (Prentice-Hall, 1973) and John Hospers, *Human Conduct* (Harcourt Brace Jovanovich, 1972). See also the articles listed under "Ethics" in *The Encyclopedia of Philosophy* (Macmillan, 1967). There are numerous anthologies, including A. Oldenquist, ed., *Readings in Moral Philosophy* (Houghton Mifflin, 1964), which has much valuable traditional material and a good introduction. Influential work on ethics by twentieth-century analytic philosophers is represented in W. Sellar and J. Hospers, eds., *Readings in Ethical Theory*, 2nd ed. (Prentice-Hall, 1970), and in G. Dworkin and J. J. Thomson, eds., *Ethics* (Harper, 1968), and P. Foot, ed., *Theories of Ethics.* For the beginner, P. Taylor, ed., *Problems of Moral Philosophy* (Dickenson, 1972), has a representative selection from recent moral philosophers.

A good introduction to the question of whether ethics is relative or absolute is the article on "Ethical Relativism" in *The Encyclopedia of Philosophy*. The position was first propounded by the ancient sophist Protagoras (590–421 B.C.). E. A. Westermarck defends ethical relativism on the basis of his anthropological findings in *Ethical Relativity* (Harcourt Brace Jovanovich, 1932).

The general issue of whether we can know the basic principles of ethics has been hotly debated throughout this century. An overview is provided in "Ethics, Problems of," "Ultimate Moral Principles: Their Justification," and "Epistemology and Ethics, Parallel Between," in *The Encyclopedia of Philosophy*. On definism and naturalism, see the article "Ethical Naturalism." Classic defenders of ethical naturalism are Aristotle (384–322 B.C.), who defends a biocentric "happiness" ethic, and Epicurus (342–270 B.C.), who is a hedonist. John Stuart Mill (1806–1873) offers a reformulation of the Epicurean concept of value in *Utilitarianism*. Mill argues that happiness or the good is desirable, that is, valuable, because it is desired. G. E. Moore (1873–1958) subjects such arguments to searching criticisms in an extremely influential work, *Principia Ethica* (Cambridge, 1903), and in "A Reply to My Critics" (in Foot). A similar objection is offered earlier by David Hume (1711–1776), who formulates it as a problem of reasoning from an "is" to an "ought." A number of important essays on Hume's "is"–"ought" problem and Moore's "naturalistic fallacy" are found in W. D. Hudson, *The Is–Ought Question* (St. Martins, 1969), and in the Foot, Sellars and Hospers, Tayler, and Thomson and Dworkin anthologies.

Noncognitivism is introduced in the *Encyclopedia* articles "Ethical Subjectivism" and "Emotive Theory of Ethics." The view is defended by David Hume and by the twentieth-century philosopher C. L. Stevenson in *Ethics and Language* (Yale, 1943).

Nonfactual ethical knowledge theories have been expressed in a variety of ways. *The Encyclopedia of Philosophy* article "Ethical Objectivism" surveys a number of alternative approaches: that we know ethical rules by purely formal reasoning (Immanuel Kant), by intuition (Richard Price and W. D. Ross) and moral sense (Francis Hutcheson), through conscience (Joseph Butler), or by appeal to an ideal observer (Adam Smith and, on some interpretations, Aristotle).

Until recently in the controversy over egoism and altruism, philosophers have on the whole supported some version of altruism. This is evident in the *Encyclopedia of Philosophy* article, "Egoism and Altruism." Many philosophers have even denied that ethical egoism qualifies as a serious ethical theory. But a new generation of philosophers has come to the defense of egoism; for example, Ayn Rand in *The Virtue of Selfishness* (Signet, 1964) argues that serving one's own self-interests is consistent with recognizing the rights of others. The liveliness of the issue today is evident from the selections in D. P. Gauthier, ed., *Morality & Rational Self-Interest* (Prentice-Hall, 1970), in the sympathetic discussion of egoism in J. Hospers, *Human Conduct,* and in T. Machan, "Recent Work on Ethical Egoism," *American Philosophical Quarterly* (1979).

Utilitarianism remains a very influential theory. The classical statements are Mill's *Utilitarianism* and Bentham's *Principles of Morals and Legislation.* The *Encyclopedia of Philosophy* article "Utilitarianism" is quite sympathetic. Valuable essays on classical utilitarianism are found in J. B. Schneewind, ed., *Mill: A Collection of Critical Essays* (Doubleday, 1968). Essays on current issues in the debate over utilitarianism are found in the anthologies of Foot, Thomson, and Dworkin; Sellars and Hospers; and M. Bayles, ed., *Contemporary Utilitarianism* (Doubleday, 1968). Powerful objections to utilitarianism have been raised recently by John Rawls, in *A Theory of Justice* (Harvard, 1971).

SOCIAL ETHICS:

Is politics necessary?

"A human being is a political animal." The Greek philosopher Aristotle made this claim over two thousand years ago, and it would seem that things have scarcely changed since then. The observation may seem trivial or even simplistic. But this is misleading. "A human being is a political animal" contains conceptual snares for the unwary philosopher.

One snare involves the fact–value problem, discussed in Chapter 7. You should consider the point of the statement, "A human being is a political animal." One might say this and simply be *describing* certain *facts* we observe about human beings, such as the fact that they could not survive for long without social arrangements. But the person making this statement could also be *prescribing* certain *values* which humans should pursue, such as the value of self-actualization that a person can find by pursuing the political life. This is a crucial distinction. For philosophers called *anarchists* agree with the factual claim that people tend to live in political units and depend on them for their well-being, yet they reject the *value judgment* that people *should* live in political systems or that it is *right* to establish states. Thus, the anarchist is raising a basic question in normative ethics: is the state good or bad?

A second snare involves the word "political," which comes from the ancient Greek word *polis* or city-state. The Greeks used this word not merely for the government but also for the whole complex of social relationships within the city-state. So the words "political animal" can mean "an animal with a government" or they can mean "an animal living in a *social* system." This distinction is, again, very important for the anarchist, who agrees that humans are *social* animals, but denies that they are *governmental* animals. By this the anarchist does not mean that people are like unreasoning "social insects." People reason and make self-governing decisions (and thus are "political" in Aristotle's sense) without establishing a formal structure of government.

The anarchist agrees that you, as a human being, have to live at least part of your life in a community with other human beings. The benefits of social life are obvious. You have inherited a vast amount of wealth, wisdom, and technology from your ancestors, and you are able to join with other people in mutually beneficial projects. (It is estimated, for example, that the average American employs the technological equivalent of *eighty* human slaves every day.) But the anarchist denies that it is a good thing to have a state: to have a president, a legislature, judges, governors, bureaucrats, police officers, soldiers, and tax collectors. There are important differences between the two value questions, "Is *society* a good thing?" and "Is the *state* a good thing?" For an *anarchist* answers the first question with a firm *"Yes"* but the second question with a resounding *"No!"* Often anarchists argue that any sort of state will violate basic human freedoms. On the other hand, a proponent of *political theory* maintains that the state is a good thing, and has some definite views as to the sorts of laws such a state should enforce. Science fiction is very useful for understanding and evaluating the claims of the anarchist. Anarchism has been seriously defended by influential thinkers such as William Godwin, Proudhon, Lysander Spooner, and Robert Paul Wolff. But, since an anarchy is radically unlike anything in our everyday experience, it helps to have detailed flesh-and-blood representations of anarchistic experiments in a fictional form to decide whether the anarchistic ideal is really desirable.

This chapter examines the controversy between these two quite different approaches to social ethics. After completing this chapter, you should be able to do the following:

- Explain the differences between the state and the community.

- Contrast the basic positions of anarchism and political theory.

- State why the anarchist finds the concepts of individual responsibility and political obligation incompatible.

- Explain how, according to anarchists, the economic needs that people attempt to satisfy by living in a community can be met without a state.

- Explain how, according to the anarchist, the rights and freedoms of individuals living in the community can be safeguarded without a state.

- Evaluate the claims of anarchism on the basis of conceptual experiments.

8:1 COMMUNITY AND STATE

8:1.1 Human beings depend on communities for their existence. People depend on each other for the satisfaction of many needs: *material* needs, such as food, clothing, and shelter, and higher *spiritual* needs, which may be emotional, aesthetic, or intellectual. In general, people perpetuate their communities by marrying and raising children. Through education, each member of the community learns *rules* governing language, etiquette, religion, and morality. Often we are not aware of these rules, which need not be written down. Yet they are necessary for the survival of the community as such and for the people living in it. The community may be quite small and primitive, for example, a small tribe or settlement, or it may be quite large and complex, for example, a modern nation.

Most people in a community feel threatened when others do not conform to widely accepted customs. Nonconformists may violate standards of dress, speech, or diet. Or they may deviate from marital or sexual customs. Someone may fail to honor certain obligations. For example, a parent may fail to feed a child. Even more seriously, one may actually act aggressively toward other members of the community, using force or fraud to deprive them of values.

As you might expect, others in the community will try to put a stop to this. They may simply complain to the wrongdoer. They may "blackball" and refuse to have anything to do with the person. In a primitive community, this may well lead to the person's death. Or other individuals may take it upon themselves to use force against transgressors: driving them out of the community, depriving them of their property, physically abusing or killing them.

8:1.2 The "state" has, in contrast, been precisely defined by modern social scientists like Max Weber.[1] It consists of the individuals in the community who claim a monopoly on the use of coercive force. The rules enforced by the government within the community are *laws* rather than mere customs. In a primitive village a chief may function as the whole state, whereas in a modern state there will be legislators, executives, police, and other persons salaried out of tax money. But in every case the state of a

---

[1]This is, of course, not a universally accepted definition. The definition of anarchism will have to be adjusted if another definition of "state" is used.

community will countenance no competitors within the community. It forbids other persons from using physical coercion to enforce laws—for example, from using force to collect taxes. A state is viable only to the extent that it can carry out its claim to *a monopoly over the use of force in the community.*

8:1.3   The difference between a community and a state is fundamentally important from the point of view of normative ethics. Suppose it is right for the state to exist. It follows that it is morally proper for certain people within the community to claim that they should be able to do things that others may not do, such as wage war, inflict punishments on rule-breakers, use force to collect taxes, and so forth. Further, other members of the community (whether they want to or not) should obey the commands of people who make up the state. Consequently, if you think there should be a state, you will agree with the following principles:

1. The members of the community should obey the laws and commands issued by a group within the community; and

2. This group (and only this group) should be able to use coercive force to enforce its rules over the community.

The question "Is the existence of the state morally justified?" really comes down to the question, "Are principles 1 and 2 correct?"

8:2   ANARCHISM VERSUS POLITICAL THEORY

8:2.1   These principles are the fundamental working assumptions for all political theory. Of course, there are many radically different viewpoints in political theory. Political theorists disagree among themselves on many important questions: How should members of the community be recruited into the government? (Are they born into the job? Are they elected?) How should the government be organized? (Should the same persons function as lawmakers, judges, and enforcers—or should these duties be assigned to different people?) What limits, if any, should there be on the power of the government to issue and enforce commands over the community? (Should the government respect freedom of speech, property rights, religious liberty, and so forth?) What primary moral goals should be promoted by the laws of the state? (Should the primary concern be to enhance individual freedom? to establish a just distribution of benefits? to promote the greatest happiness of the greatest number?) But all these theories are united in the prior assumption that the state, in some form, is morally justified.

8:2.2   These theories are conceptual light-years away from the theory of *anarchism,* which rejects the fundamental assumptions of all political theory. Anarchists reject the state's claim to moral validity. They deny that any group within the community should be able to *establish rules* which everyone else has an obligation to obey. They deny that such a select group is entitled to *enforce obedience* to its rules over the whole community. It is important to understand that the anarchists are not naïvely denying the descriptive factual claim that states exist or that modern governments exert vast power over their subject populations. They know that it would be risky if not suicidal for people in many countries even to voice criticism of their rulers. They are not denying that if you break the law you will suffer the penalty if apprehended. But they *do* deny the prescriptive, normative ethical claim that you have a *moral obligation* to obey the government as such.

8:3 ARGUMENT FOR ANARCHISM FROM RESPONSIBILITY

8:3.1 The theory of anarchism may still seem strange to you. Nearly all of us simply take it for granted not only that we *have* to pay our taxes, obtain licenses to do business, or abstain from buying certain illegal drugs because "it's the law"—but also that we *should* do so. Speculative fiction is a valuable remedy for this feeling of strangeness. Novels such as Robert A. Heinlein's *The Moon Is a Harsh Mistress* and Ursula LeGuin's *The Dispossessed* provide conceptual experiments in which sophisticated communities operate on essentially anarchistic principles. Heinlein's novel describes a revolution by anarchistic colonists on the moon in 2076 against an Earth-based Authority. Except for external controls, the Lunar colony, which is composed of former exiled convicts from Earth and their descendants, is, in effect, an anarchistic community before the revolution, since the Authority has not permitted the development of internal political institutions. A visitor from Earth, Stuart LaJoie, who has difficulty adjusting to the customs of the "Loonies," complains, "I seem to have wandered into Looking Glass Land." There are customs but no written laws or police or judges to enforce them. There are no taxes, and all the members of the community satisfy their needs and preferences without benefit of government. The Loonies are not surprised at LaJoie's incredulity: "An Earthworm expects to find a law, a printed law, for every circumstance."[2]. Ultimately, however, LaJoie finds himself emotionally and morally committed to the Loonies' struggle for freedom.

8:3.2 The spokesman for the revolution in Heinlein's novel is Professor de la Paz, who presents an argument for what he calls *rational anarchism*. The professor is arguing with a heroine of the novel, Wyoming Knott, who wants to establish a state on Luna and who has taken their mutual friend, Manuel O'Kelly, to task for saying that there "are no circumstances under which the state is justified in placing its welfare ahead of mine." The professor asserts the "dilemma of government." He asks Wyoh, "Under

[2]Robert A. Heinlein, *The Moon Is a Harsh Mistress* (New York: Putnam/Berkley, 1966), p. 130.

what circumstances is it moral for a group to do that which is not moral for a member of that group to do alone?" The basis for his argument is the assumption that "I know that I *alone* am morally responsible for everything I do." You are responsible for the actions you perform when you act as an individual. The dilemma arises from the fact that "concepts such as 'state' and 'society' and 'government' have no existence save as physically exemplified in the acts of self-responsible individuals." But insofar as concepts such as responsibility or obligation have application, they must apply to *individual* moral agents. "In terms of morals *there is no such thing as 'state.'* Just men. Individuals. Each responsible for his own acts."

You are responsible for the actions *you* perform even when you are performing them as a member of a group. The fact that you are performing an action in cooperation with others or as an agent of the government does not relieve you of the responsibility for your action. For example, suppose you were a soldier at war ordered by your superior to execute innocent noncombatants. You would be responsible for performing an immoral action if you were to do such a thing as an individual. But, if you protest, "I'm not responsible. I was acting under orders," the anarchist is not impressed. You cannot transfer *your* responsibility for your actions to the "group." There is no passing the moral buck.

Will the anarchist disobey the law or refuse to conform to the custom? Not necessarily. "I am free," asserts the professor, "no matter what rules surround me. If I find them tolerable, I tolerate them; if I find them too obnoxious, I break them."[3] From the point of view of the anarchist, if you are a soldier ordered to perform an action, you should obey the order *only if* you are ordered to perform the sort of action which you should perform. Similarly, the anarchist believes that you should obey the law only if it is a morally justified rule; the fact that a rule is a law does not *make* it a morally justified rule.

8:3.3   As you may suspect, this sort of argument is not without its critics. Jean-Jacques Rousseau contends that a *democracy* avoids this dilemma because the people govern themselves. The anarchists find no difficulty with this suggestion as long as the democracy acts only on the basis of *unanimous agreement* of everyone in the community. But they will not agree in advance to abide by the decisions of a *majority,* because the majority may arrive at an immoral decision. When Wyoh asks the professor, "You would not abide by a law that the majority felt was necessary?", he responds, "Tell me what law, dear lady, and I will tell you whether I will obey it."

Political theorists have also argued that a person should keep his promises and that, when you voluntarily live in a community you, in effect, promise to obey the law. This places you under the moral obligation to obey the state. This argument from "tacit consent" has been set out with great rigor by Socrates in Plato's dialogue *Crito* and by John Locke in his *Second*

[3]Ibid., pp. 63–65.

Treatise on Government. You may suspect that Professor de la Paz would not be moved by this sort of argument either. Some have doubted whether, simply by continuing to live in a community, you can really make a "promise" to obey the rules of the people in the community who call themselves "the government." But even if you have recited by rote, "I pledge allegiance . . ." from childhood on, can you become morally obligated by a promise of this sort? Can a promise place you under the moral obligation to obey a law or order which is immoral or to abide by a legal decision which is unjust? There is something paradoxical about this sort of blank-check promise.

The argument of the rational anarchist seems to be that, because moral responsibility and moral obligation attach to people only *as* individuals, the fact that the government orders you to do something is irrelevant from the moral point of view. If the concept of moral obligation and responsibility has any application at all, the concept of *political* obligation is absurd.

8:4 PROBLEMS FOR ANARCHISM: MEETING HUMAN NEEDS

8:4.1 We have so far only considered one sort of argument for anarchism, the argument of the rational anarchist, invoking fundamental normative concepts such as *responsibility* and *obligation.* But the philosophical battle between anarchism and political theory also rages on other grounds. Anarchists often contend also that the basic *needs* and *values* of individuals living in a community can be satisfied and realized just as efficiently (if not more efficiently) and more humanely if there is no state. How will this happen? You shouldn't expect all anarchists to agree on the answer. The specific versions of anarchism are as varied as are those of political theory. Anarchists disagree in their views as to what goals should prevail in the community (though they generally agree that these goals should not be imposed upon everyone) and as to what forms of nonpolitical organization should prevail. The anarchistic communities depicted in the novels of Heinlein and LeGuin differ in fundamental ways in terms of their structure and value orientations.

8:4.2 Heinlein depicts a society which is highly *individualistic.* The institution of private property continues to exist on the basis of custom rather than of law. Economic relationships are essentially contractual, although contracts are not enforced by law. "If a man's word isn't any good, who would contract with him? Doesn't he have a reputation?" The result is a condition of complete *laissez-faire,* an economic system sometimes referred to as *anarchocapitalism.* The individual has to provide for his own needs, since nothing, not even the air, is free. (The favorite slogan of the Loonies is "Tanstaafl," meaning, "There ain't no such thing as a free lunch.") Individuals purchase insurance against disease and other mishaps by placing bets with bookies. They resist the view that there should be a government to protect them. "There is no worse tyranny than to force a man to pay for what he does not want, merely because *you* think it would be good for him."[4]

In addition to commercial transactions, the Loonies place a great value upon the family. In place of the nuclear family of our society—a man, woman, and their 1.6 children—there are complex communal marriages offering companionship and security from sperm to worm. Heinlein's anarchist also tends to resist the suggestion of "morals legislation" which would regulate people's personal habits. They believe that individuals should be allowed to consume what they want, to engage in what private relationships they want. There is no necessity for a government to raise the moral tone of the community.

8:4.3   Ursula LeGuin takes a somewhat different approach in describing life on the desertlike planet of Anarres in *The Dispossessed.* Her anarchistic community, which like Heinlein's survives under conditions of extreme scarcity, follows the teachings of Odo, a theoretician long deceased. Her protagonist Shevek seems to agree with Professor de la Paz in placing fundamental emphasis on individual responsibility: "It's . . . our common nature to be Odonian, to be responsible to one another. And that responsibility is our freedom. To avoid it would be to lose our freedom. Would you really like to live in a society where you have no responsibility and no freedom, no choice, only the false option of obedience to the law, or disobedience followed by punishment? Would you really want to go live in a prison?"[5] All social relations are to be voluntary and cooperative. There are accepted standards of behavior, but these have the force of custom rather than of law, and they are not to be imposed on anyone against his will. Like Heinlein's Loonies, the Anarresti don't believe you should force others to accept your personal preferences in such areas as sex and marriage.

But the Anarresti do have some moral ideals which are quite different from those of the Loonies. In contrast to the radical individualism of Heinlein's revolutionaries, the ideal of the Odonians is the *social organism.* Each individual should assume a functional role within the organic community. This enables him to promote his own interests and those of the whole community at the same time. The Odonian condemns both "egoizing"—a preoccupation with your own interests and an overinflated picture of your own importance—and "altruism"—the sacrifice of your interests to others' and excessive self-effacement. The economy of Anarres is radically unlike the Lunar anarchocapitalism. "All the operations of capitalism" are as meaningless to Shevek of Anarres "as the rites of a primitive religion, as barbaric, as elaborate, and as unnecessary." There is no system of money

---

[4]Ibid., pp. 130, 242.

[5]Ursula LeGuin, *The Dispossessed: An Ambiguous Utopia* (New York: Harper & Row, 1974), p. 36.

or credit, and, as the title suggests, no private property. A concern with privacy is discouraged except for the sexual privacy of couples. (Public display of sex would be "egoizing.") People live in dormitories and eat in public cafeterias; sleeping quarters are shared. The excessive consumption and accumulation of material goods is condemned as "excremental" and "propertarian." "Excess is excrement," said Odo. The Odonian society is complex and industrialized, but also decentralized: it is a network of cellular communities linked by computers. The workers in various industries belong to voluntary syndicates which make all decisions collectively. Necessary and disagreeable community labor is done on a "tenth-day" rotational basis. Workers are "posted" or assigned to jobs on a voluntary basis by a computerized system which identifies socially necessary work, such as transportation, forestation, health care, and education. Nobody is forced to work: "work is done for work's sake. It is the lasting pleasure of life. The private conscience knows that. And also the societal conscience, the opinion of one's neighbors. There is no other reward on Anarres, no other law. One's own pleasure, and the respect of one's fellows. That is all. When that is so, then you see the opinion of the neighbors becomes a very mighty force."[6] LeGuin's richly detailed novel deals with the life of Shevek, who grows up on Anarres and then travels to a bizarre "propertarian" planet quite similar to our own. Both Heinlein and LeGuin use their great descriptive and narrative skills to make a theory of social ethics, which is utterly alien to our Earth-bound experience, plausible and even hauntingly attractive.

8:4.4 You may remain skeptical as to whether either of these economic systems would really work as well as the anarchist claims they would. It is not possible to deal with this issue more fully without investigating a host of very technical issues in economics—issues on which economists themselves are deeply divided. An economist, Murray Rothbard, has defended an anarchocapitalist scheme along Heinlein's lines in *Man, Economy and State* and *For a New Liberty*. A philosopher, Robert Paul Wolff, has defended an approach closer to LeGuin's in *The Poverty of Liberalism* and *In Defense of Anarchism*.

8:5 PROBLEMS FOR ANARCHISM: HUMAN RIGHTS

8:5.1 Many critics of anarchism believe that it has a still more serious problem to solve: How should individuals be protected from violations of their rights by others—whether by external enemies or by criminals from within? There is also a related problem: How should conflicts of interest between honest and well-meaning members of the community be resolved so that they won't end up resorting to force? These problems seem to go to the heart of anarchism, which places paramount importance on the freedom and responsibility of the individuals living within the community. If they

[6]Ibid., pp. 105, 121.

don't enjoy protection from others who would initiate force against them, they will not be *able* to exercise the responsibility that anarchism assumes everyone *should* exercise.

8:5.2 The solution of political theory to this problem is obvious: The government should provide such protection to people who live in the community. The government should maintain a standing army or militia to provide for defense against external enemies. The police, criminal courts, and penal system should protect people from murderers, thieves, rapists, and the like. Civil courts should serve to resolve disputes or conflicts of interest between private individuals. According to one version of political theory, the *limited government* theory, the state should provide these services and *only* these services. The government should intervene only to prevent or punish acts of violence or fraud and should otherwise not interfere in people's lives. Although many anarchists are sympathetic to these moral constraints, they are unwilling to allow even a limited state. In part they are persuaded by the argument that "having a little government is like being a little pregnant." Nevertheless, anarchism must find a solution to the problem of rights.

8:5.3 Fictional (as well as philosophical) treatments of anarchism sometimes seem to evade or underestimate such difficulties. For example, the problem of military defense hardly arises in LeGuin's novel because there is only one community on the planet, the anarchistic community. In Heinlein's novel, when the forces of the Authority invaded, "Loonies rushed in like white corpuscles—and fought. Nobody told them. Our feeble organization broke down under surprise. But we Loonies fought berserk and invaders died."[7] No explanation is provided as to how the Loonies could achieve the level of organization necessary to withstand a prolonged siege or a sophisticated attack. Fortunately, Heinlein introduces a powerful, humanlike computer as a *deus ex machina* to rescue the Loonies.

8:5.4 Equally unsatisfactory is the treatment of the problem of crime. Odo tries to sidestep the problem of crime with pronouncements such as, "To make a thief, make an owner; to create crime, create laws." Odo assumes that, if there is no property, there will be no crime. This isn't completely convincing. If you assume that "to commit a crime" is *defined* as "to deprive someone of his property," it follows that you cannot commit a crime against someone who doesn't have any property and, further, that crime cannot exist in a community in which nobody has any property. But this seems to be a narrow and rather arbitrary way of defining "to commit a crime." If persons do not possess "property," they do not have an exclusive right to use or dispose of certain objects. But you can still do things to a person without "property" which look like crimes. You might act violently against the person, as in the case of murder, assault, or rape. You

[7]Heinlein, op cit., p. 251.

might use force to interfere with the person's work. You might use force to prevent other members of the community from satisfying *their* needs—for example, you might use force against anyone besides yourself and your friends who tried to take food from a community storehouse.

Both Heinlein and LeGuin assume that the "force" of public opinion will, in most cases, serve to inhibit criminal action. The community on Anarres also contains rehabilitation centers to which people with criminal tendencies go, voluntarily though under social pressure. But both authors indicate that in extreme cases the members of the community will enforce their customs themselves. On Heinlein's Luna, wrongdoers may be summarily ejected out of conveniently located airlocks into the Lunar vacuum. More often, however, a trial is conducted by both plaintiff and defendant. If the judge "could not get them to agree that his settlement was just, he would return fees and, if they fought, referee their duel without charging . . . ."

8:6 CONCEPTUAL EXPERIMENT

Many critics believe that the difficulties of anarchism cannot simply be swept under the rug or thrown out of an air lock, like alleged wrongdoers on Heinlein's Luna. The story by Larry Niven, "Cloak of Anarchy," develops a conceptual experiment in which the anarchistic ideal is quite literally put to the test. The excerpt that follows from Robert Nozick's influential book, *Anarchy, State and Utopia,* presents a careful philosophical argument leading to similar conclusions.

Conceptual Experiment 8:

CLOAK OF ANARCHY

Larry Niven

Square in the middle of what used to be the San Diego Freeway, I leaned back against a huge, twisted oak. The old bark was rough and powdery against my bare back. There was a dark green shade shot with tight parallel beams of white gold. Long grass tickled my legs.

Forty yards away across a wide strip of lawn was a clump of elms, and a small grandmotherly woman sitting on a green towel. She looked like she'd grown there. A stalk of grass protruded between her teeth. I felt we were kindred spirits, and once when I caught her eye I wiggled a forefinger at her, and she waved back.

In a minute now I'd have to be getting up. Jill was meeting me at the Wilshire exits in half an hour. But I'd started walking at the Sunset Boulevard ramps, and I was tired. A minute more . . .

It was a good place to watch the world rotate.

A good day for it, too. No clouds at all. On this hot blue summer afternoon, King's Free Park was as crowded as it ever gets.

Someone at police headquarters had expected that. Twice the usual number of copseyes floated overhead, waiting. Gold dots against blue, basketball-sized, twelve feet up. Each a television eye and a sonic stunner, each a hookup to police headquarters, they were there to enforce the law of the Park.

No violence.

No hand to be raised against another—and no other laws whatever. Life was often entertaining in a Free Park.

North toward Sunset, a man carried a white rectangular sign, blank on both sides. He was parading back and forth in front of a square-jawed youth on a plastic box, who was trying to lecture him on the subject of fusion power and the heat pollution problem. Even this far away I could hear the conviction and dedication in his voice.

South, a handful of yelling marksmen were throwing rocks at a copseye, directed by a gesticulating man with wild black hair. The golden basketball was dodging the rocks, but barely. Some cop was baiting them. I wondered where they had got the rocks. Rocks were scarce in King's Free Park.

The black-haired man looked familiar. I watched him and his

horde chasing the copseye . . . then forgot them when a girl walked out of a clump of elms.

She was lovely. Long, perfect legs, deep red hair worn longer than shoulder length, the face of an arrogant angel, and a body so perfect that it seemed unreal, like an adolescent's daydream. Her walk showed training; possibly she was a model, or dancer. Her only garment was a cloak of glowing blue velvet.

It was fifteen yards long, that cloak. It trailed back from two big gold disks that were stuck somehow to the skin of her shoulders. It trailed back and back, floating at a height of five feet all the way, twisting and turning to trace her path through the trees. She seemed like the illustration in a book of fairy tales, bearing in mind that the original fairy tales were not intended for children.

Neither was she. You could hear neck vertebrae popping all over the Park. Even the rock-throwers had stopped to watch.

She could sense the attention, or hear it in a whisper of sighs. It was what she was here for. She strolled along with a condescending angel's smile on her angel's face, not over-doing the walk, but letting it flow. She turned, regardless of whether there were obstacles to avoid, so that fifteen yards of flowing cloak could follow the curve.

I smiled, watching her go. She was lovely from the back, with dimples.

The man who stepped up to her a little farther on was the same one who had led the rock-throwers. Wild black hair and beard, hollow cheeks and deep-set eyes, a diffident smile and a diffident walk . . . Ron Cole. Of course.

I didn't hear what he said to the girl in the cloak but I saw the result. He flinched, then turned abruptly and walked away with his eyes on his feet.

I got up and moved to intercept him. "Don't take it personal," I said.

He looked up, startled. His voice, when it came, was bitter. "How should I take it?"

"She'd have turned any man off the same way. She's to look at, not to touch."

"You know her?"

"Never saw her before in my life."

"Then—?"

"Her cloak. Now you *must* have noticed her cloak."

The tail end of her cloak was just passing us, its folds rippling an improbable deep, rich blue. Ronald Cole smiled as if it hurt his face. "Yah."

"All right. Now suppose you made a pass, and suppose the lady liked your looks and took you up on it. What would she do next? Bearing in mind that she can't stop walking even for a second."

He thought it over first, then asked, "Why not?"

"If she stops walking she loses the whole effect. Her cloak just hangs there like some kind of tail. It's supposed to wave. If she lies down, it's even worse. A cloak floating at five feet, then swooping into a clump of bushes and bobbing frantically—" Ron laughed helplessly in falsetto. I said, "See? Her audience would get the giggles. That's not what she's after."

He sobered. "But if she really wanted to, she wouldn't *care* about . . . oh. Right. She must have spent a fortune to get that effect."

"Sure. She wouldn't ruin it for Jacques Casanova himself." I thought unfriendly thoughts toward the girl in the cloak. There are polite ways to turn down a pass. Ronald Cole was easy to hurt.

I asked, "Where did you get the rocks?"

"Rocks? Oh, we found a place where the center divider shows through. We knocked off some chunks of concrete," Ron looked down the length of the Park just as a kid bounced a missile off a golden ball. "They got one! Come on!"

The fastest commercial shipping that ever sailed was the clipper ship; yet the world stopped building them after just twenty-five years. Steam had come. Steam was faster, safer, more dependable and cheaper.

The freeways served America for almost fifty years. Then modern transportation systems cleaned the air and made traffic jams archaic and left the nation with an embarrassing problem. What to do with ten thousand miles of unsightly abandoned freeways?

King's Free Park had been part of the San Diego Freeway, the section between Sunset and the Santa Monica interchange. Decades ago the concrete had been covered with topsoil. The borders had been landscaped from the start. Now the Park was as thoroughly covered with green as the much older Griffith Free Park.

Within King's Free Park was an orderly approximation of anarchy. People were searched at the entrances. There were no weapons inside. The copseyes, floating overhead and out of reach, were the next best thing to no law at all.

There was only one law to enforce. All acts of attempted violence carried the same penalty for attacker and victim. Let anyone raise his hands against his neighbor, and one of the golden basketballs would stun them both. They would wake separately, with copseyes watching. It was usually enough.

Naturally people threw rocks at copseyes. It was a Free Park, wasn't it?

"They got one! Come on!" Ron tugged at my arm. The felled

copseye was hidden, surrounded by those who had destroyed it. "I hope they don't kick it apart. I told them I need it intact, but that might not stop them."

"It's a Free Park. And they bagged it."

"With my missiles!"

"Who are they?"

"I don't know. They were playing baseball when I found them. I told them I needed a copseye. They said they'd get me one."

I remembered Ron quite well now. Ronald Cole was an artist and an inventor. It would have been two sources of income for another man but Ron was different. He invented new art forms. With solder and wire and diffraction gratings and several makes of plastics kit, and an incredible collection of serendipitous junk, Ron Cole made things the like of which had never been seen on Earth.

The market for new art forms has always been low, but now and then he did make a sale. It was enough to keep him in raw materials, especially since many of his raw materials came from basements and attics. Rarely there came a *big* sale, and then, briefly, he would be rich.

There was this about him: he knew who I was, but he hadn't remembered my name. Ron Cole had better things to think about than what name belonged with whom. A name was only a tag and a conversational gambit. "Russel! How are you?" A signal. Ron had developed a substitute.

Into a momentary gap in the conversation he would say, "Look at this," and hold out—miracles.

Once it had been a clear plastic sphere, golf-ball sized, balanced on a polished silver concavity. When the ball rolled around on the curved mirror, the reflections were *fantastic.*

Once it had been a twisting sea serpent engraved on a Michelob beer bottle, the lovely vase-shaped bottle of the early 1960s that was too big for standard refrigerators.

And once it had been two strips of dull silvery metal, unexpectedly heavy. "What's this?"

I'd held them in the palm of my hand. They were heavier than lead. Platinum? But nobody carries much platinum around. Joking, I'd asked, "U-235?"

"Are they warm?" he'd asked apprehensively. I'd fought off an urge to throw them as far as I could and dive behind a couch.

But they *had* been platinum. I never did learn why Ron was carrying them about. Something that didn't pan out.

Within a semicircle of spectators, the felled copseye lay on the grass. It was intact, possibly because two cheerful, conspicuously large men were standing over it, waving everyone back.

"Good," said Ron. He knelt above the golden sphere, turned it with his long artist's fingers. To me he said, "Help me get it open."

"What for? What are you after?"

"I'll tell you in a minute. Help me get—Never mind." The hemispherical cover came off. For the first time ever, I looked into a copseye.

It was impressively simple. I picked out the stunner by its parabolic reflector, the cameras, and a toroidal coil that had to be part of the floater device. No power source. I guessed that the shell itself was a power beam antenna. With the cover cracked there would be no way for a damn fool to electrocute himself.

Ron knelt and studied the strange guts of the copseye. From his pocket he took something made of glass and metal. He suddenly remembered my existence and held it out to me, saying, "Look at this."

I took it, expecting a surprise, and I got it. It was an old hunting watch, a big wind-up watch on a chain, with a protective case. They were in common use a couple of hundred years ago. I looked at the face, said, "Fifteen minutes slow. You didn't repair the whole works, did you?"

"Oh, no." He clicked the back open for me.

The works looked modern. I guessed, "Battery and tuning fork?"

"That's what the guard thought. Of course that's what I made it from. But the hands don't move; I set them just before they searched me."

"Aah. What does it do?"

"If I work it right, I think it'll knock down every copseye in King's Free Park."

For a minute or so I was laughing too hard to speak. Ron watched me with his head on one side, clearly wondering if I thought he was joking.

I managed to say, "That ought to cause all *kinds* of excitement."

Ron nodded vigorously. "Of course it all depends on whether they use the kind of circuits I think they use. Look for yourself; the copseyes aren't supposed to be foolproof. They're supposed to be cheap. If one gets knocked down, the taxes don't go up much. The other way is to make them expensive and foolproof, and frustrate a lot of people. People aren't supposed to be frustrated in a Free Park."

"So?"

"Well, there's a cheap way to make the circuitry for the power system. If they did it that way, I can blow the whole thing. We'll see." Ron pulled thin copper wire from the cuffs of his shirt.

"How long will this take?"

"Oh, half an hour—maybe more."

That decided me. "I've got to be going. I'm meeting Jill Hayes at the Wilshire exits. You've met her, a big blond girl, my height—"

But he wasn't listening. "O.K., see you," he muttered. He began placing the copper wire inside the copseye, with tweezers. I left.

Crowds tend to draw crowds. A few minutes after leaving Ron, I joined a semicircle of the curious to see what they were watching.

A balding, lantern-jawed individual was putting something together—an archaic machine, with blades and a small gasoline motor. The T-shaped wooden handle was brand new and unpainted. The metal parts were dull with the look of ancient rust recently removed.

The crowd speculated in half-whispers. What was it? Not part of a car; not an outboard motor, though it had blades; too small for a motor scooter, too big for a motor skateboard—

"Lawn mower," said the white-haired lady next to me. She was one of those small, birdlike people who shrivel and grow weightless as they age, and live forever. Her words meant nothing to me. I was about to ask, when—

The lantern-jawed man finished his work, and twisted something, and the motor started with a roar. Black smoke puffed out. In triumph he gripped the handles. Outside, it was a prison offense to build a working internal combustion machine. Here—

With the fire of dedication burning in his eyes, he wheeled his infernal machine across the grass. He left a path as flat as a rug. It was a Free Park, wasn't it?

The smell hit everyone at once: black dirt in the air, a stink of half-burned hydrocarbons attacking nose and eyes. I gasped and coughed. I'd never smelled anything like it.

The crowd roared and converged.

He squawked when they picked up his machine. Someone found a switch and stopped it. Two men confiscated the tool kit and went to work with screwdriver and hammer. The owner objected. He picked up a heavy pair of pliers and tried to commit murder.

A copseye zapped him and the man with the hammer, and they both hit the lawn without bouncing. The rest of them pulled the lawn mower apart and bent and broke the pieces.

"I'm half sorry they did that," said the old woman. "Sometimes I miss the sound of lawn mowers. My dad used to mow the lawn on Sunday mornings."

I said, "It's a Free Park."

"Then why can't he build anything he pleases?"

"He can. He did. Anything he's free to build, we're free to kick apart." And my mind finished, *Like Ron's rigged copseye.*

Ron was good with tools. It would not surprise me a bit if he knew enough about copseyes to knock out the whole system.

Maybe someone ought to stop him.

But knocking down copseyes wasn't illegal. It happened all the time. It was part of the freedom of the Park. If Ron could knock them all down at once, well—

Maybe someone ought to stop him.

I passed a flock of high school girls, all chittering like birds, all about sixteen. It might have been their first trip inside a Free Park. I looked back because they were so cute, and caught them staring in awe and wonder at the dragon on my back.

A few years and they'd be too blasé to notice. It had taken Jill almost half an hour to apply it this morning: a glorious red-and-gold dragon breathing flames across my shoulder, flames that seemed to glow by their own light. Lower down were a princess and a knight in golden armor, the princess tied to a stake, the knight fleeing for his life. I smiled back at the girls, and two of them waved.

Short blond hair and golden skin, the tallest girl in sight, wearing not even a nudist's shoulder pouch: Jill Hayes stood squarely in front of the Wilshire entrance, visibly wondering where I was. It was five minutes after three.

There was this about living with a physical culture nut. Jill insisted on getting me into shape. The daily exercises were part of that, and so was this business of walking half the length of King's Free Park.

I'd balked at doing it briskly, though. Who walks briskly in a Free Park? There's too much to see. She's given me an hour; I'd held out for three. It was a compromise, like the paper slacks I was wearing despite Jill's nudist beliefs.

Sooner or later she'd find someone with muscles, or I'd relapse into laziness, and we'd split. Meanwhile . . . we got along. It seemed only sensible to let her finish my training.

She spotted me, yelled, "Russel! Here!" in a voice that must have reached both ends of the Park.

In answer I lifted my arm, semaphore-style, slowly over my head and back down.

And every copseye in King's Free Park fell out of the sky, dead.

Jill looked about her at all the startled faces and all the golden bubbles resting in bushes and on the grass. She approached me somewhat uncertainly. She asked. "Did you do that?"

I said, "Yah. If I wave my arms again, they'll all go back up."

"I think you'd better do it," she said primly. Jill had a fine poker face. I waved my arm grandly over my head and down, but, of course, the copseyes stayed where they had fallen.

Jill said, "I wonder what happened to them?"

"It was Ron Cole. You remember him. He's the one who engraved some old Michelob beer bottles for Steuben—"

"Oh, yes. But *how?*"

We went off to ask him.

A brawny college man howled and charged past us at a dead run. We saw him kick a copseye like a soccer ball. The golden cover split, but the man howled again and hopped up and down hugging his foot.

We passed dented golden shells and broken resonators and bent parabolic relectors. One woman looked flushed and proud: she was wearing several of the copper toroids as bracelets. A kid was collecting the cameras. Maybe he thought he could sell them outside.

I never saw an intact copseye after the first minute.

They weren't all busy kicking copseyes apart. Jill stared at the conservatively dressed group carrying POPULATION BY COPULA-TION signs, and wanted to know if they were serious. Their grim-faced leader handed us pamphlets that spoke of the evil and the blasphemy of Man's attempts to alter himself through gene tampering and extra-uterine growth experiments. If it was a put-on it was a good one.

We passed seven little men, each three to four feet high, traveling with a single tall, pretty brunette. They wore medieval garb. We both stared; but I was the one who noticed the makeup and the use of UnTan. African pigmies, probably part of the UN-sponsored tourist group; and the girl must be their guide.

Ron Cole was not where I had left him.

"He must have decided that discretion is the better part of cowardice. May be right, too," I surmised. "Nobody's ever knocked down *all* the copseyes before."

"It's not illegal, is it?"

"Not illegal, but excessive. They can bar him from the Park, at the very least."

Jill stretched in the sun. She was all golden, and *big*. She said, "I'm thirsty. Is there a fountain around?"

"Sure, unless someone's plugged it by now. It's a—"

"Free Park. Do you mean to tell me they don't even protect the *fountains?*"

"You make one exception, it's like a wedge. When someone ruins a fountain they wait and fix it that night. That way . . . If I see someone trying to wreck a fountain, I'll generally throw a punch at him. A lot of us do. After a guy's lost enough of his holiday to the copseye stunners, he'll get the idea sooner or later."

The fountain was a solid tube of concrete with four spigots and a hand-sized metal button. It was hard to jam, hard to hurt. Ron Cole stood near it, looking lost.

He seemed glad to see me, but still lost. I introduced him— "You remember Jill Hayes." He said, "Certainly. Hello, Jill," and, having put her name to its intended purpose, promptly forgot it.

Jill said, "We thought you'd made a break for it."

"I did."

"Oh?"

"You know how complicated the exits are. They have to be, to keep anyone from getting in through an exit with—like a shotgun." Ron ran both hands through his hair, without making it any more or less neat. "Well, all the exits have stopped working. They must be on the same circuits as the copseyes. I wasn't expecting that."

"Then we're locked in," I said. That was irritating. But underneath the irritation was a funny feeling in the pit of my stomach. "How long do you think—"

"No telling. They'll have to get new copseyes in somehow. And repair the beamed power system, and figure out how I bollixed it, and fix it so it doesn't happen again. I suppose someone must have kicked my rigged copseye to pieces by now, but the police don't know that."

"Oh, they'll just send in some cops," said Jill.

"Look around you."

There were pieces of copseyes in all directions. Not one remained whole. A cop would have to be out of his mind to enter a Free Park.

Not to mention the damage to the spirit of the Park.

"I wish I'd brought a bag lunch," said Ron.

I saw the cloak off to my right: a ribbon of glowing blue velvet hovering at five feet, like a carpeted path in the air. I didn't yell, or point, or anything. For Ron it might be pushing the wrong buttons.

Ron didn't see it. "Actually I'm kind of glad this happened," he said animatedly. "I've always thought that anarchy ought to be a viable form of society."

Jill made polite sounds of encouragement.

"After all, anarchy is only the last word in free enterprise. What can a government do for people that people can't do for themselves? Protection from other countries? If all the other countries are anarchies, too, you don't need armies. Police, maybe; but what's wrong with privately owned police?"

"Fire departments used to work that way," Jill remembered. "They were hired by the insurance companies. They only protected houses that belonged to their own clients."

"Right! So you buy theft and murder insurance, and the insurance companies hire a police force. The client carries a credit card—"

"Suppose the robber steals the card too?"

"He can't use it. He doesn't have the right retina prints."

"But if the client doesn't have the credit card, he can't sic the cops on the thief."

"Oh." A noticeable pause. "Well—"

Half-listening, for I had heard it all before, I looked for the end points of the cloak. I found empty space at one end and a lovely red-haired girl at the other. She was talking to two men as outré as herself.

One can get the impression that a Free Park is one gigantic costume party. It isn't. Not one person in ten wears anything but street clothes; but the costumes are what get noticed.

These guys were part bird.

Their eyebrows and eyelashes were tiny feathers, green on one, golden on the other. Larger feathers covered their heads, blue and green and gold, and ran in a crest down their spines. They were bare to the waist, showing physiques Jill would find acceptable.

Ron was lecturing. "What does a government do for *anyone* except the people who run the government? Once there were private post offices, and they were cheaper than what we've got now. Anything the government takes over gets more expensive, *immediately*. There's no reason why private enterprise can't do anything a government—"

Jill gasped. She said, "Ooh! How lovely."

Ron turned to look.

As if on cue, the girl in the cloak slapped one of the feathered men hard across the mouth. She tried to hit the other one, but he caught her wrist. Then all three froze.

I said, "See? Nobody wins. She doesn't even like standing still. She—" and I realized why they weren't moving.

In a Free Park it's easy for a girl to turn down an offer. If the guy won't take No for an answer, he gets slapped. The stun beam gets him and the girl. When she wakes up, she walks away.

Simple. The girl recovered first. She gasped and jerked her wrist loose and turned to run. One of the feathered men didn't bother to chase her; he simply took a double handful of the cloak.

This was getting serious.

The cloak jerked her sharply backward. She didn't hesitate. She reached for the big disks at her shoulders, ripped them loose and ran on. The feathered men chased her, laughing.

The redhead wasn't laughing. She was running all out. Two drops of blood ran down her shoulders. I thought of trying to stop the feathered men, decided in favor of it—but they were already past.

The cloak hung like a carpeted path in the air, empty at both ends.

Jill hugged herself uneasily. "Ron, just how does one go about hiring your private police force?"

"Well, you can't expect it to form spontaneously—"

"Let's try the entrances. Maybe we can get out."

It was slow to build. Everyone knew what a copseye did. Nobody thought it through. Two feathered men chasing a lovely nude? A pretty sight; and why interfere? If she didn't want to be chased, she need only . . . what? And nothing else had changed. The costumes, the people with causes, the people looking for causes, the people-watchers, the pranksters—

Blank Sign had joined the POPULATION BY COPULATION faction. His grass-stained pink street tunic jarred strangely with their conservative suits, but he showed no sign of mockery; his face was as preternaturally solemn as theirs. Nonetheless they did not seem glad of his company.

It was crowded near the Wilshire entrance. I saw enough bewildered and frustrated faces to guess that it was closed. The little vestibule area was so packed that we didn't even try to find out what was wrong with the doors.

"I don't think we ought to stay here," Jill said uneasily.

I noticed the way she was hugging herself. "Are you cold?"

"No." She shivered. "But I wish I were dressed."

"How about a strip of that velvet cloak?"

"Good!"

We were too late. The cloak was gone.

It was a warm September day, near sunset. Clad only in paper slacks, I was not cold in the least. I said, "Take my slacks."

"No, hon, I'm the nudist." But Jill hugged herself with both arms.

"Here," said Ron, and handed her his sweater. She flashed him a grateful look, then, clearly embarrassed, she wrapped the sweater around her waist and knotted the sleeves.

Ron didn't get it at all. I asked him, "Do you know the difference between nude and naked?"

He shook his head.

"Nude is artistic. Naked is defenseless."

Nudity was popular in a Free Park. That night, nakedness was not. There must have been pieces of that cloak all over King's Free

Park. I saw at least four that night: one worn as a kilt, two being used as crude sarongs, and one as a bandage.

On a normal day, the entrances to King's Free Park close at six. Those who want to stay, stayed as long as they like. Usually there are not many, because there are no lights to be broken in a Free Park; but light does seep in from the city beyond. The copseyes float about, guided by infrared, but most of them are not manned.

Tonight would be different.

It was after sunset, but still light. A small and ancient lady came stumping toward us with a look of murder on her lined face. At first I thought it was meant for us; but that wasn't it. She was so mad she couldn't see straight.

She saw my feet and looked up. "Oh, it's you. The one who helped break the lawn mower," she said—which was unjust. "A Free Park, is it? A Free Park! Two men just took away my dinner!"

I spread my hands. "I'm sorry. I really am. If you still had it, we could try to talk you into sharing it."

She lost some of her mad; which brought her embarrassingly close to tears. "Then we're all hungry together. I brought in a plastic bag. Next time I'll use something that isn't transparent, by d-damn!" She noticed Jill and her improvised sweater-skirt, and added, "I'm sorry, dear, I gave my towel to a girl who needed it even more."

"Thank you anyway."

"Please, may I stay with you people until the copseyes start working again? I don't feel safe, somehow. I'm Glenda Hawthorne."

We introduced ourselves. Glenda Hawthorne shook our hands. By now it was quite dark. We couldn't see the city beyond the high green hedges, but the change was startling when the lights of Westwood and Santa Monica flashed on.

The police were taking their own good time getting us some copseyes.

We reached the grassy field sometimes used by the Society for Creative Anachronism for their tournaments. They fight on foot with weighted and padded weapons designed to behave like swords, broad-axes, morningstars, et cetera. The weapons are bugged so that they won't fall into the wrong hands. The field is big and flat and bare of trees, sloping upward at the edges.

On one of the slopes, something moved.

I stopped. It didn't move again, but showed clearly in light reflected down from the white clouds. I made out something man-shaped and faintly pink, and a pale rectangle nearby.

I spoke low. "Stay here."

Jill said, "Don't be silly. There's nothing for anyone to hide under. Come on."

The blank sign was bent and marked with shoe prints. The man who had been carrying it looked up at us with pain in his eyes. Drying blood ran from his nose. With effort he whispered, "I think they dislocated my shoulder."

"Let me look." Jill bent over him. She probed him a bit, then set herself and pulled hard and steadily on his arm. Blank Sign yelled in pain and despair.

"That'll do it." Jill sounded satisfied. "How does it feel?"

"It doesn't hurt as much." He smiled, almost.

"What happened?"

"They started pushing me and kicking me to make me go away. I was *doing* it, I was walking away. I *was*. Then someone snatched away my sign—" He stopped for a moment, then went off at a tangent. "I wasn't hurting anyone with my sign. I'm a Psych Major. I'm writing a thesis on what people read into a blank sign. Like the blank sheets in the Rorschach tests."

"What kind of reactions do you get?"

"Usually hostile. But nothing like *that*." Blank Sign sounded bewildered. "Wouldn't you think a Free Park is the one place you'd find freedom of speech?"

Jill wiped at his face with a tissue from Glenda Hawthorne's purse. She said, "Especially when you're not saying anything. Hey, Ron, tell us more about your government by anarchy."

Ron cleared his throat. "I hope you're not judging it by *this*. King's Free Park hasn't been an anarchy for more than a couple of hours. It needs time to develop."

Glenda Hawthorne and Blank Sign must have wondered what the hell he was talking about. I wished him joy in explaining it to them, and wondered if he would explain who had knocked down the copseyes.

This field would be a good place to spend the night. It was open, with no cover and no shadows, no way for anyone to sneak up on us.

And I was learning to think like a true paranoid.

We lay on wet grass, sometimes dozing, sometimes talking. Two other groups no bigger than ours occupied the jousting field. They kept their distance, we kept ours. Now and then we heard voices, and knew that they were not asleep; not all at once, anyway.

Blank Sign dozed restlessly. His ribs were giving him trouble, though Jill said none of them were broken. Every so often he whimpered and tried to move and woke himself up. Then he had to hold himself still until he fell asleep again.

"Money," said Jill. "It takes a government to print money."

"But you could get IOUs printed. Standard denominations, printed for a fee and notarized. Backed by your good name."

Jill laughed softly. "Thought of everything, haven't you? You couldn't travel very far that way."

"Credit cards, then."

I had stopped believing in Ron's anarchy. I said, "Ron, remember the girl in the long blue cloak?"

A little gap of silence. "Yah?"

"Pretty, wasn't she? Fun to watch."

"Granted."

"If there weren't any laws to stop you from raping her, she'd be muffled to the ears in a long dress and carrying a tear gas pen. What fun would that be? I *like* the nude look. Look how fast it disappeared after the copseyes fell."

"Mm—m," said Ron.

The night was turning cold. Faraway voices, occasional distant shouts, came like thin gray threads in a black tapestry of silence. Mrs. Hawthorne spoke into that silence.

"What was that boy really saying with his blank sign?"

"He wasn't saying anything," said Jill.

"Now, just a minute, dear. I think he was, even if he didn't know it." Mrs. Hawthorne talked slowly, using the words to shape her thoughts. "Once there was an organization to protest the forced contraception bill. I was one of them. We carried signs for hours at a time. We printed leaflets. We stopped people passing so that we could talk to them. We gave up our time, we went to considerable trouble and expense, because we wanted to get our ideas across.

"Now, if a man had joined us with a blank sign, he would have been *saying* something.

"His sign says that he has no opinion. If he joins us, he says that we have no opinion either. He's saying our opinions aren't worth anything."

I said, "Tell him when he wakes up. He can put it in his notebook."

"But his notebook is *wrong*. He wouldn't push his blank sign in among people he agreed with, would be?"

"Maybe not."

"I . . . suppose I don't like people with no opinions." Mrs. Hawthorne stood up. She had been sitting tailor-fashion for some hours. "Do you know if there's a pop machine nearby?"

There wasn't, of course. No private company would risk getting their machines smashed once or twice a day. But she had reminded the rest of us that we were thirsty. Eventually we all got up and trooped away in the direction of the fountain.

All but Blank Sign.

I'd *liked* that blank sign gag. How odd, how ominous, that so basic a right as freedom of speech could depend on so slight a thing as a floating copseye.

I was thirsty.

The park was bright by city light, crossed by sharp-edged shadows. In such light it seems that one can see much more than he really can. I could see into every shadow; but, though there were stirrings all around us, I could see nobody until he moved. We four, sitting under an oak with our back to the tremendous trunk, must be invisible from any distance.

We talked little. The Park was quiet except for occasional laughter from the fountain.

I couldn't forget my thirst. I could feel others being thirsty around me. The fountain was right out there in the open, a solid block of concrete with five men around it.

They were dressed alike, in paper shorts with big pockets. They looked alike: like first-string athletes. Maybe they belonged to the same order, or frat, or ROTC class.

They had taken over the fountain.

When someone came to get a drink, the tall ash-blond one would step forward with his arm held stiffly out, palm forward. He had a wide mouth and a grin that might otherwise have been infectious, and a deep, echoing voice. He would intone, "Go back. None may pass here but the immortal Cthulhu—" or something equally silly.

Trouble was, they weren't kidding. Or: they were kidding, but they wouldn't let anyone have a drink.

When we arrived, a girl dressed in a towel had been trying to talk some sense into them. It hadn't worked. It might even have boosted their egos: a lovely half-naked girl begging them for water. Eventually she'd given up and gone away.

In that light her hair might have been red. I hoped it was the girl in the cloak.

And a beefy man in a yellow business jumper had made the mistake of demanding his Rights. It was not a night for Rights. The blond kid had goaded him into screaming insults, a stream of unimaginative profanity, which ended when he tried to hit the blond kid. Then three of them had swarmed over him. The man had left crawling, moaning of police and lawsuits.

Why hadn't somebody done something?

I had watched it all from sitting position. I could list my own reasons. One: it was hard to face the fact that a copseye would not zap them both, any second now. Two: I didn't like the screaming fat man much. He talked dirty. Three: I'd been waiting for someone else to step in.

Mrs. Hawthorne said, "Ronald, what time is it?"

Ron may have been the only man in King's Free Park who knew the time. People generally left their valuables in lockers at the entrances. But years ago, when Ron was flush with money from the sale of the engraved beer bottles, he'd bought an implant-watch. He told time by one red mark and two red lines glowing beneath the skin of his wrist.

We had put the women between us, but I saw the motion as he glanced at his wrist. "Quarter of twelve."

"Don't you think they'll get bored and go away? It's been twenty minutes since anyone tried to get a drink." Mrs. Hawthorne said.

Jill shifted against me in the dark.

"They can't be any more bored than we are. I think they'll get bored and stay away. Besides—" She stopped.

I said, "Besides that, we're thirsty *now.*"

"Right."

"Ron, have you seen any sign of those rock throwers you collected? Especially the one who knocked down the copseye."

"No."

I wasn't surprised. In this darkness? "Do you remember his . . ." and I didn't even finish.

" . . . Yes!" Ron said suddenly.

"You're kidding."

"No. His name was Bugeyes. You don't forget a name like that."

"I take it he had bulging eyes?"

"I didn't notice."

Well, it was worth a try. I stood and cupped my hands for a megaphone and shouted, *"Bugeyes!"*

One of the Water Monopoly shouted, "Let's keep the noise down out there."

"Bugeyes!"

A chorus of remarks from the Water Monopoly. "Strange habits these peasants—" "Most of them are just thirsty. *This* character—"

From off to the side: "What do you want?"

"We want to talk to you! Stay where you are!" To Ron I said, "Come on." To Jill and Mrs. Hawthorne, "Stay here. Don't get involved."

We moved out into the open space between us and Bugeyes' voice.

Two of the five kids came immediately to intercept us. They must have been bored, all right, and looking for action.

We ran for it. We reached the shadows of the trees before those two reached us. They stopped, laughing like maniacs and moved back to the fountain.

Ron and I, we lay on our bellies in the shadows of low bushes. Across too much shadowless grass, four men in paper shorts stood at parade rest at the four corners of the fountain. The fifth man watched for a victim.

A boy walked out between us into the moonlight. His eyes were shining, big, expressive eyes, maybe a bit too prominent. His hands were big, too—with knobby knuckles. One hand was full of acorns.

He pitched them rapidly, one at a time, overhand. First one, then another of the Water Monopoly twitched and looked in our direction. Bugeyes kept throwing.

Quite suddenly, two of them started toward us at a run. Bugseyes kept throwing until they were almost on him; then he threw his acorns in a handful and dived into the shadows.

The two of them ran between us. We let the first go by: the wide-mouthed blond spokesman, his expression low and murderous now. The other was short and broad-shouldered, an intimidating silhouette, seemingly all muscle. A tackle. I stood up in front of him, expecting him to stop in surprise; and he did, and I hit him in the mouth as hard as I could.

He stepped back in shock. Ron wrapped an arm around his throat.

He bucked. Instantly. Ron hung on. I did something I'd seen often enough on television: linked my fingers and brought both hands down on the back of his neck.

The blond spokesman should be back by now; and I turned, and he was. He was on me before I could get my hands up. We rolled on the ground, me with my arms pinned to my sides, him unable to use his hands without letting go. It was lousy planning for both of us. He was squeezing the breath out of me. Ron hovered over us, waiting for a chance to hit him.

Suddenly there were others, a lot of others. Three of them pulled the blond kid off me, and a beefy, bloody man in a yellow business jumper stepped forward and crowned him with a rock.

The blond went limp.

The man squared off and threw a straight left hook with the rock in his hand. The blond kid's head snapped back, fell forward.

I yelled, "Hey!" Jumped forward, got hold of the arm that held the rock.

Someone hit me solidly in the side of the neck.

I dropped. It felt like all my strings had been cut. Someone was helping me to my feet—Ron—voices babbling in whispers, one shouting, "Get him—"

I couldn't see the blond kid. The other one, the tackle, was up and staggering away. Shadows came from between the trees to play pileup on him. The woods were alive, and it was just a *little* patch of woods. Full of angry, thirsty people.

Bugeyes reappeared, grinning widely. "Now what? Go somewhere else and try it again?"

"Oh, no. It's getting very vicious out tonight. Ron, we've got to stop them. They'll kill him!"

"It's a Free Park. Can you stand now?"

"Ron, they'll *kill* him!"

The rest of the Water Trust was charging to the rescue. One of them had a tree branch with the leaves stripped off. Behind them, shadows converged on the fountain.

We fled.

I had to stop after a dozen paces. My head was trying to explode. Ron looked back anxiously, but I waved him on. Behind me the man with the branch broke through the trees and ran toward me to do murder.

Behind him, all the noise suddenly stopped.

I braced myself for the blow.

And fainted.

He was lying across my legs, with the branch still in his hand. Jill and Ron were pulling at my shoulders. A pair of golden moons floated overhead.

I wriggled loose. I felt my head. It seemed intact.

Ron said, "The copseyes zapped him before he got to you."

"What about the others? Did they kill them?"

"I don't know." Ron ran his hands through his hair. "I was wrong. Anarchy isn't stable. It comes apart too easily."

"Well, don't do any more experiments, O.K.?"

People were beginning to stand up. They streamed toward the exits, gathering momentum, beneath the yellow gaze of the copseyes.

Analysis:

HOW TO BACK INTO A STATE
WITHOUT REALLY TRYING
excerpts from
ANARCHY, STATE, AND UTOPIA

Robert Nozick

Note to the Reader: Part I of Robert Nozick's *Anarchy, State, and Utopia,* entitled "State-of-Nature Theory, or How to Back into a State Without Really Trying," contains an important defense of the state against the objections of the anarchist. There is no way that a few brief excerpts can do full justice to this powerful and original argument, which includes an analysis of political theory and of the nature of basic moral principles, a treatment of animal rights, an extended, subtle theory of punishment, and a clarification of the principle of fairness. This selection is intended only to suggest one extremely important thread of Nozick's refutation of anarchism. Even here important qualifications which the author makes have been omitted in order to make the argument easier to grasp. We strongly recommend that the reader turn to Nozick's book for a full appreciation of the argument.

    Nozick accepts the main premise of the individualist anarchist: "Individuals have rights, and there are things no person or group may do to them (without violating their rights)." He takes seriously the anarchist's arguments that the operations of a state necessarily involve violations of the rights of certain individuals living in the jurisdiction of that state. His strategy is to give the anarchist enough rope to hang himself: Nozick starts from an ideal situation which John Locke called "The State-of-Nature": it is "a state of perfect freedom" in which individuals may do whatever they please so long as they abide by the "law of nature" that "no one ought to harm another in his life, health, liberty, or possessions." In addition to these basic rights, individuals share the right to protect themselves and to punish those who have infringed on their rights. According to the anarchist, weaker members of society have the right to combine forces and form "protective associations" in order to protect themselves against would-be rights violators. But the anarchist will not recognize the right of anyone to establish a State to protect rights. Why not? The objectionable characteristic of a State is that it maintains a *monopoly* over the enforcement of rights within its jurisdiction. Your local police and courts simply do not permit the operation of private vigilante committees. Nozick distinguishes several types of States: The *minimal state* operates like a "night watchman" of a society, protecting its clients against murderers, muggers, burglars, bunko artists, and so forth. It

Basic Books, New York (1974), pp. 51–52, 54–56, 66–67, 105, 110–111, 113–115.
Permission by the author and Basic Books, Inc. Copyright © 1974 by Basic Books, Inc.

does not perform the many functions of our *welfare state* to "promote the general welfare" by regulating the economy, redistributing income by taxing the rich in order to give assistance to the poor, and so on. The *ultraminimal state* does even less than the minimal state, for the ultraminimal state provides support only to clients who buy "protection policies" from it, whereas the minimal state protects everyone within its jurisdiction, even those who cannot afford to pay for it.

The Individualist Anarchist's Objections Against the State

A system of private protection, even when one protective agency is dominant in a geographical territory, appears to fall short of a state. It apparently does not provide protection for everyone in its territory, as does a state, and it apparently does not possess or claim the sort of monopoly over the use of force necessary to a state. In our earlier terminology, it apparently does not constitute a minimal state, and it apparently does not even constitute an ultraminimal state.

These very ways in which the dominant protective agency or association in a territory apparently falls short of being a state provide the focus of the individualist anarchist's complaint *against* the state. For he holds that when the state monopolizes the use of force in a territory and punishes others who violate its monopoly, and when the state provides protection for everyone by forcing some to purchase protection for others, it violates moral side constraints on how individuals may be treated. Hence, he concludes, the state itself is intrinsically immoral. The state grants that under some circumstances it is legitimate to punish persons who violate the rights of others, for it itself does so. How then does it arrogate to itself the right to forbid private exaction of justice by other nonaggressive individuals whose rights have been violated? *What right does the private exacter of justice violate that is not violated also by the state when it punishes?* When a group of persons constitute themselves as the state and begin to punish, *and forbid others from doing likewise,* is there some right these others would violate that they themselves do not? By what right, then, can the state and its officials claim a unique right (a privilege) with regard to force and enforce this monopoly? If the private exacter of justice violates no one's rights, then punishing him for his actions (actions state officials also perform) violates his rights and hence violates moral side constraints. Monopolizing the use of force then, on this view, is itself immoral, as is redistribution through the compulsory tax apparatus of the state. Peaceful individuals minding their own business are not violating the rights of others. It does not constitute a violation of someone's rights to refrain from purchasing something for him (that you have not entered specifically into an obligation to buy). Hence, so the argument continues, when the state threatens someone with punishment if he does not contribute to the protection of another, it violates (and its officials violate) his rights. In threatening him with something that would be a violation of his rights if done by a private citizen, they violate moral constraints.

To get to something recognizable as a state we must show (1) how an ultraminimal state arises out of the system of private protective associations; and (2) how the ultraminimal state is transformed into the minimal state, how it gives rise to that "redistribution" for the general provision of protective services that constitutes it as the minimal state. To show that the minimal state is morally legitimate, to show it is not immoral itself, we must show also that these transitions in (1) and (2) *each* are morally legitimate.

Nozick believes that the minimal state can be defended against the anarchist's objections. His argument starts from the following claim.

Independents Who Take the Enforcement of Their Rights into Their Own Hands Impose Risks on Other Members of Society

Let us suppose that interspersed among a large group of persons who deal with one protective agency lives some minuscule group who do not. These few independents (perhaps even only one) jointly or individually enforce their own rights against one and all, including clients of the agency. This situation might have arisen if native Americans had not been forced off their land and if some had refused to affiliate with the surrounding society of the settlers. Locke held that no one may be forced to enter civil society; some may abstain and stay in the liberty of the state of nature, even if most choose to enter.

How might the protective association and its members deal with this? They might try to isolate themselves from the independents in their midst by forbidding anyone permission to enter their property who hadn't agreed to forgo exercising rights of retaliation and punishment. The geographical territory covered by the protective association then might resemble a slice of Swiss cheese, with internal as well as external boundaries. But this would leave acute problems of relations with independents who had devices enabling them to retaliate across the boundaries, or who had helicopters to travel directly to wrongdoers without trespassing upon anyone else's land, and so on.

Instead of (or in addition to) attempts at geographically isolating independents, one might punish them for their misenforcements of their rights of retaliation, punishment, and exaction of compensation. An independent would be allowed to proceed to enforce his rights as he sees them and as he sees the facts of his situation; afterwards the members of the protective association would check to see whether he had acted wrongly or overacted. If and only if he had done so, would they punish him or exact compensation from him.

But the victim of the independent's wrongful and unjust retaliation may be not only damaged but seriously injured and perhaps even killed. Must one wait to act until afterwards? Surely there would be some probability of the independent's misenforcing his rights, which is high enough (though less than unity) to justify the protective association in stopping him until it determines whether his rights indeed were violated by its client. Wouldn't this be a legitimate way to defend their clients? Won't people choose to do business only with agencies that offer their clients protection, by announcing they will punish anyone who punishes a client without first using some particular sort of procedure to establish his right to do this, independently of whether it turns out that he *could* have established this right? Is it not within a person's rights to announce that he will not allow himself to be punished without its first being *established* that he has wronged someone? May he not appoint a protective association as his agent to make and carry out this announcement and to oversee any process used to try to establish his guilt? (Is anyone known so to lack the capacity to harm another, that others would exclude him from the scope of this announcement?) But suppose an independent, in the process of exacting punishment, tells the protective agency to get out of his way, on the grounds that the agency's client deserves punishment, that he (the independent) has a right to punish him, that he is not violating anyone's rights, and that it's not his fault if the protective agency doesn't *know* this. Must the agency then abstain from intervening? On the same grounds may the independent demand that the person himself refrain from defending himself against the infliction of punishment? And if the protective agency tries to punish an independent who punished a client, independently of whether their client *did* violate the independent's rights, isn't the independent within his rights to defend himself against the agency?

Nozick next carries out a painstaking inquiry into the nature and justification of punishment. He is especially concerned with the question of when we should *prohibit* certain actions and when we should merely require *compensation* from someone in case the rights of others have been violated. To prohibit an act is to exact an additional penalty, such as a fine or jail sentence, independent of the question of compensation. Nozick argues that certain acts should, in fact, be prohibited on the following grounds:

Actions Which Cause General Apprehension and Fear
Should Be Prohibited

Even some acts that *can* be compensated for may be prohibited. Among those acts that can be compensated for, some arouse fear. We fear these acts happening to us, even if we know that we shall be compensated fully for them. X, learning that Y slipped in front of someone's house, broke his arm, and collected $2,000 after suing for compensation for injuries, might think, "How fortunate for Y to have that happen; it's worth breaking one's arm in order to get $2,000; that completely covers the injury." But if someone then came up to X and said, "I may break your arm in the next month, and if I do I will give you $2,000 in compensation; though if I decide not to break it I won't give you anything," would X dwell upon his good fortune? Wouldn't he instead walk around apprehensive, jumping at noises behind him, nervous in the expectation that pain might descend suddenly upon him? A system that allowed assaults to take place provided the victims were compensated afterwards would lead to apprehensive people, afraid of assault, sudden attack, and harm. Does this provide a reason to prohibit assaults? Why couldn't someone who commits assault compensate his victim not merely for the assault and its effects, but also for all the fear the victim felt in awaiting some assault or other? But under a general system which permits assault provided compensation is paid, a victim's fear is not caused by the particular person who assaulted him. Why then should this assaulter have to compensate him for it? *And who will compensate all the other apprehensive persons, who didn't happen to get assaulted, for their fear?*

Some things we would fear, even knowing we shall be compensated fully for their happening or being done to us. To avoid such general apprehension and fear, these acts are prohibited and made punishable. (Of course, prohibiting an act does not guarantee its noncommission and so does not ensure that people will feel secure. Where acts of assault, though forbidden, were frequently and unpredictably done, people still would be afraid.) Not every kind of border crossing creates such fear. If told that my automobile may be taken during the next month, and I will be compensated fully afterwards for the taking and for any inconvenience being without the car causes me, I do not spend the month nervous, apprehensive, and fearful.

This provides one dimension of a distinction between private wrongs and wrongs having a public component. Private wrongs are those where only the injured party need be compensated; persons who know they will be compensated fully do not fear them. Public wrongs are those people are fearful of, even though they know they will be compensated fully if and when the wrongs occur. Even under the strongest compensation proposal which compensates victims for their fear, some people (the nonvictims) will not be compensated for *their* fear. Therefore there is a legitimate public interest in eliminating these border-crossing acts, especially because their commission raises everyone's fear of its happening to them.

If this argument of Nozick's is sound, it would seem to apply to risky actions in general. For example, if I were penalized for drunk driving, I could not protest on the grounds that as it happened, I did not cause an accident. For in driving in an intoxicated state I run a high risk of causing an accident, and the presence of such high risks on the highway causes "general fear and apprehension" in sober drivers. A similar argument is now applied to would-be private enforcers of rights.

Independents Who Take the Enforcement of Their Rights into Their Own Hands Should Be Prohibited from Using Unreliable Methods

The person who uses an unreliable procedure, acting upon its result, imposes risks upon others, whether or not his procedure misfires in a particular case. Someone playing Russian roulette upon another does the same thing if when he pulls the trigger the gun does not fire. The protective agency may treat the unreliable enforcer of justice as it treats any performer of a risky action. We distinguished earlier a range of possible responses to a risky action, which were appropriate in different sorts of circumstances: prohibition, compensation to those whose boundaries are crossed, and compensation to all those who undergo a risk of a boundary crossing. The unreliable enforcer of justice might either perform actions others are fearful of, or not; and either might be done to obtain compensation for some previous wrong, or to exact retribution. A person who uses an unreliable procedure of enforcing justice and is led to perform some *unfeared* action will not be punished afterwards. If it turns out that the person on whom he acted was guilty and that the compensation taken was appropriate, the situation will be left as is. If the person on whom he acted turns out to be innocent, the unreliable enforcer of justice may be forced fully to compensate him for the action.

On the other hand, the unreliable enforcer of justice may be forbidden to impose those consequences that would be feared if expected. Why? If done frequently enough so as to create general fear, such unreliable enforcement may be forbidden in order to avoid the general uncompensated-for fear. Even if done rarely, the unreliable enforcer may be punished for imposing this feared consequence upon an innocent person.

It is worth noting that Nozick does take into account more difficult cases. Consider the example of a character like the protagonist of the film *Death Wish*, who decides to take the law into his own hands and punish his wife's murderers. Suppose that he acts in secret, and, in spite of the use of very unreliable methods, he happens to apprehend and punish the real murderer. He will evidently not have violated the murderer's rights and he will not have contributed to a climate of general fear. There are different ways of dealing with this case. Some would argue that even a murderer has a right to due process and a fair trial, a right which the avenging husband is violating. Nozick takes a slightly different line: The husband *knows* that, if he punishes the suspect, he will be violating the suspect's rights if it turns out that the suspect is really innocent; so, postulates Nozick, the husband should not punish the suspect unless he has established that the suspect is guilty by using the most reliable methods available. He must make certain that he is not violating the suspect's rights. In conclusion, then, the unreliable enforcer should be prohibited.

Independents Prevented from Private Enforcement Should Be Compensated

If the protective agency deems the independents' procedures for enforcing their own rights insufficiently reliable or fair when applied to its clients, it will prohibit the independents from such self-help enforcement. The grounds for this prohibition are that the self-help enforcement imposes risks of danger on its clients. Since the prohibition makes it impossible for the independents credibly to threaten to punish clients who violate their rights, it makes them unable to protect themselves from harm and seriously disadvantages the independents in their daily activities and life. Yet it is perfectly possible that the independents' activities including self-help enforcement could proceed without anyone's rights being violated (leaving aside the question of procedural rights). According to our principle of compensation . . . in these circumstances those persons promulgating and benefiting from the prohibition must compensate those disadvantaged by it. The clients of the protective agency, then, must compensate the independents for the disadvantages imposed upon them by being prohibited self-help enforcement of their own rights against the agency's clients. Undoubtedly, the least expensive way to compensate the independents would be to *supply* them with protective services to cover those situations of conflict with the paying customers of the protective agency. This will be less expensive than leaving them unprotected against violations of their rights (by not punishing any client who does so) and then attempting to pay them afterwards to cover their losses through having (and being in a position in which they were exposed to having) their rights violated. If it were *not* less expensive, then instead of buying protective services, people would save their money and use it to cover their losses, perhaps by jointly pooling their money in an insurance scheme.

Conclusion: The Minimal State Has Been Successfully Defended Against the Objections of the Individualist Anarchist.

We set ourselves the task . . . of showing that the dominant protective association within a territory satisfied two crucial necessary conditions for being a state: that it had the requisite sort of monopoly over the use of force in the territory, and that it protected the rights of everyone in the territory, even if this universal protection could be provided only in a "redistributive" fashion. These very crucial facets of the state constituted the subject of the individualist anarchists' condemnation of the state as immoral. We also set ourselves the task of showing that these monopoly and redistributive elements were themselves morally legitimate, of showing that the transition from a state of nature to an ultraminimal state (the monopoly element) was morally legitimate and violated no one's rights and that the transition from an ultraminimal to a minimal state (the "redistributive" element) also was morally legitimate and violated no one's rights.

A protective agency dominant in a territory does satisfy the two crucial necessary conditions for being a state. It is the only generally effective enforcer of a prohibition on others' using unreliable enforcement procedures (calling them as it sees them), and it oversees these procedures. And the agency protects those nonclients in its territory whom it prohibits from using self-help enforcement procedures on its clients, in their dealings with its clients, even if such protection must be financed (in apparent redistributive fashion) by its clients. It is morally required to do this by the principle of compensation, which requires those who act in self-protection in order to increase their own security to compensate those they prohibit from doing risky acts which might actually have turned out to be harmless, for the disadvantages imposed upon them.

We noted earlier that whether the provision of protective services for some by others was "redistributive" would depend upon the reasons for it. We now see that such provision need not be redistributive since it can be justified on other than redistributive grounds, namely, those provided in the principle of compensation. (Recall that "redistributive" applies to reasons for a practice or institution, and only elliptically and derivatively to the institution itself.) To sharpen this point, we can imagine that protective agencies offer two types of protection policies: those protecting clients against risky private enforcement of justice and those not doing so but protecting only against theft, assault, and so forth (provided these are not done in the course of private enforcement of justice). Since it is only with regard to those with the first type of policy that others are prohibited from privately enforcing justice, only they will be required to compensate the persons prohibited private enforcement for the disadvantages imposed upon them. The holders of only the second type of policy will not have to pay for the protection of others, there being nothing they have to compensate these others for. Since the reasons for wanting to be protected against private enforcement of justice are compelling, almost all who purchase protection will purchase this type of protection, despite its extra costs, and therefore will be involved in providing protection for the independents.

We have discharged our task of explaining how a state would arise from a state of nature without anyone's rights being violated. The moral objections of the individualist anarchist to the minimal state are overcome. It is not an unjust imposition of a monopoly; the *de facto* monopoly grows by an invisible-hand process and *by morally permissible means,* without anyone's rights being violated and without any claims being made to a special right that others do not possess. And requiring the clients of the *de facto* monopoly to pay for the protection of those they prohibit from self-help enforcement against them, far from being immoral, is morally required by the principle of compensation . . . .

CHAPTER 8 PROBES

1. What precisely happens that makes the Free Park really free? Does Larry Niven think this is an improvement? Why or why not?

2. What is the sole law of the Free Park? How is it enforced? Do you think that any other laws should have been included? If not, why not? If so, which and why?

3. Is the organization (or lack of it) in Niven's story a "welfare state," a "minimal state," or an "ultraminimal state"? Is it none of these? Explain.

4. According to Nozick, what is the basis of the anarchist's objection to the state? How does he reply to it? Do you agree or disagree?

5. Are the "copseyes" in Niven's story fair or just in their treatment of violence? Do you suppose that they would control all serious injustices? Why or why not?

6. Consider Nozick's discussion of fear and apprehension. Would these be prevented in Niven's Free Park? Why or why not? Do you agree with Nozick that they should be prevented?

7. How would Nozick argue for employing what is called "due process" in the treatment of criminals? Would his argument be the standard one? Why or why not?

8. Nozick claims that the minimal state can be defended against the claim that individual rights are violated by such a state. How does he argue this? Are his arguments successful? Does this mean that no argument for anarchy can be made?

9. Another argument one might consider is whether or not individual rights would predictably be violated more often, or in a more severe fashion in an anarchistic setting. Do you think they would or not? Consider a few instances of basic rights in this regard.

10. Which state do you think preferable, Nozick's "minimal state" or our own "welfare state"? What are the virtues of each? What are their vices?

11. If you were to write a story about an ideal society, what sort of state or political system would be found in it? How might you argue for that system rather than for any of its alternatives? What would be against the law in that state? How would the law be enforced?

12. Now that you have considered the issues of anarchism and political philosophy more carefully, what are your views on the matter? In what way(s) is (are) your views different from those of Niven or Nozick? In what way(s) is (are) your views the same?

RECOMMENDED READING

Science Fiction and Social Values

A central issue in much of science fiction is the conflict between the individual and the state. Few writers are happy with the political setups in the world today. Political leaders, bureaucrats, and warriors are generally presented as shortsighted, malicious bunglers who are dragging the world down to destruction. Ancient philosophers had a similar view toward the state. Like modern thinkers, the ancients offered strikingly diverse solutions to the problem. The *utopian,* collectivist solution is to reconstruct and strengthen the state so that it functions in a virtuous way. The *libertarian,* individualist solution is to dismantle the state as it exists today and permit individuals a greater range of individual freedom. Modern science fiction writers also tend to champion one of these extremes or the other. Like theoretical philosophers, the science fiction writers also square off on crucial issues of today: the issue of whether the economy should be regulated by the government (pro-socialism) or left unregulated (pro-capitalism), and the issue of whether the values of technological progress should take precedence over the values of a safe, unpolluted environment.

Pro-Utopian Science Fiction.   The utopian tradition in science fiction goes back to Plato's *Republic* (fourth century B.C.) and Thomas More's *Utopia* (sixteenth century A.D.). A "utopia" is a society strictly controlled by government which aims to produce the greatest happiness of its members. A seasoned science fiction reader who peruses these philosophical classics will find many standard motifs, such as rule by an elite class of intellectuals, scientifically controlled education, a eugenics program, subtle "programming" of the individual through music, dress and speech, and so forth. A very influential (if somewhat plotless) pro-utopian modern novel is Edward Bellamy, *Looking Backward* (available in many editions). This work has spawned a multitude of novels seeking to discover a utopian dreamworld—for example, Mack Reynolds, *Looking Backward from the Year 2000* (Ace, 1973); Frederik Pohl, *The Age of the Pussyfoot* (Ballantine, 1977); and Stanislaw Lem, *The Futurological Congress* (Avon, 1976). The utopian Thomas More makes a personal appearance in R. A. Lafferty's *Past Master* (Ace, 1977). An important contribution to the utopian science fiction tradition was made by H. G. Wells in stories and novels such as *A Modern Utopia.* One of his novels inspired Alexander Korda's important film *Things to Come* (1936), in which a utopian society is constructed by scientists out of the ruins of a world war. In general, Wells's pro-utopian novels (like Korda's film) are insipid by comparison with his earlier masterpieces such as *The Time Machine* and *The War of the Worlds.* Significantly, these are works of social criticism. It is much easier to write an exciting story about individuals rebelling against an intolerable social situation than to describe them frolicking in the Elysian fields. An exception, a pro-utopian story that really *works* and challenges the reader, is Frank Herbert's *Hellstrom's Hive* (Bantam, 1974), in which, through mutation, there emerges a new race of human beings who live like social insects. The book makes a powerful case for traditional utopian ideals, as the hive struggles for survival against the CIA.

Anti-Utopian Science Fiction.   The "revolt against utopia" theme tends, for the reasons indicated, to be more exciting, but the reader must always be careful to ascertain that stories of this sort treat the utopian ideals fairly. For example, you might compare *Hellstrom's Hive* with T. J. Bass's *Half Past Human* (Ballantine, 1975), which has a similar premise of future humans as social insects but which has an anti-hive theme. A hilarious takeoff on the "sleeper awakes" formula with an anti-utopian twist is Woody Allen's film *Sleeper* (1973). More serious novels with an essentially anti-utopian theme are Ray Bradbury, *Fahrenheit 451* (Ballantine, 1978), which criticizes the use and obsession with pleasure in utopianism; Ira Levin, *This Perfect Day* (Fawcett, 1978), an excitingly plotted novel with sex and violence, which contends that utopianism contradicts human "nature"; and Ayn Rand, *Anthem* (Signet, n. d.), which emphasizes the sanctity of the individual. Extremely influential also has been George Orwell's *1984* (Signet, 1971), which is not a critique of utopianism as such, but of the grim realities of the twentieth-century "Big Brother" as Orwell perceived him. A fine film with anti-utopian devices is *THX 1138* by George Lucas (1970).

Libertarian Science Fiction. Some of the critics of utopianism just mentioned favor a strongly individualistic social philosophy. The most radical of these are anarchists who repudiate the state altogether. The anarchistic position is represented in some important works of science fiction, some of which were mentioned earlier in this chapter. For example, Robert A. Heinlein's Hugo-winning *The Moon Is a Harsh Mistress* (Berkley, 1968) describes an anarchistic revolution on the moon from the point of view of a strongly individualist, "rational anarchist" perspective. Ursula LeGuin's Hugo- and Nebula-winning *The Dispossessed: An Ambiguous Utopia* (Avon, 1975) represents anarchism from the radically different perspective of a philosopher named Odo, who has sought to define a moral theory midway between egoism and altruism. Eric Frank Russell's *The Great Explosion* (Avon, 1975) describes a pacificistic anarchistic planet based on Gandhi's teachings; an earlier version is ". . . And then There Were None," in Ben Bova, ed., *The Science Fiction Hall of Fame IIA* (Avon, 1974). Larry Niven's "Cloak of Anarchy" in this chapter is the only work of science fiction we know of that attempts to refute the anarchistic ideal.

Another important branch of libertarianism favors a minimal state limited to the protection of individuals from the initiation of force or fraud from other individuals. A very important work in this tradition is Ayn Rand's *Atlas Shrugged* (Signet, 1970), in which intellectuals and business people go on strike against a collectivized, welfare–warfare state. Rand's defense of rationality and individualism has influenced a number of contemporary philosophers as well as science fiction writers. A firmly pro-capitalist attitude is also expressed in Poul Anderson's stories about the Poleosotechnic League; a bibliography for this entire series is contained in *The Earth Book of Stormgate* (Putnam, 1978). Anderson's *Tales of the Flying Mountains* (Collier, 1971) also contains libertarian themes. A. E. van Vogt's *The Weapon Shops of Isher* (Pocket Books, n.d.), defends, in a more simplistic manner, the values of free trade and technology against the evils of collectivism. See also van Vogt's "The Weapon Shop," in Robert Silverberg, ed., *The Science Fiction Hall of Fame I* (Avon, 1970).

Social Criticism. There has been no dearth of critics of capitalism and unregulated technological progress among science fiction writers. Some writers focus on what they perceive as the evils of capitalism as such. (As in the case of anti-utopian science fiction, you should read these works with care to see that they treat opposing ideals fairly.) *The Space Merchants* (Ballantine, 1976) and *Gladiator at Law* (Ballantine, 1955) by Frederik Pohl and C. M. Kornbluth criticize many features of corporate capitalism: the unequal distribution of wealth, monopolies, advertising, pollution of the environment. Aldous Huxley's *Brave New World* (Harper, 1978), a very influential novel, seems to be directed against a perverse fusion of capitalism and utopianism, in which individuals have become enslaved to an advanced technology involving the media, drugs, and eugenics. John Brunner's Hugo-winning supernovel, *Stand on Zanzibar* (Ballantine, 1976), describes a near future under the control of powerful governments and mammoth corporations, focusing on potential problems of escalating Cold War, mind control, and uncontrolled reproduction.

Other science fiction tends to focus its social criticism on issues such as the population boom, the dangers of war, and the harmful by-products of uncontrolled technology. The population problem is the subject of Lester del Ray's *The Eleventh Commandment* (Ballantine, 1976), which lays the blame on the Roman Catholic Church; of Brian Aldiss's "Total Environment," in Donald A. Wollheim and Terry Carr, ed., *World's Best Science Fiction 1969* (Ace, 1969), in which Hinduism is also a source of trouble; and of Harry Harrison's *Make Room! Make Room!* (Berkley, 1967) and Richard Fleischer's film, *Soylent Green* (1973), where the state and big business exacerbate the problem. Early science fiction tended to be strongly pro-technology. Frederic Brown's paean to space exploration, *The Lights in the Sky Are Stars* (Dutton, 1953), is typical. But H. G. Wells's depiction of the Morlocks dehumanized by technology in *The Time Machine* was a cautionary note. Even John Campbell, Jr., who was strongly pro-technology as editor of *Astounding* and *Analog*, warned under the pseudonym "Don A. Stuart" against overreliance on machines in "Twilight," in Robert Silverberg, ed., *The Mirror of Infinity* (Harper, 1973). Harry Malzberg's *Beyond Apollo* (Pocket Books, 1979), which was critical of the American space program, won the first award in honor of John Campbell in 1973. Interestingly, this provoked an angry protest from Poul Anderson (letter to *Analog,* October 1973), who denounced the book as "gloomy, involuted, and technophobic." Many science fiction critics and writers leaped to Malzberg's defense. Thomas Disch's anthology, *The Ruins of Earth* (Berkley, 1971), is also filled with science fiction critical of technology, especially emphasizing threats to the environment. "Doom and gloom" forecasts of the impact of technology on our environment are also found in John Brunner, *The Sheep Look Up* (Ballantine, 1976); in J. G. Ballard, ed., *The Burning World* (Berkley, 1964), and *The Drowned World* (Penguin, 1967); and in Michael Crichton's *The Andromeda Strain* (Dell, 1978), the basis for a well-known film (1971). Some science fiction writers take strong exception to the pro-military values of writers like Robert Heinlein in *Starship Troopers* (Putnam/Berkley, 1959). Aside from a large crop of "mainstream" antiwar novels and films like Stanley Kubrick's *Dr. Strangelove*, which appeared in 1963, many hard-core science fiction writers have become critical of militarism, most notably Joe Haldeman's *The Forever War* (Ballantine, 1975).

Haldeman uses the same rapid-paced setting of interstellar warfare as Heinlein, but the values projected are far different. It is a significant comment on changing attitudes of science fiction fans and writers that, whereas *Starship Troopers* won a Hugo in 1960, *The Forever War* won the Hugo and Nebula in 1976.

Philosophy and Social Values

Surveys of political philosophers are found in two articles in the *Encyclopedia of Philosophy* (Macmillan, 1967): "Political Philosophy, History of" and "Political Philosophy, Nature of." A comprehensive history is G. H. Sabine, *A History of Political Theory* (Holt, Rinehart and Winston, 1973). Philosophers discuss the moral relationship of the individual to the state in terms of key concepts, which are the subjects of further articles: "Authority," "Equality," "Freedom," "General Will," "Justice," "Natural Law," "Rights," "Social Contract," and "Sovereignty." (See also the articles listed under the special heading, "Law, Philosophy of.")

Collectivistic social ideals are discussed in the *Encyclopedia* articles "Utopias and Utopianism," "Philosopher-Kings," "Progress, The Idea of," "Communism," "Marxist Philosophy," and "Socialism." The classic statements of utopianism are the *Republic* and *The Laws* of Plato (427–347 B.C.) and *Utopia* by Thomas More (1478–1535). Karl Marx (1818–1883) is the most influential proponent of social revolution and collectivism in modern times. Useful anthologies are M. Rubel and T. B. Bottomore, eds., *Selected Writings in Sociology and Social Philosophy* (McGraw-Hill, 1963); L. S. Feuer, ed., *Marx & Engels: Basic Writing on Politics* (Peter Smith, n.d.); and D. McLellan, *Karl Marx Selected Writings* (Oxford, 1979). See also the *Encyclopedia* articles "Alienation," "Dialectic," "Dialectical Materialism," and "Historical Materialism." The fascistic version of collectivism is discussed in *Encyclopedia* articles "Fascism" and "German Philosophy and National Socialism." A controversial critical history of the collectivistic tradition is Karl Popper's *The Open Society and Its Enemies.*

Libertarian social ideals are defended by traditional philosophers such as William von Humboldt (1767–1835) in *The Limits of State Action;* John Stuart Mill (1806–1873) in *On Liberty;* and Herbert Spencer (1820–1903) in *Social Statics* and *Man Against the State.* In addition to Robert Nozick, whose *Anarchy, State, and Utopia* is represented in *Thought Probes*, contemporary philosophical defenders of libertarianism include Ayn Rand, in *Atlas Shrugged* (New American Library, 1970) and *Capitalism: The Unknown Ideal* (New American Library, 1967). A good anthology of recent work is T. Macham, ed., *The Libertarian Alternative* (Nelson Hall, 1974). The anarchistic position is surveyed in "Anarchism," in *The Encyclopedia of Philosophy.* Seminal works are P. J. Proudhon (1809–1865), *What Is Property?*, and William Godwin (1756–1836), *Enquiry Concerning Political Justice.* Ursula LeGuin's description of anarchism in *The Dispossessed* is reminiscent of the teachings of anarchists such as M. Bakunin (1846–1876) and P. Kropotkin

(1842–1921). A statement of contemporary anarchocapitalism like Robert Heinlein's version in *The Moon Is a Harsh Mistress* is Murray Rothbard's *For A New Liberty* (Macmillan, 1977). A useful general survey is G. Woodcock, *Anarchism: A History of Libertarian Ideas and Movements* (New American Library, 1962).

Liberalism and conservatism, the dominant ideologies of the Western world today, are democratic and advocate a mixed, capitalistic economy. See the *Encyclopedia* articles, "Democracy," "Conservatism," "Liberalism," and "Economics and Rational Choice." The roots of these ideologies are to be found in the *Politics* of Aristotle (384–322 B.C.), *The City of God* of St. Augustine (A.D. 354–430), the *Leviathan* of Thomas Hobbes (1588–1679), *The Second Treatise of Government* of John Locke (1632–1704), and the American *Federalist Papers.* Classic statements of conservatism include Edmund Burke (1729–1797), *Reflections on the Revolution in France,* and Michael Oakeshott, *Rationalism in Politics* (Rowman, 1962) and *On Human Conduct* (Oxford, 1975). Important recent defenders of the liberal welfare state are John Dewey (1859–1952), especially in *Democracy and Education* (Macmillan, 1966); John Rawls, *A Theory of Justice* (Harvard, 1971); and Ronald Dworkin, *Taking Rights Seriously* (Harvard, 1977). A valuable overview of this tradition is S. I. Benn and R. S. Peters, *Social Principles and the Democratic State* (Macmillan, 1959).

INDEX